THE PREACHER AND THE PRESIDENTS

"Nancy Gibbs and Michael Duffy's smartly written, thoroughly researched book . . . represents a major advance in our understanding of Graham and, more broadly, religion in modern American political life. The authors, both prize-winning journalists at *TIME* magazine, not only know how to tell a fast-paced story, but also know how to ask the right questions of the many people—including Graham and former presidents—they interviewed."
—*Chicago Tribune*

"Nancy Gibbs and Michael Duffy, both veterans at *TIME* magazine, have that peculiar gift among newsmagazine writers for being able to shape masses of complex and contradictory information into a compelling narrative."
—*Newsweek*

"THE PREACHER AND THE PRESIDENTS . . . is invaluable."
—*New York Times*

"A fresh view on how evangelical Christianity gained such influence in politics."
—*Washington Post*

"Gibbs and Duffy maintain a balance between the political and the personal . . . [They] marvelously dramatize Graham and Nixon's fraught, intimate relationship."
—*Publishers Weekly*

"Long before Jerry Falwell and Pat Robertson roiled politics from the edges, Billy Graham towered over the centers of political and religious power, and presidents genuflected before his influence. THE PREACHER AND THE PRESIDENTS tells the story that needed to be told and tells it splendidly. Gibbs and Duffy write with a shrewd sense of how politics works, a sure grasp of history, and a genuine appreciation for the power of religious faith."
—E. J. Dionne, author of *Why Americans Hate Politics*

"A fascinating book that exposes the many dangers when representatives of the kingdom 'not of this world' become too close to representatives of an earthly kingdom."
—Cal Thomas, syndicated columnist

THE
PREACHER
★★★★ AND THE ★★★★
PRESIDENTS

Billy Graham in the White House

NANCY GIBBS
AND MICHAEL DUFFY

CENTER
STREET.

New York   Boston   Nashville

Center Street
Hachette Book Group USA
237 Park Avenue
New York, NY 10017

Visit our Web site at www.centerstreet.com.

Printed in the United States of America

Originally published in hardcover by Hachette Book Group USA.

Center Street is a division of Hachette Book Group USA, Inc. The Center Street
name and logo are trademarks of Hachette Book Group USA, Inc.

First Trade Edition: June 2008

10 9 8 7 6 5 4 3 2 1

The Library of Congress has cataloged the hardcover edition as follows:

Gibbs, Nancy Reid.
    The preacher and the presidents : Billy Graham in the White House / Nancy
Gibbs and Michael Duffy.—1st ed.
        p. cm.
    Includes index.
    ISBN-13: 978-1-59995-734-0
    ISBN-10: 1-59995-734-5
    1. Graham, Billy, 1918–   2. Presidents—United States—Religion.   3. Chris-
tianity and politics—United States.   I. Duffy, Michael, 1958–   II. Title.

BV3785.G69G53 2007
269'.2092—dc22
[B]   2007009393

ISBN 978-1-59995-104-1 (pbk.)

Contents

Contents

The Lions and the Lamb

Montreat, North Carolina, is a cove made of rocks and woods tucked at the foot of Greybeard Mountain, where it is easy to feel safe. A tourist who stopped and asked where Billy Graham lived was likely to be told, "Gee, I don't really know." But everyone knew. He lived with his wife, Ruth, on the mountaintop, in the house she had built out of pieces of old log cabins more than half a century ago; this was where he came home after his travels, and where in twilight he finally came home to stay.

Maybe everyone needs a sanctuary, a place to find peace, reflect on a life well lived and what lies ahead. But this life was like no other; it was lived, perhaps more than any in modern times or any time, in full view, unguarded. Billy Graham is believed to have spoken face-to-face with more people in more places than anyone in history, having preached the gospel to 210 million people in 185 countries in 417 crusades over the course of more than half a century. Not even Billy Sunday or Dwight L. Moody or any of the great evangelists going back to Saint Paul had spread their message so far; it was Billy Graham alone, inserted into history at just the ripe moment, who became the unrivaled global ambassador for Christ.

His crusades took something out of him. It was not unusual for him to drop fifteen, twenty pounds over the course of several weeks of preaching every night. "I have often gone on a three- or six-month crusade," he told Lyndon Johnson, who was adjusting to postpresidential exile, "I jet home to the quietness of this mountain, and for the first few days I hardly know what to do with myself. There even come times of depression. However, that all soon passes."

The road to his house is tight and winding; two cars would have to

inhale to pass in opposite directions. On a winter day the clouds hang
below the treeline, and the branches stretch old and bony as far as you can
see. The final, steep stretch of road ends with a weather-beaten shingle
sign reading "Private Drive," then chain link topped with barbed wire and
a set of automatic iron gates. These were installed in 1968, at the insis-
tence of J. Edgar Hoover, because the death threats were becoming so
common, and American icons were being shot that year. Before that the
Grahams had been content for protection with signs that said "Trespassers
will be Eaten."

At the top of the drive is a rain-soaked, brown-logged, stone-and-
shingle place that looks like it rose up naturally, as though someone
dropped some timber and it grew up to be a house. There's no sign, no
post, no box, no indication that anyone of note lives inside, other than a lot
of room for cars and what seems like a lot of dogs.

The first time we visited, we walked in the side door into a long hall
that smelled of something we couldn't place, sweet and spicy, not quite
dessert, like some kind of perfect incense of home. There were American
antiques everywhere, sturdy and hand-hewn and crafted with purpose,
thick chairs, a spinning wheel, as well as a Chinese cabinet, porcelains,
photos and paintings on the walls, a life's collection of travels. A lazy Susan
table stood in front of the oven in the dark wood kitchen/family room, and
cookies and a pie sat on the stovetop. Discreet but central on one wall was
a huge flat-screen television, and all the papers lay on the table, not just
the *New York Times* but the London *Telegraph*. Under the piano in the living room was a big basket of books, with Thomas Friedman's *The World
Is Flat* on top. Over the immense brick fireplace, a mantel had been hewn
out of an old diving board, stained dark and etched in German with the
message "A Mighty Fortress Is Our God."

Billy Graham was sitting in the darkened family room, his walker
beside him, and rose slowly to greet his guests. He was frailer than we'd
expected; he had Parkinson's disease and prostate cancer, and a shunt in
his brain to drain the extra fluid. There came a time most days when a
powerful pain came over him, a feeling he described as being like an octo-
pus had wrapped itself around him and begun to squeeze. So he timed his
visits carefully, to see guests only during his good hours, typically around
midday. His eyes were failing: once, many years before, when a mysterious
arterial spasm affected his vision, people wrote to Graham headquarters

offering to donate their eyes to him. His voice was quiet, sweet in greeting, his manner somehow friendly and courtly at the same time. "I'm honored you've come," he said, and he suggested, almost urgently, that we go
back to his office and get started.

He led the way down halls that veered at odd angles, the tennis balls
gripping the feet of his walker, heading past the living room and bedrooms
and back to his private study, a prefabricated room shipped to the mountaintop and attached to the log house where he could write his sermons,
escape the noise, the visitors, the children. It was not a big room, but it
had a big window and deep chairs, bookcases full of Bibles and memoirs.
There were no photographs of the vast crowds at his crusades, a hundred
thousand in Yankee Stadium, a quarter million in Brazil, well over a million in Seoul. But there was one of the plain white spire of the chapel in
the woods near where he and Ruth had planned to be buried. There were
no souvenirs of his glory, only reminders of his friends: not only the presidents but the queen of England, who invited him to visit a dozen times,
all the former prime ministers of Britain, the chancellors of Germany, the
movie stars and sports icons—Muhammad Ali had come here to the house,
and Bono, who sat in the living room and played the piano and sang—and
an unimaginable variety of people seeking answers to the most simple of
all questions.

The walls were a window into Graham's other ministry, so public and
so private at the same time: Graham the friend of the famous and, above
all, the pastor to presidents. We had written about politics for years, covered campaigns, watched White House warriors come and go. But no one
had done what Graham had done, no statesman, no wise man, no professor or fixer or fund-raiser or image maker: befriend eleven presidents in
a row, men vastly different from one another who all found both a need
and a use for this one man. He knew every president from Harry Truman
to George W. Bush, and while it is impossible to know who valued the
arrangement more, there had never been anything like it in any generation. It reflected some quality, maybe some measure of power he had that
even they couldn't match.

We wanted to know why they all called: what was it about him, and
about them, and about the presidency, that explained this abiding attention? Quite apart from the mutually useful public alliance, we wondered
what happened when these men who spent their lives onstage, preacher

and presidents, retreated behind the curtain and talked in private for hours. We wanted to learn how Graham managed to be so close to the white-hot center for so long and still maintain his honor and reputation; we wondered if there was a price he paid.

And finally, we came at a time when the country was having one of its recurring arguments over the role of faith in public life. Mahatma Gandhi said that those who believe that religion and politics aren't connected don't understand either. Billy Graham more than anyone had moved in both realms, tried for decades to bring them closer together, and by doing so learned the value of keeping them apart. Reporters had tried and failed in recent years to get him to enter the ring, weigh in on abortion and stem cells, gay marriage, the right to die: "I don't give advice," he said again and again. "I'm going to stay off these hot-button issues." He was inclined to leave it at that, embracing his role as God's servant, not His lawyer. He had come a very long way since the day in 1952 when he declared with youthful enthusiasm that he could swing sixteen million evangelical votes just by saying the word. We wanted to understand how he had changed, and what he would tell anyone who hoped to follow his path.

From long experience came a firm judgment: he did not want to be dividing people by using faith as a political test or a trap or a weapon. He had come by his conviction fitfully, after encounters with some presidents that threatened to wreck his ministry. On matters of faith his certainty had never faltered; on matters of politics he now had his doubts. "As I look back I feel even more unqualified, to think I sat there and talked to the president of the United States. I can only explain that God was planning it in some ways but I didn't understand it." He prayed for them still; he and Ruth did daily devotions, and whoever was president was in their prayers.

The White House Covenant

We knew that there were millions of people inclined to see Graham as a saint; we'd also encountered those who dismissed him as a showman, a sycophant, or a pawn of powerful men, with a mass-market message too silky and simple to merit further study. Graham agreed to talk to us without any conditions or control over what we would write.

He had one challenge to us as we set out: "I hope it will just be fair and honest and tell the bad and the good."

Unless you've been in his presence, it's hard to capture its effect. Many people said he was the most charismatic man they ever met. His was not a dazzling intellect—as he often said, "I don't care who you are. Your intellect alone will never get you into heaven." It was a different quality, a sincerity like paint stripper, removing any pretense and pride. He volunteered regrets before we probed for them. In the hours of discussion that followed our first meeting, he was perfectly transparent about his own failures, but slow to pass judgment on anyone else. We are all sinners, he said, in search of grace.

The presidency giveth and it taketh away, and the first thing it removes is the possibility of uncomplicated friendship: but Billy Graham was wired for simplicity, not skepticism. "I'm not an analyzer," he told us. "I don't analyze people. I got a son that analyzes everything and everybody. But I don't analyze people." His critics called him gullible, naïve to the point of self-delusion; his defenders, of whom there were a great many more, called him trusting, always seeing the best in powerful people and often eliciting it as a result. Where both agreed was that his agenda—to spread the gospel of redeeming love—applied as much to his Oval Office ministry as to his global one. "I think at times they turn to things that are far beyond them," he said, referring to the occupants of the White House, "and they have nowhere else to go."

Of the eleven presidents he'd known, ten became friends, and seven of them close ones. They entered into an unspoken covenant of private counsel and public support. The presidents called for comfort; they asked the simplest questions: How do I know if I'll go to heaven? Eisenhower wanted to know. Do you believe in the Second Coming? Kennedy wondered. Will I see my parents when I die? Johnson asked. They asked about how the world would end, which was not an abstract conversation for the first generation of presidents who had the power to make that happen. They recalled their mothers' strong faith, and looked to linger a while with their childhood certainties; when jaded aides smirked at the mention of Graham's name, presidents from Eisenhower to Clinton dressed them down. By 1969, Graham was so important—and so well positioned—with both political parties that he could seamlessly spend the last weekend of Johnson's presidency in the White House and stay over to spend the first night with Nixon as well. The week before Gerald Ford pardoned Nixon, he tracked Graham down to talk it through; that conversation, Ford said later, was crucial. Nancy Reagan called him to the hospital the day her husband was shot; twenty-three years later he was the first person outside the family she called when he died. When Hillary Clinton felt no one in the world understood how she could forgive her husband, Graham pointedly praised her for it. Graham was uniquely able to give presidents what they needed most, Bill Clinton observed. "I don't think presidents need anything from pastors other people don't. They need prayers, support, counsel, and honest, often vulnerable conversation," he said. But "those things are harder for presidents to get because they're busy, protected, often isolated, and understandably reluctant to share their frailties and fear. Billy was a great pastor to me and other presidents because he was wise, trustworthy, politically astute, and generous in spirit." The presidents, and the First Ladies, could summon Graham to the White House confident that there would never be an unpleasant conversation, never a rise in temperature, never a leak to the press; that was the safe zone he tried to create. "I think they began to realize that if I didn't quote them, they could talk to me about their personal feelings and problems and pray with me," he said. "Their personal lives, some of them, were difficult. But I loved them all, I admired them all. I knew that they had burdens beyond anything I could ever know or understand."

One price of holding the most powerful job in the world is the residue of regret when it's over. "Every president I think I've ever known, except Truman, has thought they didn't quite get what they wanted done," Graham said. "And toward the end of their administration, they were disappointed and wished they'd done some things differently." He saw the job grow more crushing with each administration, particularly as his great friend Nixon collapsed under the weight of Watergate. We've turned our presidents into kings, he said then: "Every president needs some people around him who still call him by his first name and tell him exactly what they think. . . . He becomes isolated partially because even his friends are afraid to tell him the truth. Everybody needs some friends around him who will just say, 'You are *wrong*!' And that includes me."

Had the convenant stopped there, had he been an unknown pastor slipping into the White House through some back door to hear their confessions and swap war stories, the whole transaction might have been a private matter. But Graham was the most famous preacher on earth, and nothing he did went unnoticed. The very fact of his presence was news.

And no matter how discreet he was about the private conversations, he invariably sent a public message, sometimes inadvertently, and sometimes because he couldn't resist.

This is where the temptation came in, on both sides. Every president had political troubles that Graham was uniquely positioned to relieve, often simply by standing next to him. Eisenhower enlisted religion's rising star in the war against "Godless Communism"; Kennedy invited him down for a round of golf four days before his inauguration to reassure Protestants about the prospect of a Catholic president. Johnson used him to convince conservative Baptists that the War on Poverty was scripturally sound. Reagan sent him to help persuade pro-Israel evangelicals that it was safe to sell AWACS to Saudi Arabia. George Herbert Walker Bush wanted him by his side the night before the first Gulf War, Clinton at Oklahoma City, George W. Bush after 9/11, and just about every one of them on Inauguration Day. They may have come to love him and need him; but that didn't mean they couldn't also use him. And many presidents were surrounded by men who had little scruple about drafting so willing and valuable an ally into their army.

Graham rejected the charge that he was being exploited on such occasions. He believed completely in the supreme and sacred nature of the presidency—not that presidents weren't human, as he had plainly seen. He just believed they would always put the public interest over partisan ones once in office. He told them each that he believed they were God's choice to lead the country, even when he didn't quite understand God's thinking. Graham's was a gospel of obedience, above all to the Almighty, but there always seemed to be a natural transfer to the man in power, a deep predisposition to trust and obey and "build a wall of prayer around him."

And the covenant worked both ways. In return he got to indulge what he admitted was a deep fascination with politics. He told Truman after they met—he was only thirty-one, but a rising evangelical star already—that "I follow political trends carefully and would be delighted at any time to advise you on my findings among the people." He advised Eisenhower and Nixon about which states to focus on, how to use their television ad budgets to best effect. Decades later when he was with candidates, he still wanted to talk about campaigns, political strategies, styles of leadership. However divided the country became, Graham remained close to politicians from across the spectrum. Even in twilight, he kept up with the debates—and he lived in a house divided: "I watch CNN a great deal," he said. "My wife watches Fox." His eyes twinkled. "That gives us something to talk about sometimes."

More important, he saw how much his political ministry served his spiritual one. His relationships with presidents and prime ministers helped him revive evangelicalism at midcentury and usher it into the American mainstream. He fought to witness in places no evangelist ever had, hold immense, integrated rallies in South Africa, preach behind the Iron Curtain, in the former Soviet Union, in North Korea, to all the ends of the earth. "If I had not been a friend of the presidents," he argued, "in most of these places, they wouldn't have invited me to see them. The reason Yeltsin invited me was because he knew I knew the president. . . . And so it was a way of the Lord using presidents for me to reach other people for Christ."

Most important of all, the friendship opened the most tightly guarded door of all: the one to the Oval Office. "Very few people will tell the president about spiritual things and religious things or have prayer with him," Graham said, "and I felt that this was a way that God used me."

So at what price was he willing to preserve that opportunity? He knew pride was a sin; but what about sycophancy? If Jesus' message at its heart was about radicalizing love, how blind an eye did Graham have to turn to win the allies he felt he needed? He wasn't looking for money or power in his alliances with princes and politicians; but in using them to promote his message, did he have to water it down? Graham believed that by helping bring godly men to power and ministering to them in office, he could strengthen God's kingdom here on earth. Yet Satan, ever subtle, had tempted Jesus with temporal power, offered to tangle him so in the institutional business of the world that he would take his eyes off of heaven. "It had a tendency to creep into my own spiritual life," Graham admitted of his political engagement, "to use media coverage and the ability to pick up the phone and call the president."

How many people have that access and don't use it? How many use it, without it turning their heads? His fiercest critics testified to his honesty, sincerity, and the depth of his commitment to Christ. Yet some of his greatest fans would admit that his was a cautionary tale. If a man so obviously decent could still be sometimes thrown off balance during his political encounters, despite his best intentions, his lack of agenda, his

North Star wife, and hard experience, if even he could not always resist the temptations of power and reconcile the Two Kingdoms, then you wonder about the wisdom of anyone else ever trying.

Graham's relationship with presidents was never the same after his painful passage through the Nixon years; and yet it would be wrong to say that the covenant was broken. He simply worked more quietly, lowered his expectations, and chose his friends more carefully. But he never left the White House orbit in part because the men who followed Nixon into the White House would not permit it. Both Ford and Carter, who had strong spiritual backgrounds and their own religious advisers, nonetheless sought out Graham for help with political problems. His meetings with Reagan—the president with whom he says he was closest of all— were almost entirely private, under the radar. The vow to be a spiritual adviser but not a political ally was renewed, and generally honored thereafter. As it happened, there were among his oldest friends and acquaintances several presidents in waiting, and he would be tested and tested again.

He remained far and away the most respected evangelical leader in the world; but at a time when other evangelical leaders crowded into the public arena, organizing voters, promoting candidates, elevating social issues as litmus tests, Graham was someplace else entirely, resolutely welcoming to all believers, all over the world. God, he said, did not favor one nation over another. The message of his final years, of suffering and of reconciliation, is a kind of witness all its own. A long and extraordinary journey approached its sharpest turn. "I don't have much longer," he told us, without fear or regret. But he had lived an enormous life and he was a curious man, who believed as sure as he believed anything that there's another adventure ahead, the greatest of all.

So in the time he had left he would take the time to look back, tell his story, and let his lessons live long after he was gone.

ONE

The Invocation

*I didn't have any other motives throughout my life but to proclaim the gospel.
I'm amazed myself that I was able to see all those men become president.*

—Graham on his calling

SEPTEMBER 23, 1949

The sky was dark and spitting hailstones on Friday morning just before 11 a.m., when secretary Myrtle Bergheim from the White House press office passed by the pressroom. "The Boss says don't go away," she told the loitering reporters. "He might have a little something later."

A few minutes later, a dozen reporters gathered around the walnut desk of Charles Ross, Harry Truman's old friend and press secretary. "Close the doors," he said. "Nobody is leaving here until everybody has this statement." He handed out copies. The reporters started reading, whistled through their teeth, then bolted for the door and sprinted through the White House lobby, ripping the nose off a stuffed deer as they raced to the pressroom telephones. Two minutes later the bells on the tickers in newsrooms signaled a flash; by 11:08 the Associated Press bulletin was on the wires.

"We have evidence," the White House statement announced, "that within recent weeks an atomic explosion occurred in the U.S.S.R."

Closing the books on an innocent age, *TIME* declared that "the news hit the nation with the jarring impact of a fear suddenly become fact. . . . For the first time, U.S. citizens would know, as much of the world had known since 1945, how it feels to live under the threat of

sudden destruction—coming like a clap of thunder and a rattle of hail."
Some in Congress raised the question of transferring government agen-
cies out of Washington. Veterans dryly nudged each other: "Better get out
your old uniform." Secretary of Defense Louis Johnson urged the newspapers not to overplay the story and fuel panic, guidance that the Hearst
papers at least found easy to ignore. The *New York Journal-American* ran a
half-page picture showing Manhattan engulfed in atomic "waves of death
and havoc."

The news came at the end of an unsettling summer, one that had
weighed heavily on Truman. His triumphs of the first half of 1949—the
signing of the NATO treaty in April, the ultimate success of the Berlin
airlift at breaking the Soviet blockade a month later—had given way to a
woozy economy and rising fears. The perjury trial of accused Soviet spy
Alger Hiss ended in a hung jury in July, with a new trial scheduled for fall.
The China lobby, watching the collapse of Chiang Kai-shek's national-
ist forces in the face of Mao's million-man communist army, was hurling
abuse at Truman and Secretary of State Dean Acheson. Unemployment
was rising; business profits were down 13 percent. People talked, extravagantly, about depression, the fear that was never far away even in the
midst of postwar prosperity. To a group of visiting Girls Nation delegates
Truman referred, only half joking since he did it so often, to "this terrible
job" that allowed him to live "over there in that great white jail, with the
balcony and everything." More seriously, to his cousins Nellie and Ethel
Noland, he wrote that he had succeeded in getting himself into "more
trouble than Pandora ever let loose in the world."

Now the Soviets had the bomb. And one week later, on October 1, a
communist country comprising one-fifth of the human race inaugurated
itself as the People's Republic of China. It was all enough to make a country stop dead and fall on its knees for a moment.

As it happened, that was just what Billy Graham had in mind.

Now thirty years old, Graham had been having a hard summer himself. Five years out of Wheaton College, he'd spent most of that time
crisscrossing the country to preach at independent revivals and Youth for
Christ rallies. The experience had built his reputation and broadened his
ministry; but some private encounters had shaken his faith. That year his
talented friend and fellow evangelist Charles Templeton had decided to
suspend his preaching and head to Princeton Seminary, to put his beliefs

to a tough intellectual road test. Whenever he had the chance, he tried to pull Graham along with him.

"Billy," he said, during one visit to Graham's house in North Carolina, "it's not possible any longer to believe the biblical account of creation. The world wasn't created; it has evolved over millions of years. It's not a matter of speculation, it's demonstrable fact."

"I don't accept that," Graham said, "and there are reputable scholars who don't."

"Who are they?" Templeton asked. "Men in conservative Christian colleges?"

"Most of them, yes. But that's not the point." And then Graham went on to explain what he had learned in his young ministry, something he knew for certain, could "prove" because it happened inside and in front of him whenever he preached—even at the raucous Youth for Christ rallies that he and Templeton had led, which typically featured Bible quiz shows, magic acts, ventriloquists, close-harmony quartets, and a kneeling horse who would tap his hoof twelve times when asked how many apostles there were.

"When I take the Bible literally, when I proclaim it as God's Word, I have power," Graham explained. "When I stand before the people and say, 'God says,' or 'The Bible says,' the Holy Spirit uses me. There are results. People respond. Wiser men than you or I have been arguing questions like this for centuries. I don't have the time or the intellect to examine all sides of each theological dispute, so I've decided, once and for all, to stop questioning and to accept the Bible as God's Word."

Templeton was troubled by this. He called it intellectual suicide to actively decide not to question or explore. "Billy, you cannot refuse to think. To do that is to die intellectually." He tried to phrase it in Graham's own scriptural terms: this would amount to rebellion, a breach of faith. "You cannot disobey Christ's great commandment to love God 'with all thy heart and all thy soul and all thy *mind.*'"

And so it went between them all year long; they met in New York when Graham came to town, and then one more time in August, at a retreat center just outside Los Angeles. Graham was preparing for his most ambitious crusade yet in the City of Angels. Preachers weren't trying anything like this anymore; there had been few large-scale evangelistic meetings in the United States since World War I and the heyday of Billy Sunday and Aimee Semple McPherson. "We are tired of religious revivals as we have known them," announced the Reverend Willard Sperry, dean of Harvard Divinity School, in 1946. "Among all but the most backward churches it is now agreed that education is the best way of interesting our people in religion."

Graham's Los Angeles team thought otherwise; they had been organizing local churches and business groups, and the prayer groups had been praying. Organizers spent $25,000 on posters and ads: "Visit the Canvas Cathedral with the Steeple of Light" and hear "America's Sensational Young Evangelist." But first Graham had some demons to lay to rest.

At the conference center, Templeton confronted him with their growing theological rift, and leveled charges that would follow Graham for years to come. "Billy, you're fifty years out of date," he said. "People no longer accept the Bible as being inspired the way you do. Your faith is too simple. Your language is out of date. You're going to have to learn the new jargon if you're going to be successful in your ministry."

It was, as they say, a moment of truth. What could be more tempting, to a rising preacher trying to reach young people, a preacher who stressed being approachable and relevant, than to tailor his theology to the tastes of the times, especially if the latest scholarship allowed wider appeal? But to Graham, the choice was not between believing in the Bible's inerrancy or going down a more modern, popular road. For him it came down to this: Believe the Bible or leave the ministry. "It was not too late to be a dairy farmer," he concluded.

What followed was an event that became so central to Graham's life and ministry that a plaque on the grounds marks the spot where it happened. As he often did when he couldn't sleep and his mind was burning, he went for a walk and wound up in the woods near the retreat center. He opened the Bible on a tree stump and prayed in the moonlight. There was too much in there he couldn't understand, confusion and contradiction and mystery. And finally, he felt the spirit release him, to say, "Father, I am going to accept this as Thy word—by *faith*."

He recalled feeling God's presence as he hadn't in months, and sensed that a spiritual battle had been fought and won. In years to come, when Winston Churchill asked him about heaven, or Eisenhower about salvation, or Johnson about sin and damnation, he could answer them with a kind of certainty that made men in authority sit back and listen. He was the messenger; he was not scripting the message, and his power was perfect so long as he did not embellish or interpret the word he had been given to transmit. His strength was absolute in this role. So was his confidence.

THE CANVAS CATHEDRAL

And so he descended on Los Angeles just as the news of the Russian bomb was breaking, with a message for a shaken city. A "Fact Sheet" prepared by the Christ for Greater Los Angeles sponsors described him as "tall, slender, handsome, with a curly shock of blond hair, Graham looks like a collar ad, acts like a motion picture star, thinks like a psychology professor, talks like a North Carolinian and preaches like a combination of Billy Sunday and Dwight L. Moody. He makes no pretensions to fame—says he's just a North Carolina hill-billy—believes in the literal interpretation of Bible truths—wears loud ties and socks because 'you don't need to be a long-hair to be good' and is recognized as America's outstanding evangelist. . . . He uses few illustrations, no sob stories, absolutely no deathbed stuff. His illustrations are usually current events."

A local Salvation Army public relations man, helping with the crusade publicity, had persuaded some reporters to come to Graham's first press conference. In the papers the next day, no one wrote a word.

Graham immediately wrapped the breaking news into his sermons. "Russia has now exploded an atomic bomb. Do you know the area that is marked out for the enemy's first atomic bomb? New York! Secondly, Chicago; and thirdly, the city of Los Angeles." Would God protect "this city of wickedness and sin, this city that is known around the world because of its sin, crime and immorality"? Graham paced the stage, using a lapel mike for the first time, wearing argyle socks and bright hand-painted ties and a double-breasted suit that flapped on his lanky frame, waving his arms as he hurled God's wrath over the crowds. He surveyed their sins—divorce, gambling, false prophets, and treachery. "Do you know that the Fifth Columnists, called communists, are more rampant in Los Angeles than any other city in America? We need a revival."

Graham's universe was drawn by hand in black and white. For people wrestling with all kinds of new uncertainty in the postwar shadows, his conviction and the simplicity of his message were bracing and new. In the opening meetings, he preached to about three thousand people a night, which was a respectable number, except that he suspected that most were already Christians. That would change, however, as the days passed. Maybe it was something in the air, something about the time. Maybe it was normal curiosity, in a city that likes a good show, that drew people down to the converted eight-peaked Ringling Brothers circus tent. And this was Hollywood, where a high-profile convert can make all the difference in the world. Among those answering the call were a Mob wiretapper, an Olympic runner, and a famously sinful radio cowboy who found Jesus and went on to run for president as a Prohibitionist.

One night Graham and his team arrived at the tent to be greeted by a herd of photographers and reporters. What on earth had happened? "You've just been kissed by William Randolph Hearst," one newsman explained.

Graham had never met the newspaper baron; he was later told that Hearst and Marion Davies had attended a crusade in disguise, after learning about it from a housekeeper named Hedla who used to listen to Graham on the radio. It is just as likely that Hearst came around because he was acutely interested in anything that a great many people were interested in. As the legend goes, he returned to his office and sent a two-word telegram to all his papers: "Puff Graham." The Hearst papers began running stories about the crusade all across the country, and it was not long before other news organizations noticed. By the final weeks of the crusade, all the wire services as well as *LIFE*, *Newsweek*, and the major papers were running stories.

Reporters called it the greatest revival in the history of Southern California. "Thousands Hit Sawdust Trail" was the headline in the *New York Sun*. "Old-style religion is sweeping the City of Angels with an evangelistic show overshadowing even Billy Sunday." And with that, Graham's words became national news. They were consumed by an audience hungry for explanations about how, in the space of four years, America had gone from an astounding victory over fascism to a global military and political struggle against a communist enemy with the potential to blow up their cities. As Truman reminded people, the Soviet nuclear breakthrough had been foreseen. But that it came several years earlier than expected seemed to confirm the fears that Joe McCarthy had been fanning all year, that communist spies had infiltrated the deep reaches of American power and stolen her secrets.

Graham warned of the spies in their midst and then addressed the most dangerous foe of all, against whom Christ alone offered protection. "Western culture and its fruits had its foundation in the Bible. . . . Communism, on the other hand, has decided against God, against Christ, against the Bible and against all religion," he said. "Communism is a religion that is inspired, directed and motivated by the Devil himself."

In the end the Los Angeles crusade lasted not three weeks but eight. Some 350,000 people attended, including stars like Jane Russell and Gene Autry. One movie star, not yet converted, told Graham bluntly, "Billy, you can't compete with us in entertainment. We know all the ropes. If you get up there and preach what's in the Bible, I'll be on hand every night."

Graham emerged a full-fledged celebrity; on the train back east people stopped and recognized him. His next crusade, in Boston starting on New Year's Eve 1949, was covered by the Boston papers as front-page news. They heralded the arrival of the "swashbuckling southerner" who shared, quite precisely, the dimensions of heaven as "sixteen hundred miles long, sixteen hundred miles wide and sixteen hundred miles high," with streets of gold that they'd drive down in a yellow Cadillac, and gates of pearl and trees bearing a different kind of fruit every month. "We became the object of a circulation war between the newspapers," Graham said, and each paper tried to outdo the others with its coverage. Years later, when confronted with some of his statements from these heady months, Graham would refer to his "boy preacher" days and note wryly that some of his theology had evolved.

Graham's own political career was also launched. He was invited to pray at the Massachusetts House of Representatives; reporters wanted to hear his positions on everything from the death penalty to foreign aid to the Marshall Plan. "What I said was being quoted all of a sudden, and I knew I wasn't really qualified," he admitted later. "I didn't really have the experience yet to say the right things, but the people expected me to speak with that authority. I was just scared to death." He told reporters that he thought a revival would do more than the Marshall Plan to combat evil, and warned that "we are going to spend ourselves into a depression. We can't keep on taking care of the whole world." Seeing the reporters scribbling his words, he quickly added, "But don't anybody tell Mr. Truman I said so."

As it happened, Truman would hear anyway.

THE OPENING WEDGE

Years later, when asked how it was that an unknown preacher became the best-known evangelist of the ages, he said there were two men most responsible: Hearst was one; but the other was Henry Luce, founder of Time Inc. and the nation's most powerful publisher. Hearst and Luce didn't much like each other—battling media barons rarely do—but they both very much liked Billy Graham.

Preachers, like presidents, have a message they are looking to transmit. For a traveling evangelist like Graham, who after 1945 did not have a pulpit to call his own, drawing people to his crusades depended on getting the word out. During their exile following the disasters of the Scopes trial and the collapse of Prohibition, fundamentalists had communicated underground. They were ignored by the national media but quick to see the power of radio and magazines, pamphlets, and, in decades to come, television and cable and the Internet. Since Graham was aiming to build a much wider audience, he needed to reach the secular press, something few religious leaders and virtually none as theologically conservative as Graham had managed.

Graham had an instinctive sense that something was changing in the way people learned about their world. He discovered the power of the photo op early on: Templeton recalled how once at Chicago's O'Hare Airport, on their way to tour battered Europe in 1946, hundreds of people had gathered to send them off—along with a flock of photographers. So they kneeled on the tarmac, asking God's blessing for their mission as the cameramen scuttled around, looking for angles, calling, "Keep prayin', fellas! That's it—hold it! Just one more prayer!" which they obligingly provided. "In the photographs," Templeton recalled, "it can be seen that Billy and I are having trouble restraining our laughter."

Hearst sent a photographer to cover that European tour and then helped again by promoting the Los Angeles crusade. But it was Luce who quickly took up the role of Graham's premier publicist. Graham understood how much farther his message would travel with allies such as this. God was opening a door for him, Graham thought, when powerful men like Luce were taking him seriously.

Luce was a missionary's son, whose love of country and faith in its goodness was of the kind sometimes peculiar to people who did not grow up in it. He had founded *TIME* as a vessel for his belief that it was great men who made history, in all their valor and vanity. He took his Calvinist Presbyterianism seriously, which was just one of many things that distanced him from other media moguls of the day. He was awkward, lonely, restless, rude, innocent, and endlessly curious, a collector of remarkable characters, with an acute instinct for what people wanted to read about. He and Graham, in other words, were perfect for each other.

In the spring of 1950, his friend Bernard Baruch was staying at his South Carolina vacation home, a plantation at Hobcaw Bay; the local paper was carrying the sermons that Graham was preaching in Columbia. "There's a young fellow down here that's not only preaching some good religion," Baruch told Luce, "but he's giving some good common sense." Luce decided to go see for himself.

TIME's Atlanta bureau chief, William Howland, met Luce in Charleston, South Carolina, having arranged dinner with Governor Strom Thurmond at the Governor's Mansion after the crusade service. The crowds, Howland observed, were typical for a southern revival: "earnest, discouraged by lack of success in this life, not well dressed nor well educated, it was a sort of southern American gothic crowd; denominationally it was almost entirely Baptist, Methodist and Church of God." There were bobby-soxers and old people, "lintheads and farmers," not many big cars in the parking lots but they came from all over the state, and Georgia, Florida, North Carolina. Thurmond and his wife were frequent guests on the platform, along with Senator Olin Johnson and Supreme Court justice James Byrnes, Truman's former secretary of state, who said of the service, "I've been with statesmen, presidents, and kings . . . but this is the most inspiring moment of my life."

And yet it was the idea of Luce in the audience that made Graham nervous. He worried that the sermon he had prepared on Divine Judgment might be off-putting to him, and was strongly tempted to change his text. But he feared that God would disapprove of him pulling his punches to appeal to a powerful man, and would punish him for it. As it turned out, Luce was all the more intrigued.

"All you have to do to go to heaven is to put your faith in Jesus," Graham proclaimed. "When they talk of the hydrogen bomb, my heart grows heavy, but I am not afraid. I know that when the bomb drops and I've disintegrated, I'll go to heaven." And on he talked, and down the aisles they came, some weeping, some just quiet and sure, old women with burning eyes, girls in pigtails, young men in overalls, as the choir sang Graham's trademark hymn, "Just As I Am," and Graham stood and welcomed them home.

Back at the Governor's Mansion, Luce and Graham stayed up late into the night, talking theology. "I think he was trying to pull me out," Graham said, "to see if I was genuine or honest."

Among other things, the encounter had an impact on *TIME*'s coverage. In February the magazine had reported that "admirers of glib, armflailing Evangelist Dr. Billy Graham, 31, swear his voice can penetrate a case-hardened conscience like a jackhammer." But after Luce's visit, the tone was less mocking. Now he was "hawk-nosed, handsome Evangelist Billy Graham," whose old-time religion he "spruces up with streamlined metaphors of his own. Said he of Judgment Day: 'God is going to say "Start up the projector!" Because from the cradle to the grave God has had His television cameras on you. God has every sinful word on His recording. . . . Are you ready?'"

Graham wrote to tell Luce how honored he had been by his presence; he noted that he had been invited to Washington to open the House of Representatives with a prayer the next month, and to address a group of senators, who were urging that he bring his crusade to the capital. "The Lord is working on our behalf," Graham told Luce. "It may be the opening wedge that I spoke to you about. If Washington could experience a spiritual revival and our national leaders turn to Christ for the answer to our dilemma, the course of history may be changed."

That was it; the hope that drove the journey that now commenced. Change the hearts of men of influence and then influence many more people through them. Much to the frustration of future social reformers, the faith that he expressed to Henry Luce never faded: install Christ in the Oval Office and on Capitol Hill, and the nation's problems would take care of themselves.

TWO

Harry and Billy

I know that I didn't have any fear—and I should have, because I asked him
about his personal faith. He said he believed in the Sermon on the Mount, tried
to live by the Golden Rule. And I told him, "I don't think that's enough!"
—Graham on his first meeting with Harry Truman

It would be easy to imagine Harry Truman and Billy Graham hitting it off just great. Both were devout sons of strong farm families whose lives had taken a surprising turn. Though of different generations—Graham was thirty-one, Truman sixty-six when they met—they were both, in their values and tastes, anchored in an earlier age. It's true that Graham never drank anything stronger than buttermilk, while Harry liked his bourbon and his poker games; yet the president was, compared to his peers, an upright though not self-righteous fellow. He never embraced the Jazz Age, never learned to dance, never really left the moral upholstery of a nineteenth-century small-town America, the America whose visions and values Graham invoked at every turn when calling his listeners home to their better natures and a simpler time.

Above all, they were two men whose personal modesty was tested over time by achievements that surprised no one more than themselves. Truman, the man Winston Churchill said had "more than any other man . . . saved Western Civilization," was derided as one of history's wild accidents. A great reader and student, he dreamed of being a concert pianist; as a young man with a new job he spent twenty-five dollars he didn't have for a complete set of Mark Twain. Yet he never made it to college, after his father lost everything betting on wheat futures. His path to the

White House moved from the mailroom at the *Kansas City Star* to time-keeper on the Santa Fe Railroad, to bank clerk to farmer to soldier to haberdasher to machine politician in Kansas City; even as a senator, he was sliding toward obscurity at fifty. He achieved ultimate power thanks to a few flips of the lever by the Democratic power brokers in 1944, which hoisted him into the vice presidency.

Graham was, by comparison, a prodigy, preaching to millions of people all across the country and Europe by the time he was thirty. And yet his ascent was no less surprising; he often said that the first question he planned to ask God when he got to heaven was, "Why me?" A mediocre student from a dairy farm outside Charlotte, North Carolina, he wanted to date girls and play baseball—he once shook Babe Ruth's hand—and said the local minister reminded him of a mortician. Since in those days, in those parts, a son who grew up to preach the gospel was more to be prized than one who grew up to be president, it can't have cheered his pious parents when a visiting preacher at their home told the rambunctious twelve-year-old Billy, "Run along, little fellow, you'll never be a preacher." He was, however, a great salesman, as he learned selling Fuller brushes door to door the summer before college: "Sincerity," he concluded, "is the biggest part of selling anything—including the Christian plan of salvation." He preached his first sermon at the age of seventeen to a cluster of drunks, thieves, and vagrants in a Monroe, North Carolina, jail.

Graham's first attempt at college had been a semester spent at Bob Jones University in Cleveland, Tennessee; it was the kind of strict, fundamentalist education that Morrow Graham had dreamed of for her son, where even once they got permission to go on a date students were not permitted to sit on the same sofa. He couldn't take it, and when he went to see Dr. Bob to tell him he was planning to transfer, Jones pronounced him a failure who would never amount to anything. "I left his office disillusioned and dejected," Graham said. Though raised a Presbyterian, Graham enrolled in the Florida Bible Institute instead, and in 1939 was ordained a Southern Baptist minister. Four years later he graduated from Wheaton College in Illinois, with his degree in anthropology and his new wife, Ruth. It took but a year and a half as pastor of a small church in Western Springs, Illinois, for Graham to discover his evangelical call and leave his pastorate to barnstorm for Youth for Christ.

Truman and Graham shared some habits of mind: corny, unspoiled, optimistic, curious, deeply patriotic, self-made men. Neither spoke in the plummy vowels of a Harvard Club, neither was big on nuance or sarcasm or cleverness for its own sake. Both were called simple, but neither actually was. There were plenty of wily veterans of the sawdust trail, and Truman's predecessor in the White House was a study in subtlety. But neither Truman nor Graham was an operator, though they did not necessarily believe this of each other.

In the beginning Graham was impressed by Truman's skills and eager to win his respect. It was during the final heat of the presidential campaign of 1948, when Graham was staging Youth for Christ rallies in Des Moines, that he rose at dawn and went with his colleague Cliff Barrows to hear Truman speak. Truman and Thomas Dewey had both brought their campaigns to the farm belt that September, with the Democrats determined to pull Iowa into their column. "I'm going to fight hard," Truman told the reporters with him as he set off, "and I'm going to give 'em hell." Graham went to one of the "platform stops," where a few hundred people gathered to hear the candidate talk off the back of the train. Whatever Graham had learned about capturing a crowd's imagination, at that moment he got to see a master at work, a secular version of the revivals he was holding every night, and feel for himself the gusts of a different kind of power. Truman talked about plowing, about farm life and the economy, introduced his wife, Bess, and daughter Margaret, and it was all so real and raw, slapping those Republicans as "gluttons of privilege," who had "stuck a pitchfork in the farmer's back." "I told Cliff," Graham recalled, "'if he gets before enough people with that message he's going to win!'"

Years later Graham said he couldn't remember whom he voted for—he'd been raised a Democrat, but Dewey did go on to become his friend and personal lawyer. But a year later, even before his national breakout in Los Angeles, Graham was intent on leveraging the president's attention for his cause. At that time he had the distinction of being the youngest college president in the country, having been recruited by a storied fundamentalist leader named William Riley to succeed him as president of the Northwestern Schools, a strict Bible college in Minnesota. One of his early initiatives was to launch a religious radio station. In February 1949, Truman received a telegram noting that "new unique powerful radio station KTIS on air this week in Minneapolis." The dedication program was to be held Sunday afternoon, with all kinds of local civic and religious leaders in attendance, Graham wrote. "Would deeply appreciate a congratulatory telegram. This station noncommercial and dedicated to the building of good will in the Midwest. Eagerly awaiting your telegram."

Such an act gives a clue to Graham's sense of himself and his destiny. Truman's secretary Charlie Ross wrote back, with characteristic tact, that the president regretted being unable to help, but he received so many such requests that he did not want to be playing favorites. Graham cabled back that he understood, and added, "Please be assured of this, that over 1100 students here at these Northwestern Schools are praying daily that God will give him wisdom and guidance in the strenuous days ahead. . . . We believe him to be God's choice for this great office."

That last could be dismissed as mere spiritual flattery—except that all through his career Graham would, without reserve, offer his prayers and support for whoever was in office, whatever their political disagreements. Come election time, he prayed that God's will would be done; and the man who emerged victorious, whether or not he was Graham's choice, received the evangelist's public and prayerful support. That pattern gave weight to his claims of political neutrality, but also left him reluctant to challenge any decision by a man whom he believed had been chosen by God.

Truman himself was too modest to have imagined himself as "God's choice." But it was true that over the course of his unlikely rise to power, as David McCullough chronicles in his epic biography, his faith was seldom far from his sleeve. At his moment of ascension to the presidency in April 1945 after Roosevelt's sudden death, Chief Justice Harlan Stone held a cheap Gideon Bible, scavenged from a drawer of the White House head usher; at the end of the ceremony, Truman reached for it and kissed it. When, against all odds and predictions, things went well in the early days, Truman wrote in his diary, "I can't understand it—except to attribute it to God. He guides me, I think." He would sometimes slip across Lafayette Park to St. John's Church and sit in a back pew, where no one paid him much mind.

He did harbor some suspicions about itinerant preachers: "It used to be you couldn't go downtown in the evening without running into a half dozen evangelists ranting and raving and carrying on," he said of his days growing up in Independence. Graham's style back then was at its most flamboyant, not just the radiant ties and lively socks, but an equally flashy preaching style that appealed to ever larger crowds but would have been way too extravagant for Truman's more austere taste.

Graham was undaunted by Truman's first rebuff and emboldened by the attention being paid his every move after Los Angeles; he sent Truman another telegram, this one from Boston at 7:30 on New Year's Day 1950. For all the focus on his Los Angeles triumph, the reception in Boston by "God's frozen people" was even more remarkable. This was not a city where a southern preacher could succeed just by putting on a good show. The skeptical *Boston Herald* headline on New Year's Eve read, "Evangelist here to vie with New Year's Fun," and mocked the idea that Graham thought he could draw a crowd to hear a sermon with no champagne involved. But it turned out that no hotel or nightclub drew a bigger crowd, and the assembly approved a resolution that Graham now passed along to the president. History was watching, it said, as the American way of life was "seriously threatened by anti-God forces from without and moral disintegration from within." But America was on the brink of a mighty revival, which could perhaps benefit from a presidential endorsement. "We urge you to call America to her knees in a day of prayer and repentance of sin, and as a nation renew our faith in the God our forefathers stamped on our coins."

One could lose count over the whole span of his ministry how many times Graham predicted that a great revival was stirring, but in 1950 the evidence was on his side. In the postwar search for something that felt familiar and safe, churches of all species saw their congregations growing, sales of Bibles doubled between 1947 and 1952, seminaries were crowded, new churches rose across the sprawling new suburbs. There was a hunger, and Graham felt it, and all he wanted to do, he told an AP reporter in Boston, was "to get President Truman's ear for thirty minutes, to get a little help."

This was a new priority for a preacher of old-time religion: for the past generation fundamentalist Christians had largely separated themselves from worldly affairs, tending their individual souls, leaving society's business to be straightened out when Christ came again to reign in glory. But Graham cleared the way for a new breed, and by throwing himself headlong into the public debate, befriending politicians, and discussing social and economic trends, he invited evangelicals to emerge from pious isolation and join him: keep believing the Bible, keep the faith, but enter into the mainstream of postwar American success and suburban prosperity and public citizenship.

AN OVAL OFFICE ENCOUNTER

Graham liked to think that politicians were responding to his message, but often they were responding to how *other* people responded. Among those struck by the great Boston revival was Massachusetts congressman John McCormack, who would eventually ascend to be House Speaker. He could hardly miss the headlines when forty thousand people turned up on the Boston Common to hear Graham: "Huge Crowd Braves Rain and Chill at Greatest Prayer Meeting in Common's History as Evangelist Launches Five-Point Program for World Peace." It was he who managed, after a number of attempts, to get Graham his appointment with Harry Truman, on the fourteenth of July, at noon.

As fate would have it, Truman's hopes for peace came crashing down in the weeks between making that date and keeping it. On June 25, the North Korean army stormed across the 38th parallel into South Korea. Truman confronted a challenge from a communist-backed power that risked either widening into a larger Asian war, or demonstrating that the United States was not prepared to meet such aggression. Truman was home in Independence when word of the invasion came. As his daughter Margaret recalled it, "My father made it clear from the moment he heard the news, that he feared this was the opening of WWIII."

The American people generally favored a strong response. And Graham himself, whose wife had been educated in Korea during some of the years when her parents served as missionaries in China, weighed in with his own counsel. Knowing he was to see the president in a few weeks, Graham sent a cable to Truman that day, putting the Korean invasion in a spiritual and demographic context. "Millions of Christians praying God give you wisdom in this crisis," Graham wrote. "Strongly urge showdown with communism now. More Christians in southern Korea per capita than any part of the world. We cannot let them down." Now, the telegram was signed not "President of Northwestern Schools," but rather "Evangelist Billy Graham."

Graham understood intuitively how anxious people felt. With something of a residual war reflex, there was a rush on nylons, soap, tires, washing machines, even toilet paper. On June 30, when Truman, with United
Nations support, agreed to commit ground forces, he called it the hardest
decision of his presidency—harder than Hiroshima. The deadly slaughter
of the days that followed was one of the grimmest chapters in American
military history, as a small band of inexperienced but valiant GIs tried to
slow the North Korean advance until reinforcements could arrive. Truman lauded it as one of the most heroic rearguard actions ever undertaken.
But however brave and necessary, that was not the kind of war Americans
were used to fighting. Defense Secretary Louis Johnson was called incom-
petent or worse; some said General MacArthur should be allowed to drop
the bomb and be done with it.

All the pressures came together in a historic cabinet meeting on July 14.
Faced with the facts on the ground and the realities of U.S. resources,
Truman committed himself to battle. Embracing the recommendations of
NSC-68, the blueprint for the cold war, he asked Congress for an emergency appropriation of $10 billion, in a year when the whole military bud-
get was supposed to be $13 billion. Before the year ended it would reach
$50 billion. He was accelerating the draft—later that summer he called
for doubling the size of the armed forces to three million. On that day,
in that meeting, was born the arms race that would shape U.S. policy for
decades to come.

The cabinet meeting took place at ten that morning. And at noon,
Truman was paid a visit by Billy Graham.

"It was quite an event for a country boy to go calling on the President
of the United States." That was how Truman described his first time calling on Franklin Roosevelt as a rookie senator in 1935. Graham felt just
the same way; as the visit approached he was nervous, not sleeping well,
debating what he and his three colleagues—song leader Cliff Barrows,
publicist Jerry Beaven, and his childhood friend and fellow evangelist
Grady Wilson—should wear. Like the president, Graham was a careful
dresser, neat to the point of obsession. Truman struggled when he came
to Washington to find a dry cleaner who could press his suits properly;
Graham was known to take three showers in a day. He was determined
to make a good impression: "After all, the President was a haberdasher
himself."

He remembered a picture he had seen in the paper, of Truman vacationing in his Little White House in Key West, Florida, wearing casual clothes and white bucks. That was it; Graham sent Wilson down to Florsheim's to buy white bucks for everyone. *TIME* described him as wearing a "pistachio green suit," the others similarly lively. Judging from the look on his face, Graham recalled, "the chief executive of our nation must have thought he was receiving a traveling vaudeville team."

There was Truman, slight, bespectacled, modest, with his thin, transparent hair and a voice that was high and pinched as if there was a strap fastened too tightly around his neck. He was five foot nine but could seem smaller than he was, and critics liked to call him that "little man." Everything he said tended to be anchored in sense and substance, especially on a day when he was weighing the prospect of yet another war.

And then there was Graham, six foot two, his features fiercely beautiful where Truman's were gently wise, his voice an instrument of vast range and power as he spoke of all things seen and unseen and the kingdom eternal.

As Graham remembered it, the two men made polite conversation for a while. Truman said he had heard good things about the meetings, and Graham told him about the crowds in Los Angeles and Boston. They talked about Korea; Graham told him that people were gripped by "a fear you could almost call hysteria," and urged him to "get a microphone and encourage the people at this hour." We can't come through this crisis, Graham told him, "unless we turn to God."

After fifteen minutes or so Graham realized his time was running out, and he had to seize the moment. "I know that I didn't have any fear," he recalled of his attitude, "and I should have, because I asked him about his personal faith."

"Mr. President," he said, "tell me about your religious background and leanings." "Well," Truman replied, "I try to live by the Sermon on the Mount and the Golden Rule."

That simple moral road map had been drawn back when he had memorized the Sermon on the Mount as a child; by the time he was five his mother had taught him to read the large-print family Bible. But that didn't mean he was comfortable talking about it with a stranger. "I am by religion like everything else," he once wrote to Bess Wallace during their courtship. "I think there's more in acting than in talking." (It is worth noting that Bess was a Presbyterian, Harry a Baptist, which put her higher up the ecclesiastical pecking order, a status gap that her mother at least was not inclined to overlook even when he became President Harry the Baptist.)

As for living by the Golden Rule, that had provided ammunition for Truman's many critics, who charged that he was naïve to place much faith in the basic goodness of people. A lethal verse accompanying a cartoon from the *Chicago Tribune* went:

Look at little Truman now,
Muddy, battered, bruised—and how!
Victim of his misplaced trust,
He has learned what good boys must.
In the alley after school,
There just ain't no golden rule.

Years later, Graham was abashed at what he said next. "I said, 'I don't think that's enough!'" He went on to explain that it was faith in Christ and His death on the Cross that mattered. The president stood up. Graham realized that his time was up—"we were only supposed to stay twenty minutes"—and stood up too.

"And as he got up to see us to the door, I put my arm around him, and I said 'Mr. President, could we pray?'"

"Well," Truman replied, "I don't think it could do any harm."

And so Graham put his long arm around Truman's shoulder, drew him close, and prayed with him and for him:

"Our Father, we thank thee for the privilege of being here today, and we pray for thy blessing on this man on whose shoulders rest perhaps the most important responsibility in the world.

"We pray that thou wouldst give him wisdom, strength and courage for these critical days. Bless this nation at this hour and if it be thy will, give victory to our armed forces. Amen."

"Amen," Cliff Barrows kept muttering as Graham prayed, "do it Lord."

And then they stepped outside into a flock of hovering cameras and pencils. The reporters wanted to know everything. "What did the president say?"

Graham told them everything he could remember, "like a fool—nobody had briefed me that you don't quote the president." Truman, he said, was giving "serious thought" to going on the radio to reassure the country and to call on church leaders to arrange that national day of repentance and prayer.

"What did you say?"

And Graham told them. He described Truman as being "very gracious, very humble, very sweet."

"Did you pray with the president?"

"Yes, we prayed with the president."

"What did he think about that?"

Graham explained that they had stood with their heads bowed, and "I just prayed to the Lord, and asked God to give him wisdom."

"Would you pray out on the lawn and let us take a picture?" a photographer asked. "We couldn't get in to take a picture."

"Kneel down, kneel down," other reporters shouted.

Since Graham and his team had intended to thank God for their visit anyway, they went down on one knee in their ice-cream-colored suits there on the White House lawn. "I prayed, a real prayer," Graham said. "I didn't try to redo something that I'd done. And of course the next day the press had that picture. I was so embarrassed."

"It began to dawn on me a few days later," Graham would write, "how we had abused the privilege of seeing the president. National coverage of our visit was definitely not to our advantage." In fact Truman was furious. Columnist Drew Pearson reported a few days later that Graham was no longer welcome at the White House.

Truman's hostility was personal; he was the only president who suspected Graham might be a phony or a cynic. "He's . . . well, I hadn't ought to say this," Truman later told oral historian Merle Miller, "but he's one of those counterfeits I was telling you about. He claims he's a friend of all the Presidents, but he was never a friend of mine when I was President. I just don't go for people like that. All he's interested in is getting his name in the paper."

Graham came away more impressed than Truman, though that wasn't saying much. Four days later he wrote to Matthew Connelly to ask for an autographed picture, "that I might proudly display in my office." On July 31 he wrote directly to Truman to thank him, and to offer himself as a kind of political canary in the coal mine. This letter represented his first real effort to reach out to a president and offer his assistance, and it gave a clue about the kind of relationship he envisioned. He was not proposing a public alliance, a shared spotlight that would reflect well on both men. It was a private offer, a suggestion that Graham's ministry might give him a special insight into the mood of the country that a president might want to hear.

You seldom see any signs of vanity in Graham: with the arrival of fame, pride was the sin he most feared. But when it came to politics, to reading the public mood and riding it, he often just could not resist. "It is my privilege to speak to from five to twenty thousand people a night in every section of America. I believe I talk to more people face to face than any living man," he reminded the president, who particularly in the course of his whistle-stop campaigns had spoken to plenty of people himself, perhaps more than any president ever had. "I know something of the mood, thinking and trends in American thought."

He offered spiritual advice certainly, about the value of a national day of prayer. But there was political guidance as well, urging a "total mobilization" against communism. "The American people," he assured Truman, "are not concerned about how much it will cost the taxpayer if they can be assured of military security."

He made Truman the offer he would make to each president who followed. He could act as a kind of private pollster of the nation's mood and spirit. "I have every confidence in you," he said, "and that confidence was strengthened in my conversation with you a few days ago. If at any time I can be of service to you personally or to our country, please do not hesitate to call. Also, I follow political trends carefully and would be delighted at any time to advise you on my findings among the people."

Truman would never take him up on the offer, though Graham persisted in trying to win him over. No other president would ever put up the same resistance.

THREE

Truman's Rejection

I became strongly anticommunist; that was almost my gospel for a while. That was wrong. I shouldn't have done that. But that was the way I felt at that time. I was young and inexperienced.

—Graham on his early years

For Truman the months that followed his July 1950 meeting with Graham were as wild a ride as any in his presidency. MacArthur's daring landing at Inchon turned the war around; a counterattack by 260,000 Chinese troops pouring into Korea turned it again. MacArthur wanted a naval blockade of China, permission to bomb Manchuria and mainland cities: "WWIII moves ever closer," warned *LIFE*.

When Truman met with his cabinet on November 28, 1950, he reminded them in the grimmest of terms what was at stake. Graham sent a message of support. "I am praying for you during these critical hours that will decide the future of the world," he wrote to Truman. "With complete trust and confidence in the God of our fathers I believe he will give you wisdom and strength." And Truman would now hear from others as well, who took more comfort in Graham's prayers than from anything they were hearing from policymakers.

One Edward Lindley of Emporia, Kansas, a "retired minister of the Methodist persuasion," wrote to the president that he would inspire more confidence in people during these hard times if he embraced someone like Graham, whom he referred to as "a virile young Baptist minister." Graham had captured the country's confidence and imagination, Lindley said: "My suggestion is that in your 'Emergency Address' you mention him with approval." This would mark the first of what would be countless letters to the presidents recommending Graham for commissions, committees, cabinet positions, ambassadorships, the Supreme Court, and, a couple of times, the vice presidency of the United States.

The challenge for Truman was that it was harder to be subtle than strident, to ease the public into a new way of looking at the world, now that a mistake could mean annihilation. The idea of fighting a limited war was a new and for some people an uncomfortable one, and Graham was influenced at that time by those who were calling for an all-out showdown with the communists. He came to echo many of those whom Truman found himself at war against: the brass-knuckled cold warriors who were quick to see weakness rather than wisdom in any act of restraint; the hawks of the China lobby, Graham's mentor Luce high among them, who exalted Chiang Kai-shek as a great leader however unreliable he'd proven as an ally; the red-baiters in the Senate who threw down a gauntlet: fall in line, or be called a traitor.

In December Graham was concluding a six-week Atlanta crusade, where he devoted part of his sermons to events in Korea. He denounced the State Department for not listening to the wise men on Far Eastern affairs—a list that included MacArthur, Luce, and Chiang Kai-shek. "The State Department wouldn't listen to these people," he said, "and sent out diplomats and 'smart boys' there to be wined and dined." Of the British prime minister, Graham said, "It seems that nothing Mr. Truman and Mr. Attlee now can say will preserve Asia and keep Europe safe unless something miraculous happens. Wouldn't it be good if they would hold a little prayer meeting, telling God 'We don't know where to turn.'" On top of everything else, he warned of something rotten in the administration, referring to "a moral collapse—the recent investigations by congressional committees only scratch the surface of immorality in high places—we are breaking apart from the inside."

The warnings typically came on his *Hour of Decision* radio broadcasts, launched that fall on 150 ABC radio stations just days after the Chinese intervention in the war. Within a month Graham's was the biggest religious show on the air. Graham promised to present the news in a biblical context. "We shall keep you abreast of fast-moving events and try to interpret them for you in the light of the Scripture." Graham said, "From the first I decided to use a lot of current illustrations from national and international affairs as well as from social issues. For a while, I even had a teletype machine in our house so I could keep abreast of the latest events for these messages." In January of 1951 he warned about Truman's economic policy, though he avoided mentioning the president by name. "The vultures are now encircling our debt-ridden inflationary economy," he said, "with its fifteen-year record of deficit finance and its staggering national debt, to close in for the kill."

Graham even dipped a toe into the fetid waters of Joe McCarthy's witch hunts. Though they never met or corresponded, Graham almost sounded like an ally of the senator when he told audiences about "over 1100 social sounding organizations that are communist or communist operated in this country. They control the minds of a great segment of our people; the infiltration of the left wing . . . both pink and red into the intellectual strata of America" has gone so far that "our educational [and] religious culture is almost beyond repair." Even as McCarthy's fires were fading, Graham defended the cause of virulent anticommunism. "While nobody likes a watchdog," he said, "I thank God for men who, in the face of public denouncement and ridicule, go loyally about their work of exposing the pinks, the lavenders and the reds who have sought refuge beneath the wings of the American eagle and from that vantage point, try in every subtle, undercover way to bring comfort, aid and help to the greatest enemy we have ever known—communism."

Looking back, Graham saw the cost of allowing ideological battles to consume and distract him. "I became strongly anticommunist; that was almost my gospel for a while," he said. "That was wrong. . . . But that was the way I felt at that time. I was young and inexperienced." His convictions were rooted in his days at the Florida Bible Institute, when close friends of its president—evangelical firebrands, Graham called them—came to the campus and talked about communism. In later years he regretted the detours into geopolitics and red-baiting. "My job was preaching the gospel, which I did, that was the overwhelming thing of my life and my ministry." But sometimes, the pull of current events was irresistible.

Truman's firing of the insubordinate General MacArthur in April 1951, while backed by all of the military men he trusted, as well as those editorial pages that feared for the future of civilian control of the armed forces, nonetheless triggered a crisis like nothing the president had weathered during six years in office. "I fired him because he didn't respect the authority of the President," Truman explained years later. "I didn't fire him because he was a dumb son of a bitch, although he was, but that's not against the law for generals." Even politicians and columnists who had deplored MacArthur's miscalculations, winced at his ego, and questioned his judgment now reacted in horror at Truman, that little man, beheading one of the titanic figures of the age. More than two-thirds of the public came down on MacArthur's side in a Gallup poll, and images of Truman were burned in effigy.

"Ladies and gentlemen, I am not a politician," Graham declared. "I refrain from making statements on political matters; I am not choosing sides in the dismissal of General MacArthur." However, he went on, MacArthur had been especially helpful to missionaries in the Orient, and all Asian Christians would feel they had been dealt a blow. Upon MacArthur's return to the United States, Graham likened him to George Washington; when they met together in Washington, Graham declared of MacArthur, "He is one of the greatest Americans of all time."

Despite his initial support of Truman in Korea, Graham had come to criticize "this twilight war," this "half forgotten war," "this half-hearted war," "this terrible bloody tragedy." Perhaps the harshest attack, given the personal toll that managing the war took on Truman and his advisers, came in an *Hour of Decision* broadcast, when Graham charged that "some in Washington decided" that American boys were "expendable" and denounced the "diplomats who drank cocktails in Washington" while soldiers were dying in Korea.

THE GREAT WASHINGTON CRUSADE

So it should not have come as a surprise to Graham that as his historic January 1952 Washington crusade approached, his efforts to persuade the president and Mrs. Truman to put in an appearance were met with barely polite refusal. He sent Truman his first formal invitation two days before Christmas, explaining that most of the churches in the city were helping to sponsor the event, the first revival in the capital in thirty-five years, along with a long list of lawmakers serving on various crusade committees. There would be, he informed them, weekly businessmen's lunches, pastor workshops, and television and radio coverage, and already "the newspapers of the city are promising excellent cooperation and editorial support." A change of tone and subject couldn't do the president any harm: "Due to the recent unpleasant headlines that have emanated from Washington, more people than ever before are praying that Washington will have a spiritual and moral revival."

It was enormously important to Graham that Truman be there, that the crusade bring people together from both parties, all branches of government, a demonstration that the spiritual dimension of life was bigger and more powerful than any political agenda. "The opening meeting will begin at 3:00 January 13. I would count it a high privilege and distinct honor if you could bring a few words of greeting, and, if possible, stay for the entire service. . . . I believe millions of Americans would rejoice if you could take time out of your busy schedule to lend your presence to an event that millions of persons of every faith, race, color and creed will have their eyes upon."

Graham deeply believed in the good it would do for the nation to see the president calling the capital to prayer. But he was also alert to the political pressures. That October Truman had broached the idea of naming a U.S. ambassador to the Vatican, which among other things, he argued, would "assist in coordinating the effort to combat the Communist menace." To Republicans, this amounted to pandering to Catholic voters; to Truman's fellow Baptists, it would divide the country and destroy the separation of church and state. It was in that context that Graham, who did not share the anti-Catholicism of many evangelicals, wrote that Truman might be wise to show up that opening Sunday. "You may be interested to know I have refused to make any comment on the Vatican appointment because I didn't want to be put into the position of opposing you."

He closed in a spirit of sympathy and respect. "Your burdens are extremely heavy," he wrote. "I am certain that no one has any understanding of the responsibilities which press upon you." He wanted the president to know that he would be in his prayers.

In the private memos of the White House, Truman's hostility was plain. He was not the type to use a preacher for window dressing, and he wasn't up for reelection anyway: he needed someone like Graham neither for personal pastoring nor public protection. "At Key West," adviser William Hassett wrote to Matt Connelly, "the President said very decisively that he did not wish to endorse Billy Graham's Washington revival meeting and particularly said he did not want to receive him at the White House. You may remember what a show of himself Billy Graham made the last time he was here. The President does not want it repeated."

Connelly gently wrote back to Graham on New Year's Eve, saying how sorry he was to have to "send a disappointing reply." With Congress convening in early January, he said, the president's schedule was just too full.

About eleven thousand people came to the opening service at the Washington, D.C., Armory. While the capital was in many ways a southern city, the meetings would not be segregated. "In church there is no color line," Graham told reporters. In the days that followed, most audiences included several dozen members of Congress and a handful of senators. He preached on everything from dirty magazines to home and family life to the cheating scandal that had led to the expulsion of ninety cadets from West Point. Vice President Alben Barkley told him admiringly, "You're certainly rockin' the old capital."

Graham hoped that the prospect of the service at the capital might yet lure the president out of the White House and into the pew. "The eyes of the Christian world," not to mention ABC television, would be upon it, Graham told one White House aide in yet another plea to get Truman there. He added his belief that "the president will go down in history as one of the most courageous men of all times," and that he was eager to share his feelings publicly. Truman's principled resistance to Graham's courtship was remarkable given the letters coming into the White House from Graham's many admirers. Mrs. Mary Schmit of Trenton, Michigan, wrote, "Your burden, Mr. President, is very heavy. But we have a great burden bearer in our Lord Jesus Christ. In this hour of our greatest need, God is sending you help in the person of his servant, Billy Graham. Mr. President, see the hand of God in this move and give your assistance in every way, yea even by attending one or more of his meetings. Lead our people back to God."

But Truman was unyielding, and the service at the capital went ahead without him. "This country needs a revival," declared Speaker Sam Rayburn, "and I believe Billy Graham is bringing it to us." The House sergeant at arms estimated that the crowd surpassed that at Truman's inauguration. With the help of his faithfully steadying team, Graham handled his acclaim as a preacher by directing the praise heavenward; but when it came to politics, he talked as though God might toss the ball right back to him. Assessing the current political climate, he told the crowd, "If I would run for president of the United States today on a platform of calling people back to God, back to Christ, back to the Bible, I'd be elected. There is a hunger for God today." The news reports noted that Truman, while specially invited, did not attend.

This was becoming an embarrassment; Truman might be retiring, but other Democrats were going to have to face elections again, and as the crusade gathered momentum, more calls came from party leaders to urge the president to reconsider. "I believe we are missing a great opportunity by not inviting Dr. Billy Graham down to see the Boss," Alabama congressman Frank Boykin wrote to Connelly. "I see he is invited all over the world, Eisenhower in Paris, and somebody else in London, and I understand he is going to New York next week, at an invitation from General MacArthur."

This was a clear political warning. Graham had spoken at a congressional lunch for about sixty-five lawmakers from both parties. Boykin called it "the greatest hit I have ever heard of." He and his wife had gone to hear Graham at the Armory the night before, then had dinner with him and talked until midnight. "He is a great man, and I believe he can be very helpful. He has something, Matt, and I think it would be a wonderful thing, if President Harry Truman could invite Billy Graham down, and have a good heart to heart talk with him." But, he said, it would be even better if Truman would join the other VIPs on the stage. "I sat on the platform with him last night, and we had Senators and Congressmen from just all over the land, and I never saw so much enthusiasm in my life."

Graham certainly made an impression on politicians he encountered during his first deep immersion in the national political culture. He visited Capitol Hill almost every day; Lyndon Johnson, Richard Nixon, Sam Rayburn all sought him out. "There's an absolute change in the cloakrooms," South Carolina's Joseph Bryson told Graham. "You don't hear any more swearing or cursing, or off-color stories since you were here." At least three lawmakers came forward to accept Christ. "Once I spoke at a luncheon meeting in the Washington Hotel," Graham told a reporter, "to 100 congressmen and Senators, on the subject 'Communism and Christ.' After the lunch several came up and told me they'd never really understood communism until then." Graham saw a new and powerful opportunity in his ministry "to present Christ to the leadership of America at this crucial hour. I know them now," he said, "and I can walk into their offices and sit down and talk."

Many suggested he should run for office himself; maybe senator? He announced that he hoped to interview all the presidential candidates. "I want to give them the moral side of the thing. Of course, I do not intend to endorse any candidate." He had already predicted that "the Christian people of America will not sit idly by during the 1952 presidential campaign. [They] are going to vote as a bloc for the man with the strongest moral and spiritual platform, regardless of his views on other matters. I believe we can hold the balance of power."

The one disappointment of the whole experience was that the president never did come around. But Graham was understanding, at least publicly. The wire services ran a headline, "President Rebuffs Billy Graham." "I don't think it was that bad," Graham told a *TIME* correspondent. "I guess he was just too busy or something." But he added that "one congressman told me, 'Truman lost five million votes when he failed to see you.' I don't think the Administration realizes the tremendous impact this meeting has had across the entire nation."

Graham had, however, discovered the impact he could have, as had the politicians of that era. He learned that he would have to be more circumspect about what he said, for he had an enormous megaphone now. He was still a very young man who had risen very, very quickly. "I did not know how to conduct myself in front of the reporters," he said, looking back on those days. "Sometimes in my innocence I made statements on politics and foreign affairs that were outside my jurisdiction as a preacher. But experience was gradually teaching all of us to be more careful."

As for Truman, the accidental president, Graham would come to a greater appreciation as time passed. America found, somewhat to its surprise, a man of great personal and political courage, with no patience for political hacks, florid speech, airs, attitude, or ego that got in the way of action. He was, famously, the great unbending one, resistant to pressure, indifferent to popularity; the buck stops here. Looking back generations later, it's easy to forget how tender was that midcentury peace, how frail the institutions that initially rose to keep it, how much in need that postwar world was of leaders with nerves of iron. "I think history," Graham said, "is beginning to show him now as a great president."

One could say that Truman did Graham a favor; he gave him a sharp lesson in the importance of discretion. In years to come, Graham became more respectful of the presidents, more circumspect in what he said in public, which allowed the private ministry to flourish. Years later, in 1967, he visited Truman in Independence. The first thing out of his mouth was an apology for that notorious photograph. By this time the president had mellowed; Truman had once said that photographers were the only people in the world who could boss him around. "That's all right," he told Graham graciously. "I knew you hadn't been briefed." And then he took him on a tour of the Truman Library.

FOUR

Christian Soldier

I didn't even know if he was a Democrat or a Republican. It was his views that I was interested in.

—Graham on his first meeting with Eisenhower

It became part of the Graham legend that he was the one who convinced the eternally reluctant General Eisenhower to run for president in 1952. The real story is a little more complicated. While it was remarkable that a Texas billionaire arranged to send him to Paris to lobby Eisenhower in person, it's also true that by the time Graham and Eisenhower met, a long line of petitioners had laid the groundwork—and Eisenhower had already won the New Hampshire primary without actually shaking a single voter's hand.

The man who played matchmaker was one of the richest in the world, a reclusive Texas oil baron named Sid Richardson who met Billy Graham during his Fort Worth crusade in 1951 and adopted him. "Mr. Sid" didn't have much use for preaching, but he made an exception for Billy Graham. A man who loved money with great tenderness and judged talent with great shrewdness, Richardson introduced Graham to his whole stable of Texas protégés, including Lyndon Johnson and John Connally. He also passed along to his friend General Eisenhower a letter from Graham that laid out the reasons the preacher thought the general should run for president.

Eisenhower was sufficiently taken with Graham's letter that he wrote back directly in November 1951, only a week after noting in his diary how little interest he had in running for office. In a letter marked "Personal and Confidential" since he didn't want it quoted, he congratulated Graham on his efforts to "fight for the old-fashioned virtues of integrity, decency and straightforwardness in public life. I thank the Almighty that such inspired persons as yourself are ready and willing to give full time and energy to this great purpose."

Having said that, Eisenhower still begged off the idea of running. His NATO mission was too important, he said, to be dividing people by allying with one party or another. Graham wrote back and pressed his case, noting that a district judge "confided in me that if Washington were not cleaned out in the next two or three years, we were going to enter a period of chaos that could bring about our downfall. Sometimes I wonder who is going to win the battle first; the barbarians beating at our gates from without, or the termites of immorality from within." He added that he'd be praying for the general that God would "guide you in the greatest decision of your life. Upon this decision could well rest the destiny of the Western World." As Graham wryly noted later, "No one could accuse me of understatement."

"That was the damnedest letter I ever got," Eisenhower wrote to Richardson, and wanted to know more.

"I'll send him over so you can meet him."

There may not have been five people alive who thought Billy Graham and Dwight Eisenhower had much to say to each other, raised a generation apart and on different planets, one a man of arms, one a saver of souls. Ike was all stature and strength; Graham was eager gospel spirit. Both had been scooped up by some of the most powerful businessmen in the country, men like Richardson, who gave them gifts, lent them vacation homes, flew them in private planes to the best golf courses. While both were accused of being too much in awe of the rich, it was often the other way around. Like Graham during those years and unlike other politicians, Eisenhower faced the challenges that came with a certain kind of fame, not mere celebrity, but adulation. He had saved the Western world, and Billy would save your eternal soul. It was hard for anyone else to touch that.

Both men had faces that cameras loved, and there is no way to measure the impact that had on their success at the dawn of the television age: in 1950 just over four million households had TVs; by the end of the decade forty-five million did. Both men knew how to beguile reporters. Both could come across as simple country boys with a gift for putting people at ease—though Eisenhower cultivated his artlessness while Graham's was innate and impermeable. Eisenhower's wondrous grin could mask deep doubts and depressions, for he felt a leader had to project optimism. Graham went through passages of hypochondria when his closest friends had to work hard to assure him that he was not about to die.

But one thing Eisenhower was not exactly known for was his piety. He had never been much for churchgoing as he moved from army post to post. He had plenty of friends already. So why go out of his way to ally himself with a flamboyant young preacher at that particular moment? Why did Ike seem as interested in promoting religious revival as Graham was himself?

One thing this was not, aides insisted, was a matter of electoral politics. "He was not a hypocrite," said his speechwriter William Ewald. "He was not trying to display something that wasn't there, for the sake of votes or appealing to a constituency." Eisenhower knew something about the pressures of war—but was every bit as respectful of the pressures of the Oval Office. "He said he didn't see how in the world he could bear the burdens of the presidency without a belief in divine providence and leadership," Ewald recalled. "It couldn't be done. That was a very genuine feeling of his."

But any pastor could have helped him bear his burdens. Graham could also offer something more strategically valuable. Facing the prospect of a cold war, Eisenhower had come to a clear, hardheaded conviction about the role of religion in national survival. As he launched his run for the presidency, he talked about America's challenges and strengths. "In spite of the difficulties of the problems we have, I ask you this one question," he said. "If each of us in his own mind would dwell more upon those simple virtues—integrity, courage, self-confidence and unshakable belief in his Bible—would not some of these problems tend to simplify themselves? Would not we, after having done our very best with them, be content to leave the rest with the Almighty?"

You could say that the two men became friends, with the understanding that they were both men with a great many friends. Yet what they did together was less important than the extraordinary things they did separately but in parallel.

Getting to Know You

Half a century later Graham remembered most the smile, the handshake, the way Eisenhower looked at him, "very curious." He told reporters over the years that during that first meeting in Paris they spent a couple of hours together, but, intent on correcting the record, he'd say later that it was more like half an hour, "because he knew I had come all the way to see him."

If Truman's Baptist roots were not enough to win Graham over, Eisenhower's allergy to churches was not enough to keep him away. Up to this point, whatever he knew of the general's character, Graham knew next to nothing about the state of his soul. This encounter gave him his first clues. Eisenhower asked about the Washington crusade and what message Graham had been preaching; most people never actually bothered to ask about what he preached, since they assumed they already knew. They talked about America's spiritual health, and Eisenhower described his own family's roots among the fundamentalist River Brethren, an offshoot of refugee Swiss Mennonites, whose men wore beards and women kept their heads covered. "You know, what you stand for is my mother's faith," Graham recalled Eisenhower telling him.

Such a simple observation, such a complicated story. While Eisenhower had a more strict religious upbringing than other modern presidents, he did not have an easy story to tell, unlike the procession of Presbyterian and Episcopalian politicians who preceded him. He often praised his devout parents for the values they had instilled; but anything much more specific would have required a careful explanation, especially about his respect for a mother whose faith rejected much of what her son stood for. So not even Graham heard the whole story, then or later.

Though the extended Eisenhower family was River Brethren, both of Eisenhower's parents became active in the Bible Students, which years later would be known by a different name: Jehovah's Witnesses. Gatherings were held at members' homes, including the Eisenhowers', rather than any church, and his mother, Ida, often played the piano for the meetings, which were devoted to serious adult Bible study.

There was no talk of politics in the house, at least in any organized sense. "They felt that if each person were individually good, society could then take care of itself," brother Milton Eisenhower observed of their parents. "I think they were more concerned with the millennium, which unfortunately hadn't come in their day, than they were with contemporary social institutions." In accordance with Jehovah's Witness teaching, Eisenhower called his mother "the most honest and sincere pacifist I ever knew."

That, of course, could pose a problem to a devoted son who was also commanding the Western Alliance in World War II. In the spring of 1943 he wrote to his brother Arthur about a front-page story trumpeting his mother's antiwar views. "Some reporter made a point of the fact that our dear old Mother likes to go to conventions of her beloved Jehovah's Witnesses," he wrote. "As far as I am concerned, her happiness in her religion means more to me than any damn wisecrack that a newspaperman can get publicized—I know full well that the government is not going to measure my services as a soldier by the religious beliefs of my Mother."

That conviction did not prevent some extremist groups in the 1952 race from using Ida's faith to denounce Eisenhower as an "anti Christian Cultist" and a "foe of patriotism." It was a somewhat complicated situation for Eisenhower to have had parents obsessed with Armageddon when he was running to preside over the emerging nuclear age; parents who had named him after the nineteenth-century revivalist Dwight Moody, the Billy Graham of his age, who famously said, "I look upon this world as a wrecked vessel. God has given me a lifeboat and said, 'Moody, save all you can.'"

While the extremist charges were plainly ridiculous, Eisenhower did need some help constructing a more mainstream religious identity for himself after a childhood on the outer fringes of Protestantism and an adulthood largely free of churches of any kind. "I didn't go to church in the chapels in the military," he admitted to Graham, who recalled the salty language of that first conversation. "He used a lot of army language. It sort of shocked me at the time. I spoke to him a couple years later about that."

The alliance was forged that day in Paris; two days later, Eisenhower wrote a long, confidential letter to Drew Pearson that affirmed his religious agenda: "The more intimately I become familiar with the desperate difficulties that abound in the world today, the more convinced I am that solutions must be firmly based in spiritual and moral values." Graham told reporters in Paris about Eisenhower's interest in an American revival. He said that they had not talked politics at all and that he would not get involved in the campaign himself, other than to go on the air before election day reminding people that it was their Christian duty to vote.

But Graham came back from Europe clearly thrilled with finding himself in the political whirl. The 1952 campaign was the first in decades to be wide open on both sides, with no incumbents, no heirs apparent, and Graham was unabashed about his interest in the debate. He spoke to the convention of the National Association of Evangelicals in Chicago, the group born a decade earlier to help ease evangelicals back into the mainstream by breaking with the more barbed strands of fundamentalism. This was not a group that was used to having preachers roaming the halls of power or weighing in on the earthly issues of the day, and Graham knew he needed to explain his agenda.

"Many people have said to me, 'Why do you go and talk to all these political leaders?'" he told them. "Do you know the reason? I sit down with them and give them the Gospel of Jesus Christ straight from the shoulder. God has opened the door, and I believe it is my duty to talk to these leaders for Christ. I've had prayer with most of them."

But then he went further, inviting his brethren into the arena with him and educating them about how the game was played. "In the coming campaign," he told the group, "there's going to be the Jewish bloc, there's going to be the Roman Catholic bloc, there's going to be the Labor bloc, there's going to be the Negro bloc, there's going to be the Polish bloc, there's going to be the Irish bloc. They will put on tremendous pressure. . . . Some of them will almost hold the balance of power. Why should not evangelicals across America be conditioned and cultured and instructed until we, too, can make our voice known?"

This might be called the baptism of the religious right, though in nothing like the form in which it would emerge some three decades later. To the extent that Graham and his allies had an agenda, it was a very general one: a strong stance against godless communism, and promotion of spiritual values at home. There was no litmus test for candidates, no wedge issues or explicit plans to ally the faithful with one candidate or party.

It was, rather, the time for "good Christian men" to come out of the shadows and take an active role in politics. "The people are hungry for a moral crusade, and they need a Moses or a Daniel to lead them in this hour." Graham, of course, was sure that the people had found their Daniel.

The Great Crusade

That spring, Eisenhower officially hung up his uniform and returned to the States to re-create himself as a presidential candidate. The first week of June he went home to Abilene, Kansas, trailing clouds of glory and a whole host of reporters, to pay homage to the parents who had instilled in him the beliefs that would now anchor his run for the White House. *TIME* called it his political debut; standing in a field across from the white clapboard house where he and his brothers were raised, he had no prepared text, but spoke in the tones of a revivalist. *New York Times* reporter James Reston likened him to William Jennings Bryan and the preachers of the Chautauqua circuit. "He appealed not to the mind but to the heart," Reston wrote, "and his language was filled with the noble words of the old revivalists: frugality, austerity, honesty, economy, simplicity, integrity."

Eisenhower was nominated on the first ballot at the Republican convention in Chicago, and vowed to lead "a great crusade." During the convention Kansas senator Frank Carlson, whom Graham had met during the Washington crusade, called and said that Eisenhower wanted to see him, having sold Eisenhower on the idea of approaching the preacher again. "He [Carlson] thought I'd be a good speechwriter," Graham said.

They met at the Blackstone Hotel, which still had its original smoke-filled room where the party bosses chose Warren G. Harding for president. Eisenhower asked Graham if he'd be interested in pitching in. Graham said he'd be glad to, as long as it was understood, he insisted, that he wouldn't be getting tangled in partisan battles. That was fine, since Eisenhower didn't have much use for partisan politics either. As the candidate was leaving Chicago, he revealed the race he wanted: "I hope to bring a message of militant faith and hope to the American people in what they have got the capacity to do, gol darn it, rather than go into details of a specific program."

Graham too gave a press conference while the Republicans were meeting, reassuring his followers that he was committed to a moral agenda, but alarming some friends who now thought he was getting in too deep. He boldly announced that he could swing sixteen million votes with a word. He had had "a number" of offers of backing in the event he wanted to run for the Senate—or the White House—himself. For now he was content to remain on the sidelines, but he put both parties on notice. If he felt they were not fighting the moral deterioration he saw, or were allowing communism to gain the upper hand, "I will not hesitate to step to the forefront. I will offer myself in any capacity to lead the Christian people of this country in the preservation of their God-given democratic institutions." Future political recruiters who tried to get Graham to run for the White House could always say he'd opened the door.

An old friend was inspired to issue a warning. "You have won so many people in this country because you have a spiritual message," he wrote. "Given even the slightest intimation that there are political aspirations and this influence for righteousness will be dispelled in large measure." His ministry, the writer said, had met a great need: but if people "become disillusioned about your motives, or your estimation of your following for other than spiritual purposes, it is bound to do harm."

To which Graham replied in a way he often would to critics he respected. "I want and need your suggestions, counsel, advice," he wrote back. "And any time you feel like jacking me up and kicking me in the pants, please do. I have enough people patting me on the back. . . . I need some real friends from time to time who will talk turkey to me."

That would be the last occasion for some time that Graham talked about his own political prospects. But his fans were still urging Eisenhower to make him an ally. Eisenhower wrote back to one of them, Washington governor Arthur Langlie, in August. Graham had a real gift for reaching people, Eisenhower said, and he was pleased that the preacher was mentioning Ike's "crusade" for honest government in his broadcasts. The problem was one of appearances. "Since all pastors must necessarily take a non-partisan approach, it would be difficult to form any formal organization of religious leaders to work on our behalf." But maybe something "informal?" Eisenhower suggested.

Graham went out to Denver to spend a few days at the Brown Palace Hotel, where Eisenhower, always a quick study, was getting a crash course in farm policy, labor relations, the budget. Graham was consulted on the places where those questions intersected matters of the spirit. They talked about Bible verses that might be useful in the campaign, and Graham once again told him the story of his own spiritual journey. Eisenhower admitted that he had grown disillusioned with the church—Graham later recalled his saying that this was because the preachers seemed less interested in spiritual than social issues, a charge that Graham would make often in years to come to account for the decline of mainline churches and the appeal of the evangelicals' Christ-centered message. "If I get elected, and I go to Washington," Eisenhower said, "is there a church you'd recommend?"

By that time Eisenhower had concluded that the American people would not easily follow a president who did not go to church. "I won't join one during my candidacy, because people will think I'm doing it for votes," he told Graham. "But win or lose in November, I'm going to join a church." Since Mamie was a Presbyterian and they'd been married in a Presbyterian service, that seemed a safe choice. Graham recommended National Presbyterian, whose officers included J. Edgar Hoover and whose pastor, Edward Elson, had been a chaplain in Europe in the war.

Graham and his team seldom left home without a supply of their trademark silk-sewn red Moroccan leather Bibles, which he autographed and handed out to people who had worked especially hard at his crusades. (The color, Graham's boisterous associate Grady Wilson liked to say, was chosen because "I think a Bible should be read.") Graham presented Eisenhower with such an inscribed red Bible, which he would keep by his bedside at the White House throughout his presidency. Graham had marked up the margins and put in notes about special scriptures and how to study them.

For a party claiming the moral high ground against the communist-appeasing, crony-rewarding Democrats, what followed was an awfully nasty campaign. The Republican platform charged that Democrats had fostered class strife, promoted socialism, debased the dollar, "shielded traitors to the nation in high places," and "shamed the moral standards of the American People." And that was just the preamble.

The Eisenhower campaign embraced no clear political philosophy; but when a moral hero who has defeated the greatest evil the world had known invites citizens to join his next crusade—well, that's hard to vote against. Billboards read, "Faith in God and Country; that's Eisenhower—how about you?"

Graham echoed the theme that character counted most. The *Houston Post* reported, "Emphasizing that he does not become involved in politics, the Rev. Mr. Graham said that the country needs a President who has the fortitude and moral courage to clean out the 'grafters and hangers-on' who come out in every business." Other times he would ask, "How many of you voted to go into the Korean War? I never did." America went in because "one man sitting in Washington made the decision." ("Back then," Graham would later confess, "I was not averse to publicly criticizing the U.S. State Department for its many blunders, but how foolish and presumptuous that appears now!")

In late October, just days before the vote, Graham revealed the results of his "survey of churchmen" and religious editors, which found that 77 percent of them favored Eisenhower. With no trace of irony, the press release noted that "Mr. Graham is not taking sides in the political campaign. He is remaining neutral."

When it was all over, Graham wrote to his friend Henry Luce, praising *TIME*'s coverage of the campaign and asking to see him when Graham got back from a trip to Korea. "Thanks again for backing Ike," he wrote. "I have had the privilege of talking with him twice during the last few months and believe him to be a man of great personal integrity and moral principle. I believe a new day is dawning."

It would be a new day for both men. Eisenhower's presidency would be distinguished by the fact that he liked Billy Graham but never exploited him. He welcomed his counsel; he sought his pastoral care; but it would be left to other members of his administration to see the political advantages that an alliance with the evangelist might bring.

As for Graham, his crusade literature after 1953 included a picture of him and Eisenhower on a sofa reading the Bible together. His association with a popular president gave him credibility in secular circles that no evangelist in decades, maybe ever, had enjoyed.

FIVE

One Nation, Under God

He said "Billy, could you explain to me how a person can be sure when he dies he's going to heaven?" I didn't feel that I could answer his question as well as others could have.

—Graham on Eisenhower's spiritual journey

W hy was it, upon winning the presidency, that Eisenhower made religious revival such a priority?

Eisenhower's faith had always been private; but once elected he decided to take it public, almost in the spirit of Lincoln, another biblically fluent but unchurched president with whom Eisenhower identified so strongly that he painted a portrait of him and gave colored prints of it to the White House staff for Christmas one year. "I have been recently studying the life of Lincoln and am convinced that the reason he is so revered today is that he talked about God . . . more than any other president in American history," Graham would write to Eisenhower. "Like Lincoln, you have put a spiritual emphasis in the White House; and like Lincoln you have been dedicated to a cause."

But Lincoln and Eisenhower parted ways when it came to faith as a strategic tool. America's destiny, as Lincoln saw it, was that of "God's almost chosen people." He viewed those who disagreed with him over slavery as sincere—just sincerely wrong. As for whose side God was on, Lincoln famously prayed that he might be on God's side.

Eisenhower needed for God to be on America's side, for that was how he framed the cold war. The essential difference between the American and Soviet systems was less economic or political than spiritual; they were "godless" while America was "chosen." Graham agreed completely and saw a clash of civilizations: "Either Communism must die, or Christianity must die," he wrote, "because it is actually a battle between Christ and anti-Christ." Eisenhower even made faith a weapon on the battlefield that counted most, where every single citizen could be called to arms. "Our forefathers proved that only a people strong in Godliness is a people strong enough to overcome. . . . What is our battle against communism if it is not a fight between anti-God and a belief in the Almighty."

In decades to come Americans would fight over saying prayers in school and posting the Ten Commandments in courthouses and observing a moment of silence before the football game. No future president, even the born-again evangelicals, would present themselves as the country's spiritual commander in chief in quite the way Eisenhower did.

FAITH IN ACTION

G raham suggested that one of Eisenhower's first acts as president be to declare a national day of prayer. "General," Graham told him, "you can do more to inspire the American people to a more spiritual way of life than any man alive." Eisenhower agreed, and also arranged for a special church service for his incoming administration. At the last minute inaugural parade organizers realized that among all the floats, "nowhere was there any representation that this was a nation whose people believed in God." So officials raced to put together a new float, and decided that it should lead the whole parade. "God's Float," as it was called, had huge photographs of churches and worship scenes with the legends "Freedom of Worship" and "In God We Trust." Anticipating the criticism that would soon attend the new civil religion, the *Episcopal Church News* remarked that, "Standing for all religions, it had symbols of none," and observed that it looked like something left over from a dental exhibit.

Three-quarters of a million people came out on a propitiously balmy day to greet the new president. They were packed along Pennsylvania Avenue, perched in trees like they were awaiting the Messiah's triumphal entry, or watching through cardboard periscopes. Graham, attending the first of many presidential inaugurations, watched Eisenhower place his hand on the Bible passage he had commended to him two weeks before, 2 Chronicles 7:14: "If my people, which are called by my name, shall humble themselves, and pray, and seek my face, and turn from their wicked ways; then I will hear from heaven, and will forgive their sin, and will heal their land."

But Graham claimed to be as amazed as everyone else when Eisenhower, without warning, reached into his pocket and pulled out a prayer.

"My friends, before I begin the expression of those thoughts that I deem appropriate to this moment, would you permit me the privilege of uttering a little private prayer of my own?" He asked that they bow their heads, and prayed that they might dedicate themselves to the country's service, see clearly right from wrong, serve all people regardless of race or station—or belief.

Ike's brother Edgar said he was taken totally by surprise—and was angry the next day to read the critics dissect the prayer. "I don't believe God cared what words Dwight used," he said. "Dwight was saying to the world . . . 'I don't think I am so big, so smart that I can handle this great task alone. Therefore I am calling upon my Creator.'" Rumors that Graham had written it for him were so persistent that, years later, Graham wrote Mamie Eisenhower a note assuring her that all he had done was suggest some Bible verses. "Please do not give that newspaper account another thought," she replied. "Of course I personally saw Ike write his own little prayer, so why worry what other folks say?"

Eisenhower would soon become the first president to be baptized in office, and the second, after Calvin Coolidge, to join a church after being elected. True to his Denver conversation with Graham, he joined National Presbyterian; it was, however, nearly a short-lived association. A few weeks later, Ike wrote angrily in his diary that "we were scarcely home before the fact was being publicized, by the pastor, to the hilt." Reverend Elson had promised that there would be no publicity. "I feel like changing at once to another church of the same denomination. I shall if he breaks out again."

What followed was a burst of official religious promotion such as America had not seen in years. Eisenhower announced that cabinet meetings would begin with a moment of silence. (This took some getting used to; appointments secretary Tom Stephens recalled the time the president emerged from the cabinet room when he suddenly realized, "Jesus Christ, we forgot the prayer!") The first National Prayer Breakfast was held in 1953, with Eisenhower and Graham both in attendance.

In 1954 the phrase "Under God" was added to the Pledge of Allegiance. A newly formed Foundation for Religious Action in the Social and Civil Order brought together all the pillars of Eisenhower's civil faith; its board included Graham, Norman Vincent Peale, Henry Luce, Henry Ford Jr., Herbert Hoover, and Charles Wilson of General Electric. In 1955 Congress opened a prayer room in the Capitol, and ruled that all coins and bills had to have the phrase "In God We Trust" on them. The following year that became the national motto, an improvement, lawmakers felt, on "E Pluribus Unum."

On the eve of the four-power Geneva Summit that summer, over the doubts of even his secretary of state, Eisenhower used his national address to enlist the entire American public in refuting Soviet propaganda that portrayed the United States as bent on war. He called on all 165 million Americans to go to church that Sunday and pray for peace. "To see the President of the United States kneeling in prayer at a church in Geneva brought tears of joy to my eyes," Graham declared at the time, "and I said 'God will be with that man in the Big Four conference,' and He was."

It was easy to be skeptical about the ways Eisenhower called the nation to her knees. The phrase "a deeply felt religious faith" appeared again and again in Eisenhower's speeches. ("Our form of government has no sense unless it is founded in a deeply felt religious faith, and I don't care what it is.") That line invited commentators like William Lee Miller to observe wryly that "one might say that President Eisenhower, like many Americans, is a very fervent believer in a very vague religion." Radio commentator Elmer Davis noted that "the greatest demonstration of the religious character of this administration came on July fourth, which the president told us all to spend as a day of penance and prayer. Then he himself caught four fish in the morning, played 18 holes of golf in the afternoon, and spent the evening at the bridge table."

But Eisenhower's private thoughts, expressed in his letters and diaries, offer another way to look at his call for revival. Trying to win the cold war by force of arms was an invitation to bankruptcy, if not national suicide. He poured out these concerns in an extraordinary diary entry in his first summer in office, as the stakes became clear to him. Every day, he wrote, he was struck by "the shortsightedness bordering on tragic stupidity" of people who claimed to support capitalist democracy but then pursued short-term policies that would destroy it over time. Get people to think of the long term, he said, and communism would not have to be destroyed by arms; it would self-destruct. But keep aiming for maximum immediate gain and "the so-called enlightened areas of Western Europe, Britain, the U.S. . . . will . . . actually commit suicide." Faith, he believed, was what allowed human beings to overcome their essential selfishness, to rise to heroism, to suffer for the larger good—to function, in other words, in the ways a democracy needs its citizens to function. To Eisenhower, there was a direct spiritual line between "In God We Trust" and "E Pluribus Unum."

The president thought that at the very least he had to lead by example. He had never had much use for churchly ritual, his brother Milton said, because he viewed faith as more a matter of mind and heart. But things changed when he became the leader of the free world. "Ours is a religious nation," Milton said, and a president had to offer some "spiritual stimulation as well as political and social leadership. . . . This being so, it is good and right for the president of the United States to go to church regularly and to stimulate others to do likewise."

Graham observed all this with almost giddy delight. "We are no longer going to be pushed around by the communists," he said, and the president was setting an excellent spiritual example. He wrote to Eisenhower in June 1953 from Dallas, where his crusade was drawing twenty-five thousand a night, and enclosed some newspaper clippings. "I am only informing you of these things to indicate the great spiritual hunger there is in America. Your interest in spiritual matters has helped tremendously, and I believe there is a great ground-swell of religious revival that must take place if our country is to be spared."

The problem was that not everyone reacted that way to the sudden swells of public piety. Graham himself would sometimes sound skeptical, as when *McCall's* asked whether the religious revival was real: "God is interested in the quality of converts, not quantity." Hollywood was churning out religious movies, with Hedy Lamarr as Delilah and Charlton Heston as Moses. Jane Russell talked about God as "a livin' doll." There were popular religious songs on the radio, best-selling religious novels in the stores. But in many cases this faith was safe, tame, friendly, less hellfire, more self-help, less sin, less Satan, more ten-step paths to success, the vanilla faith of Peale. Religion became more socially respectable, if less spiritually intense.

Some Christians worried about a faith that was so embracing as to be meaningless, that exalted not the Almighty so much as the American Way of Life. This was not yet God's kingdom, and when civil religion bleached the challenge from faith and left behind a watery patriotism, there was room for concern all around. Civil religion can be a partner to other expressions of complex faith, Eisenhower's critics argued, but when it becomes a substitute the churches have a problem.

Eisenhower and Graham shared a critic in the theologian Reinhold Niebuhr, perhaps the most outspoken opponent of a faith too easily understood and deployed. He warned against the notion of America as an innocent nation, whose blessings and prosperity were taken as evidence of its virtue. A patriotism hoisted into the realm of the sacred was too reassuring; this was chauvinism, not faith, and counterproductive as well if it blinded people to the kinds of problems and injustice that had given communism its appeal in the first place.

But whatever rebellions and disturbances lay below the surface, along with the urgent calls for social action, these would have to wait for another decade, another president, to burst out.

GRAHAM'S ASCENDANCE

In February 1954, Graham's patron Henry Luce wrote to *TIME*'s man in London, the legendary correspondent Andre Laguerre, to prepare him for what was about to come when Graham landed in London for a spring crusade. He explained with some pride that *TIME* and *LIFE* had been "the first national papers in the US to take note of Billy and he remembers that gratefully." But others had more than caught up in their coverage—*Newsweek* had recently put Graham on the cover.

For all his admiration, Luce was clear-eyed about Graham's significance at this stage. "While it is true that Billy has had really big audiences," he wrote, "it is not my impression that his influence has really entered into the main stream of American thought and feeling." His impact was hard to measure because religious experience is impossible to quantify. "In the last 10 years . . . there has been a great increase in interest in religion. I say 'interest' because 'interest' is all a journalist can judge: journalists can hardly, if at all, judge of the quality of true religion."

Whatever you think of Graham, Luce said, he is sincerely motivated by bringing people to Jesus—which is why Laguerre and all of Britain should brace themselves. "Religion in Britain is near death," Luce noted, "so Billy's impact will be worth watching." Indeed, church membership at the time was between 5 and 15 percent of the population, as opposed to 59 percent in the United States. "Surely he will be scorned by all the people you know. Whether the common people—the very common people—will hear him gladly, I couldn't guess."

Luce was by no means alone in watching with interest what would happen. Before Billy and Ruth set sail, Supreme Court chief justice Earl Warren led a prayer rally of high-ranking officials in Washington to wish the evangelist godspeed. But nothing could protect him from the sharpened knives of the British press corps that lay in wait. "Silly Billy," they called him. The *People* newspaper wrote that "being bulldozed into loving God by ecstatic young men who talk about Him with easy familiarity is something which makes the biggest British sinner shudder." "Now This Yank Says We're Heathens," read one headline. Another paper turned over much of its front page to a close-up of one of Graham's more exuberant outfits, with the caption "WHO WOULD WEAR THIS TIE???"

The people, however, appeared to feel differently. The advance team, the prayer groups, and the local sponsors had been preparing for years. The crowds that came to greet him at Waterloo Station were so big that one dazed girl exclaimed, "My! You'd think it was the Queen!" So many people came the first week that from then on he held three meetings at Harringay Stadium on Saturdays. "Harringay Full" read the signs on the Underground; people started singing hymns on the trains as they headed out. Night after night eleven thousand people sat and another thousand stood, in rain or sleet or cold, to hear him preach. As the weeks went on, members of Parliament came, an admiral of the fleet, the navy chief of staff; he was invited to Clarence House to visit with the Queen Mother, and eventually would be invited for the first of a dozen private meetings with the queen herself.

He was welcomed at the House of Commons by both Labour and Conservative members. "I have done my best to make a small contribution to Anglo-American relations," Graham wrote to Eisenhower. He had also been following France's growing problems in Vietnam and the demands that America come to the rescue. "I have been praying a great deal for you in the last few days as you wrestle with the Indo-China problem," Graham wrote, and then volunteered his pulpit to the president. He shared his views—but if Eisenhower chose a different path, Graham promised to fall faithfully in line. "Whatever your ultimate decision, I shall do my best through radio and television to make my contribution in selling the American public. My private opinion is that Indo-China must be held at any cost."

Graham came under particular fire from the *Daily Mirror* columnist "Cassandra," a man named William Connor, who called Graham "Hollywood's version of John the Baptist." As he often did with prominent critics, Graham suggested they meet in person; Connor mischievously suggested a rendezvous at a pub called the Baptist's Head. He was struck by how worn-out Graham looked; he had lost fourteen pounds since the crusade started. "But this fact he can carry back to North Carolina with him," Connor wrote, in a long account that showed him clearly won over. "It is that in this country, battered and squeezed as no victorious nation has ever been before and disillusioned almost beyond endurance, he has been welcomed with an exuberance that almost makes us blush behind our precious Anglo-Saxon reserve. . . . I never thought that friendliness had such a sharp cutting edge. I never thought that simplicity could cudgel us sinners so damned hard. We live and learn."

When it was all over, Graham was heading to Scotland for a holiday to recover, but on the morning of May 25 he got a surprise call. Could he come have a visit with Prime Minister Churchill? And so years later Graham would have another tale to tell of a weary world leader looking for a sense of peace.

Churchill struck him as being in one of his dark moods. They talked about the state of the world: "I am a man without hope," Churchill said. "Do you have any real hope?" Whether he was talking about the world or himself was not clear, so Graham acted as pastor.

"Are you without hope for your own soul's salvation?"

"Frankly, I think about that a great deal," Churchill said. And so Graham pulled out his New Testament and did what he always did, explaining the possibilities of grace and God's plan.

And then, Graham said, he prayed for the prime minister, and as he was leaving they shook hands. "Our conversations are private, aren't they?"

"Yes sir," Graham said, having learned his lesson.

By the time Graham had swept through Germany, Scandinavia, and France as well, he had become, as *TIME* declared in a cover story called "The New Evangelist," "the best-known, most talked-about Christian leader in the world today, barring the Pope." The *Chicago Daily News* wrote that Graham had "the unique distinction of being just about the only living American to whom Europeans seem willing to listen. He is certainly a far bigger attraction than anybody the Commies can produce." He had matured in the process; he retired the more outrageous ties, adjusted the volume in the preaching though not the message; he appeared more sober and statesmanlike, more seasoned somehow by the whole experience.

Which was fortunate, since he returned home to a kind of fame he could scarcely have imagined. Some twelve million people had heard him preach in person; but many millions more heard him or saw him in the mass media channels that earlier generations of evangelists could only have dreamed of. When a publisher asked the great revivalist George Whitefield for permission to print his sermons, he replied, "Certainly . . . if you will include the fire and the lightning." Graham was a powerful presence in print—his 1953 book *Peace with God* sold well over a million copies, his newspaper column appeared in nearly a hundred papers, with fifteen million readers. But fire and lightning traveled more easily over the airwaves. His radio show was now on a thousand stations; he turned down a million-dollar offer from NBC to host a television show. He had appeared in five full-length evangelistic movies, which were yielding many "decisions for Christ" themselves. Cecil B. DeMille offered him the part of Samson, to which Graham replied that he'd stick with the sawdust trail. "And Mr. DeMille told me afterward that he knew all along that I would say that, and he said it had restored his faith."

He was embraced by the Hollywood stars who first brought his crusades into the spotlight, the press barons who kept them there, and the moguls who helped fund them. The titans of industry were grateful for his defense of capitalism and commerce and a Main Street American work ethic. In his early days Graham came down clearly on the side of management, describing the Garden of Eden as a paradise with "no union dues, no labor leaders, no snakes, no disease." As *TIME* wrote in its cover profile, "upper-crust Christians tend to regard the sweaty urgency of evangelistic Christianity as frequently hypocritical and always in bad taste. Billy

Graham is different." Or as Graham's associate T. W. Wilson would put it, "Too much work done in the name of Christ is rundown, baggy trousers stuff. Billy believes in going first class."

There had been predictions that old-time fundamentalist religion would fade away, and even religion more generally, pushed aside by progress into a tidy corner. Instead Graham was soon taking note of the fact that more was written about him than about Eisenhower himself. In 1956 he was photographed more than Marilyn Monroe, or Richard Nixon.

It is a very human thing, to want to be liked. But among the rare experiences that Graham and the presidents shared was being the object of so much attention, often adoration, of the kind that precludes privacy and tests pride. Graham's ambition was forever doing battle with his fears; fear that too much success would twist him somehow; then he would be lost, his gifts reclaimed by God, his heart broken because he had not kept it humble.

The ambition too had to somehow belong to God; he argued that he pursued fame because it allowed him to reach more people, spread the gospel farther. But that doesn't explain why, once he was arguably more famous than any president, with more invitations to preach than he could accept in a lifetime, he still circled back into the Oval Office, always welcome and always protecting that welcome by protecting the man.

Fascination with power would forever be his weakness; and against its lure he often had no protection beyond the ever levelheaded Ruth telling him that he needed to stay away from politics and keep his eye on his evangelical mission. She was in every way his earthly anchor and rock: the beautiful, bright souled, bighearted daughter of missionaries, Ruth never planned to marry, and might have easily followed her parents' path had not Billy swept her off her feet at Wheaton. She was his peer and partner, sharing both his charm and energy and teasing him without mercy. Ruth knew her Bible inside out, wrote books and poetry, and brought to their union just the right skill set to manage a household and particularly a husband as unusual as hers. She liked to tell their five children that "there comes a time to stop submitting and start outwitting"—a rule that applied to herself as well, such as when she tried to hide a broken arm from Billy because she didn't want him to know that she had gone hang gliding. When it came to the other fatal attractions that have destroyed so many preachers and politicians alike, he was well defended.

To keep his finances transparent, he insisted that crusade accounts be audited and published in the local papers when the crusade was finished. Having founded the Billy Graham Evangelistic Association in 1950, he took a straight salary, comparable to that of a senior minister of a major urban pulpit, no matter how much money his meetings brought in. As for other forms of temptation, he never allowed himself to be alone in a room with a woman other than Ruth. One society doyenne swooned at Graham at a luncheon. "He is so eloquent and so handsome," she said. "Isn't it a shame that he isn't in politics?" To which Ruth Graham dryly replied, "Maybe the Lord thought politics had its share and decided to give the ministry a break." He and his team often shared rooms in hotels as they traveled, just in case. Eventually he would send someone in first to search the room, to make sure no overeager fan or tabloid bait was lying in wait.

Perhaps the greatest safeguard was another lesson he took from the Gospels. Graham had his band of disciples, a small group of life-long friends, like Grady Wilson and Cliff Barrows and Bev Shea, who remained at his side, kept him humble and honest, played practical jokes, teased him, trusted him, and in Shea's case was still living in a house just down the mountain in Montreat when he was ninety-seven years old. Wilson especially was clear about his calling in life: "If the Lord keeps Billy anointed," he liked to say, "I'll keep him humble."

Just as Graham had addressed the risks of sex and money and pride that brought other evangelists down, so did he evolve in attitude. Moderate evangelical Protestantism needed a voice, and was not necessarily any more comfortable with the increasingly liberal social teachings of the mainline churches than with the hard-liners. Graham founded *Christianity Today* in 1956 to challenge the influential but modernist *Christian Century*; his goal was to "restore intellectual respectability and spiritual impact to evangelical Christianity." "We would attempt to lead and love rather than vilify, criticize and beat," he declared. "Conservative Christians had failed with the big-stick approach; now it was time to take a more gentle and loving direction."

A GROWING INTIMACY

None of this was lost on Eisenhower. If at first his reaction to Graham, like Truman's, was bemused curiosity, he gave their acquaintance time to ripen. Graham changed as he traveled the world and climbed a steep learning curve in judgment, human nature, power, celebrity, and the distribution of justice. And Eisenhower grew more comfortable seeking both political counsel and personal comfort, to the point that at times Graham found himself veering into purely pastoral territory.

It was during the summer of 1955 that Eisenhower first reached out to Graham as an intimate rather than a public ally. On his way home from Europe, Graham was passing through Washington when Eisenhower called; he offered to send a car to bring Graham out to his farm in Gettysburg for the day. Graham assumed this would be a purely social visit. As they sat and talked, he told the president that both of his grandfathers had fought there during the Civil War.

"Well," Eisenhower offered, "maybe we can take you over there and we'll look around." He had studied the Battle of Gettysburg as a West Point cadet and in his obsessive readings of military history, even before he bought his farm adjoining the land. So Graham called his mother on the spot and asked about his grandfather's regiment. Then they drove around the battlefield in a golf cart, the Secret Service trailing behind, Eisenhower narrating the tale of Pickett's charge.

When they headed back to the house, Graham recalled, Eisenhower asked him to come upstairs to see Mamie, who had not been well.

"I didn't know her at that time very well," Graham said, but they went and visited with her in bed, and prayed with her. Then they went down for lunch. "I knew he was thinking about something," Graham said. "I knew there was a reason why he had me up there and he hadn't come to it yet."

They were in the den, Graham seated, Eisenhower pacing in front of the fireplace, when he got to what was on his mind.

"Billy," he said, "could you explain to me how a person can be sure when he dies he's going to heaven?"

Surprised, Graham said, "I'll try," pulled out his New Testament, and walked him through those passages that explained salvation and its terms. He hoped he had provided some reassurance that salvation came through grace, and "not by anything we can do for ourselves." But many years later he was still weighing the conversation. "It was an interesting visit. And a very humbling one for me," Graham said. "I didn't feel that I could answer his question as well as others could have."

They also discussed the more immediate concerns on Eisenhower's mind that day. He was heading into an election year, and the Republicans had no clear successor if he chose not to run again. He had a 69 percent approval rating; it was not like the campaign would be an uphill fight. But he would be sixty-five in October and had been in public service his whole life.

Graham made his case in writing when he got home, and once again he pulled no punches. It was not just that the people needed Ike: God had called him to the presidency. "I realize that both you and Mrs. Eisenhower have paid a tremendous personal price," Graham wrote. "However, you are the only American on the horizon who has any possibility of uniting the American people. . . . It seems to me that the next five years are going to be the most crucial in our history. In my opinion, your leadership is absolutely essential, no matter what price you must pay.

"I realize this is a hard thing to say—you have already given so much of your life to your country—yet in probably the most unique way in American history you have been placed in the office of president, not only by the overwhelming confidence of the American people but also by Divine Providence."

Despite the heart attack Eisenhower suffered that fall ("I think you are a better president from a sick bed than all of the other candidates in the field," Graham wrote to him during his recuperation), he did decide to run again. As one Republican put it, "He just could not take it—sitting up there in Gettysburg and watching Adlai Stevenson or Averell Harriman unraveling everything he's just got started."

That decision had a profound impact on the party and the country; but also on another friend in the White House whose future depended on Eisenhower's favor, and with whom Billy Graham was growing ever closer.

SIX

The Man Who Was Going Places

Oh, I thought he was easy to know.
—Graham on meeting Nixon

As a rising political star, Richard Nixon made enemies and friends in equal measure, so one would think that the last person Billy Graham would embrace so eagerly during the 1950s was a man who practiced the politics of division as energetically as the vice president.

Their relationship was the most complex of any that Graham nurtured with a politician, the most ardent and the most wounding. "There are few men whom I have loved as I love you," he would write to Nixon in 1962. "My friendship for you was never because you were Vice President or an international figure. It was far deeper than that." One could say that Graham brought out the best in him, seeing a spiritual side that some Nixon scholars argue has been overlooked. He had stories of a thousand kindnesses that Nixon showed him over the years, and when he at last confronted the evidence of the Californian's dark side, Graham's reaction would be a mix of bewilderment, humility, and heartbreak.

You could also say that Nixon brought out the worst in Graham, both then and later when he finally became president. That was not a calculated scheme to destroy him: in fact, Nixon often sounded more protective of Graham's image than the preacher himself. But Graham could not resist the temptation to offer advice to a friend he admired, and Nixon could not resist taking it and asking for more, for a blanket benediction from the man who would forgive just about anything.

They met in the Senate Dining Room in 1952, when Graham was the toast of the capital during his Washington crusade. North Carolina senator Clyde Hoey invited him to lunch to introduce him to members curious about the new force in town. "He knew I hadn't been there much and he was pointing out people, senators, he thought I'd like to know," Graham recalled. "And he said, 'There's young Nixon'—that's what he called him, 'young Nixon, from California.'" Hoey waxed prophetic: "Keep your eyes on that young man," Graham recalls him saying, "he is going places."

Elected to Congress in 1946, the same year as John F. Kennedy and the rest of the first World War II class, Nixon was something of a prodigy; his extravagant anticommunism and national profile as the Man Who Saved America from Alger Hiss made him one of the GOP's most sought-after speakers.

"I'd like to meet him," Graham said, so Hoey called him over. It turned out that Nixon had heard about Graham from his mother, Hannah, who'd gone to hear him preach in Whittier after the 1949 Los Angeles crusade. "He was so warm, shook my hand and looked me in the eye, and a few minutes later he said, 'Do you play golf?'"

"Well I try," Graham replied, at which point Nixon invited him to join a round with Florida senator George Smathers that afternoon; Graham seized the invitation. After they played, they were heading back into town when Nixon suggested they stop by his house. "So I went home with him, I met Pat, his two daughters, and they just struck me as ordinary people, an ordinary house." They talked for a long time, until Nixon offered to drive Graham back to his hotel. "And that was the beginning."

The beginning of a relationship that would test them both; Graham himself called it "bittersweet." He encountered Nixon right at the place where the politician's nature cleaved. One Nixon loved and protected the evangelist, one deceived and used him. One Nixon was an austere, thoughtful Quaker who never missed a chance to help his friend, the other a profane manipulator of people and principle whom Graham could scarcely recognize decades later when the incriminating tapes exposed him.

"When Nixon's public and private personalities meet," his critics liked to say, "they shake hands." The notion that there were two Nixons forever conspiring to divide and conquer emerged from his very first race for Congress in 1946 and shadowed him from that point on. His admirers saw a righteous public servant who pursued the public interest even at personal political cost. To his critics he was a creature of phony piety and pure calculation—in fact Smathers called him "the most calculating man I ever knew"—and he was a friend. "If he ever wrestled with his conscience," Nixon's enemies charged, "the match was fixed."

When critics painted Nixon as the most ruthless of operators, Graham rose to his defense. "His mind doesn't reach for political gimmicks," he said, "he has no characteristics of a demagogue." Graham stated at a news conference during an Indianapolis crusade that "Mr. Nixon is probably the best trained man for President in American history, and he is certainly every inch a Christian gentleman." He defended Nixon's lack of spiritual flamboyance as both a sign of Quaker modesty and rectitude: "He has been extremely reticent to speak out on his personal faith for fear that people will think he's using it politically." But in private, Graham would come to have doubts, and would push Nixon to pray, to read scripture, to place his trust in God. It was only much later that he suspected that Nixon would not talk much about faith because there wasn't much to talk about.

A Spiritual Journey

On January 20, 1953, the day Richard Nixon was inaugurated as vice president of the United States, his mother slipped him a piece of paper. He did not read it until that night, but he carried it with him long after.

To Richard,

You have gone far and we are proud of you always—I know that you will keep your relationship with your maker as it should be for after all that, as you must know, is the most important thing in this life.

With love, Mother.

Nixon's spiritual journey was both more complex than that of many presidents, and more relevant. Hannah Nixon was a particularly pious woman even in the devout Quaker farming colony of Whittier, where her family moved in 1887. Regularly referred to as a Quaker "saint," she was serious to the point of joyless, intent on serving others and on seeing her sons succeed. The last thing she wanted, Nixon wrote in his first memoir, *Six Crises*, was for him to enter "the warfare of politics." She hoped he might become a Quaker missionary in Latin America. But "true to her Quaker tradition, she never tried to force me in the direction she herself might have preferred." Hannah once described her son as "an intensely religious man, but he shuns even the restrained rituals of the faith. I am sure other Quakers understand my son. They know why he has been the center of so many controversies. Quakers are gentle and tolerant people, but they are also stubborn in defending their opinions and high-minded in pursuing their ideals."

Religion was the center of family life, with daily prayers, Bible readings at bedtime, and four worship services on Sundays. Nixon played piano at church and taught Sunday school. His mother took literally the injunction from Matthew to pray behind closed doors and not flaunt one's piety; she actually went into a closet to say her prayers before going to bed at night. When Nixon became vice president, Eisenhower urged him to work God into his speeches more energetically, but, citing his mother's example, Nixon could not quite bring himself to do it.

Nixon's father, Frank, who never made it past sixth grade, was in every way louder, rougher, more fervent and combative about his faith. Raised a Methodist, he embraced Quakerism when he won Hannah Milhous; but if her God was gentle, his was fierce. "I tried to follow my mother's example of not crossing him when he was in a bad mood," Nixon recalled, and mused that both his skills at debate and his dislike for personal confrontation went a long way back.

In the death of Nixon's brother Harold of tuberculosis after a long struggle that rent the family, Frank Nixon saw a harsh judgment from God. He stopped opening his grocery store on Sundays and became even more flamboyantly devout, standing up in church and declaring, "We must have a reawakening! We've got to have a revival!" Years later when Graham was exploring his friend's spiritual journey, Nixon told him he had made his commitment to Christ as a teenager at a rally held by evangelist Paul Rader.

But unlike Graham's own teenage conversion at the hand of the evangelist Mordecai Ham, Nixon's did not lock him into a traditional faith based on biblical literalism. During his senior year in college, he wrote the closest thing to a statement of personal faith, for a class subtitled "What Can I Believe." His parents had raised him to accept the Bible as the literal word of God: "the miracles, the whale story, all these I accepted as facts when I entered college four years ago." He had been warned to be wary of liberal-minded college professors who might dilute his conviction. And yet, he went on, many of those "childhood ideas" had been "destroyed." He still believed in God the Creator; he believed that Jesus was God's son, though perhaps not in the physical sense of the term. In Nixon's revised view, the literal accuracy of the Resurrection was not as important as its profound symbolism. "The important fact is that Jesus lived and taught a life so perfect that he continued to live and grow after his death—in the hearts of men." But he would never talk about Jesus in these or any other terms as a politician. Orthodox teachers, he noted, insist on the physical resurrection as a cornerstone of Christian faith. "I believe that the modern world will find a real resurrection in the life and teachings of Jesus."

Of course, one of those orthodox teachers would be Billy Graham, who would gently work almost from the day they met to bring Nixon back to the certainty and clarity of his youth.

The men shared, in addition to their passionate anticommunism, a personal primness, fidelity to their wives, and yet a tireless pursuit of their goals at the expense of time with their families. They could tell jokes as needed, but neither had the edge or eye for irony that made for sharp humor. Graham had not the remotest notion of Nixon's profane and coarse side, or his capacity for brutality. In the early years of their friendship many of Nixon's demons had not yet burrowed into him. Whenever Graham was called to testify to Nixon's personal nature, he described him as one of the most likable men he'd ever known: warm, sincere, an excellent listener. "When he shakes your hand," Graham said, "he has a way of making you feel you are the only person in the world that matters. He has the rare gift of communicating genuine interest in you, your work, your problem."

But for all the mutual affection, the differences bonded them as much as the similarities. Where Nixon was stiff and awkward, Graham was liquid charm. Nixon seemed to wonder at Graham's disarming grace; he saw an American icon "who lets the people of the world see what Americans are at their best." "Oh, I thought he was easy to know," Graham said of Nixon, but Graham made it easy, created a safe place. If Nixon was given to brooding introspection, Graham brought equanimity. If Nixon trusted no one, Graham trusted everyone. Nixon was incapable of small talk of any kind; Graham could talk to anyone about anything.

Graham's shoulders had no chips; life had treated him kindly and he lived in gratitude, looking for the best and finding it. Nixon seemed to have been born bitter; but even apart from that his cynicism was fed by the opposition of the Truman administration as he pursued Alger Hiss; by the evaporation of "friends" when he wrestled with the scandal that climaxed with his legendary Checkers speech; by Eisenhower's persistent coldness toward him even as he relied on his loyalty as hatchet man. The beloved Ike, Nixon charged, was "a far more complex and devious man than most people realized."

And Ike was just as wary of Nixon as a human being. Nixon was, famously, a man without friends, a pattern that began long before he entered public life. Despite a close family and a generally placid youth, he somehow lost, or never found, the ability to confide in people. Through his rise in Washington he made allies as needed; but he did not have the kind of trusted inner circle that politicians depend on as they become more isolated by power. When Eisenhower visited him once at the hospital he came back and marveled to his secretary Ann Whitman that he couldn't see how a man could live without friends. In her diary Whitman mused on the difference between the two men: "The President is a man of integrity and sincere in his every action . . . he radiates this, everybody knows it, everybody trusts and loves him. But the Vice President sometimes seems like a man who is acting like a nice man rather than being one."

It was a painful twist that a man who so desperately wanted to be liked had so little ability to make that happen. "No one," Republican chairman Len Hall observed, "would look forward to spending a week with Nixon fishing." One exception was Nixon's trusted friend Bebe Rebozo, whom Pat Nixon described as "a sponge; he soaks up whatever Dick says and never makes any comment. Dick loves that." And the other was Billy Graham. "Nixon admired Billy tremendously," said Nixon's longtime press handler Herb Klein, "and liked him as a friend." Spending time with Graham "gave him a lot of comfort." This was not a purely pastoral bond; Nixon had a strong religious sense, Klein said, but he was not one to talk theology, even with an evangelist. "He just enjoyed the man. Billy Graham sees the best in people." And so it was natural that Graham would try to broker a peace between his friends, president and vice president, the Republicans' reigning hero and their rising star.

1956

Nixon was the first real friend that Graham coached through a national campaign, first as vice president and eventually as president. Then and later he would always profess his neutrality; but he was quickly caught up in watching candidates try to judge the terrain, find their allies, shape a message. As he had told Truman, he followed political trends carefully, listened closely when he traveled around the country, and was always eager to sit in as amateur strategist in the most high-stakes game ever played.

Graham began shepherding Nixon toward the Oval Office virtually from the start of their friendship; but it was Eisenhower's heart attack in 1955 that inspired Graham, along with practically every politician in both parties, to consider how Nixon's prospects had brightened now that Eisenhower's future was uncertain. Even as he was writing to Eisenhower urging a second term, he was noting to Nixon in October 1955 that "your political position has tremendously changed," and advised that he look to God for strength and guidance during the coming months, which would be "the most critical of your entire career."

Now playing what would become a familiar role, as the transmitter of political messages, Graham relayed a conversation he had had with New York governor Thomas Dewey, the failed 1948 GOP candidate who became the elder statesman of the moderate Republicans. Dewey considered Nixon the most able man in the party, Graham explained, but "seems to be a little fearful that you may be taken over unwittingly by some of the extreme right-wingers. He feels that in order to be elected President . . . a man is going to have to take a middle-of-the-road position. I think he is right!"

Nixon wrote back to say, "I think your political advice was right on the beam and, as you probably have noted, I have been trying to follow the course of action you recommended during the past few weeks."

But those weeks and months that followed were a kind of slow political torture for Nixon, largely at Eisenhower's hand. Despite his vice president's steady conduct during the aftermath of the heart attack, his careful balance between being reassuring without overreaching, Ike was torn about keeping Nixon on the ticket. The day after Christmas he called him into the Oval Office. He talked about how he hadn't planned on a second term, but he didn't see anyone on the bench who could take his place. It was unfortunate, he said, that Nixon's standing had not risen "as high as he had hoped it would." Now that his health was an issue, the Democrats were sure to make Nixon a target. And so, he proposed, maybe it would be best for Nixon to take a cabinet post, gain some administrative experience. To a sitting vice president this sounded like a suggestion that he call a press conference and commit political suicide.

Watching this, Graham looked for ways to help. Look to God, he advised, He will guide you. While Eisenhower was working to ease Nixon aside, Graham was trying to raise him up, both with Eisenhower and other influential Republicans, and with the most powerful religious leaders. He put the word out quietly, suggesting that they invite Nixon to speak at their conferences that summer. When both the Presbyterians and Southern Baptists confirmed a Nixon appearance, Graham made sure he understood the stakes. "This will put you before two of the largest summer religious conferences in America," he said. "People come to these two conferences from all over the world." And after the meetings, Nixon could come back to Montreat for a private lunch with the Protestant titans, the Episcopal and Methodist bishops, the moderator of the Presbyterian Church, the president of the Southern Baptist Convention. "Very frankly, you are in need of a boost in Protestant religious circles," Graham advised. "I am asked about you almost everywhere I go. I think it is time that you move among these men and let them know you." He even sent along some suggested remarks for Nixon to offer the Baptists.

As the nomination fight reached a boil and Harold Stassen, who had supported Nixon in 1950 and 1952, now worked to unseat him, Nixon was safely sequestered in the arms of Graham and his fellow clergy. The Democrats, meeting to nominate Adlai Stevenson once again, let loose on Nixon. "From the opening crack of the gavel in Chicago until the last lusty cheer echoed and died, Nixon was the target," *Newsweek* reported. "Speakers pronounced his name with a sneer, as though it were an obscene epithet." He was attacked as "the vice-hatchet man," "the White House pet midget," a traveler of "the low road." Remember, they suggested at every turn, if anything happens to Ike, you'll be left with Nixon.

As the Democrats' convention wound down and the Republicans prepared to convene in San Francisco, Stassen wrote to Nixon, who was in North Carolina with Graham, and urged him to withdraw from the ticket. "It is my deep conviction that if you decide to take this step it would be best not only for our country but, in the long run, for your future career." Nixon ignored the letter, set off for San Francisco, and rode to victory at the convention and then once more at Eisenhower's side in November.

Having been returned to office by a magnificent margin, he found the path was now open to him. And Graham and Nixon had bonded in victory: the letters now began, "Dear Billy" and "Dear Dick." Writing to congratulate him, Graham told Nixon that his prestige was now "higher than ever. I think some of the possibilities we talked about concerning the future are definitely in the making."

Graham and Nixon were already talking about his path to the Oval Office in November 1956.

SEVEN

Ambassador at Large

I met all the [British] prime ministers except the current. . . . I had a very good relationship with all of them, and with the German chancellors. I knew all of them except the last two. But the primary one was the queen; she had me, I think, twelve times. . . . I've never told that, never quoted any of those people.

—Graham on other world leaders

It became clear to close White House observers that something had changed during a press conference in the spring of 1956. Eisenhower's remarks covered predictable ground—the reorganization of the Defense Department, the upcoming visit of Indian prime minister Nehru, the fate of the farm bill, and the implications of building a nuclear bomb with the force of a billion tons of TNT. But then reporters got a little more personal. Why, they asked, was the president spending so much time with the evangelist Billy Graham? asked first William Lawrence of the *New York Times*, then May Craig, an intrepid columnist with the *Portland* (Maine) *Press Herald*. "I wondered if you would tell us why you feel the interest in him?" she asked. "Are you thinking of mobilizing the religious countries of the world against communism?"

Eisenhower's first reflex was to dodge. They were merely acquaintances, he suggested. "Actually this is the first time I had realized I had given a great deal of time to him," he said. "I see him normally—a matter of a few minutes, and yesterday, I believe, was probably the longest visit I ever had with him." But then he caught himself. "No, he did visit me at my farm; I had lunch with him."

Still, the president did wrap his arms around the evangelist as someone to listen to, if only because so many other people did. "He carries his religion to the far corners of the earth, trying to promote peace, trying to promote . . . tolerance instead of prejudice," Eisenhower told the reporters. "Therefore, because of the very great crowds that he attracts to listen to him, I am very much interested in Billy Graham's activities."

Ms. Craig, however, was not satisfied: what about mobilizing the Christian world to fight godless communism? Here was the moment of truth, and Eisenhower saw the opportunity. The United States, he said, was engaged in "a battle between those people who believe that man is something more than just an educated animal, and those who believe he is nothing else," he said. "It is atheism against some kind of religion." And yes, it was important to rally believers because the "underlying basic fact is this: that religion ordinarily tries to find a peaceful solution to problems."

As he went on, a Time Life correspondent named John Steele was struck by what he was seeing. "This was a long speech by a president at a news conference," he wrote back to his editors in New York. "Somehow, though, it came through. Billy, for all his showmanship, his Pepsodent smile, his many charms and his well-cut clothes, had struck a responsive note in the President of the United States." However different the two men might be, they had formed some kind of alliance. "The common denominator," Steele guessed, "seemed to be, if not a love, an understanding of the heartstrings of the 20th century man. The pastor and the president seemed, indeed, to have much in common."

Even some members of Eisenhower's administration were surprised to discover how strongly he felt. One of the president's aides practically snorted as he ran down the day's call list and noted that "evangelist Billy Graham" had called asking to see the president. Eisenhower leveled his gaze and told him, dead serious, "I'm delighted to hear from him. I'll be glad to see him," and as the assistant, Robert Gray, began to leave, he said it again. "I'll be glad to see him any time." Gray saw not just a willingness but "an anxiety to talk with him." When Gray met Graham himself, he found that "the fellow has something about him that is hauntingly capturing," and as they talked, he thought he understood what Ike was responding to.

Quite apart from the personal attraction, the strategic value of this alliance became clear during Graham's historic journey through Asia that winter. Secretary of State John Foster Dulles summoned Graham to

Washington before he embarked to be sure he was fully briefed: he would be touring India just weeks after a triumphant goodwill visit by Communist Party leader Nikita Khrushchev and premier Nikolay Bulganin, during which Prime Minister Nehru had arranged for sightseeing, state banquets, formal receptions, folk festivals. But Graham's reception was astonishing in its own way, in a country of 380 million with perhaps 5 million Protestant church members. The crowds were immense, curious, captivated: a hundred thousand people came to hear him in Kottayam— a town of forty thousand. William Stoneman, head of the foreign service of the *Chicago Daily News*, noted that "objective observers" had concluded that "no American in this postwar period has made so many friends for America and gone so far toward offsetting the widespread conviction that material rather than spiritual matters are America's sole significant concern as Billy Graham during his amazing tour of Asia."

When Graham returned to brief Eisenhower, Nixon, and Dulles, he tried his own hand at diplomacy. Khrushchev's gift to Nehru of a magnificent white horse made the front pages of every paper in India; when Dulles offered $50 million in aid, that merited only a small mention inside. The average Indian, Graham said, had no concept of $50 million but understood the horse. He argued that more care be given to appearances; give not just wheat, but maybe a distinctive white train to transport it from one end of the country to the other, so people would associate the benevolence with the United States. Or maybe a Cadillac. Such gifts would "do more to demonstrate the friendliness of the Americans than all the millions of dollars given in economic aid."

Such advice, born of Graham's instincts about sales and seduction in a worthy cause, inspired the *Christian Century* to snort that Graham "hasn't a glimmer of a notion about what is really going on in the world. . . . If there were any sense at all of the real nature of the world's revolution, a man couldn't even think of such irrelevance as a train or a car, much less utter them. . . . It is wretched politics and impossible Christianity."

But Nixon was more than willing to promote Graham's efforts overseas that year and in years to come. He had cabled the U.S. envoy in India to help arrange Graham's meeting with Nehru, and wrote to the Australian ambassador in 1958 instructing him to help Graham's advance team in any way they needed. The next year he wrote to Raymond Hare, ambassador to Egypt, to arrange for Graham to meet with Egyptian president Nasser, with the guidance that "in his meetings with other world leaders, I know that Dr. Graham has made a very favorable impression, and I can strongly recommend such an appointment. . . . I feel sure that a discussion between them would advance the cause of peace and understanding in the Middle East."

During those years, however, peace and understanding at home were just as pressing a priority, and this time it would be Eisenhower who enlisted Graham as emissary. Civil rights was one area where Eisenhower was not inclined to provide moral, much less political, leadership. He acted, or reacted, when his hand was forced. He was respectful of the Supreme Court's *Brown vs. Board of Education* decision in 1954 that desegregated public schools, but he made it clear that he was defending the authority of the court, not the substance of their ruling. He counseled patience; the black community was trying to move too fast. "Not enough people know how deep this emotion is in the south," he argued. "Unless you've lived there, you can't know . . . we could have another civil war on our hands."

"He was not a racist," his speechwriter William Ewald said. "But he was a southerner by birth, and had lots of southern friends, whom he admired." There was a political piece as well. During the 1952 campaign, when advisers essentially proposed that he skip campaigning in the solidly Democratic South, he rejected that advice—and the crowds that turned out for him were vindication. "He thought it was high time that someone in the Republican party say something nice about people in the South," Ewald said. He noted that Eisenhower was the first president to appoint a black special assistant to his presidential staff.

On this issue Graham, also a southerner with many southern friends, had nonetheless pulled way out ahead of the president. His typical need to unite people and avoid controversy in this case found a prophetic edge— at least for a while. "The Christian looks through the eyes of Christ at the race question and admits that the Church has failed in solving this great human problem," he argued in 1954. "We have let the sports world, the entertainment field, politics, the armed forces, education and industry outstrip us. The Church should have been the pace setter." The solution, he concluded, could be found only at the foot of the cross, "where we come together in brotherly love." In fact he affirmed his profound belief in equality every time he gave the invitation at the end of a service: "Old or young, white or colored, man or woman, rich or poor, educated or uneducated, you come quickly right now."

So in 1952 at the annual meeting of the Southern Baptist Convention, he had argued that it was the Christian duty of Baptist colleges to accept qualified black students. In Jackson, Mississippi, he called segregation, along with alcohol, the two biggest problems in town. The next year, when organizers of the Chattanooga crusade refused to desegregate the arena, Graham went to the tabernacle and walked up and down the aisles, tearing down the ropes. Horrified ushers ran over and protested, "No, no, please Reverend Graham, this will be misunderstood." Graham replied, "Either these ropes stay down or you can go and have this revival without me."

He talked about Christian life as being both horizontal and vertical—the vertical referring to what one draws from one's relationship with Christ, the horizontal being its application in daily life. Ever the synthesizer, he suggested that people take care not to stress one or the other too much—Baptists being inclined toward the vertical, Methodists to the horizontal. Get the mix right, he'd explain, and you are following the shape of the cross.

Graham did share with Eisenhower a belief that you can't change hearts in a hurry, and that true social change would take some time. "I believe the Lord is helping us," he told the president, "and if the Supreme Court will go slowly and the extremists on both sides will quiet down, we can have a peaceful social readjustment over the next ten year period."

But to many civil rights leaders, calls for patience were just cover for inaction. By 1956 much of the South was in open rebellion against *Brown*. Four legislatures announced that the ruling had no force in their states. In March, 101 senators and congressmen signed a manifesto declaring that they were determined to reverse the verdict. Martin Luther King Jr., meanwhile, was leading the historic bus boycott in Montgomery, where black churches were being bombed—but it was the boycotters being arrested.

Eisenhower was determined to stay out of the fight and let the courts take the lead. But Alabama congressman Frank Boykin proposed that Graham might be a useful undercover agent. Graham "could do more on this than any other human being in the nation," he wrote—though what Boykin was looking for was a calming force, not a revolutionary one. "I mean to quiet it down and to go easy and in a God-like way, instead of trying to cram it down the throats of our people all in one day, which some of our enemies are trying to do. I thought maybe if you and Billy talked . . ."

Eisenhower wrote back the next day. "What you say about Billy

Graham interests me a great deal," he said. "The reports I have had on his activities abroad correspond with your own comments. He is remarkably gifted and has accomplished much good.

"Today he was in my office, and we talked over some ideas about how he might, from time to time, turn his talents to the easing of some of the more serious human problems in our country."

Eisenhower sat down to write Graham a long, thoughtful letter; but this time it was not "Dear Rev. Graham" but "Dear Billy," and in tone and depth it was very different from the perfunctory good wishes and courtesies of the years before. There was real attention and urgency this time, since the more that was done from the pulpits, the less he would have to do in the courts, the Congress, or with soldiers in the streets.

"I have been urgently thinking about the matters we discussed in our conversation the day before yesterday," he began, and proceeded to lay out what he referred to as "gratuitous advice."

Ministers, Eisenhower suggested, were in a unique position to promote both tolerance and progress, while defusing confrontation. "Ministers know that peacemakers are blessed; they should also know that the most effective peacemaker is one who prevents a quarrel from developing, rather than one who has to pick up the pieces remaining after an unfortunate fight."

He was hoping Graham could help him gather evidence of progress that would reassure federal district judges they did not need to step in. He proposed some first steps: "could we not begin to elect some qualified Negroes to school boards . . . ? City commissioners? Maybe universities could begin basing graduate admission purely on merit; admissions boards would be unaware of race of applicant?" These were all ideas, he suggested, that could appropriately be addressed from the pulpit. Maybe a good word for the Louisiana archbishop who had desegregated his parochial schools. In all, if Graham could urge ministers to express approval of whatever advances were being made on any front, "these things would be called to the attention of Federal Judges, who themselves would be inclined to operate moderately."

Graham immediately responded that of course these discussions would remain private. But he would gather the major southern religious leaders together, lay out Eisenhower's ideas, and "come up with concrete suggestions for ministers to take back to their pulpits."

At no point in his letter had Eisenhower veered into the political fallout of his efforts on civil rights. But even on something he viewed as a profound moral imperative, Graham couldn't resist slipping on his secular robes as well. "Immediately after the election," he advised, "you can take whatever steps you feel are wise and right. In the meantime, it might be well to let the Democratic party bear the brunt of the debate." Let your deeds speak for you, he advised, and float above the fray. "I hope particularly before November you are able to stay out of this bitter racial situation that is developing."

Eisenhower was as aware of the political quandary as anyone. "I have read with great care what you have to say about the political situation," he wrote back. "I think it a great pity that this crucial matter will, almost inescapably it seems, be dragged into the arena of partisan politics. For myself, I shall always, as a matter of conviction and as a champion of real, as opposed to spurious, progress, remain a moderate in this regard." The "foolish extremists" on both sides, he noted, "will never be won over."

In June Graham sent Eisenhower a progress report. He'd had private meetings with leading clergy in the South, black and white, urging a stronger stand in calling for desegregation "and yet demonstrating charity and above all, patience." He had spoken at Protestant conferences and black universities, laying out what he considered a sensible program on race relations. But he was disturbed by rumors that the Republicans would go all-out for the black vote in the North, whatever the price among whites in the South. "Again I would like to caution you about getting involved in this particular problem. At the moment, to an amazing degree, you have the confidence of white and Negro leaders. I would hate to see it jeopardized by even those in the Republican party with a political ax to grind."

Graham may have sincerely believed that Eisenhower's reelection was the best way to promote the cause of civil rights. But it is worth noting that in the first of many presidential campaigns in which Graham was close to a candidate, he was the one monitoring political gossip, introducing political calculations, weighing the cost of standing up for principles. Eager as he was to help out on race relations, he was clearly even more eager to help get Ike reelected.

In August Graham wrote to praise Eisenhower's convention speech and remarked on the prayer of dedication at the end. "I am absolutely convinced that the great contrast between what went on in Chicago and the convention in San Francisco won millions of thoughtful Americans. As you,

Mrs. Eisenhower and the Nixons were bowing in prayer, all of us seemed to sense that here were dedicated people to a cause that cannot lose."

And then he closed with a promise that made no pretense of neutrality: "I shall do all in my power during the coming campaign to gain friends and supporters for your cause." It was a testimony to Graham's reputation for bipartisanship that he was suspected of ghostwriting part of both conventions' keynote speeches, for his good friends Frank Clement, the Democratic governor of Tennessee, and Arthur Langlie, the Republican governor of Washington. "I did write a brief note to each of them suggesting that they inject a moral and spiritual note . . . to present a spiritual call to arms to millions of Americans." But no, he said, he had not written their speeches.

Eisenhower wrote back that he was glad Graham liked the speech. ("I know I really can't compete with some of you people in the latter department.") But more interesting was the letter he sent to Republican chairman Len Hall. "Below I give you the last two paragraphs in a letter I have from Billy Graham, the evangelist. It occurs to me that some time during the campaign we might want to call on him for a little help."

He would never need Graham's help getting reelected: he managed that with 57 percent of the vote to Stevenson's 42 percent. But a year later the tensions had only grown, especially as a new school year began and many communities saw mob violence and open rejection of desegregation. Most defiant of all was Arkansas governor Orval Faubus, the shrewd hillbilly from Greasy Creek, who called out the National Guard carrying bayonets and gas masks to surround Little Rock's Central High School and prevent a dozen black students from entering. This was Eisenhower's nightmare scenario. He worried that if he used federal troops to enforce desegregation, some southern communities would shut down their public schools completely, shifting to a system of private and parochial schools that would hurt poor white children as well as black ones. Faubus's defiance had spooked parents in communities that had been desegregating peacefully; now both white and black parents pulled back, waiting to see what would happen in Little Rock.

On September 23, with a howling mob around the school, nine brave black students actually managed to slip in the back door. Now the crowd was inflamed. "Lynch them!" people cried, as the mayor of Little Rock, Woodrow Wilson Mann, sent Eisenhower a telegram: "The immediate need for federal troops is urgent. . . . Situation is out of control."

Graham was in New York when Eisenhower called. What did he think the president should do about sending troops? "I think you have no alternative," Graham told him. "The discrimination must be stopped." Nixon called an hour later and Graham said the same thing. The next day he told reporters that "all thinking southerners" were appalled at the violence and venom of the mobs, whatever their opinions on integration.

Eisenhower had to move; he called out the army, federalized the National Guard, and some five hundred paratroopers of the 101st Airborne were in Little Rock by nightfall. Under heavy guard, the next day nine black students entered Central High. While Eisenhower explained in an address to the country that he was using federal troops to enforce the law, not force desegregation, that distinction was lost on segregationists throughout the South who called it an "invasion." Eisenhower called the day one of the saddest of his life. When he appealed to southern moderates to step forward and provide some leadership, few took up the cause.

But Graham did; he continued to identify himself as a pronounced desegregationist. Senator Estes Kefauver and columnist Drew Pearson challenged him to preach to an integrated audience in Clinton, Tennessee, after the bombing of the high school. He agreed, urging that they come and join him on the platform. He heard that the White Citizens Council warned he wouldn't get out of town alive. But in the end no violence occurred.

Graham was now confronting white opposition across the South—and defying it, even when it came from the highest levels. South Carolina governor George Bell Timmerman expressed outrage at the notion of an integrated Graham rally on the grounds of the State House. "As a southerner," he said of Graham, "his endorsement of racial mixing has done much harm." With Eisenhower's blessing, Graham moved his crusade to the Fort Jackson army base, where the sixty thousand in attendance were described as the first unsegregated mass meeting in South Carolina's history. "God pity us [Christians]," he told reporters, "if we let our differences [on segregation] prevent us from presenting Christ and his message to a lost world."

In 1959 Graham went to Little Rock, for a week that began with another bombing and ended with crusades in War Memorial Stadium. Governor Faubus himself came but couldn't find a seat. He settled down on the steps way in the back. "I have not come to make any inflammatory statements or preach on the subject of race," Graham said. "I don't think we're ever going to solve our basic social problems apart from the Cross of Christ."

In the audience was another watchful attendee, a young man from Hot Springs who had talked a Sunday school teacher into taking him along to the crusade, named Bill Clinton.

The Ultimate Breakout: New York

Graham was now officially important enough to come under fire from all sides. The more entranced he seemed with the size of the crowds, the numbers of converts, the embrace of his mission by the pillars of the social and economic and political establishments, the more he alienated critics on both the left and the right. They saw America's religious strength as being drawn from her rebellious, searching nature. A country founded by religious dissidents, settled by pioneers, subject to periodic social reformations, was now mass-producing the new faithful.

Graham's critics were divided between those who complained about his fame and those who disliked how he used it. The very fact of his wide appeal alarmed fundamentalists, who charged that he was selling out the true faith in pursuit of bigger crowds and broader acceptance. On the left, meanwhile, his focus on personal salvation gave rise to charges that he was not doing enough to promote social change. It all came together—outrage from the right, condescension and criticism from the left, and sustained attention from the very center of media and business—when he took on the ultimate City of Sin with his Madison Square Garden crusade in New York in 1957.

The planning had been years in the works: twenty-four-hour prayer chains in fifty different countries, including a tribe of former headhunters in Assam who reported that they were praying every morning at sunrise. There were mass mailings, 650 billboards, 40,000 orange-and-black bumper stickers, half a million leaflets. *Variety* predicted that the crusade would be the biggest "full-chorus, hallelujah, oldtime religion, monster revival" since Billy Sunday's invasion of New York in 1917. As in England, Graham was reaching out to the unchurched: more than half of New York's population of eight million was unaffiliated with any faith; 27 percent were Catholic, 10 percent Jews, 7.5 percent Protestants. So rather than ally himself with only conservative evangelical church sponsors—of which there would have been few—he cast wide his arms and welcomed church sponsors from across the theological spectrum.

On April 3 Graham laid down the terms that shaped all his efforts to widen his ministry. He told the National Association of Evangelicals, "Our New York Campaign has been challenged by some extremists. I would like to make myself clear. I intend to go anywhere, sponsored by anybody, to preach the Gospel of Christ, if there are no strings attached to my message."

It was all too much for Graham's former fundamentalist supporters. Bob Jones Sr. just three years earlier had told *TIME* he thought Graham was a prophet: "God almighty wanted him to call attention to the troubles of our time. You can't explain him any other way." Now he denounced Graham for saving souls only to send them to theologically corrupt churches, like Norman Vincent Peale's Marble Collegiate. Students at Bob Jones University were forbidden to pray for the crusade's success. Even Graham's movies had come under fire; conservatives feared that if Graham's name drew devout Christians into these houses of sin for the first time—indeed, the *Hollywood Reporter* estimated that as many as forty-three million Protestants did not go to see movies—the taboo would be broken and bad habits formed.

Graham's defenders argued that he was successfully infiltrating the liberal reaches of Protestantism and culture and drawing people back to traditional roots and values; that modernists who allied themselves with Graham were the ones compromising their positions, not he. "If by fundamentalist you mean 'narrow,' 'bigoted,' 'prejudiced,' 'extremist,' 'emotional,' 'snakehandler,' 'without social conscience'—then I am definitely not a fundamentalist," Graham argued. "However, if by fundamentalist you mean a person who accepts the authority of Scriptures, the virgin birth of Christ, the atoning death of Christ, His bodily resurrection, His second coming, and personal salvation by faith through grace, then I am a fundamentalist." Indeed, as one reluctant sponsoring pastor told *Reader's Digest* religion editor Stanley High, "Personally I don't care too much for Billy Graham or for what he preaches or for the way he preaches it. But I'm inclined to think the Almighty does."

But other skeptics weren't so sure. The editors of the *Christian Century*, and Niebuhr in particular, abhorred this "new junction of Madison Avenue and the Bible Belt." They acknowledged Graham's decency and sincerity; it was the simplicity and digestibility of his message that troubled them, the lack of any real wrestling with the ambiguities of life and soul and suffering and duty. "His plans and his methods show no faith in the caprice of the Holy Spirit," the *Century* charged. "There is something horrifying in this monstrous juggernaut rolling over every sensitivity to its sure triumph. . . . The most worrisome aspect of the whole Graham phenomenon, perhaps, has been the failure of nerve in men who know better, the atrophy of critical faculties. Worst of all has been the drive to smother opposition, to engulf critics, to surround criticism. In the good name of unity, Billy and his friends have pressed for a dangerously anti-Protestant uniformity and conformity."

Thus was the stage set for the great showdown, Billy versus Satan in the Garden. On his way to New York Graham stopped in Washington to see Eisenhower. In a White House reception room a *Newsweek* reporter told Graham that the magazine had been planning a cover on chief of staff Sherman Adams, but editors were talking of switching to a New York crusade cover instead. Graham used the visit to tell Eisenhower of his plans. It was a short visit, but as he was leaving, the president called him back to have his picture taken, which Graham decided was a signal. "That was, I think, one way he felt he could indirectly endorse what we were doing."

The circus moved out of the Garden the night before Graham arrived, and in came whole meadows' worth of flowers, and a tall pulpit with a lattice fence around it, like a sweet suburban oasis in the heart of Sodom. There was, for once, no smoky haze over the arena; ushers were polite; the beer signs at concession stands were covered in cardboard and a checkroom was turned into a Bible shop. The *New York Times* ran the full text of his opening sermon, like it was a State of the Union speech. Over the next ninety-seven days some two million people would attend, the largest evangelistic effort in the country's history. In the VIP box on any given night might be Jerome Hines, Pearl Bailey, Gene Tierney, Ed Sullivan, Dale Evans, Sonja Henie, Walter Winchell.

To the fury of Graham's southern critics, Martin Luther King Jr. gave the opening prayer one night. Graham told the *New York Times* that the civil rights leader was "setting an example of Christian love." The next day King sent off a letter to Graham. "The discussion period that we shared together will remain one of the high points of my life," King wrote. "I am deeply grateful to you for the stand which you have taken in the area of race relations. . . . You, above any other preacher in America, can open the eyes of many persons on this question. . . . Your message in this area has additional weight because you are a native southerner." The next step, he urged, would be to take his nonsegregated crusades to the "hard-core states in the deep south. . . . The impact of such a crusade would be immeasurably great."

On the first night of June, ABC broadcast the crusade live for the first time. *Variety* now hailed Graham as "tremendous box office." He won the highest ratings—some seven million viewers—for the network in the impossible time slot against Jackie Gleason and Perry Como. (Said Perry, "Very fine rating." Said Jackie, "No comment.") It all ended after sixteen weeks with a rally in Times Square; 1,941,200 people attended; 56,426 made decisions for Christ, and another 30,523 as a result of the TV shows.

By now Graham had more in common with the presidents and movie stars than just celebrity. The loss of privacy, the death threats, the pressures and isolation of fame, descended on him as well. As his ministry extended into radio and television, it could all evolve into the Church of Billy Graham, with all the financial and personal temptation that would bring: pride and distance from individuals and normal daily life; a huge strain on the family; and an eternal struggle to keep his eyes on heaven and not on the crowds before him.

Nixon was the first president or vice president to experience that power directly. Truman had of course adamantly refused to attend the Washington meetings. Eisenhower had many more opportunities, although somehow never managed it, maybe because members of the White House staff advised him it would be politically dangerous to endorse "any religious promoter," especially any organization or leader that "smacked of evangelism and proselytizing."

Nixon's moment came on a July evening in 1957, when Graham moved his crusade outdoors to Yankee Stadium and a hundred thousand people came to see him in the 105-degree heat, with another ten thousand turned away. People stood in the aisles, they crowded the field itself, at that time the biggest crowd ever in the stadium or ever in the United States for Graham. Nixon had called the crusade "one of the most courageous spiritual ventures in our generation." But as the two men walked side by side across the infield toward the speaker's platform, and the crowd swelled and roared and sang out "All Hail the Power of Jesus' Name," it was Graham's power that Nixon saw.

It must be incredible, he told Graham, to have been able to summon such a crowd, to earn such adulation. But to say this was to touch Graham's nerve at its most raw, the place where he feared pretense and pride, and he swatted back Nixon's praise. "I didn't fill this place; God did," Graham said, and he repeated that to the enormous crowd. "They said Yankee Stadium wouldn't be filled. But it is. God has done this," he declared, "and all the honor, credit and glory must go to him. You can destroy my ministry by praising me for this. The Bible says God will not share his glory with another."

But as the months and years ahead would show, there were other ways for Nixon to destroy Graham's ministry.

Eisenhower left office in 1961 and retired to Gettysburg to write his memoirs and at last enjoy some well-earned rest. He and Graham corresponded occasionally. But it was not until his last illness put him back in Walter Reed Army Hospital in 1968 that they truly came together again. Graham was on his way to Vietnam when he stopped to see the dying president.

Graham recalled how Eisenhower was concerned about Nixon; Julie was engaged to marry David Eisenhower. "He asked me to go see Nixon for him, and tell Nixon that 'I'd like to see him, there's some things he and I have to get right.' And so I did, I went to Nixon's apartment in New York and we sat in front of the fire and ate steaks. And he said, 'I'll go down there tomorrow,' and he seemed to be very happy and relieved, that Eisenhower had asked me to do that."

During Graham's final visit, Eisenhower asked the doctors and nurses to leave after he had been there about fifteen minutes. "Billy," he said, "I want you to explain once again what you did in Gettysburg, about how you can *know* you're going to heaven?"

So Graham told him one more time, and they prayed together. He told him his whole past had been forgiven and he had nothing to worry about. "I'm ready," Eisenhower said. "And before I left the room," Graham said, "he gave this big smile, big wave, and he said 'You tell those fellows over there that there's an old doughboy here, thinking about 'em and praying for them.'"

EIGHT

The Holy War

I did give political advice, and I shouldn't have. But during that period of time I was strongly for Nixon.

—Graham on the 1960 campaign

Nineteen sixty was the first closely contested presidential race for Graham's generation, the young, postwar nation-builders whose sense of promise and purpose had been sedated by Eisenhower's careful stewardship. America was in motion, redrawing the map between cities and suburbs, redefining the relationship between races, rethinking its role in the world. Voters were looking for change, for action and energy, which gave Jack Kennedy, young and raw and inexperienced compared to Richard Nixon, his greatest advantage. Nixon had to play the statesman who had helped shape the peaceful, prosperous decade that had just ended; but he also needed to break enough from Eisenhower to assure voters that he would represent a fresh start.

Nixon versus Kennedy offered a study in contrasts: Protestant versus Catholic, poor boy versus rich, the awkward loner against the gregarious charmer, the prude against the playboy. And yet when it came to actual policy, there was little to choose: they both promised a hard line against the communists, progress on civil rights, action against poverty, lower taxes, higher defense spending. That meant the outcome would turn on the voters' instincts about what the two men were made of and which one could be trusted to lead.

This time Graham would be even more deeply involved: as election day approached it brought obsessive concern, constant prayer, and as he later recalled it, at least one miracle. His wife, his closest friends, even Nixon warned him that he endangered his ministry by becoming too entangled in politics. What saved him—at least this time—was that unlike some other prominent clerics, he played his part largely in private, offering a constant stream of encouragement and strategic advice. Even at the time Graham seemed to know he had crossed a line; he asked that Nixon destroy one particularly conspiratorial letter after reading it. Asked years later about his role, he said plainly, "I did give political advice, and I shouldn't have. But during that period of time I was strongly for Nixon."

There was, not coincidentally, never a campaign in which religion mattered more. Of course a race decided by a micromargin can be said to have turned on any number of things, including the weather. But any account of the 1960 race has to account for the central role of religious leaders and the beliefs they brought onto the stage.

Both candidates understood the taboos surrounding any kind of public discussion of faith. The country may have just finished an eight-year revival, but when it came to partisan politics, religion was still an untouchable subject. This was a strange feature of America's hunger for generically pious leaders: declaring one's faith in God was a condition for entry, but anything more specific than that—about the actual content of one's faith or how it might relate to policy—was off-limits. "There is only one way I can visualize religion being a legitimate issue in an American political campaign," Nixon declared. "That would be if one of the candidates for the presidency had no religious belief."

Like so many presidents, Kennedy and Nixon were raised by devout mothers who tried, with mixed success, to shape their sons' spiritual lives. Yet Kennedy's religious inheritance would play an immense role in his public life, Nixon's almost none. Rose Kennedy was serenely devoted to the rituals of the Catholic Church, but Jack Kennedy wore his faith lightly, skidded past theological inquiry, and explored matters of the spirit as they interested him. He was "casual about religious rituals and observances," said his sister Eunice, and "a little less convinced about some things than the rest of us." Getting to the heart of his faith was not easy even for those close to him. He didn't think the Catholic Church had a monopoly on virtue, or that nonbelievers went to hell. "He made it a point to attend mass every Sunday when he was on the road, and while he was in the White House," said his adviser and "intellectual bloodbank" Theodore Sorensen. "But as the saying goes, he did not wear his religion on his sleeve. He did not make a point of crossing himself before big moments."

In all their conversations over the years, he never once talked to Sorensen about his personal views on man's relationship to God.

The first time Americans had to reckon with the implications of a Catholic president was in 1928 with Al Smith's candidacy, when perhaps 16 percent of the country was Catholic. When Herbert Hoover crushed him, 58 percent to 40 percent, Billy Graham, who would turn ten the next day in Democratic North Carolina, remembers everyone celebrating the outcome in school without really understanding why. But by 1960 the U.S. Catholic population had more than doubled, and urban Catholics dominated the machinery of the Democratic Party from New York across to Illinois. This time, instead of the exuberantly ethnic, cigar-chewing, rubber-faced Al Smith, who had left school at fourteen and learned politics at the Fulton Fish Market, they presented Harvard's elegant son, all round vowels and a Pulitzer Prize—a Catholic prince claiming his throne. The Eisenhower landslides had swept up many Catholics, and Democrats were determined to bring them home in 1960.

Graham saw the race taking shape long before its contours became clear to most analysts. "Senator Kennedy is getting a fantastic buildup in certain elements of the press," he warned Nixon back in December 1957. "He would indeed be a formidable foe. Contrary to popular opinion . . . I think the religious issue would be very strong and might conceivably work in your behalf." Nixon's faith and understanding of scripture were much on Graham's mind at the time. He recalled a visit with Nixon and Senator George Smathers, in which they had discussed biblical prophecy and the end times. "Sometime perhaps we will have opportunity to go over them again privately," he wrote, "because it may help you in determining future courses of action in case added responsibilities are yours."

Graham often talked to Nixon this way, weaving together the role faith should play in his private decisions and his public demeanor, to the point of telling him he needed to be more consistent about getting to church on Sundays. As the 1960 campaign approached and Graham declared publicly that he thought Nixon was the best-qualified candidate, it made the front pages of many papers. Angry letters poured in: how could he be supporting such a casual Christian? "I have taken my stand and intend to go all the way," he assured Nixon. But apart from any desire to worship, there were good strategic reasons for Nixon to be a bit more conspicuously faithful about his church attendance. "I am convinced that you are going to have the support of the overwhelming majority of the religious minded people in America. It would be most unfortunate if some of your political enemies could point to any inconsistency."

Nixon's Protestantism, however diluted, was an asset to him at this time. While it is difficult from the distance of nearly fifty years to remember the kind of alarm that the prospect of a Catholic president raised, pure anti-Catholic bigotry was only beginning to fall out of fashion. In February *Christianity Today*, which since Graham founded it had become the most influential evangelical magazine, ran an unsigned editorial declaring that it was "perfectly rational" for Protestants to oppose election of a Catholic for president. This was not "irrational prejudice," it explained, given the Vatican's methods: "Where the Romanists are strong enough, they persecute. Where less strong, they oppress and harass; where they are in the minority, they seek special privileges, Government favor and more power."

Kennedy knew he couldn't afford to be angry or defensive. He could say all the right things in public: affirm his commitment to church/state separation, oppose federal aid to parochial schools or appointment of a Vatican ambassador. But much of the conversation about religion was going to be conducted quietly, in pamphlets handed out on Sundays outside churches. He needed to find a way to talk about his faith in a way that would reassure Protestants and rally Catholics. And for a moment at least, there was a chance maybe Billy Graham could help him do it.

Though Graham's friendship with Nixon was well-known, he talked at least about keeping a safe distance from the battle. "It would be a tragedy," he said, "if through the wiles of Satan, I should be led into anything that could be construed as political." He spent the first three months of 1960 in Africa, where, when asked his opinion of nuclear weapons, he declared, "That's political. We are in a political year in the U.S. and I want to make as few political statements as possible." He went to Brazil in July, then toured Europe from August to October. "As you probably have noted, I am desperately trying to stay out of the political situation in the United States," he wrote to Henry Luce. "That is one of the reasons why I have spent the last few months abroad." This spoke to his own experience of political temptation. The best way to resist it was to apply the same strategy as he did to sexual temptation: don't be alone with any woman other than your wife, and stay out of the country during election years.

But the fray had a way of finding him wherever he went.

Summer of Decision

Graham was in between his foreign trips and back in the United States in the spring, boarding a train in Cincinnati on his way to Chicago, where he was to address the National Association of Evangelicals. A young man came up and introduced himself as Pierre Salinger—Kennedy's press secretary. Kennedy was hoping that Graham would consider making a statement about the importance of religious tolerance in the election, for release before the West Virginia primary, which was two weeks away. West Virginia was about 95 percent Protestant. Hubert Humphrey was leading by twenty points, and newspaper polls suggested that half of his support was based purely on religion. (His campaign song was sung to the tune of "Give Me That Old-Time Religion.") The pastor of the United Brethren Church in Parkersburg told the congregation that if Kennedy won, "The Pope will be running the country."

It was in West Virginia that Kennedy found his lines and his strategy: make the issue not religion, but tolerance; voters who were undecided between the candidates could at least enjoy the satisfaction of showing they were not bigots by voting for Kennedy. Sorensen had quietly drafted a letter to be signed by prominent Protestant clergy, urging their colleagues to fight religious prejudice; he made it clear to the ministers he approached that the statement would not come from Kennedy's office or have Sorensen's fingerprints: it was just a nonpartisan appeal for tolerance. So when Salinger crossed paths with Graham, he came back to sit with him and argued his case "earnestly and charmingly." But in the end Graham refused to make any statement, or sign any letter. "I was afraid some might interpret anything I said as an implied political endorsement," he said, though as the campaign went on he showed less caution, at least when it came to implicitly endorsing Nixon.

Graham was no bigot. His message was about coming to Christ; which road you traveled to get there mattered much less to him than that you set out on the journey. While some Catholic leaders during his New York crusade had accused him of promoting "false doctrines" and urged Catholics to stay away, he was used to Catholic priests telling him that they had come to his crusades without their collars—and spotted half a dozen colleagues similarly disguised. He was taking his crusades to more Catholic countries, and finding a warm response. So he was unwilling to openly oppose a Catholic candidate, for all the pressure from some Protestants to do so; but neither would he endorse one.

"We regarded Graham as a conservative who was at least implicitly if not explicitly backing Nixon," Sorensen recalled. Kennedy's team was more successful with other ministers, like the Very Reverend Francis Sayre, the dean of Washington's Episcopal Cathedral and grandson of Woodrow Wilson. The ministers' letter won 144 signatures from clerics testifying, "We are convinced that each of the candidates has presented himself before the American people with honesty and independence, and we would think it unjust to discount any one of them because of his chosen faith." A copy went to every Protestant minister in West Virginia. In the end Kennedy carried all but seven of fifty-five counties in the primary, and Humphrey stood down.

Many Republicans were delighted; they thought Kennedy would be the easiest to beat. But Nixon had no such illusions; he had thought JFK would get the nomination all along. He knew his rival; they had been close to friends once. When Nixon was running for the Senate in 1950, Kennedy had stopped by his office one day with a $1,000 contribution from his father. Now Kennedy had virtually unlimited money, a skilled staff, and a party that was bigger and more united than the GOP. Nixon thought Kennedy's religion would help him in key swing states and hurt only in states he could afford to lose anyway. He told other Republicans and everyone on his team to stay far away from the issue, since any overt anti-Catholic effort would just drive Catholics and independents to the Democrats. Nixon would have to scoop up independent voters to have a chance of winning.

Conservative Protestantism was not exactly cooperating, however. In May, thirteen thousand delegates gathered in Miami for the annual meeting of the Southern Baptist Convention; at the same time the great power summit in Paris between France, Britain, the United States, and Russia, more than two years in the making, was dissolving in vitriol over the Russians shooting down what Eisenhower was finally forced to admit was an American U-2 spy plane. Graham offered a major address on the eve of the convention that reviewed the disaster in Paris: "We may be living at the end of history," he warned. "We Christians are losing the world, and we're losing it fast. Prime Minister Macmillan of England said that if this conference fails we may be on the verge of the extinction of civilization, and the conference has already failed." One more false move, he said, "and the city of Miami could be wiped out by the Russian subs sitting off our shores."

Graham was always willing to draw his audience into a discussion of the impending Apocalypse; but that spring much convention business was devoted to matters nearer at hand. The convention unanimously adopted a resolution affirming the Baptist commitment to church/state separation and warning that "the implications of a candidate's affiliations, including his church, are of concern to the voters in every election." All the more so if he was a member of a church that "maintains a position in open conflict with our American pattern" of religious freedom.

In the middle of all this Graham spoke at a news conference and offered what the *New York Times* called "an implied, though unmistakable, endorsement of Vice President Nixon." He would be voting this time, he said, out of "deep personal convictions." Could that have anything to do with his long friendship with Nixon?

"Might be," he said with a grin. But there was something much larger than friendship at stake, he argued. "The next four years will be the most critical in world history, and we need a president of world stature and experience. This is no time to experiment with novices."

Then he smiled and added, "But I'm not taking sides." And fifty reporters laughed.

During the convention Graham talked to Len Hall, who was now Nixon's campaign manager, letting him know that as he would be in South America he would not be able to accept the invitation to pray at the GOP convention. "He went on to say," Hall wrote in a memo to Nixon, "that after deep and long consideration, he had made up his mind to come out for you publicly." Graham was going to be on *Meet the Press* in early June and, if Nixon thought the time was right, could use that forum.

That would have been a first; and Graham was still ambivalent about an outright endorsement, having been raised in a culture that favored a certain pious distance between candidates and clergy. He sent Nixon clips from the Baptist Convention, noting his veiled statement of support. "I think this strategy carries greater strength than if I came all out for you at the present time." He had encouraging news about the depth of Nixon's strength among the Baptists, and predicted that if Kennedy got the nomination, Nixon could have a real shot at some traditionally Democratic southern states.

In another bit of advice that was characteristic of Graham's counsel when it came to controversy, he warned Nixon about the fallout from the U-2 mess. Graham called the incident "political dynamite. My advice for what it's worth would be to keep as quiet as possible. It is difficult to tell which way sentiment is going to turn." Khrushchev, he warned, seemed intent on inserting himself into the campaign. But he also thought that by criticizing Eisenhower's handling of the incident, Kennedy, Stevenson, and other Democrats might have alienated people who wanted a bipartisan approach to foreign policy.

Nixon was now treating Graham with great respect and care. On the question of an endorsement, he assured him, "I think you handled the subject with great skill," and that the time was not right. As for the summit fallout, Nixon said, "I agree completely with your recommendation as to the proper way to handle the U-2 incident." He enclosed a recent speech he had made that, he said, "I think follows the line you suggested." And maybe they could grab a round of golf soon?

For a man determined to avoid being pulled into politics, Graham was tempting fate by holding a weeklong crusade in Washington the following month. "This is a politically explosive town," he said, "and I am staying away from politics as much as I can." The postmaster general threw a party for him; 56 senators came for a lunch hosted by Lyndon Johnson, Smathers, and two others; 125 representatives came to a breakfast. He prayed at the Pentagon, visited Mamie Eisenhower in the hospital, opened a session of the House with prayer, and helped Pat and Richard Nixon celebrate their twentieth wedding anniversary at his crusade.

Graham had a chance to check in with his best political sources—which included Johnson, who was still clinging to the hope that he could get the nomination—and he wrote to Nixon with his findings. While Graham was only passing along political scuttlebutt among friends, Nixon knew that the titans of the Democratic Party were not exactly looking out for his interests. "Senator Johnson invited me to his office the other day and I spent nearly two hours," Graham told him. "He and Speaker Sam Rayburn are both convinced that the religious issue is THE paramount issue." Whatever Nixon might be tempted to do to win over wavering Catholics would be a waste of time, he said. Johnson, Smathers, and Rayburn all agreed that Kennedy had the Catholic vote totally locked down. "In my opinion, if you make the mistake of having a Catholic running mate, you will divide the Protestant vote and make no inroads whatsoever in the Catholic vote." Better to pick someone around whom Protestants could rally. Minnesota congressman Walter Judd, a much-admired former medical missionary to China like Graham's father-in-law, was the only candidate that both liberal and conservative Protestants would freely support; he could gain Nixon voters in the southern and border states as well. "They don't all agree with him but they deeply respect him. Being on the ticket with you would give you a dedication and enthusiasm among Protestants as no other man in the Republican party." Graham called Judd "almost a *must*."

When he was finished, Graham seemed to realize that he had splashed deep into dangerous waters. "I would appreciate your considering this letter in utter confidence," he concluded. "You would do me a favor by destroying it after reading it." Three days later, Nixon arranged for a quiet lunch with Graham and his top political staff.

In July the Democrats gathered in Los Angeles to nominate Kennedy and Johnson for their ticket. Graham wrote to Johnson, assuring him that "I hold you in the highest personal esteem," and swatting down the rumors that he was going to weigh in on religion. "This is not true," he said, adding that he planned to "stay out of the political campaign as much as possible." Then it was the Republicans' turn in San Francisco, where, having been turned down by Judd and Nelson Rockefeller, Nixon turned to Henry Cabot Lodge, and they set off together down the campaign trail.

Graham was still in Europe, making decisions that, while largely secret, would have an immeasurable impact on the race. On August 4 he wrote to Eisenhower, making his case for why the president needed to get off the sidelines. He urged Ike to swing through key southern states, where he was much admired. "I believe you could tip the scales in a number of key states from Kentucky to Texas," Graham wrote, sounding every bit the inside strategist. "I believe that Nixon has a fighting chance only if you go all out. I know this would mean two months of hard work, but I believe the rewards to the Nation would be as great as when you led the armies at Normandy." That analogy suggests the level of alarm with which Graham viewed the prospect of a Kennedy victory, though this was more a measure of his total faith in Nixon than his lack of faith in the Democrats.

From here on out Graham would travel a different road than some other prominent Protestant leaders. He continued to transmit advice to Nixon behind the scenes; but he never really stepped out in front of the cameras. When other religious leaders came onstage, the shape of the race quickly changed.

NINE

"I Am for You"

I wasn't necessarily involved. Norman Vincent Peale was involved.
—Graham on the campaign's great religious confrontation

On August 10 Graham wrote a letter to Kennedy, promising not to cause trouble—in public, at least. He would probably vote for Nixon, he said, but based on their long friendship, not any religious concerns. And if Kennedy won, he could count on Graham to help him unite and rally the country behind him: "In the event of your election, you will have my wholehearted support."

A week later he hosted a meeting of evangelicals in Montreux, Switzerland, and the general discussion of their common spiritual mission quickly turned into a debate about the U.S. campaign. The details of that meeting were known to few people at the time; but as the contest unspooled, Graham's gathering would help produce the most notorious eruption of the entire race.

Graham wrote to Nixon about it in a letter marked personal and confidential. The twenty-five or so clergy had come up with a plan of action: "First: a highly financed and organized office is being opened September 8 in Washington to supply information to religious leaders throughout the nation," he wrote. "This will be operated on the highest level and is to be free from the type of bigotry and intolerance that often hurts rather than helps." The ministers felt that the Democrats were better organized and much better at getting out their message, placing favorable stories in the papers; this new office was meant to level the field.

The meeting mattered because among those in attendance was Nixon's most conspicuous religious ally, Norman Vincent Peale. He had approached Graham earlier in the summer to share his concerns about Kennedy, and so Graham invited him to come to Montreux.

Peale was sometimes called "the rich man's Billy Graham"; more than any figures of the time, they had carved the religious profile of that anxious age. Like Graham, Peale had his huge best-seller in the early 1950s, *The Power of Positive Thinking*. Both preachers had extensive radio and TV ministries and a syndicated newspaper column that reached millions of people every week. Both were favorite targets of theologians like Niebuhr, who charged them with contributing to the spiritual bankruptcy of bourgeois life. Both were friends of businessmen and politicians, and especially of Nixon, who as a young naval officer stationed in New York used to worship at Peale's Marble Collegiate Church. Through Graham's 1957 New York crusade, Peale's church received more new members than any other in the city.

Graham and Peale were not exactly theological kindred spirits; Graham's message was more gospel-driven, Peale's the seminal self-help manual. As for their political instincts, if Graham wrestled with how to balance the demands of his ministry to reach out to all, and the desires of his heart to help his friend get elected, Peale showed less ambivalence. During the West Virginia primary he had gone to Charleston and declared that it was essential to talk about Kennedy's Catholicism. He was planning to come out squarely for Nixon in a Sunday sermon in October, when it would have the greatest impact, and his wife had already looked into what it would cost to print 350,000 copies of it.

So after Montreux, Graham told Nixon that he and Peale had been commissioned by the group to "urge you to say more on religion in your addresses." This was not so much about defeating Kennedy as about defining Nixon: there was "a running question" throughout Protestantism about what exactly Richard Nixon believed. "I informed them of your reticence to use religion for political purposes. They all agreed that it would not be so interpreted but that the people have a right to know of a candidate's religious convictions, particularly at this uncertain hour of history."

Graham urged Nixon to testify so often that one wonders whether he was among those needing to hear it; whether for all his defenses, even then he was uncertain about the actual depth of Nixon's faith. The irony of their relationship as it unfolded in 1960 was that Graham was so attentive to Nixon's political needs, he sometimes failed to address the spiritual ones. Graham's immense flock became a constituency, not a cloud of witnesses: he told Nixon he had written a letter to his mailing list of two million households, urging them to organize Sunday school classes and churches to get out and vote. They in turn would bring in other religious groups as well. "It is felt that the majority of people on these lists are Democratic or independent voters. It was also felt that this would bring about a favorable swing among these voters to you."

Graham also revealed that he had had a letter from Eisenhower in which the president said he was trying to help. "He could have a tremendous influence if he would make some fighting speeches such as he gave at the convention."

Finally, Graham invited Dick and Pat to North Carolina for a visit when he was back in the States in October—an open invitation for Nixon to use his friendship with Graham as political theater: "This would certainly be a dramatic and publicized event that I believe might tip the scales in North Carolina and dramatize the religious issue throughout the nation without mentioning it publicly." In this case one could hardly accuse Nixon of exploiting Graham when doing so was Graham's idea.

Nixon wrote back gratefully, promising to incorporate Graham's suggestions into his speeches and noting that he'd passed Graham's proposed deployment plan on to Eisenhower. As for church attendance, he said, that was not as easy as it looked. "Since the nomination, the press, of course, regularly covers me on Sundays as well as other days and, consequently, pictures have appeared showing me going to church with Pat and the two girls virtually every week. A Kennedy supporter complained bitterly to one of my friends that I was deliberately injecting the religious issue into the campaign by allowing my picture to be taken going to church. This shows that you just can't win on that issue."

But he approved of Graham's effort to rally his followers, as long as it didn't step over a line. "I think that the most effective thing ministers can do in this campaign is to urge all their members to vote," Nixon wrote. "This completely avoids any so-called religious prejudice and simply assures that the decision on November 8 will be made by a majority of all the people."

In his public comments, however, Graham did go a bit further than "everyone should vote." Catching up with him in Geneva, reporters pressed him to explain the role he thought religion would play in the race. He replied that he thought it would be "the decisive issue." "A man's religion," he said, "cannot be separated from his person; therefore, where religion involves political decision, it becomes a legitimate issue. For example, the people have a right to know the views of a Quaker on pacifism or a Christian Scientist's view on medical aid, or a Catholic's view on the secular influences of the Vatican."

That was enough to prompt *TIME* to declare that Graham had "plunged into politics" by saying that Kennedy's Catholicism was a legitimate issue. Graham protested in a letter to the editor, which he copied to Nixon as well. But his fingers had been burnt, and it may have saved him from much greater harm. "As you can see, I am withdrawing myself from public involvement on the religious issue," he assured Nixon on September 1. "I am also detaching myself from some of the cheap religious bigotry and diabolical whisperings that are going on. I am not so much opposed to Kennedy as I am *for you*."

His strategy going forward, he told Nixon, was aimed at protecting both of them. "Privately, I intend to do all in my power to get you elected. I think by refusing to be associated with bigotry and intolerance I can be of far greater importance and support to you." It wasn't just that bigotry was wrong; it was stupid. The open attacks by Protestants, he said, were serving mainly to solidify the Catholic vote. "At all costs you must stay a million miles away from the religious issue at this time. I read a very dangerous letter yesterday. A Protestant leader said that he had established underground communication with the Republican National Committee. Even if it were true, I was shocked to see it in a letter for fear that if it ever got into the wrong hands it would do the Republicans great damage."

Then he passed along news from the Kennedy camp: they were taking the religious issue extremely seriously, he said, and had hired "a clever, brilliant Protestant attorney by the name of Wine who is going to organize Protestants for Kennedy. I am informed that a debate is now going on within the Kennedy camp as to whether this should be an open move or kept underground."

In fact it was Sorensen's assignment to open a "community relations" division. At Bobby Kennedy's suggestion, he had hired lawyer James Wine, a former staff member at the National Council of Churches, who as a West Virginia native had helped with the ministers' letter in the spring. "We thought he was a very knowledgeable straight shooter and had good credentials," Sorensen said. With a team of secretaries and stenographers, they answered hundreds of letters each week from people asking about Kennedy's beliefs. "The mail that poured into the office was not about issues like contraception," Sorensen recalled. "People said that the pope will control this country, that Catholics are subject to a rigid hierarchy." Wine's operation counseled local Democrats about how to answer inquiries and distributed leaflets and films of the senator's statements. They came to suspect that much of the ugly literature was being created and circulated by wealthy Nixon backers. "We knew after a while that they were not anti-Catholic," Wine said of his conservative antagonists. "They were anti-Kennedy."

As Nixon sent out warnings in every direction for people to stay clear of religion, the issue erupted all across the map. Running his brother's campaign, Robert Kennedy followed his canny motto to "hang a lantern on your problem" when he spoke from the newly expanded offices of the DNC: "Right now, religion is the biggest issue in the South, and in the country." Harry Truman accused Nixon of playing a double game: "While he stands at the front door proclaiming charity and tolerance," Truman declared, "his supporters are herding the forces of racial, religious and anti-union bigotry in by way of the back door. And no one will ever make me believe he is not smart enough to know what is going on." That salvo brought Eisenhower to his feet. "I not only don't believe in voicing prejudice," the president said at his press conference, "I want to assure you that I feel none. And I am sure that Mr. Nixon feels exactly the same. . . . I would hope that religion could be one of those subjects that could be laid on the shelf and forgotten until after the election is over."

At that moment, however, Peale was across town at the Mayflower Hotel with 150 other Protestant leaders, sending a very different message to the world. It was, Nixon said, "a disastrous political development . . . over which I had no control."

THE PEALE EXPLOSION

The meeting of the Citizens for Religious Freedom was actually organized by neither Peale nor Graham, but by a man named Donald Gill, a thirty-two-year-old Baptist minister on leave from the National Association of Evangelicals, and a seventy-year-old Congregational minister named Dr. Elwin Wright. Graham was still in Europe that September, so he could not even attend. Peale, while he had nothing to do with the group's creation, agreed to preside at the meeting and serve as its official spokesman. And that act nearly ruined him.

Before the meeting convened he was already on record with his views. Democrats, he said, "should not have nominated a man, no matter how fine a person he is, who would cause this divisiveness among Americans," a statement that effectively disqualified any Catholic, or anyone of any background that could "divide" people. "Personally I don't know anything about Mr. Kennedy," Peale said. "I respect Mr. Nixon and feel that he should be President at this time. That has nothing to do with religion."

There were no Catholics or liberal Protestants in attendance and the meeting was closed to the press, but two reporters managed to sneak into an adjoining sound booth and listened in on the whole event. "Our American culture is at stake," they reported Peale saying. "I don't say it won't survive, but it won't be what it was." Among those attending were Daniel Poling, editor of the influential *Christian Herald* and a longtime Kennedy antagonist, and Graham's father-in-law, L. Nelson Bell, who declared that Protestants were too "soft" on Catholicism. To him, there was not much to choose between Rome and Moscow: "The antagonism of the Roman church to Communism is in part because of similar methods."

The assembly approved a 2,000-word manifesto, and when it was over Peale prepared to meet with reporters. "Say one wrong word," one conferee warned, "and the press will murder us—by next week we'll be out of business." Peale laughed. "Pray for us," he said, "while we are talking to those reporters."

Given the hostility of the comments the hidden reporters had overheard, Peale was finished before he started. In front of a sea of microphones, he tried to characterize the meeting as a "philosophical discussion" of the nature of the Catholic Church. Nixon did not know about the meeting, he told reporters, "and probably would have disapproved of it had he known." But Peale then shared the manifesto, which called religion "a major factor" in the campaign and questioned whether Kennedy or any Catholic candidate could truly be trusted to operate free from Vatican pressure, given Rome's "determined efforts . . . to breach the wall of separation of church and state."

The reaction was blistering: columnist Murray Kempton inveighed against the bland spiritual flavor of the Eisenhower era and the "priests of the empty temple," including both Graham and Peale: "We have been afflicted with a state religion which is so diluted as to be no religion at all," he wrote, "and whose true conviction was abstracted neatly by Peale when he said of the Quaker birth of his candidate, Richard Nixon: 'I don't know that he ever let it bother him.'" He noted that Graham, the "Pope of lower

Protestantism," was more discreet than Peale in public, but "Graham certainly prays Republican; he has prayed at the White House and Gettysburg with the President and totes his good friend the vice president around to Bible conferences." Kempton lashed them both for hypocrisy in charging Catholics with ignoring church/state separation when Graham felt free to denounce Supreme Court decisions removing compulsory religious education from schools.

That was the exception. By and large Graham remained invisible, and Peale was the celebrity whipping boy of what was instantly christened the Peale Group. Kennedy accused the group of challenging "my loyalty to the United States." Johnson denounced the "hate campaign." Niebuhr and John Bennett, the vice chairmen of the Liberal Party in New York, denounced the efforts of the "Protestant Underworld." "What kind of country do these Protestants want?" Bennett asked. "A country where 40,000,000 citizens feel that they are outsiders?" Jewish leaders deplored what amounted to a religious test for political office; the *Philadelphia Inquirer* dropped Peale's column. Senator Henry Jackson, chair of the Democratic National Committee, called on Nixon to repudiate him.

The meeting had taken place on a Wednesday: Nixon's first public appearance upon escaping from the hospital, where he'd been sidelined by a serious knee infection, was that Sunday on *Meet the Press*. There he proceeded to defend Kennedy's honor, patriotism, and service. "I have no doubt whatsoever about Senator Kennedy's loyalty to his country," Nixon declared. It would be "tragic" if the election were decided on religious grounds. And he repeated his orders to everyone connected to his campaign "not to discuss religion, not to raise it, not to allow anybody to participate in the campaign who does on that ground, and as far as I am concerned, I will decline to discuss religion."

Kennedy had his own political decision to make, and he seized the opportunity the next day. Nixon was now trapped: every time he came out with a statement against prejudice, Kennedy could say, "There goes Tricky Dick again, raising the religious issue." But Kennedy's next move was the boldest of all: he accepted an invitation to address the Greater Houston Ministerial Association, perhaps the least friendly audience imaginable at a time when the religious issue was white-hot. Sorensen was recruited to draft answers to whatever the ministers might ask. "We can win or lose the election right there in Houston on Monday night," he told a friend.

The ministers gathered in the pink-and-green-carpeted ballroom of the Rice Hotel, three hundred strong with three hundred more spectators come to see the fireworks. The national press corps was there, looking for a showdown. "Kennedy came out of the back room all by himself. . . . No one was there to guard him," recalled Johnson's adviser Jack Valenti. "It's as if he said 'Okay, you bastards. You want me—here I am.' By that simple act of one lonely man ready to take on the hordes, he threw the first punch, and it was about as brilliant a performance as I've ever witnessed, as a clinical observer."

He had come, Kennedy said, not to talk about what kind of church he believed in, "for that should be important only to me—but what kind of America I believe in.

"I believe in an America where the separation of church and state is absolute—where no Catholic prelate would tell the president (should he be Catholic) how to act, and no Protestant minister would tell his parishioners for whom to vote . . . where religious liberty is so indivisible that an act against one church is treated as an act against all."

He drew into his tent not just fellow Catholics but all religious minorities, a late insert in the final draft. This time a Catholic might be considered suspect, but next time it could be the Jew, or the Unitarian. "Today I may be the victim—but tomorrow it may be you—until the whole fabric of our harmonious society is ripped at a time of great national peril.

"I believe in a president whose religious views are his own private affair, neither imposed by him upon the nation or imposed by the nation upon him as a condition to holding that office." This was the America he had fought for, he said, and his brother had died for. And when they were fighting and dying, "No one suggested then that we may have a 'divided loyalty,' that we did 'not believe in liberty,' or that we belonged to a disloyal group that threatened the 'freedoms for which our forefathers died.'"

Finally, a promise: as president he would make decisions based on the country's interest, not any outside pressures. "But if the time should ever come—and I do not concede any conflict to be even remotely possible—when my office would require me to either violate my conscience or violate the national interest, then I would resign the office; and I hope any conscientious public servant would do the same."

The sullen, hostile audience was moved, some to tears. "It was the best speech of his campaign," Sorensen said, and a film version was distributed over the weeks that followed, so that millions of people saw it for themselves. It helped reshape the battlefield from that point on. Kennedy having answered eloquently all the reasonable concerns, anyone who continued to challenge his fitness for the office could be doing so only out of blind prejudice.

"As we say in my part of Texas," said Sam Rayburn, "he ate 'em blood raw."

Nixon, seeing what had occurred and desperate for the issue to go away, said that the Houston statement "should be accepted without questioning."

As for Peale, he had been hit by a hurricane. Republican friends wrote to tell him how much he had hurt Nixon's campaign. Within days Peale had publicly cut his ties with the Citizens group, though as Sorensen wryly noted, "He had no disagreement with what was said and done but wanted everyone to know he had nothing to do with it." Then he went into seclusion, canceled all his speeches, offered to resign the pulpit of Marble Collegiate. He told a friend he had ruined himself, and even thought about making a public statement urging support for Kennedy—anything to repair the damage he had done.

For all his suffering, Peale never implicated Graham. Neither man had actually organized the Washington meeting, which was already in the works when Graham's group met in August. The organizers said that they had intentionally kept Graham out of it, because it could have hampered his ability to hold crusades in Catholic countries in the future.

But some of their mutual friends felt that Graham had abandoned Peale when the issue exploded. The *Christian Herald*'s Daniel Poling told Graham he had attended the Washington meeting because he thought Graham was a sponsor. Even decades later, Graham remained sensitive about the whole issue. To the suggestion that he was involved in the religious issue during the campaign, he insisted, "I wasn't necessarily involved. Norman Vincent Peale was involved. The first letter came to me *from* Norman Vincent Peale, saying that he was disturbed about the fact that there was going to be a Catholic candidate." As he recalled it, when someone present at Montreux brought up the Washington meeting, Graham had said he couldn't go, but urged Peale to be there. "That was the only involvement I had." Graham knew that Peale had been damaged, personally and professionally, by the whole thing, and later apologized to him for having urged him to attend.

COUNTERING KENNEDY

Painful as it was for Peale and Nixon, watching those September weeks unfold was a near-death experience for Graham as well. He had been saved from public disgrace by the fact that no one who knew about the Montreux meeting was talking and he had not been directly involved in the Washington meeting. But his next letters to Nixon have a desperate feel to them.

"I cannot possibly get involved in the religious issue," he wrote on September 24. "Not only would they crucify me, but they would eventually turn it against you. . . . I have been avoiding the American press during these last few weeks like the plague; but when I arrive home next week I will make statements by implication that will be interpreted as favorable to you without getting directly involved. As the campaign moves on, I may be forced to take a more open stand if I feel it will help your cause, but we shall await further developments."

But in the meantime, given Kennedy's triumph in Houston, someone had to do something to reset the debate. Graham sensed that Nixon was losing momentum, that religion was hurting him. The Democrats' goal, he argued, was to solidify the Catholic vote and split the Protestant vote. Kennedy became a martyr, evoking people's sympathies, while the important issues in the campaign, the ones that played to Nixon's advantage, were obscured. "They are successfully accomplishing all four of these objectives," Graham warned. "As I recall a conversation with a high-ranking Democratic leader in June, this was precisely what he told me would happen if Kennedy were nominated. He said 'Kennedy can be elected solely on the religious issue.'"

Nixon himself could not fight back, Graham acknowledged, but that just made it all the more important to get Eisenhower involved, as well as Rockefeller and Dewey. "No one could ever accuse them of religious bigotry or prejudice."

On a more tender subject, Graham suggested that Kennedy was making a lot of sense when he talked about strengthening U.S. defenses and taking a harder line against Cuba. He knew that Nixon couldn't oppose Eisenhower's policies, "but I think toward the end of the campaign you can be as strong on these points as Kennedy and thus take away one of his great weapons." He of course had no idea that there were plans for an invasion of Cuba already on the drawing board—which of course Nixon could not discuss.

When he got that letter, Nixon spoke by phone and sent a memo to his aides Bob Finch and Len Hall, enclosing Graham's advice. "I think it makes a hell of a lot of sense," Nixon told them, and wanted to know how it could be implemented. "Please note the paragraph where he is talking about the Cuban situation. I would like you, Len, to go over and have a chat with the President about that situation. I don't know whether anything can be done about it, but it does show what the reactions are."

Nixon was now using Graham as a barometer. He was surrounded by talented, experienced GOP political advisers, but they seldom felt they got through to him—"he reduced us all to clerks," one complained. Graham, on the other hand, got a close hearing and easy access. In early October Graham finally flew home from Europe, and immediately got on the phone with political, religious, and business leaders around the country, taking soundings. He found himself listening closely to Kennedy, and agreeing with more and more of what he was saying. Kennedy's talk of sacrifice and dedication to meeting the challenges of the 1960s appealed to him—which helped him understand why it was appealing to a lot of other people as well.

The fate of Nixon's campaign was hanging in the balance, and Graham told him his sources were unanimous on several points. First, on Cuba: maybe U.S. foreign policy needed to be recast in electoral terms. "I am wondering if the President could not take some strong dramatic action even to the breaking of diplomatic relations." It was time to remind people how many countries had gone communist under Democratic administrations. "I believe there are at least twenty countries. This would be tremendously impressive and would shut the mouth of your opponent on this point."

Next, some respected Republican leader had to show how the Democrats were exploiting religion. "Truman and Johnson have been in North Carolina during the past few days," he said, "and the main theme of their talk is religion." And now Graham cut a bit closer to the bone. Nixon had a religion problem of his own, he said. There was still a strong undercurrent among Protestants that the vice president needed to speak out more forcefully about the need for revival, about dependence on God and prayer—to talk, in other words, the way Eisenhower had in the course of reinjecting religious rhetoric into public life. The bar had been raised, and Nixon was now the victim of higher expectations for public piety.

"I wonder if you couldn't say in your next debate that whoever is elected should look to God for strength, guidance and leadership as Washington and Lincoln did," Graham suggested, and then invoked Eisenhower directly. "I know from my private conversations with the President that he feels most strongly on this point."

That brought up another tender subject: Nixon's reluctance to deploy his greatest weapon by getting Eisenhower more engaged. Send him to Texas, Pennsylvania, Ohio, and California, Graham urged. "He is not too effective on television, but his personal appearance in an area does something remarkable to the people." That would help send the message that a Kennedy victory would be a personal repudiation of Eisenhower.

Nixon agreed: Eisenhower was raring to go. But on the eve of their meeting to discuss a big presidential push, Mamie Eisenhower called Pat Nixon, pleading with her to limit her husband's participation; his doctors feared what a heavy campaign schedule could do to his health. Nixon agreed, and lost whatever help Ike could have given him in some key states.

Finally, Graham offered some spiritual support as well. Thousands of prayer meetings had been organized across the country, he said, to pray for the election. "I am certain that during the next few days you are going to sense supernatural strength and wisdom in answer to prayer."

As it happened, however, a third religious figure was about to join Graham and Peale on the campaign stage, and Nixon, yet again, proved unable to win credit for instincts of which he had always been proud.

DR. KING COMES ONSTAGE

If religion was one fault line in the 1960 campaign, race was the other. Civil rights presented both a moral and political challenge to the candidates. Both were committed to seeing progress; whatever his private feelings—and in years to come the White House tapes showed they could be deeply racist—Nixon's record during the past eight years had been stronger than Kennedy's, and the vice president had worked to engage Eisenhower in the issue. Some of his mother's teachings had gotten through: he sent his daughters to an integrated school, and refused to sign a restrictive covenant when he bought his house. After meeting Martin Luther King during a trip to Ghana in 1957, Nixon invited him and Ralph Abernathy to the White House during debate over the civil rights bill: King estimated that even with its flaws, it could help add two million black voters to the rolls by the 1960 election. When it passed, King wrote to the vice president, thanking him for "your assiduous labor and dauntless courage. . . . This is certainly an expression of your devotion to the highest mandates of the moral law. It is also an expression of your political wisdom. . . . The Negro vote is the balance of power in so many important big states that one almost has to have the Negro vote to win a presidential election."

As 1960 unfolded Graham kept an eye on King, seeing a potent political force in the making. They spent three days together in Rio de Janeiro in June, at the World Baptist Alliance, where Graham gave a dinner in King's honor. He wrote to warn Nixon that King's expressions of political neutrality did not preclude dropping some conspicuous hints, rather like Graham's own: "Kennedy had just invited him to his home for three hours. King was greatly impressed and just about sold. I think I at least neutralized him. I think if you could invite him for a brief conference it might swing him. He would be a powerful influence."

Nixon faced a great temptation: since most northern blacks were already leaning Democratic, would a more restrained approach to reform give the GOP a shot at winning the South? But under pressure from moderates, Nixon held his ground; Barry Goldwater would later say that Nixon's support for civil rights cost him the South, and hence the election. So it was all the more striking that when the crucial moment came to take a stand on race, Nixon managed to alienate both northern blacks and southern whites.

On October 19, Martin Luther King was arrested at Atlanta's Magnolia Room restaurant, along with more than fifty other people who were conducting sit-ins across the city. While the others were all released on bail, King was held on a technicality—a traffic violation—and sentenced to hard time at the state penitentiary in Reidsville.

When he heard the news, Nixon told his spokesman Herb Klein, "I think Dr. King is getting a bum rap." He called the Justice Department: weren't Dr. King's civil rights being violated, and was that grounds to act? An official drafted a statement supporting an application for his release, but it was never acted upon. Eisenhower said nothing. When asked about the incident, Klein, leaving matters to the Justice Department, said the vice president had "no comment."

Kennedy, meanwhile, at the urging of his brother-in-law Sargent Shriver, put in a call to Coretta Scott King, who was six months pregnant and wondering about the odds of her husband surviving a four-month sentence of hard labor in a rough Georgia jail. "I know this must be very hard for you, and I just wanted you to know that I was thinking about you and Dr. King," Kennedy told her. "If there is anything I can do to help, please feel free to call on me." The call lasted perhaps two minutes. The next day Bobby called the sentencing judge, a Democrat, to cut a deal that would end with King's release.

In the final heat of the campaign, most people in the country had little idea what had occurred. But Coretta King, alight with gratitude, told her family and friends, who told others, who spread the word. Kennedy was initially furious that word had gotten out, fearing it would hurt him with southern Democrats. But Dr. King's father, himself a renowned Baptist preacher, gave him reason to relax. He had come out a few weeks before for Vice President Nixon, mainly on religious grounds. ("Imagine," Kennedy remarked, King's father is a bigot. But then, he added wryly, "We all have our fathers, don't we.") This act of compassion was enough to convince Daddy King that he could vote for a Catholic candidate after all. "I've got a suitcase of votes, and I'm going to take them to Mr. Kennedy and dump them in his lap."

Kennedy's campaign went on to print a million pamphlets on blue paper, outlining the candidate's support for the civil rights leader and his family, which they handed out in front of black churches all around the country: "The Case of Martin Luther King: No Comment Nixon versus a Candidate with a Heart, Senator Kennedy." Ralph Abernathy declared, "I earnestly and sincerely think that it is time for all of us to take off our Nixon buttons." It was later referred to as "the blue bomb." Two days before the vote, Dr. King himself went on the radio to praise Kennedy and denounce the Republicans for "disagreement and double-talk." It was not quite an endorsement—but it was enough. Where Republicans had carried black voters by a three-to-two margin in 1956, Kennedy won them seven to three. In the end, Eisenhower complained, the race was decided by "a couple of phone calls" from the Kennedy brothers.

In a fit of understatement, Nixon called the King episode "one incident . . . which, in retrospect, might have been avoided or at least better handled."

So Peale had his turn, and King had his, to sway the course of the race. The last decision, however, fell to Graham—and this time it would take God answering his prayers to keep him safely out of the fire.

TEN

The Meaning of LIFE

He was so dejected. I mean he just, his shoulders drooped and he was almost haggard. And I could see he was very discouraged. And I put my arm around him and I said, "Dick," I said, "The American people will call on you again."
—Graham on Nixon after his defeat

Billy Graham called what happened next "possibly the greatest inward conflict since my conversion to Christ over twenty years ago." And all over a magazine story.

Among his first stops when he arrived back in the country in October was the Time and Life Building in New York, where he went to see Luce. Still scorched by the Peale bonfire, he told the publisher he wanted to help Nixon, but without making an outright endorsement.

Luce had a proposition. "Why don't you write an article about Nixon the man, as you know him? If it works, we'll use it in *LIFE* magazine," he suggested. Graham was hesitant. "Don't write whom you're going to vote for," Luce said. "Just what you think of Nixon as a man."

Still doubtful, Graham said he would try. He went back home to North Carolina, and one afternoon sat down to dictate; it took less than an hour, start to finish. It was one of the easiest things he'd ever done.

"I was determined to stay out of politics, especially when religion became an issue in the campaign," he wrote in his article. But he had studied scripture and prayed, and concluded that it was his duty as a citizen to speak out. "Labor leaders, movie stars, newspaper columnists and editors and people of all walks of life are expressing themselves on each side, should not I?"

In making his case, he played on the experience theme: he had talked with leaders in more than fifty countries, who reminded him that "you are electing the leader of the free world." Nixon, he said, had the qualities to become another Lincoln. He was warm, sincere, and of course, genuinely devout. His home life was above reproach. "I can testify that he has a deep personal faith in God springing from devout Christian parents," he wrote, which was a surprising argument from one who preached that faith had to be personal, not inherited. "Although he doesn't flaunt his faith publicly, I know him to be a deeply religious man."

Graham's devotion to Nixon would not supersede his loyalty to the country and the presidency: he promised to support Kennedy if he won, and in the end he turned everything over to God, urging Americans to pray that "Thy Will be Done."

He hadn't told Nixon he had written the story; he did talk to some Nixon staffers, who were undecided, which just confounded Graham even more. But Luce was thrilled when he read it. "I'm running it this coming week—going to feature it." That would put it in the hands of more than six million readers two weeks before the election.

Graham was glad Luce was pleased, but he was increasingly miserable. Still the voice of caution when it came to his political activities, Ruth was adamantly opposed. Like his other friends, she argued both principle and pragmatism: plunging into politics, she warned, would jeopardize his ministry and would probably hurt Nixon in Catholic areas that he needed to win. Then the calls started coming from Graham's Democratic friends, as rumors about the story seeped out. Governor Luther Hodges of North Carolina called. "It's getting you into politics, and you've stayed out of politics," he said. Next were Graham's good friends Senator Smathers and Governor Clement. He was making a terrible mistake, they told him. "I'll love you no matter what you do," Clement said, "but I hope you don't publish it."

The day before the story was due to go to press, reporter Bill Furth wrote a memo to Luce and *LIFE* editor E. K. Thompson, warning that the *Boston Globe* had gotten wind of the story, and asked whether *LIFE* would run a companion piece by someone writing on Kennedy's behalf— and whether it was true that Kennedy had called to protest.

LIFE went to press on Thursday night, October 20. That night, the Grahams were on their knees. Graham wasn't prepared to ask Luce to drop it, but he'd be glad if God did. They prayed that if it was God's will that the story not appear, He would find some way to stop it.

Whether or not God intervened directly, Kennedy certainly did. Luce had alerted him that it was coming, and he fought back hard. In fairness, Kennedy argued, Niebuhr or someone like him should have a chance to write a contrasting piece. (That promised to be an interesting article as well: "I never thought I'd be voting for a compulsive adulterer," Niebuhr told the Reverend William Sloane Coffin, "but he certainly has a better grasp of the situation than Nixon.")

Given the opposition, and the fact that he still had one more week left to run it, Luce pulled the story at midnight.

The next morning he called Graham at ten. He hadn't been able to sleep last night, he said, and told Graham what he'd done. He was already regretting the decision; but Graham was ecstatic. He was convinced that God had heard their prayers, and that a miracle had been performed. This was hard for Luce to argue with, but he said he'd give Graham the weekend to think it over.

Graham wouldn't budge. "I fear that an article by me telling people who to vote for would have a reverse reaction," he wrote to Luce. He offered to compose something safe, on why it was every Christian's duty to vote. He had read a version to his friend Stanley High on the phone: "He thinks it will accomplish our objective without being accused of engaging in partisan politics." And then he reminded the publisher of the stakes of getting this decision right, of keeping their priorities straight. "At this fateful period of history God in His sovereign will has given me a world-wide hearing. I shall always be convinced that He used you more than any single factor in this open door around the world. Therefore when I preach the gospel, in a sense you are participating."

Luce wasn't especially keen on a watered-down version and suggested that Graham simply stand down; but Graham wrote it anyway and sent it off. Luce didn't think it was as strong as the first, but agreed to run it instead. "I really felt that the Lord had intervened in some strange and mysterious way," Graham concluded. "I may never know why until I stand before Him at the Judgment."

Of course the message in the *LIFE* article that finally ran was not exactly subtle. Voting, Graham argued, is part of one's Christian duty. As for how to decide, "Certainly we should not decide on the basis of which candidate is more handsome or more charming. Neither should we follow the dubious path of tradition and say 'I'll vote for my Party, right or wrong.' That is bigotry at its worst." It was also bad for Republicans who were heavily outnumbered.

There is no telling what difference it would have made if Billy Graham had come out for Nixon in the headlines leading up to election day. It's not likely that anyone would have been surprised: that last week was a dance of seven veils, in which Graham in news conferences and interviews flirted with commitment and repeated lines from the article he had just pulled: "I see that citizens from all walks of life—movie stars, clergy, business leaders, labor leaders—are supporting candidates," he told the *Charlotte News.* "I think it may be not only the right but the responsibility of people to come out at this time." He was especially tempted since "I do have some strong convictions about this campaign that are deeper than any other since I have become of voting age." But he felt he hadn't crossed the red line so long as he didn't expressly say what they were.

Others around him were not so constrained. When Nixon came to campaign in Charlotte, Graham's parents greeted him at the airport and sat on the platform with him. His associate Grady Wilson wrote to all the Charlotte ministers, urging them to attend. Graham himself offered the invocation at Nixon's rally in Columbia, South Carolina. As the two men walked down the Capitol steps together, the band played "Dixie Is No Longer in the Bag." "My appearance in Columbia should not be politically interpreted," he told reporters. He revealed that having been tempted to make an actual endorsement of Nixon, he announced that he had decided against it. "I have come to the conclusion that my main responsibility is in the spiritual realm and that I shouldn't become involved in partisan politics."

This was not the first time he had said this, and it would not be the last.

When it was all over, Graham and Luce concluded both that they had been right not to run the original *LIFE* story—and that it could have been decisive. "The closeness of the election makes me feel that perhaps we made a mistake in not publishing my original article," Graham admitted. "Yet when I go to prayer there is great peace and this is all-important."

Luce wrote back about the dilemma they had shared. "In such a close election—so close in so many places—any number of things could have made the difference. Your intervention might have.

"I think I made a mistake just as an editor. That is, I should have sent your article into print without alerting Kennedy, simply because it was a fine article. But, inconsistent though this may seem, I think you made no mistake in the final decision."

Imagine what it meant for Nixon, to have had a man as admired as Graham testify so warmly to his character—and have no one see it. "Probably the best and most effective statement on my behalf in the entire campaign was the one which was not used—the article you wrote for *Life Magazine*," he wrote to Graham. But holding it was the right decision, he added, waxing righteous. "What is even more important than winning an election is for you to continue to maintain the respect and affection which enables you to be one of the most inspirational religious leaders in the nation's history. I would never want to do anything which would impair your effectiveness in that respect." While this was easy to say after the fact, it is worth noting that there would be occasions in the future when Nixon's men wanted to use Graham to some political advantage and he privately brushed them back.

It is also true, however, that within a year Nixon was taking public credit for saving Graham's ministry. Reprising the episode in *Six Crises*, he gave himself a starring role, despite Graham's recollection that he'd had nothing to do with it. Defending his handling of the religious issue, he said he had "even gone so far as to exercise a veto over a proposed endorsement that would certainly have given my candidacy a boost." Graham, his "close friend," endorsed him "unqualifiedly and enthusiastically," which pleased Nixon and his staff, who thought it could be a big help. But Nixon shut it down, he said, "because of my fear that, even though he was basing his support on other than religious grounds, our opponents would seize on his endorsement as evidence of religious bigotry, his own forthright denial notwithstanding."

THE FINALE

To the very end, in fact, both camps were torn about where to come out on religion. Both Kennedy's and Nixon's advisers urged them to make a major statement in the last days of the race. With polls showing a tight finish, sending the right message could be decisive. The question was figuring out what that message was, and which way it would make people decide.

Pollster Lou Harris warned Kennedy that a last-minute Republican television blitz and the belated appearance of Eisenhower on the trail were having an impact. He feared a surge of religious sentiment as the positive image of Kennedy from the debates was fading, and urged Kennedy to address religion again in a nationwide TV show. Within the Kennedy camp, the private line was that "yes, Nixon has said he's not going to raise the religious issue. In fact he has said that in every state he's been in."

Graham was saying much the same to Nixon. "There is no doubt in my mind that you would win the election hands down if it were not for the religious issue," he wrote on November 2. Though the *New York Times* had reported that billionaire Texas Republican H. L. Hunt was distributing hate literature, Graham cited suspicions that Democrats were secretly doing the same thing in heavily Catholic areas, as a means of incitement. He may not even have known about his own team's contribution: Grady Wilson claimed on a radio show that a midnight mass had been held where Catholics prayed that the military plane carrying Graham to Spain would crash.

Graham proposed a huge television push by Nixon, with a taped statement broadcast in the seven largest states all through the weekend and into election day. "In your closing television appearance Monday night," Graham told Nixon, "you [should] state that whoever is the next President of the United States, he will not have the ability to cope with the awesome problems facing the world, alone. He must have God's help. He is going to need the prayers of all the people."

For Graham, this advice was both tactical and heartfelt. He was still getting letters from "heartsick Christians" about how far short of Eisenhower's example Nixon had fallen. It was as though if he could just hear Nixon say the words, everything would turn out all right. "State frankly that you are a firm believer in God, that He directs the destiny of men, and that you put this election in His hands and that you are praying the prayer, 'Thy will be done,'" Graham urged. "Indicate also that you have little personal ambition in this matter but that you have represented a cause in which you sincerely believe. I think if you would give this personal witness it would have a tremendous effect."

This was, Graham said, a deep spiritual struggle. "There is an unseen battle waging that does not show up in the polls and statistics." And then he bore witness, shared his own prayers for Nixon and a challenge. "Dick, this is a time that you should cast yourself before the Lord and trust in Him. In Psalm 118:6 the Scripture says, 'The Lord is on my side; I will not fear: what can man do unto me?' I believe you are going through a time of testing and God may be searching your heart to see where you stand before Him. I am convinced that without this help you cannot win this election." And he quoted God's promise to Joshua: "Be strong and of a good courage; be not afraid, neither be thou dismayed: for the Lord thy God is with thee whithersoever thou goest."

Those were his last words before election day.

The rest, as they say, is history. Of his five presidential campaigns, "none affected me more personally than the campaign of 1960," Nixon wrote in his memoirs. "It was a campaign of unusual intensity."

One can lose count of how many things might have changed the result. Given the tide, if the campaign had lasted two more days, Nixon might have won. Luce wondered about having pulled the *LIFE* story. Peale had to read newspaper columns charging that he had cost Nixon the White House. Nixon wondered, what if he had spent the last Sunday in Illinois, instead of Alaska, keeping his promise to campaign in all fifty states?

And then there was all the talk of voter fraud and recounts, which was inevitable in a race decided by 113,000 votes out of more than 68 million. "You know, Dick," Len Hall told him a couple weeks after the vote, "a switch of only 14,000 votes and we would have been the heroes and they would have been the bums." Tricia Nixon gave her Christmas money that year to a recount committee checking the vote in Chicago.

When it was finally over, Nixon sent Graham a letter with the kind of praise that might have chilled his soul: "I have deeply appreciated the spiritual inspiration and guidance you have given me," Nixon said, "but, in addition to that, your political advice has been as wise as any I have received from any man I know. I have often told friends that when you went into the ministry, politics lost one of its potentially greatest practitioners."

If Graham had been able to see Nixon's original draft of the letter, he might have come to a different understanding of political intimacy. Nixon had added in a postscript that Pat joined him in "sending our very best wishes to Ruth and to you." And then, marked by hand in parentheses: "ck for sure that his wife's name is Ruth."

ELEVEN

The Fourteen-Carat-Gold Photograph

You remember when Kennedy's father had me come down there, after all the religious problems. It didn't occur to me at that time, but it did later, that I was being used. But I wanted to be used. I was happy to be used in that situation because it was a religious situation. Yes, he was trying to heal the situation at that time.

—Graham on his pivotal meeting with Kennedy

Before we are inundated in weightier matters this week, let it be noted that John Fitzgerald Kennedy launched his 1964 reelection campaign on a Palm Beach golf course Monday."

So began a dispatch from *TIME* correspondent Hugh Sidey to his editors in New York, in January 1961, a few days before Kennedy's inauguration as president. And he proceeded to describe the golf-course summit that followed between the president-elect and Billy Graham.

The post-election meeting was not Kennedy's idea; his father, Joe, made him do it, and Jack was said to have groaned at the thought. Senator George Smathers, a devoted Kennedy pal but friends with Nixon and Graham as well, played matchmaker. He was the one who called Graham a few days after the election to invite him down to Palm Beach for a friendly game, to get better acquainted with the president-elect.

Graham was not one to say no to such a summons. But this was different, given his closeness to Nixon, who was still reeling from the crushing closeness of the defeat. So he called for guidance, and talked to aide H. R. Haldeman. "Billy accepted with some hesitation," Haldeman told Nixon.

"He says he has no idea what Senator Kennedy wants, but he wanted you to know that this in no way detracted from his whole-hearted support for you."

Nixon understood very well how the game was played, and told Graham not to give it another thought. "He's the President-elect," Nixon said. "Every time he asks you, you have to go. I would go." In fact Nixon himself had met with Kennedy six days after the election. "So don't think anything of it."

And Smathers would be there to break the ice. When Sidey asked him if he was already thinking of 1964, Smathers smiled. "It doesn't hurt." Graham seemed not to analyze the motives; he just saw the opportunity. The invitation, he wrote to Luce, was "a possible providential opening" for him, "at which I may have some opportunity to express my thoughts and ideas to the president elect."

When he arrived at Joe Kennedy's Palm Beach estate, Jack was in an upstairs bedroom changing clothes. Graham remembered him leaning out a window and calling down. "Dr. Graham, my father wants to see you. He's out by the pool, would you go out to see him?"

Graham found the Kennedy patriarch waiting for him at poolside. "Do you know why you're here today?" Joe Kennedy asked.

"No sir, I'm surprised," Graham said. "And honored to be invited."

Joe proceeded to tell him a flattering story, of traveling in Germany with the president of Notre Dame and seeing signs for a Graham crusade. Curious, they went to see for themselves, tens of thousands of people crowded into a square to hear the evangelist preach. They were "astonished" at the scene. A few days later they had an audience with the pope and told him about it. "And the Pope said 'Yes, I wish we had a dozen people in my church doing the same thing.'"

So, Kennedy said, "When Jack got elected, I told him he must make you one of his friends."

Or if not friends, at least limited partners. Jack Kennedy drove Graham to Seminole Golf Club in a white Lincoln convertible, and off they went down the course. The evangelist double-bogeyed the first hole, and Kennedy teased him. "I always understood that you were a good golfer."

"Well, I am if I'm not playing with the president-elect of the United States."

As Graham recalled the day, on the way back to the club Kennedy waxed theological. Pulling up at a stoplight, he posed a question. "Billy," he said, "do you believe in the Second Coming of Jesus Christ?"

This was an odd question, since anyone who was at all familiar with Graham's ministry knew that it was a central theme in his preaching.

"I was shocked," Graham recalls. "I said, 'I sure do.'"

"Why doesn't my church teach it?"

"Well, it's in all their creeds," Graham replied.

"They don't tell us much about it," Kennedy said. "I'd like to know what you think."

Kennedy was famous for drilling into people's areas of expertise, in a way that taught him and flattered them. Graham walked him through the biblical lessons of Christ's life and death and promise to return.

"Very interesting," Kennedy replied. "We'll have to talk more about that someday." When he told the story in *McCall's* a few years later, Graham noted how "very quickly, I was impressed by the Kennedy charm. He also revealed his restless, probing intellect. He must have asked a hundred separate questions."

But even Graham had to know that the purpose of the visit was not spiritual or philosophical. The purpose was the picture. Kennedy asked Graham if he'd mind coming with him to talk to reporters waiting at a hotel. Assuming he would be there to listen rather than speak, Graham agreed. He didn't really have much choice, given that he had written that letter to Kennedy over the summer, in which he had promised to support him if he won.

Now came the test. There were hundreds of reporters waiting when Kennedy arrived. He recapped the golf match, and then seized his opportunity. "I've got the Reverend Billy Graham here with me, and I'm going to ask him to answer questions, anything you may have to ask him."

After the closest, hardest-fought campaign in American history, Graham mused later, Kennedy wanted to heal the rift. "I tried to be a healer that night."

Reporters jumped up; had religion been discussed? "It was mentioned," Billy said with a laugh. History is written of moments like these, and Graham himself did some preemptive editing. "I did not commit myself on the religious issue before the election," he insisted. "I made no statement whatsoever before the election on the matter of religion," which mainly meant that he had not said nearly as much as he might have.

But a little revision didn't bother Kennedy too much, because Graham proceeded to offer exactly the words of reconciliation that the Kennedy team was eager to hear him say. The election, Graham said, had produced a better understanding between Protestants and Catholics, and proved that "there was not as much religious prejudice in the United States as many people had feared." As for future elections, he predicted, ever wishful, that never again would religion prove so divisive. "I think that is a hurdle that has been permanently passed."

Kennedy could be confident that Graham would do what was needed; it was part of the sanctification ritual, the transfer of loyalty of the country's preeminent religious leader to its new political leader. "I think Kennedy recognized him as a powerful influence in the country, and a new president who has won by the narrowest possible margin is going to reach out to powerful influences and at least befriend or neutralize them," explained Ted Sorensen. "I don't think he regarded him as close or sympathetic ideologically or philosophically." But the deed was accomplished: by the time it was over, "JFK was calling him Billy and Billy seemed delighted," Sidey told his editors. "They shook hands, then JFK slid behind the wheel of the convertible, secret service man beside, and wheeled off to his father's place."

The next day the papers all carried pictures of the two tall, handsome men smiling together. Smathers got a call from a top Protestant leader, saying that the meeting and the picture were the best thing that could have happened to mend the breach and get the country moving forward. Eventually the captions from prayer breakfast photos would identify Graham and Kennedy as good friends—a less accurate description, perhaps, than that of Graham's relationship with any other president. But to Kennedy the pictures mattered. Writing in the Jesuit magazine *America*, Father Thurston Davis noted that a picture of the president with a cardinal "would cost Mr. Kennedy 10,000 votes in the Bible belt in 1964," whereas pictures of him with Billy Graham "are pure 14-carat gold, to be laid away at five percent interest till the day of reckoning."

From that point on Graham and Kennedy would have only limited contact, of a formal nature. Graham came to the White House occasionally, saw Kennedy at the prayer breakfasts, but was never invited to a state dinner or to stay overnight. That would have to wait until another old friend became a new president. "When your picture appears in the press two or three times a year with a president, especially if it's on the golf course, it looks as if you are old buddies," Graham said. "But I really did not get to know John Kennedy."

People close to him perceived a change in Kennedy after the Bay of Pigs and the Cuban Missile Crisis, that he became both deeper and more private about spiritual things. One quiet evening Sidey encountered him in the Oval Office, gazing out the window. He confessed at that moment that maybe God was more important in the scheme of things than he had admitted. But when Sidey pressed him, he declined to say any more.

He did find occasions to reach out to Graham. The evangelist came to the White House in December 1961 to talk about his upcoming Latin American tour: Kennedy himself was heading off on a ceremonial tour in a few weeks. "I'll be your John the Baptist," he volunteered. Graham noted that he was having trouble getting into Colombia. Kennedy intervened, and opened the way for the meetings to proceed, with crowds of twenty thousand in attendance.

There was one other occasion when Kennedy would enlist Graham as an ally. Nineteen sixty-three was the year when the fight for equality exploded, above all in the streets of Birmingham, Alabama. Martin Luther King, writing from the Birmingham jail, challenged all those who still believed that justice could come voluntarily and spontaneously. His letter was officially addressed to the eight white Birmingham pastors who had objected to an outsider disrupting their careful progress toward desegregation. But it might as well have been aimed at Attorney General Robert Kennedy, who called the action ill-timed, or the *Washington Post*, which viewed King's demonstrations as "of doubtful utility." Or at Graham himself, who told the *New York Times* that the Birmingham demonstration had complicated a situation in which real progress was being made. "What I would like to see now is a period of quietness in which moderation prevails," he said, offering some advice for King, "a good personal friend: Put the brakes on a little bit."

"Frankly," King wrote, "I have never yet engaged in a direct action movement that was 'well-timed' according to the timetable of those who have not suffered unduly from the disease of segregation." And then he threw down the gauntlet—to his fellow clergy, to the White House, to all the "white moderates" facing a moment of truth. "I have almost reached the regrettable conclusion that the Negro's great stumbling block in the stride toward freedom is not the White Citizens Counciler or the

Ku Klux Klanner, but the white moderate who is more devoted to 'order' than to justice . . . who constantly says 'I agree with you in the goal you seek, but I can't agree with your methods of direct action.'"

From the horrifying street scenes that followed, delivered into every home with blazing moral clarity by television, suddenly the country's portable conscience, there came thuds of recognition. For the White House, there was a realization that "if King loses, worse leaders are going to take his place." The president introduced a comprehensive civil rights bill that would outlaw all forms of discrimination in public accommodations. For Graham it was reason to raise his voice louder. "It is an insult to human dignity to turn a man away from a public restaurant because of the color of his skin," he said.

After the bombing in September of the 16th Street Baptist Church in Birmingham in which four black children were killed, columnist Drew Pearson organized the America's Conscience Fund to rebuild it, with Graham as one of four honorary chairmen. Kennedy, meanwhile, meeting with clergy, was urged to recruit Graham to hold an integrated crusade in the city. Graham, declared John Connally, now the governor of Texas, was "more than a preacher, more than an evangelist, more than a Christian leader. In a greater sense, he has become our conscience." It would not be the last time a president would be urged to send him to smooth the southern waters.

Three weeks later, Kennedy was dead; but Graham's Birmingham crusade proceeded. On Easter Sunday 1964, despite calls for its cancellation, warnings of violence, and threats from segregationist extremists, he preached to an integrated crowd of thirty-five thousand in Birmingham's main stadium. Authorities called it the largest fully integrated meeting in Alabama history.

For all the warnings, all the fears of a Vatican takeover of the Oval Office, the only time a Catholic mass was celebrated in the White House was on November 23, 1963.

TWELVE

Tragedy and Transition

It seems like I've always known Lyndon Johnson. He was a very complex man. But I loved him very much.

—Graham on LBJ

Lyndon Johnson insisted that Jackie Kennedy be present when he took the oath of office aboard Air Force One on November 22, 1963, ninety-eight minutes after her husband was declared dead. Continuity mattered now, and legitimacy. When everyone was gathered in the steamy, gold-carpeted presidential cabin, she had still not arrived. "We'll wait for her," Johnson said. "I want her here." He urged Lady Bird to takes notes on everything that happened, found a Dictaphone to record the ceremony, and made sure a photographer got it too. When Jackie came, she stood by him and his wife as he raised his hand; when he had finished, he turned and hugged them both, then gave his first order as commander in chief. "OK. Let's get this plane back to Washington."

On the flight, he imagined what it would be like if something suddenly happened to the pilot, and someone else had to bring the plane in, "with no plans showing how long the runways were, with no maps, no notes."

He was not alone. Churches filled with people who came to pray for Kennedy's life, and then when the news arrived, for his soul. The bells began to toll, and the country essentially stopped. Stores closed, courts shut down in the middle of hearings, theaters snuffed the marquee lights, doctors passed out sedatives, every football game, every party, was canceled; so many people reached for the phone that the system blacked out, and operators had to refuse calls.

The death of President Kennedy added, among other things, another curious legend to Graham's ministry. It was not exactly that he had seen this coming; but he did speak of a strange premonition two weeks before, when he was preaching in Houston. Governor Connally had come to see him at his hotel, and talked about his concern about Kennedy's impending trip: the mood in Texas was increasingly hostile toward the president. That conversation had stuck with Graham, to the point that he tried to reach Kennedy through their friend George Smathers and urge him not to go. But he and Kennedy never connected, so the message never got through.

"This is the most tragic day in American history since Lincoln was shot," Billy Graham declared back home in North Carolina. "All of us should be in constant prayer for Mr. Johnson as he assumes these awesome responsibilities." And he searched for some larger meaning, a chance to witness. "Perhaps the American people will be awakened by this tragedy to their spiritual needs, and we might see a spiritual revival as a result of what has happened."

Then he sent off a telegram to Johnson, praying that God would watch over him. "Your message met the need," Johnson wrote back. "The knowledge that one of God's greatest messengers was seeking Divine Counsel on my behalf provided me with a strong source of strength, courage and comfort. . . . I shall cherish this in the days ahead."

Cherish it indeed, since for Johnson this was a personal as well as a national crisis. He had loathed being the vice president, whose primary function was to remind the president of his mortality. "Every time I came into John Kennedy's presence," he told Doris Kearns Goodwin, his aide and later biographer, "I felt like a goddamn raven hovering over his shoulder." Having risen from hill-country poverty to master of the Senate, he had slid to such oblivion as vice president that *Candid Camera* had trouble finding people on the streets who recognized his name. Kennedy, though respectful of Johnson himself, always got a laugh when he'd relax with friends in the Oval Office, smile innocently, and muse, "Say, whatever happened to Lyndon Johnson?"

But now Kennedy was gone, and Johnson found himself presiding over a trauma ward. "I always felt sorry for Harry Truman and the way he got the presidency," Johnson told an aide two days into office, "but at least his man wasn't murdered." Kennedy was instantly untouchable, an impossible act to follow. Johnson had never shared that sense of mythic destiny that propelled some men into high office; now he was certain that people saw him as a usurper; two-thirds told pollsters that they wondered how the country could go on without Kennedy. "Let's see what your cracker president is going to do for you now," a bartender in Harlem told his customers when they got the news. "And then there were the bigots and the dividers and the Eastern intellectuals, who were waiting to knock me down before I could even begin to stand up," Johnson said. "The whole thing was almost unbearable."

So he reached out in every direction to reintroduce himself in those first days, bringing to the White House business tycoons and labor leaders, civil rights champions, editors and publishers, mayors and governors, close to a hundred groups visiting just in his second week in office. Graham was sitting in the chaplain's study at the Naval Academy in Annapolis, about to speak in the chapel, when the call came in.

"Billy, this is Lyndon. If I'd known about it in time, I would have been up to Annapolis to hear you preach," the president said. "I'd like for you to come over to the White House and see me tomorrow."

Which is how it came about that on December 16 Graham arrived for what he expected would be a fifteen-minute audience, which stretched to several hours. After a visit in the Oval Office, Johnson proposed a swim in the White House pool. That no one had brought a bathing suit was no deterrent; in years to come the president would often interrupt meetings to suggest a swim and needle anyone who was reluctant to strip naked and dive in a baptism in intimacy. Graham and Johnson splashed in the pool before retiring to a dinner for some newspaper publishers, at which Graham offered the prayer.

"I felt that you gave me an inside look at some of the awesome responsibilities of the presidency," Graham wrote to Johnson afterward, and offered the kind of biblical encouragement that Johnson loved. He recalled Moses' words to Joshua as he turned Israel over to him: "As thy days, so shall thy strength be. . . . Underneath are the everlasting arms." Millions of people were praying for the new president, Graham said, and so would he, preemptively elevating Johnson into the ranks of America's greatest leaders. "As God was with Washington at Valley Forge and with Lincoln in the darkest hours of the Civil War, so God will be with you. There will be times when decisions come hard and burdens too heavy to bear—that is when God will be nearest to you."

With the private benediction came a public blessing for a president all too aware of the pictures of Kennedy still hanging on the wall of every West Wing office. Listeners could draw their own contrasts when Graham called Johnson the "best qualified man we've ever had in the White House," one who would "provide moral leadership for the country. The President is a very religious person," he said, adding, with some exaggeration, that "he has attended many of our crusades and he comes from a religious family. I think he will set a tremendous example for the people of this country."

Johnson wrote back to Graham, grateful and urgent. "Pray for me, too," he pleaded. "I cannot fulfill this trust unless God grant me the wisdom to see what is right and the courage to do it." Handwritten at the bottom was: "Do come see me when you are in D.C."

This Graham proceeded to do, that year and every year Johnson was in the White House. It was as though his semi-exile from Camelot had renewed him; there was no way he could have gone from advising Nixon all through 1960 to being virtually installed as Johnson's White House chaplain. But time had passed, and Graham's own distance from Kennedy helped relieve Johnson's deep insecurity that he didn't measure up. Graham seemed to absorb Johnson's resentment of the Kennedy mythmaking machinery, never missing a chance to mention to reporters that the first time he ever heard about Vietnam was from Kennedy during that preinaugural golf game in 1961, that Johnson had inherited what Graham would come to call the Vietnam "mess," or that Johnson had succeeded in pushing through Congress historic legislation that Kennedy had not been able to manage. The regular folks were back in power now, the non-northern, non-Harvard types of the Old Frontier, who were Graham's and Johnson's natural constituency.

"Graham was using Johnson as much as Johnson was using Graham," argued Ted Sorensen, who left the Johnson White House after several months to return to law and write his Kennedy biography. "Graham wanted to be Mr. Religion in this country and show how important and powerful he was," Sorensen said. "That was part of the charisma that brought thousands of people and millions of dollars to his cause." But the relationship was more complicated than that. As the years passed and Johnson's presidency unraveled and his approval ratings sank from a high of 80 percent to 38 percent, Graham would face challenges to his loyalty—since his mission depended on his popularity as well. If Johnson would be battered to the point of surrender, Graham too felt what it was like to come under fire, not just from the fundamentalists who disapproved of his consorting with ecumenical types or elites who still thought he was a hillbilly; now it came from people of faith who shared a passion for social justice and wondered why he wasn't doing more about it.

Graham and Johnson were great believers in order, conservative in means if not in ends. "I want to be president of *all* the people," Johnson often said, the man who could forge a great consensus. But this was to be a decade of discord, civil rights leaders against segregationists, feminists against patriarchs, poverty warriors against capitalists, environmentalists against corporate polluters. Those who had paddled happily in the mainstream in Eisenhower's America would find themselves swept aside as the headlines were taken over by radicalized children and activist clergy and academic china breakers and Black Power leaders and all manner of revolutionaries who made them feel unheeded, quaint. The old-fashioned believers were Billy Graham's congregation, and would later be baptized as Nixon's Silent Majority, but it was during Johnson's presidency that their whole world changed.

Commentators who had predicted that Graham's celebrity would fade after 1960 were proven wildly wrong; both at home and abroad his appeal only grew, as he built a more global evangelical movement that spoke even more powerfully to disquieted people. He had his own pavilion at the 1964 World's Fair. "Debbie Reynolds and Billy Graham Talk Frankly about Love and Faith" was the headline in *Redbook*. His books sold millions, his film and television ministries flourished, and he took revival to even more distant and once hostile lands. When reporters wanted to know the mood of the heartland, take soundings about any of the rising social issues of the day, from school prayer to free love, it was Graham whose views they sought out. By decade's end his Minneapolis headquarters occupied 160,000 square feet of office space, and he was sending out eighty million pieces of mail a year, inspiring professionals from both the Republican and Democratic national committees to come see the operation in action.

Johnson and every president who followed watched all this, since now they would have to choose their chaplains carefully. Once liberal Protestantism embraced a clear social agenda, Graham's broad message offered presidents some protection: his agenda was eternal, not temporal, his focus on saving souls more than reforming society. He was, the historian Martin Marty suggested, "a man in transit between epochs and value systems." But he also faced his own challenge. When a man hates injustice but loves order, what does he do if the prevailing order is itself unjust? And if being valuable to his friend the president impeded being a visionary, would that be a price he was willing to pay?

THE BEST FRIEND

O f all the things to which Kennedy was born and which Johnson lacked—wealth, background, elegance," observed the author
Theodore White, "Johnson probably envied Kennedy most his capacity
for arousing love and friendship."

It was Kennedy who described Johnson as "a very insecure, sensitive
man with a huge ego." More than anything else, Billy Graham gave
Lyndon Johnson what he most craved: love without strings. The preacher's
political value to Johnson was never as great as the personal. No president
who had accomplished so much was hated so much, including by those he
felt he'd done the most to help. "Not many people in this country love me,"
Johnson told Walter Cronkite after he left office, "but that preacher there
loves me." The president described Graham's visits as being like "a new
injection" during the hard times. "When I was being called a crook and a
thug and all," Johnson said, he'd invite Graham over, "and we bragged on
each other. I told him he was the greatest religious leader in the world and
he said I was the greatest political leader."

"People in power, who are larger than life, appreciate other larger-than-
life people," observed Doris Kearns Goodwin. "Johnson could see that
Billy Graham was fantastic on TV, was a great speaker; he was doing in
his realm what Johnson hoped to do in his own. If they had both been in
the same field it could produce tension; but since Graham's was a different
field, Johnson just viewed him with fascination and respect, felt an instant
attraction to his energy and success."

Graham was also not one to disturb his peace. He'd go into the First
Bedroom late at night and see the great stack of papers that the president was determined to get through before he slept. "He'd lie in bed and
read the newspapers and watch his three television sets," Graham said.
"Every time I'd ask him to have prayer, he'd get out of bed and get down
on his knees in his pajamas."

Graham read the Bible with him, talked about scripture. When Johnson
got a massage, he'd offer Graham one as well, let him watch the therapist
try to squeeze the strain out of him. Sometimes, Johnson said, Graham
"got up at 3 in the morning and got down on his knees and prayed for
me. At 6 he'd have coffee with me, and we'd talk over the problems fac-

ing the country." When Graham was there, Johnson's daughter Luci said, the whole mood in the residence changed. "The decibels of anxiety in the household seemed to always be defused when Dr. Graham was around," she said. Lady Bird saw most clearly the effect Graham's presence had on her husband. "Lyndon had a very strong sense of need," she said, "to be sure he was on the right path . . . a need for an anchor. Billy was a comfort—and if there is ever a position in the world where you feel you need all the help you can get it's the presidency."

It was in the Johnson White House that Graham first ministered to the entire First Family. Unlike the Eisenhowers, the Johnsons were rough contemporaries of the Grahams, and Ruth and Lady Bird had much in common. Their men were seldom home; they had to shield their children from the radioactive fallout of the power and fame that defined their fathers. Johnson once proudly told Graham how he had raised his daughters to "do a little thinking of their own, be a little independent, get their own ideas, select their own schools, pay their own income taxes, do their own voting." But the girls really didn't have any choice but to raise themselves. As Senate leader, their father was rarely home before they were asleep; their mother, putting his career ahead of everything, spent her days tending to his visiting constituents, giving them tours of attractions like Mount Vernon (she stopped counting after the two hundredth), and her nights at his social events. As for Sundays, "Daddy was the kind of man who believed it was more important to invite [Johnson's mentor, Senator] Richard Russell . . . over for Sunday breakfast," daughter Lynda later said, "than to spend time alone with his family."

Political families are seldom normal households, with milk and cookies after school, and parents attending the piano recital. Instead, family vacations are campaign swings. Privacy is impossible. "People in public life, presidents, First Ladies, have to make a lot of difficult choices," Lucy observed. There's a reason that even First Families of very different political persuasions rarely criticize each other. "It's not necessarily because we're so classy and nice," she said. "It's because we all empathize with each other, with the vulnerability and exposure and the demands on family life. Who needs that kind of life?" The First Families could see that the Grahams shared similar burdens, as his travels expanded and his fame grew. "Once you've lost your privacy," Graham said later, "you realize you've lost an extremely valuable thing." And it applies to everyone. "It's hard on the children, I'm sure, because they're looked at and watched everywhere. They're expected to be saints—yet I think I can say my children have overcome this."

"I think a lot of us felt his own sense of vulnerability," Luci said of Graham, so it was natural that she turned to him when she set off down her own spiritual road as a teenager, on her way to a conversion to Catholicism. From Graham, she said, "I felt a strong expression of, 'you're not leaving us, you're celebrating the need to have your faith alive and relevant and personal and meaningful and I'm here to pat you on the back and wish you godspeed.' That's what made him so universal. It's that personal experience he believes in. He doesn't care if your path comes from the left or the right or whatever. His focus was 'Get on the Path!' There were a lot of folks who were judgmental," she said, but Graham was never one of them.

As time passed, some of Johnson's closest aides would leave him, burned out by the demands he made or discouraged by the roads he chose. But Johnson made it easy for Graham to stay: he behaved differently around him, tamed the ego, curbed the appetites, told the truth, even when it was about what scared him. Graham saw the volcanic mood swings: "He could roar like a lion on one side," Graham said, "and talk as gently as if he was talking to a little child." But clergymen always held a place of honor; Johnson had grown up relishing "long, tall preaching," and kept on the wall of the Oval Office a yellowed letter from Sam Houston to his great-grandfather, who had brought the Texas hero to Jesus. And Graham was his favorite of all: White House aides marveled at the calming and civilizing effect Graham had. When Johnson swore, he'd turn and say, "Forgive me, Preacher." He was more likely to chug buttermilk than Cutty Sark around Graham, treated Lady Bird more gallantly, pursued his Virtue Agenda to help the least among us with a mix of evangelical fervor and political cunning. "I knew he was not a saint," Graham said. "Did he intimidate me? Maybe just the opposite: I think I intimidated him a little." Graham knew Johnson liked having an "old-fashioned Baptist preacher around for personal as well as political reasons, but I did not avoid taking issue with him or probing his soul whenever I thought it necessary."

Johnson didn't need to intimidate Graham, of course, didn't need to reach into his toolbag for some blunt instrument to break his will, because he and Graham were not in a power struggle, not doing a deal. Of all the people a president encountered, said adviser Jack Valenti, "Graham was unique in American political life. He asked nothing. He wanted nothing. . . . No hidden agenda. Every president understood that and so they luxuriated in his embrace. You can't put a price on it."

Not that Johnson didn't try. Graham became a recipient of his gargantuan gift-giving, by which he baptized people into his debt: it was a way, he told Goodwin, of "engraving my spirit on the minds and hearts of my people." Graham received an album of photos, some Senokot laxative, an electric razor, an electric toothbrush. (Goodwin herself had accumulated an even dozen toothbrushes from Johnson by the time he died. White House aides used to call him the Great Wampum man, she said.) Johnson even sent two wooden rocking chairs from the ranch, which held a place of honor on the Grahams' Montreat porch. And Graham responded in kind, sending a personalized Bible, Wedgwood cuff links at Christmas, and, most extravagantly, after Johnson admired a pair of Graham's yellow pigskin golf shoes, three pairs in different colors. "If you wear them," Graham joked, "some reporters are likely to term you the 'Psychedelic President.'"

When Johnson knew Graham was coming to town he often told him to cancel his hotel reservations, come stay at the White House, or spend the weekend at Camp David. "I was present any number of times he'd come to the second-floor quarters on a Sunday and pray," Valenti recalled. Johnson would send a plane to bring Graham down to his ranch in Texas, where he installed the evangelist in a bedroom close enough to hear the snoring, then took him to count his chickens, collect eggs, eat cornbread, inspect the Herefords, the Angora goats, the antelopes. They took wild boat rides, or went ricocheting around the ranch in the Lincoln convertible, Johnson spurting scripture and Graham correcting him. Following one such visit, Johnson became the first sitting president to attend a Graham crusade, when he appeared at the final service of Graham's ten-day Houston revival in November 1965.

"I think you have to be in that Pedernales River Valley to understand President Johnson," Graham observed. "I understand a little bit of the background of where he came from . . . and what made him tick. The things people thought of as crude were not crude to me, because I had been there." Out in the hill country, described by historian Walter Prescott Webb as a place of "nauseating loneliness," where people lived "far from markets, burned by drought, beaten by hail, withered by hot winds, frozen by blizzards, eaten out by grasshoppers, exploited by capitalists and cozened by politicians," Johnson had learned what it meant to be poor. Here lay the roots of longing and legend: asked once by a foreign leader whether it was true he'd been born in a log cabin, Johnson insisted, "No no no, you're confusing me with Abe Lincoln. I was born in a manger."

His father, Sam Ealy Johnson, a five-term state legislator and cattle speculator, had little use for things spiritual; he passed along his toughness and pride and political passion. His formidably refined mother, Rebekah Baines, miserable in her marriage until her son came along to save her, taught him to quote Longfellow and Tennyson by age three, told him stories of his famous forebears, like her father, Joseph Wilson Baines, a lawyer and educator and lay Baptist preacher. She spun a vision of noble service and gentility, her expectations for her son so high that he worried to Graham, even as he reached the White House at last, about whether he could live up to them. When Johnson left office, one of his aides wrote to Graham that "he was greatly affected by your care of him. You were one of those few people who caused him not to forget certain things he had learned in his mother's lap, certain things he would occasionally call 'the unforgettables.'"

"My father was a man of enormous personal faith," Luci Johnson said. "He went off and broke his mother's heart when he was eleven—she was a Southern Baptist, he made the decision to join this Christian Church [Disciples of Christ] without full family consultation." But in a way characteristic of presidents, who have no need for extra politics in their spiritual lives, he never really cared about denominations. "My father would go to a nine o'clock Christian Church service, then turn around and go to eleven o'clock church with my mom, then try to go to mass with me at one. I would say to him, 'Daddy, go watch *Meet the Press* or whatever you need to do. You've been to church twice, you don't need to do this for me.' He said, 'You don't understand, Lucy. I'm not doing this for you. When you're in this position you need all the help you can get.'"

And that appetite, that ecumenical inclination, she suggested, was something that drew Johnson to Graham. "Though Reverend Graham is a Baptist, he has that nondenominational feel about it. He's everybody's universal man of faith. He's not about tearing people up; he's about the possibilities, not the impossibilities. That's why Lyndon Johnson loved him so much. That's what Daddy was. He belonged to his church, but he was a universal man of faith."

Yet Johnson's spiritual wanderings were costly and constant. "My faith?" he was asked one evening, standing outside under the immense White House elm trees, looking at the Washington Monument. "It's just as solid as this," he said, stamping on the concrete drive. But it was never that easy; he had, adviser Bill Moyers once said, "an exquisite hole at his center . . . an unfillable void." Terrified of assassination, he feared not just death but disability, had nightmares of being paralyzed, being dependent on others or mistaken for dead himself. Once he was scheduled to speak to an education convention in Atlantic City, and it was a fearsome day, with fog so dense that all commercial flights were canceled. He asked Graham, in town for the National Prayer Breakfast the next day, if he'd come along. During the flight, Graham said, they all prayed—and prayed hard. "He introduced me to that crowd of teachers," Graham said, "and he said the reason he had me along was the bad weather."

In fact, Johnson wanted a minister with him all the time. "He was always a little bit scared of death," Graham said, and wanted to be sure there was a preacher with him when he died. The fear, Graham suspected, arose from Johnson's doubts about whether he had ever really been saved. He had been to revival meetings as a boy, knew what conversion was supposed to look like. But still he wasn't sure, not with a lifetime's political and moral debris accumulated around him. "I think that he had a conflict within him about religion," Graham said. "He wanted to go all the way in his commitment to Christ. He knew what it meant to be saved or lost, using our terminology, and he knew what it was to be born again. And yet he somehow felt that he had never quite had that experience."

Graham recalled an evening at the ranch together, driving in the convertible, when they pulled over and sat watching the sun go down. The Secret Service pulled over behind them in another car to wait.

Johnson was very serious, very raw. "You know Billy," he said, "I know that I've received Christ." But there was still that fear that Graham heard so often. "I'm not sure in my heart that I'm really going to heaven." So Graham said he talked to Johnson very plainly. Had he ever really personally declared Christ as his savior?

"Well, Billy, I think I have. I did as a boy at a revival meeting. I guess I've done it several times."

Graham had heard that kind of thing before. "When someone says that, Mr. President, I don't feel too sure of it. It's a once-for-all transaction. You receive Christ and He saves you."

Johnson didn't say much. And Graham pushed. "I said, 'Why don't you just make this a definite moment that you can remember, that you've received Christ.'" Johnson bowed his head over the steering wheel, and they prayed together. "And he did, and I thought that was true," Graham recalled, "though only the Holy Spirit knows about that."

Maybe the most remarkable thing about the relationship was the extent to which it was largely private and pastoral. If Nixon and his successors were often looking for new ways to graft Graham's moral authority onto themselves, Johnson seldom did. This is not because Graham didn't offer his affirmations, or because Johnson was not the type to use people. It's more that he didn't know *how* to use Graham because he never fully grasped the priestly nature of the presidency; he knew political machinery better than anyone but not political mystery and majesty.

He had at best a rudimentary sense of how Graham could help ennoble him. "They were certainly not ashamed to pray with each other," said adviser Marvin Watson, "to seek God's guidance in the affairs of state." And if it became public that Johnson was talking and praying for the country with Graham, so much the better. If he was to convert to his vision of civil rights and social justice the good solid people who viewed government with a certain squinty skepticism, noted his gifted, gentle counsel Harry McPherson, "you want very much to have respected leaders like Graham to say that 'what this man's trying to do is good for all of us—and I've just been out praying with him.'"

Johnson told a *TIME* correspondent during that first spring that it was all about reaching out to everyone, "from the biggest corporation president down to the poorest sharecropper. They have a babylike faith in me . . . I want to be worthy of that faith." For that he didn't need just any minister: he wanted someone who cared about poor people but didn't scare rich ones. "Neither one of them ever saw a difference between a millionaire or a beggar in the personal value of the individual," argued Watson. "Look at the hotels Dr. Graham stayed in, compared with what he could have. Look at the price of his clothing versus what was offered to him. Look at the salary he took, compared to what was offered. You begin to see that the things of the world were not the things that influenced Dr. Graham. And it was not those things that influenced President Johnson."

Indeed, it was not very long before official Washington was taking note. "One of the most intriguing relationships to evolve from the volatile world of Great Society politics is the friendship between Democratic evangelist Lyndon Baines Johnson and Baptist Evangelist Billy Graham," wrote the columnist Marianne Means. "It is understandable that they should get along well. For there is a great deal of the preacher in Lyndon Johnson and a great deal of the politician in Billy Graham."

Johnson had a gift for honing in on people's weaknesses; he sensed Graham's delight in being at the center of things, even if Graham explained this as wanting to ensure that the men who were closest to power were themselves brought closer to God. The president gossiped about world leaders whom they both knew, pulled back the curtain on decisions he was wrestling with. Graham recalled how once around budget time, Johnson went into a cabinet meeting. "Billy, I don't know how long I'll be in there," Johnson said. "You take these pencils and see if you can trim a few billion off this budget while I'm gone." Graham actually leafed through the thick notebook and, far from trimming, added to some items. When Johnson returned and saw what he had done, he declared that "you'd have made a good congressman!"

Johnson loved to tell people how he handled complaints from irate Southern Baptists who disapproved of plans for poverty programs that would also help parochial schools. One day a call came in, and Moyers got on the line.

"What in the world has happened?" said the caller, a prominent Baptist leader. "Has the pope taken the president over?"

"No one's taken him over," Moyers replied. "The president's out swimming."

"What's the president doing swimming in the middle of the day, with all the work he has to do?"

"Well," Moyers said, "he's out there swimming with Dr. Graham."

Johnson, in the retelling, would savor the moment of revelation. "Is that . . . our Billy?" the suddenly tamed critic wanted to know.

Of course when Johnson spoke to a group of Southern Baptists, he warmed them up by saying, "I wish you could have seen Billy Graham and Bill Moyers in that pool together the other day. Everyone else was already a Christian, so they just took turns baptizing each other." There was even a time when he could surprise the guests in the pool at Camp David by turning to Graham and announcing, "Billy, you know *you're* the man to become president of the United States. You're the only one who could bring 'em all together. If you ever decide to run, I'll be your manager."

It was a fun joke, but it had an edge to anyone who watched the first test of loyalty between the two men, when Johnson was running to be elected in his own right in 1964 and finally lay the ghosts of the Kennedys to rest.

THIRTEEN

The Battle for Billy

My wife called me and said, "If you run, I don't think the country will elect a divorced president."

—Graham on rumors he might run in 1964

The notion that it was time for Billy Graham to run for president and save the country did not arise only as a response to that gunshot in November. As far back as July 1963, Gallup was conducting national polls pitting Graham as the GOP candidate against Kennedy in 1964. (Kennedy prevailed, 61 percent to 24 percent; when asked why, 17 percent said because Graham didn't have the experience, while 19 percent said he belonged to religion and should remain there.) But the world would change after November, especially for Republicans who viewed an extended Johnson presidency with a degree of alarm matched only by their own level of fratricidal discord.

From the ashes of Nixon's 1960 defeat rose Barry Goldwater, shredding with his force of conviction the Republican reflex of caution and compromise: he offered "A Choice Not an Echo." He would make Social Security voluntary, kill farm subsidies altogether, strip labor of its power, hand control of nuclear weapons over to the commanders in the field: "let's lob one into the men's room of the Kremlin," he said. So fervid were his supporters, not among the eastern internationalist solons of the party but its western, alienated grassroots activists, that when the Draft Goldwater Committee called for a rally at the Armory in Washington, buses rolled in from as far away as Chicago and Texas. The only gatherings there that had ever been bigger were the inaugurations of Eisenhower and Kennedy, and Billy Graham's crusades.

In a sense it was not so outlandish, as moderate and conservative Republicans set to tearing one another apart through the 1964 primary season, that Graham was back in play. During his Los Angeles crusade the previous fall, a high-level Republican strategy session was said to have discussed the merits of a Graham candidacy—not least that his crusade infrastructure and mailing lists would provide an excellent grassroots foundation for any White House bid—and made their case to him directly. Graham said he got telegrams from Republicans saying they would pledge their delegates to him if he ran. By that winter it had been rumored for months that he had caught the eye of the wildly rich Texas oilman H. L. Hunt, an aging billionaire curmudgeon in a clip-on bow tie. Though a longtime backer of Johnson's, Hunt allegedly told Grady Wilson that he would deposit as much as $6 million into Graham's personal bank account if he would agree to have his name floated for the GOP nomination.

Friends said it took about fifteen seconds for Graham to reject the idea flat out. There were various versions, different amounts of money on the table, different terms discussed. "As far as I can tell," said Marvin Watson, who heard the rumors as the head of the Democratic Party in Texas before Johnson brought him to the White House, "'64 was Hunt's most active year of trying to find people to run for office."

What is beyond dispute is that somehow the story leaked, suggesting that Graham had not just dismissed the idea. The morning headlines read, "Billy Graham Weighs Idea of Running for President," quoting a "source close to Graham." "He is giving earnest and prayerful consideration to the idea," said a story in the *Houston Press*, "and has spent many sleepless hours weighing it."

It was all juicy enough to make the *CBS Evening News* with Walter Cronkite, and inspired a snort from the Graham watchers at the *Christian Century*. "Why should he publicly disavow so improbable a possibility. . . . That he should feel it necessary after such reflection publicly to take himself out of the race few even dreamed he might enter indicates just how far out of touch with political reality a man who stands in front of crowds can get." The *Century* editors maybe didn't know that Gallup had been polling this "improbable" possibility for months.

But their hostility was nothing compared to Ruth's. She called and informed her husband, "If you run, I don't think the country will elect a divorced president." His father-in-law was next. "He said, 'You hold a [press] conference right now, right this minute and tell them.' I said, 'It's midnight here! I can't do it.' But I did the next morning." "If nominated I will not run," Graham declared. "If elected I will not serve. God called me to preach." He did not, however, mention as one of his reasons the fact that he had so much confidence in the leadership of his friend in the White House.

That was not the end of Graham's 1964 political career. Once Goldwater had locked down the nomination, there remained the question of his running mate. Tradition argued for some kind of healing figure, given that Goldwater and the moderates had divided up the primaries among them. He could use a southerner who would extend Eisenhower's effort to break the Democrats' hold on the South; someone with a moderate enough record on civil rights to offset Goldwater's vote against the landmark Civil Rights Act that June, but someone who also lived in Goldwater's black-and-white moral universe.

In that light there was a certain logic to the idea of a Goldwater-Graham alliance. Though they weren't close, the previous fall, as Graham was wrapping up a huge Southern California crusade and Goldwater was in town speaking to the biggest Republican rally in eighteen years, the two had met at the Biltmore for a breakfast of eggs, hominy grits, and orange juice.

It was not until much later that Johnson himself was briefed on an effort by Goldwater forces to recruit Graham for the ticket. A Texas lawyer named Earle Mayfield wrote a memo to Johnson filling in the details: just before the Republicans gathered, "several key Goldwater operators," Mayfield wrote, had flown to Montreat to see if Graham was interested. Mayfield contended that, "The matter was discussed for several hours. In declining the invitation, Graham is reputed to have said, in effect:

a) There had not been enough time allocated for the transition from minister to politician and no public buildup for it.

b) There should be a "grass-roots-draft" over a sufficient period of time to bridge the above-mentioned transition.

c) That the invitation had the appearance of being "the 'last chance' sort of thing, namely, that it was being offered to him after many other [*sic*] had declined it."

Graham said many years later that he did not remember the meeting, and the official Montreat calendar has no record of it ever taking place. And Goldwater went on to reject any whiff of conciliation; he named New York congressman William E. Miller, a northeastern Catholic, top debater, and archconservative, who gave the ticket some geographical if not ideological balance. Johnson, however, was not taking any chances that summer. He invited Billy and Ruth up to Washington for an evening of dancing under Japanese lanterns on the rooftop adjoining the East Wing, after a state dinner for the president of Costa Rica.

Johnson had his own vice presidential decisions to make. Letters poured into the White House urging that he consider Graham—though the popular favorite, by a four-to-one margin over the nearest competitor, was Bobby Kennedy, who saw himself as the true custodian of Camelot. The two men loathed each other: Kennedy considered Johnson "mean, bitter, vicious—an animal in many ways." Of Bobby, Johnson said "he skipped the grades where you learn the rules of life. He never liked me, and that's nothing compared to what I think of him." There was speculation that Jackie Kennedy might come to the Democrats' convention in Atlantic City and plead her brother-in-law's cause. Johnson was "scared to death Bobby Kennedy would maybe come out with Jackie and just take the thing by storm," Graham said. "I think I finally managed to set his mind at ease a little about that."

After Johnson preemptively ruled out any member of his cabinet, he was free to find his own man. His one concern about Hubert Humphrey, apart from thinking he talked too much, was whether he was too radioactive for white southern voters after his heroic leadership of the Senate fight for the Civil Rights Bill that summer. There are few things more flattering than to be consulted, even artificially, on a question as strategically sexy but cosmically insignificant as Who Should Be Vice President, and Johnson consulted far and wide.

Ruth and Billy Graham spent the night at the White House on the eve of the convention; Johnson thought he'd run a little focus group. They were sitting at the table, Graham recalled, and Johnson "was on the phone, back and forth. And he said, 'I've got the names of a number of people I'd like to throw at you and see what you think of them, I've got to make a choice for vice president today or tomorrow.'"

Johnson started reading off the names, more than a dozen of them, but as Graham was about to respond, Ruth kicked him hard under the table. Johnson saw it too.

"You shouldn't answer questions like that," said Ruth, ever valiant in swatting away temptations. "Your job is to give spiritual and moral advice to the president, not political." But when Lady Bird and Ruth got up from the table and went into the living room, Graham recalled, Johnson got up, quietly closed the door, then turned to him and said, "Now, tell me, what do you really think?"

Graham offered the name he knew the best, guessing who Johnson had already picked, he later said, more than advising. He liked to tell the story of how he had met Humphrey when they were both swimming nude at the YMCA in Minneapolis when he was running for mayor, back when Graham was conducting his first Youth for Christ rallies back in 1945.

"I don't know whether that had anything to do with his selection or not," Graham said. "But I always liked Hubert Humphrey." A couple days later when Johnson finally gave Humphrey the good news, he noted, "If you didn't know you were vice-president thirty days ago, maybe you're too stupid to be vice-president."

In addition to private advice, Johnson got the pictures he wanted: that Sunday before the convention assembled, Graham was the guest preacher at Johnson's church, and gave thanks for the "warm friendship" he enjoyed with the president. After church the Johnsons and Grahams took a well-photographed stroll around the White House grounds, beagles in tow.

By the time the race began in earnest, Johnson had the adversary he dreamed of and the campaign he wanted: he got to run as a consensus builder against an extremist, travel the country shaking hands until they bled, soaking in a kind of affirmation he had never inspired in his years as a Senate power broker or Kennedy understudy. In the middle of September, Gallup put him on top by 69 percent to 31 percent.

But as for Graham, some White House advisers warned Johnson that the evangelist's instinctive conservatism might yet inspire him to fall in with Goldwater. Graham told reporters at one fall press conference that his association with Johnson didn't mean anything political, and noted that he'd always been friends with people from both parties. *New York Post* liberal columnist James Wechsler wrote of attending Graham's central Ohio crusade in Columbus in September and hearing the evangelist talk about the nation's moral decay, the disintegrating toll of high taxes, the growing culture of dependency. "Suddenly, as I closed my eyes, I realized that one might have been listening to the text of Barry Goldwater. Plainly Dr. Graham felt that, as far as taxes were concerned, he was weary of being his brother's keeper."

Goldwater's great gift to Graham was to focus voters' attention on moral decay of the kind that Graham regularly deplored in his sermons. Both men described a country that was rich and unhappy and unwell: crime was rising (rape rose 28 percent in New York in the first six months of 1964); a syphilis epidemic was blamed on the loose morals of the young; hard liquor sales reached record levels. There were beach riots, hooliganism, suicide was up. When Goldwater and Graham were both in Boston, Goldwater declared that he and Graham were kindred spirits: Graham was trying to save souls through God, Goldwater through the Constitution. "Moral decay begins at the top," Goldwater warned, and if there were less immorality in the White House there would be less crime and mayhem abroad in the land.

From Boston Graham headed north, where he was scheduled to speak in Portland, Maine. But when he heard that Nixon was coming to campaign for Goldwater, he drove up to Augusta to meet him at the airport; he and Governor John Reed were on the tarmac when Nixon arrived, and Graham went to Nixon's press conference and to his speech at the Augusta Armory. It was their first visit in a while, and it had to have made Johnson nervous. "I doubt Goldwater can win," Nixon told Graham when they met privately that day, "but I'm going to do everything I can to help him."

If that was not all bad enough, Johnson's world was rocked when his closest aide, Walter Jenkins, was arrested in the basement men's room of the YMCA a few blocks from the White House and charged with indecent sexual behavior. Johnson and Jenkins had been so close for so long that one of Jenkins's six children was named Lyndon; he was the president's discreet right hand. When word of the arrest became public nearly a week later, the CIA launched an investigation into possible espionage or blackmail. Johnson ordered him to resign immediately; Jenkins was so distressed that he had to be hospitalized.

So the president tracked Graham down in Maine to talk things over, and invited him to come down to Washington to spend that weekend before the election with him at the White House. Graham told him he'd been on his knees the night before, praying that God was giving the president strength, and was hoping he'd slow down. He was worried about Johnson's health. "You've got this election, in my opinion, wrapped up, and you've got it wrapped up big." As for Jenkins, Graham declined to pass judgment. It was not his nature to elevate one sin over another. He reminded the president, "You know, when Jesus dealt with moral problems, like dear Walter had . . . he always dealt tenderly. Always. I know the weaknesses of men, and the Bible says we're all sinners . . . and I just hope if you have any contact with him, you'll just give him my love and understanding."

Graham did come for the weekend with Johnson at the White House, and received the standard instruction: "Now Billy," Johnson said, "you stay out of politics." By then, of course, the deed was done. As one columnist later noted, "Those visits spoke louder than words." Graham later admitted as much. "I sort of teased him afterwards and said 'you kept me locked up here because you were afraid I'd get out and say something about Goldwater.' He laughed."

Graham got to see up close the weapons of political warfare: he recalled chatting with Johnson in his bedroom first thing in the morning when an aide came in with a note, which the president let Graham see. It was the day's intelligence report on Goldwater, every move he'd made from breakfast to bedtime, his blood pressure, whom he talked to about what. "It was unbelievable," Graham said, "and unsettling—to realize what goes on behind the scenes in politics." After the weekend Bill Moyers wrote to an ally who had wondered about Graham's loyalties, telling him not to worry. Handwritten at the bottom Moyers noted wryly of Graham's political orientation, "you know—Both sides of the road."

But Goldwater's army was not giving up. During the closing days the telegrams began clacking into the North Carolina mountains, to the point that the Western Union manager in Asheville said they had to open five extra wires, running full tilt as the staff worked around the clock. While some people urged Graham to support Johnson or to stay out of the debate altogether, the overwhelming majority of the telegrams were from Goldwater boosters, some of them running to several feet long with hundreds of signatures appended. More than a million came in all, the similarity of the wording suggesting an organized drive. And indeed, Graham said he later met a man in Georgia who was in charge of the "telegrams to Graham" effort in the state.

Johnson's allies were also trying to get Graham to come out for the president; but they neglected to wrestle the rest of the family into line. Graham was driving home toward Charlotte from Washington when he heard the bulletin on the radio: his teenage daughter Anne had endorsed Goldwater.

Anne wasn't home when the phone rang in Montreat. It was the president calling, to apologize to Graham for any pressure put on him, and to reassure him about Anne. "We all live and learn. I just thought you handled it masterfully, that's what I called to tell you, when I read your statement in the paper."

Graham had explained how Anne had been trapped; she had gone down to a rally, he said, and "they found out she was there, they got her up on the platform and she's just sixteen and they asked her for a statement, she was caught up in the emotion of the thing and afterward she was just weeping."

"Well you just tell her not to be," Johnson said. "Tell her we want to know her better, we're all one family." He praised her independence and recalled his own daughters' mini-rebellions. Graham reported that he had just called a press conference. "I told them my high regard for you, my friendship for you, that we all ought to unite behind you and pray for you and that I intended to stand by you 100 percent." Of course he had also mentioned to reporters that he was a longtime friend of Goldwater's as well, and that while his family was "politically divided," he was maintaining strict neutrality.

The next day the newspapers relayed Graham's word: "Billy's Advice to Churches: Shun politics," ran the headline. "Sometimes I think the church is getting too involved in politics," he said. "The more we stay out of straight politics, the better. Jesus said we are to 'pray for those in authority' and President Johnson will get my prayers day and night."

For a president finally convinced of his legitimacy by winning a great landslide, Graham offered an even higher blessing. He wrote to Johnson that he was "convinced you were not only the choice of the American people—but of God. You are as truly a servant of God as was your great-grandfather Baines when he preached the Gospel."

Years later, Ruth told people she never did know whom he voted for that year.

FOURTEEN

Preachers and Protesters

Johnson really loved black people. I was with him a number of times on the ranch and he'd fill up that convertible of his with black children and take them on a ride. You could see when he talked about some of these social issues, they were really on his heart.

—Graham on Johnson's civil rights campaign

It is an American pattern that religious revivals spark social revolutions: the first Great Awakening laid the groundwork for the American Revolution, the second for the Civil War. Graham got his revival all right; but he hadn't reckoned with another revolution. His message now faced new competition as the clergy flooded the public square, called to arms by the civil rights and antiwar movements, making their entrance from the political left, not the right. Their embrace of social action would transform relations between congregations and their leaders, between the mainline and the evangelical churches, between politicians and pastors. The general mood of rebellion united Graham ever more tightly with those in power, for his was an obedient patriotism that affirmed their authority at precisely the time that people across the country were challenging it.

Graham always said that he and Martin Luther King Jr. had an understanding. It was forged during the friendly days they spent together during the 1957 New York crusade, and then on the trip to the World Baptist Conference in Brazil in 1960. As Graham recalled it many times over the years, he told King, "I certainly am not going to ever condemn you for your street demonstrations. So let me do my work in the stadiums, and you do yours in the streets." Graham was sure that King understood.

"If you go to the streets your people will desert you," he recalled King telling him, "and you won't have a chance to have integrated crusades."

But it was an awkward alliance at best. King, the moody prince of the black community, was far more the intellectual, enlisting Aquinas and Thoreau and Hegel to his cause. Graham favored natty suits and radiant ties; King's suits were deacon black. Graham's personal and financial life was pristine, King's eternally precarious. The motto of King's Southern Christian Leadership Conference (SCLC) might have been Graham's as well: "to save the soul of America." But theirs were different spiritual gifts: King was a prophet, Graham an evangelist. Graham's job was sales, King's courageous subversion; he had entered the ministry, rather than law or medicine, with the belief that sermons were a respectable means of spurring debate, "even social protest."

There was a moment early on when they might have worked together, when King shared Graham's idea of attacking segregation through mass revival; he even dreamed of a joint crusade first in the North, and then farther south. When he visited Freedom Riders in prison, he'd smuggle them writings of Gandhi disguised as Graham's books. Even Malcolm X declared that he was "taking my cue from methods used by Billy Graham," explaining to a group of clerics that he would preach the gospel of black nationalism without asking followers to join a specific organization.

But as racial tensions rose, Graham was more inclined to focus on scriptural imperatives, King on visible progress. Graham had second thoughts about the very idea of civil disobedience: "No matter what the law may be—it may be an unjust law—I believe we have a Christian responsibility to obey it. Otherwise you have anarchy." To this, King cited Saint Augustine, that "an unjust law is no law at all." Graham would never move fast enough for King, and King was being pushed by rivals whose agenda was much more fierce. Adding Johnson, the picture turned three-dimensional, relations among the men by turns warm and wary, mutually useful, and occasionally hostile.

"With King there was a certain competition involved," noted Doris Kearns Goodwin. Johnson was certainly fighting for racial justice, she said, "but that doesn't mean he's not aware that Martin Luther King is out there pressuring him. It's an interesting dance they were performing, King as the outside force arguing that government should do things, Johnson wanting to proceed in the way he thought most likely to work."

And as Marvin Watson, Johnson's chief of staff, explained, there was more than one view of King within the government, thanks in part to the relentless pursuit and toxic tactics of FBI chief J. Edgar Hoover. "There's no question that Dr. King was a most influential person," said Watson. "He got great press." But in both the Kennedy and Johnson White Houses, King's reputation would be shaped by Hoover's determination to discredit King as a dangerous, adulterous communist fellow traveler. "I have to say," Graham told biographer Marshall Frady, "that in time I became mixed up in my thinking about him. I became concerned about the people who were around him. I think it was because of Hoover and all the things he kept warning me about in regard to King."

Civil rights leaders who visited Graham years later heard him muse about what might have happened if they had taken to the streets together. "I think it would have had a great impact on people," said Reverend Joseph Lowery, who founded the SCLC with King and ran it for twenty years, "if he had applied the moral imperatives of the faith to social and economic problems. I know a lot of people called on him publicly to support the movement, but he always sort of stayed behind the pulpit."

Even before the rise of more militant leaders, Graham and Johnson were bonded, as southerners of a certain generation, in their aversion to some of King's tactics. "It was very difficult," Watson said, "for the president to believe that anyone should violate the laws and be rewarded for the violation." Johnson was proud to be the only leader to actually steer revolutionary civil rights legislation through Congress. He believed deeply in both the need for fairness and the sanctity of law; and Graham believed just as deeply in the power of grace. So what were the proper measures of force and faith to bring about radical change? It helped Johnson that Graham came to argue a middle ground: the role of the Christian was "first to proclaim the Gospel of Jesus Christ as the only answer to man's deepest needs; and second, to apply as best we can the principles of Christianity to the social conditions around us."

But Graham's stance was not shared by more liberal clerics of that era. It was the cause of racial justice more than any other that brought America's preachers into the streets. Their movement started slowly but gathered force, ministers and priests and rabbis meeting in a Washington gym to plan strategy and then swarming the Capitol to plead directly with senators about civil rights legislation. Stirred from lethargy or luxurious isolation by the images of dogs terrorizing black children, of fire hoses and cattle prods, of bludgeoned churchgoers and bombed churches, priests and rabbis marched with scripture under their arms, into the line of fire, into jail. "Some time or other," declared the Reverend Dr. Eugene Carson Blake, executive head of the United Presbyterian Church in the United States, "we are all going to have to stand and be on the receiving end of a fire hose."

Graham found himself caught between the growing activism of the mainstream Protestant churches with whom he worked and the hostility of fundamentalists whose theology was more congenial to him but who disapproved of his integrated crusades and his ecumenical outreach. That hostility, which had been growing for years, reached such a point by 1966 that Bob Jones Jr. forbade his students to attend Graham's Greenville, South Carolina, crusade or to pray for its success, and denounced Graham as a false teacher who "is doing more harm to the cause of Jesus Christ than any living man."

For many on the left, meanwhile, Graham's patient focus on mending men's souls came at too high a cost. "The Civil Rights movement operated on the theological premise that while we waited on your feelings and your heart, we wanted to change your behavior," Lowery said. "In other words, you get your foot off my neck while you're working on your heart. Oppression is no less painful because you say you're trying to get your heart straight first before you stop oppressing me."

King, however, marveled at Graham's ability to win positive headlines in whatever city he was in, even in staunchly segregationist papers that were covering his fully integrated crusades. He sent two lieutenants to Chicago to meet with Billy Graham Evangelistic Association officials and learn about fund-raising, organization, and crusade techniques. Asked how to keep King's mission in the news, media adviser Walter Bennett told them they were going about it all wrong: Graham got the coverage he did because he limited his exposure to a few crusades a year, each involving about two years and a million man-hours of preparation. King, in contrast, was spread too thin, traveling from city to city desperately raising the funds to keep the SCLC afloat. That pattern would never break through the media threshold, Bennett warned, and predicted as well that the pace would kill King within five years.

His timing was right, but not the cause of death.

JOHNSON, GRAHAM, KING, AND SELMA

W ithin days of Kennedy's assassination, King had called for the passage of the Civil Rights Bill as a tribute, and the next day Johnson appeared before a joint session of Congress. "No memorial oration or eulogy could more eloquently honor President Kennedy's memory," he said, "than the earliest possible passage of the Civil Rights Bill for which he fought so long. We have talked long enough in this country about equal rights. We have talked for 100 years or more. It is time now to write the next chapter."

King saw promise in the energies of the exuberant Texan, quite different from the cool dispassion of the Kennedy brothers. But when it came to tactics, Johnson was more of a mind with Graham: the South needed to be brought into the union for real this time, integrated economically and socially with the rest of the country. "I'm going to be the president who finishes what Lincoln began," he said, and he discouraged King from further confrontation. We'll take it from here, he promised.

Graham recalled talking to Hubert Humphrey, who had managed the floor vote on the night the historic bill passed. Democratic leaders had gathered in his office, marveling at what they had achieved, imagining how many doctoral dissertations would be written about what they had just done. What Graham remembered about the night was the vice president vindicating Graham's priorities. "He had led the fight," Graham said, "and he pulled me aside. 'Billy, we've got it done, legally, but to get it done, really done, we need your help and people like you.'"

Johnson signed the bill on July 2, 1964; one aide likened it to signing the Emancipation Proclamation, and King was there to see him do it. That day Johnson called his commerce secretary, Luther Hodges, Graham's old friend from his days as governor of North Carolina, and talked about what would happen next. Hodges said they needed to reach out to black leaders, get them to go slow, not to go out and try to get arrested. He wasn't sure the system could handle hundreds of cases just in the first few days, and there were warnings of violence already.

They needed a blue-ribbon panel, mayors and ministers and community leaders who they could call on as conciliators, Johnson said. "If we have a real roughhouse . . . we'll ask someone to go in there." He was naming former Florida governor Leroy Collins to direct the new Community

Relations Service, which would swoop in to help arbitrate disputes, and he needed an advisory board to help.

"Billy Graham turned us down, Mr. President," Hodges said.

"What'd he say?"

"He felt like he could do more good, and to tell you he was going to try to have crusades in Mississippi and two or three other places in the South. He thought this other might detract from it."

"That may be," Johnson agreed, and there appeared to be no hard feelings: a week later Graham was at the White House for that evening of dancing on the roof.

The next step, King felt, would be legislation on voting rights, as he told Johnson when he stopped to see him following his receipt of the Nobel Peace Prize that December. Johnson agreed, but warned that they should not move too quickly, since he didn't think it could pass so soon. It would take another stab into the national conscience to force the next step—which is how the battle came to Selma, where fewer than one in a hundred eligible black voters were registered, where the local police chief wore a button declaring "Never!" on his lapel and called blacks "the lowest forms of humanity."

The images of Bloody Sunday, March 7, 1965, and the days that followed, of peaceful demonstrators in Selma being teargassed and beaten, convulsed the country once more. Graham, who was in Hawaii, himself seemed ready to take up arms. "It's true I haven't been to jail yet," he said, evoking an unimaginable image. "I underscore the word yet. Maybe I haven't done all I could or should do." He called on Johnson to assemble a civil rights summit. The next day, the president appeared before Congress and gave the greatest sermon of his presidency. He compared Selma to Lexington and Concord. "Rarely in any time," he said, "does an issue lay bare the secret heart of America itself." No amount of wealth or progress or strength would matter if the issue of racial justice was unsolved. Now it was the nation's eternal soul that was at stake. "It is not just Negroes, but really it is all of us, who must overcome the crippling legacy of bigotry and injustice.

"And we shall overcome."

The men who had gathered with Martin Luther King to watch the speech watched him as well. For many it was the only time they had seen King cry.

Johnson proceeded to call Graham. "Billy," he said, "have you got guts enough to preach all over Alabama? You're the only man that can settle this thing down there." ("Johnson, you know," Graham said later, "would get quite extravagant in what he had to say.") Graham canceled his planned tour in Europe in order to head south instead, to preach in every major venue in Alabama that he could arrange and meet privately with pastors, business leaders, local politicians. "We did it surrounded by policemen," he recalled. "The KKK went around and knocked our signs down." The FBI alerted him of at least one bomb threat—which was better treatment than King received, since they typically declined to warn him when they heard about a threat on his life.

"Billy Graham Is Focusing on Rights" read the *New York Times* headline that week, announcing that Graham was spending more and more time talking civil rights and had just added George Wallace to the little black book of people he prayed for. Graham denied being a latecomer to the cause; he praised the Civil Rights Act and acknowledged that while "I have never felt that we should attain our rights by illegal means, yet I must confess that the demonstrations have served to arouse the conscience of the world." He condemned southern churches: "They should lead the way, but they are not doing it."

He believed that his Alabama crusades confirmed his argument that revival was central to reform. Black leaders were "literally shouting for joy over the new atmosphere that has been created in Montgomery." He saw a "change in the spiritual and social climate of major proportions." Watching black and white men and women receive the invitation together, he said, one of the pastors on the platform whispered, "This is the answer to our problems." Moving forward, he argued that things would all get easier and Alabama could prove a model to the nation, "if the Ku Klux Klan will quiet down, if the extremists in the civil rights organizations will give Alabama time to digest the new civil rights laws, and if the politicians will not try to exploit the situation."

Meanwhile, another Baptist preacher was having another reaction to the entire scene. At Thomas Road Church in Lynchburg, Virginia, a young preacher named Jerry Falwell told his congregation in a sermon two weeks after Bloody Sunday, "Believing the Bible as I do, I would find it impossible to stop preaching the pure saving gospel of Jesus Christ and begin doing anything else—including the fighting of communism, or participating in the civil rights reform. . . . Preachers are not called to be politicians, but to be soul winners." Had they listened closely, both Graham and King might have heard their methods and messages repudiated. But Falwell himself would come to feel differently.

Johnson had only praise for Graham's effort. "I wish I could describe adequately what your presence and your prayers are meaning for me in these days here," he told him. "Please know that this door is always open— and your room is always waiting. I hope you will come often.

"You are doing a brave and fine thing for your country in your courageous effort to contribute to the understanding and brotherhood of the Americans in the South. . . . I am praying for your success, and want you to know I am very proud of you."

WATTS EXPLODES

Selma represented one of the hinges in history, after which everything looked different. It certainly marked a high point in Graham's civil rights efforts; in the months and years that followed, as the battle grew more radical, more violent and confrontational, as a new cadre of leaders crowded the stage, Graham's natural caution and conservatism sent him into retreat.

Johnson got his Voting Rights Act passed, and signed it on August 6, 1965. But almost immediately he would confront the reality that changing lives was harder than changing laws. Better schools, better jobs, fewer slums, all would take more time; but the expectations raised by the political victories created a heady climate of hope, and anger.

Five days later a confrontation between a California Highway Patrol officer and a black motorist unleashed the six days of fire and rage in Watts that left thirty-four dead, more than a thousand people injured, four thousand arrested, and millions of dollars in property destroyed.

Johnson, for one, was stunned. "How is it possible," he asked, "after all we've accomplished? How could it be?" And he was not alone: the Urban League the year before had ranked Los Angeles first in the country in conditions and opportunities for blacks. Now Johnson saw his reforms imperiled not only by his opponents but by those he wanted to help, as a page turned in American politics.

Graham was at home in Montreat when the riots broke out. To this kind of mayhem, he did not prescribe only gospel love; the enemy now was not man's sinful nature, but a very real, subversive enemy determined to sow anarchy. "We are caught in a great racial revolution," he warned. "We may have a blood bath." He urged Congress to "immediately drop all other legislation and devise new laws to deal with riots and violence as we have witnessed in Los Angeles. I am convinced there are sinister and evil forces at work taking advantage of the race problem whose ultimate objective is the overthrow of the American government." The L.A. riots, he declared, were "a dress rehearsal for a revolution." But he still insisted that no legal remedy would be sufficient without spiritual revival; you can't legislate hatred out of people.

Graham's comments, to the extent that they echoed the accusations of John Birch Society members who insisted that the civil rights movement was a communist conspiracy, brought him directly into the line of fire from the editors at the *Christian Century*. "Evangelist Billy Graham reacted to the Los Angeles riots with a vague, emotional outburst consistent with the role he plays as a national religious leader," they said. "With words more hysteric than prophetic, Mr. Graham issued dire warnings like a man who knows something is dreadfully wrong but who hasn't the slightest idea what caused it."

But Graham was quick to condemn extremism of all kinds, from both left and right. Wary of a backlash to the rioting that could spread elsewhere, he insisted that "an entire race should not be blamed for what a relatively few irresponsible people are doing." He saw that a vacuum had opened, and invoked Dr. King as the leader of responsible black opinion, urging that King call on civil rights leaders to halt their demonstrations until people had had a chance to digest the new Civil Rights Act.

King had watched the horror unfold and wanted to go immediately to help calm the waters. But Governor Edmund Brown urged him not to come, and the local black clergy were uncertain about whether his presence would help or hurt. So King held off, until he saw the reports of Graham arriving in town, putting on a bulletproof vest, and being shown the scenes of destruction in a helicopter tour with Mayor Sam Yorty. He called Tom Kilgore, the Los Angeles head of the SCLC. "Tom, if Billy Graham can ride over them in a helicopter, why can't I come out there and talk to those young people." And so the next day King went out as well, walked the streets, and called for calm. He did not defend the destruction: the riots, he said, were "a blind and misguided revolt against authority and society," which required the use of "intelligent force" in response.

Johnson now had a different problem on his hands. As the focus of the protests shifted from the compelling moral pageant of protest against Jim Crow in the South to a broader revolt against conditions in the northern ghettos, whatever consensus had existed among people of goodwill and progressive instinct began to shred. The very word "integration" lost resonance. In 1964 only a third of people thought that black leaders were trying to move too fast. By 1966 the number was 85 percent. While leaders like King and Roy Wilkins commanded huge respect within much of the black community, the headlines were soon taken over by the next generation of militant leaders who viewed nonviolence as obsolete; We Shall Overcome became We Shall Overrun. By that year even the liberal lions of the *Christian Century* were distinguishing "good black organizations from bad black organizations," supporting the SCLC and NAACP but warning against the "personal empire building" of the Congress of Racial Equality (CORE) and the Student Nonviolent Coordinating Committee (SNCC). Graham himself called on Johnson and the FBI to expose the extremist groups that were interested in "national disorder for sinister political objectives."

To Help the Least Among Us

Johnson wanted to put the question of civil rights aside for a while, call a temporary cease-fire. He still wanted to fight poverty, even if he had no more idea of what would actually work than he had when the first waves of legislation passed in 1964–65. But King would not be his partner in the next crusade, not after what Johnson saw as a lack of gratitude for the risks he had taken and the price he had paid in fighting so hard for civil rights.

And not when Graham appeared to have had a conversion experience of his own, having gone back, he said, and studied the scriptures concerning the Christian's duties toward the poor. Though in 1966 he had fired off a round at clergy who "call for social service without also providing a solid spiritual basis for it," by 1967 he was telling the World Council of Churches that "there is no doubt the Social Gospel has directed its energies toward the relief of many of the problems of suffering humanity. I am for it!"

At one point he suggested that Johnson and the Congress might "take some of the money we are giving away abroad . . . and get rid of those ghettoes that have no place in affluent America. It has always seemed incredible to me that so much poverty should exist side by side with so much wealth in places like Manhattan."

As the director of the Office of Economic Opportunity (OEO), Sargent Shriver was the field general for the War on Poverty. One warm day in the spring of 1967, the lawn furniture at the Graham house was blown down the mountain as Shriver landed in a helicopter to pick him up for a tour of the Appalachian poverty trail. Among the people they met was a woman who lived in a spare mountain shack. They asked what she would do if she had a twenty-dollar bill. She said she would go find someone who needed it more than she did and give it to him.

From this adventure would come a film to be shown on television, *Beyond These Hills*. "I believe this is the first and only time that Dr. Graham has ever consented to so endorse a domestic program of the United States government," Shriver told press secretary George Christian, so "we are extremely pleased." That summer the House Committee on Education and Labor spent seven weeks debating whether to reauthorize the landmark 1964 act that had created Shriver's agency in the first place, and how much money to give it.

Graham came to Washington in June for the premiere of the film and to lobby the lawmakers. When Watson asked if Johnson wanted to host the lunch for him with congressmen and business leaders, Johnson declined; his budget constraints and ambivalence about the loyalty of the OEO may have limited how much he was willing to do. But he and Graham conferred beforehand, and Graham went on to argue that the War on Poverty was spiritually as well as morally motivated. "I've been before different congressional committees on 17 occasions. But I tell you today that I have never testified for anything like I do for this poverty program. I was critical of it when it started. Now I'm a convert. It's not a giveaway program."

In fact, if Congress did not continue to support the OEO, he warned, America would "pay for it spiritually, morally and in every phase of society." At least one lawmaker, Democrat Edith Green of Oregon, the bill's premier antagonist, was annoyed by Graham's efforts. "If you criticize the war on poverty," she grumped, "you're sacrilegious."

Graham immediately found himself under "tremendous pressure," as Shriver told Johnson, because he was meddling in politics. Congress was more conservative now, after the 1966 elections; southern Democrats had especially cold feet about an agency that was the most visible symbol of the Great Society, funding everything from remedial education to health care to legal services for the poor. Opponents complained of partisanship and waste and unintended consequences. Another wave of riots that summer allowed enemies to argue that the OEO was a failure. Graham even wanted to pull the film until after Congress had voted—which Shriver pointed out would look just as "political" as making it in the first place.

In November, shortly before being hospitalized with pneumonia, Graham spent a week on the phone urging lawmakers to support the bill. He was not engaged in how the money was spent, he said. "I'm just interested that none of the programs be curtailed. The poverty program is not a giveaway program, it is one of self-help, that's why I'm for it." Historian Richard Pierard argued that Graham's lobbying helped save the OEO from near-certain death. The bill passed in time for Johnson to sign before Christmas. "A few months ago," marveled one House member, "nobody would have bet a nickel we would approve a poverty program in this Congress."

But such victories, in the end, did not outweigh the great defeat, or close the gap between a domestic policy that tried to do so much for so many people and a foreign policy that would drive them away. Johnson would have only a few months left before his surrender.

FIFTEEN

"The Strong Arm of Empathy"

I knew that they had burdens beyond anything I could ever know or understand.
—Graham on presidents in war time

I t was over Vietnam that Dr. King, like so many others, completely broke with Johnson. America, King charged, had become the world's great purveyor of violence with this soul-poisoning war. He saw vital social programs "broken and eviscerated as if they were some idle political plaything of a society gone mad on war, and I knew that America would never invest the necessary funds or energies in rehabilitation of its poor so long as adventures like Vietnam continued to draw men and skills and money like some demonic, destructive suction tube."

This drew fire from the *New York Times* and other editorial pages; King wrestled with other black leaders who warned him not to conflate the issues. Graham rebuked him for wrapping the two movements together. "Surely Negroes are divided about the war as the rest of us," he said, "and it [King's protest] is an affront to the thousands of loyal Negro troops who are now in Vietnam." Johnson of course could not acknowledge this fatal tension between his foreign and domestic policies, and so fed his reputation as a conniver as he concealed the costs of the war for as long as possible.

"I knew from the start that I was bound to be crucified either way I moved," he told Doris Kearns Goodwin. "If I left the woman I really loved—the Great Society—in order to get involved with that bitch of a war on the other side of the world, then I would lose everything at home. All my programs. All my hopes to feed the hungry and shelter the homeless. . . . But if I left that war and let the Communists take over South Vietnam, then

I would be seen as a coward and my nation would be seen as an appeaser." That would yield "a mean and destructive debate, that would shatter my presidency, kill my administration and damage our democracy."

Early on Graham accepted the president's arguments and reassured his audience that America was, as always, fighting in a noble cause. But it soon became clear that Vietnam was something much more complicated, and his public comments became more equivocal. "I found that equally devout Christians were on both sides of the Vietnam question," he said. He was much more comfortable speaking out on race relations as a moral issue, however uncomfortable its political dimensions made him. The proportions were reversed on Vietnam; it was less clear to him as time passed where the moral imperatives lay.

As early as spring of 1964, George Smathers cited Graham as a barometer in warning Johnson about the lack of popular support for a major escalation. The Republicans will beat you up whatever you do, Smathers reasoned. "I heard Billy Graham on a program just the other night," he said. "He usually stays out of these things pretty well, but he said, 'I just don't understand why it is we can be so tough in that area of the world and how we can be so untough in Cuba.'" And if Graham didn't embrace the cause of confronting the communists in Southeast Asia, Smathers suggested, then no one would.

By 1965 Graham was talking about the "mess" in Southeast Asia. The president "needs our prayers that God will give him wisdom." He was in no way turning pacifist: as he told Johnson and the assembled dignitaries at the prayer breakfast in 1966, "There are those who have tried to reduce Christ to the level of a genial and innocuous appeaser; but Jesus said, 'You are wrong. I have come as a fire-setter and a sword-wielder.'" But if he still believed some wars were worth fighting, he was less sure that this one was. "There came the day when [South Carolina Democrat Mendel Rivers, who chaired the House Armed Services Committee] called me and said 'Well, I've given up on Vietnam.' This must have been way back around 1966. 'It's an unwinnable war, Billy.' This was Mendel Rivers, the Hawk of Hawks, talking. 'We've got to somehow get out of this thing without losing all of Asia.' From that moment on I began to feel the same way."

Vietnam eventually gave Graham a template for issues that would divide Americans in years to come. It was the first time he had really confronted the challenge of conflict avoidance, when the public's longing for moral guidance on a hard issue had to be weighed against the cost of giving it. "I have been extremely careful," he insisted in a letter to the *Christian Century*, "not to be drawn into the moral implications of the Vietnam war." There was, increasingly, no middle ground to occupy. "I just decided this was such a divisive and emotional issue in America that my job was to preach the gospel to the people on both sides," he said once the war was over. "If I took a stand on one of these sides or the other, half the [people] would not hear what I was saying about Christ."

Even Johnson, noted Robert Bellah in his landmark essay on civil religion in 1966, "has been less ready to assert that 'God has favored our undertaking' in the case of Vietnam than with respect to civil rights." Lady Bird Johnson told biographer Robert Dallek that "he had no stomach for it . . . it wasn't the war he wanted. The one he wanted was on poverty and ignorance and disease and that was worth putting your life into." But Johnson also hated the people who hated the war, because they talked as though he had wanted it, had gone looking for it, the armchair generals and antiwar intellectuals whose opposition, Johnson was sure, only bolstered Hanoi's resolve. So here Graham was able to maintain his usefulness and find common ground with the embattled president: he may not have been for the war, but he was against protesting it. The demonstrators, he charged, "so exaggerate our divisions over the war that they could make Hanoi confident that it will eventually win. Then what already is anticipated as a long war will be even longer."

Graham's loyalty was such that he and Johnson were attacked together. A three-act play called *America Hurrah* opened off Broadway at the end of 1967, and was considered the first major drama of the antiwar movement. In it Graham was portrayed as a fool and Johnson a hypocrite. It ran for 640 performances, received "more critical acclaim than any new American drama this year," according to the *New York Times*, and was called the watershed play of the decade.

Graham got caught in Johnson's vicious circle: if they could rally support at home it would help project U.S. resolve abroad and improve the odds of getting Hanoi to negotiate a settlement. But as the administration's rosy predictions parted company from reports from the field, his credibility suffered, his allies deserted him, and the divisions at home only deepened.

Graham felt this tension when he went to Vietnam for Christmas in 1966, to see for himself what was happening. As the trip approached Johnson sent him his encouragement: "My spirits are really lifted by the knowledge that you will bring your strength and inspiration as a Christmas gift to our soldiers in Vietnam. . . . I look forward to a full report on your return."

Graham traveled with Francis Cardinal Spellman, often called the American Pope, who was a full-feathered hawk. Spellman celebrated mass at the air base at Cam Ranh Bay; Graham held a candlelight Christmas eve service at An Khe, spent Christmas day with marines in Da Nang. "You have raised man's eyes and lifted his heart in the far corners of the world," Johnson wrote to him on New Year's. "America's sons, America's families and I, who share your prayers for peace, are proud and grateful for your inspiration."

Troop morale was very high, Graham announced upon his return. "They all seemed to have two things—a Bible or a camera. They are facing death or the possibility of death and this makes them realize how fragile human life is." Impressed as he was by the soldiers, he still emerged from the trip alarmed and pessimistic. "It is a complicated, confusing and frustrating war. I don't see an early end to it." At the same time he wasn't ready to abandon the cause. "The stakes are much higher in Vietnam than I had realized," he said at a news conference, and his reflexive fear of communist aggression had not diminished. The next day he was even more apocalyptic. "I think we are on a collision course with China," he said, and predicted that China, out to dominate the world, could land a nuclear attack on U.S. soil within ten years. They believed they could afford a nuclear war, he warned, "because they think 'We'll lose 300 million people and we'll still have 400 million left.'"

As promised, Johnson invited Graham and Spellman to the White House for a lunch that included National Security Adviser Walt Rostow and Secretary of State Dean Rusk. As Graham remembered it, Johnson asked Spellman, "Now what do you think? We can't go on with this thing. The American people are not going to take it."

Spellman favored pushing on; for his own part, Graham was hygieni-cally sealed from political comment, saying he would limit his observations to "the moral and spiritual conditions that I found among the American troops. . . . This was my main concern. I'm not going to get into the fact as to what you should do or should not do. But I agree with you that the American people are getting restless over this thing."

His public remarks prompted the *Christian Century* to hold him account-able: too much civil religion, too much talk of good Christian soldiers, turns every fight into a holy war. "Billy Graham can give the Vietnam War the blessing of the Gospel from coast to coast," read an editorial that

January, "condoning the killing, maiming and burning as indispensable to the victory of the great Christian cause, and nobody accuses him of meddling with national policy."

It was all enough to prompt Graham to back away from the whole debate. In a long interview with the *New York Times*, he acknowledged that Niebuhr "had a point" in charging him with a lack of social concern, even though "in recent years, I've preached on every social issue you can think of." He would continue to speak out on racial justice, he said, but had decided to "stop making the ridiculous and foolish statements on current events that I used to make when I didn't have all the facts." Specifically on Vietnam, "I don't know what the answer is. All Christians are for peace, but they can sincerely be on either side of the debate."

Activists would continue to try to win him to their cause, particularly given his access to the White House. One demonstrator in Los Angeles dropped a leaflet through the window of his car, asking the evangelist to "bring awareness to Lyndon Johnson of the consequences of these war crimes for his immortal soul." Nor did the Johnson White House hesitate to use him as a political asset. They kept close track of what Graham was saying: in February 1967 Marvin Watson told the president about a half-hour TV show Graham had made about his trip in which he "says some very complimentary things about the President." Johnson was eager to see it. In discussions about the military draft a little over a week later, polling expert Fred Panzer told Johnson about a Gallup poll that showed that when people heard the word "lottery," they thought of gambling, and that it would be wrong to gamble with people's lives. So he suggested calling the plan "equal service" and recruiting Graham to help relieve any concerns. Johnson proposed that Graham be part of the monitoring team that would bless the South Vietnamese elections that September. Graham declined, but did introduce his *Hour of Decision* broadcast on election day by noting that reporters were sure to jump on any rumor of "shenanigans." Just as U.S. elections are not always "totally above board," he said, Americans should give the South Vietnamese the benefit of the doubt.

Most awkwardly, in the middle of all this, *TIME* reported that a group secretly financed by the CIA had funded Graham's Latin American crusade, which came as a complete surprise to Graham and prompted a repudiation: "I would never accept funds from any government agency," he declared, "especially the CIA."

There was no prophetic role for him as a voice against the war, only a pastoral one, as he ministered to a president who was consumed by the struggle. If Vietnam alienated Johnson from his more skeptical aides like George Ball and even Humphrey, from prophets like King, from millions of Americans who shared his values of pride and patriotism but were appalled by the costs of a war that had never been debated, it brought him closer to Graham. It was not in the evangelist's nature to let reservations about the wisdom of policy prevent him from ministering to a powerful man in a deep crisis.

"Nobody could make Johnson feel he was right about Vietnam like Billy Graham could," Bill Moyers said. But that may have been less about a specific view of the war and more about Graham's almost childlike faith that whatever a president does must be right because he is in authority. He was always quick to absolve Johnson of the original sin: "I do know that President Johnson had little choice," he said in 1967. "At the time of the Kennedy assassination, thousands of American troops already had been committed, and the President was faced with the responsibility of making sure that that commitment was fulfilled." He often noted how many columnists and apostate senators had been on board at first. He blamed the change in public support on the war's length and the way it played out every night on the evening news. Johnson told him once, he said, "that television is what had killed him politically."

Johnson himself had been consumed by doubts from the moment he made the fateful decision to escalate the war with the bombing campaign Rolling Thunder—the code name from Graham's trademark revival hymn, evidence of "power throughout the universe displayed." At the time Johnson called Eisenhower to plead that he make up some excuse that would bring him to Washington so they could talk. Say that you're going to see your publisher, Johnson said, "so it doesn't look too dramatic, that we've got an emergency. It's not that deep. But it's deep enough that I want to talk to you." Johnson offered him the Lincoln Bedroom if he'd agree to spend the night. "I would love for you—I wish you would stay at the White House. I need you a little bit. I need a little Billy Graham these days. I need somebody."

In Time of Need

As he staggered toward 1968, Johnson came to view himself as the victim of a vast conspiracy of commentators and communists and Kennedys and people whom he had once trusted. Liberals seemed eager to savage the most progressive administration ever, civil rights activists to pillory the only president who had actually ever done anything for them. "The press destroyed the strongest personality that ever led this nation," argued the loyal Watson. "He was the most knowledgeable person that ever served in that office." In retirement, Goodwin observed, "Johnson sincerely believed that he would have been the greatest president in his country's history had it not been for the intellectuals and the columnists— the men of ideas and the men of words."

Always less secure on foreign than domestic affairs, Johnson in his need for reassurance rejected those who challenged and exalted those who confirmed him. "He was going around the country," said Harry McPherson, "either to military bases or colleges that are way the hell over to the right and the students are all very well behaved. I said this was so obvious it would hurt him. I thought he was sounding like a fool." Sometimes when Johnson couldn't sleep, he walked the halls with a flashlight, looked at the portrait of Woodrow Wilson, paralyzed by a stroke, and imagined his fate. "He could not rid himself of the suspicion that a mean God had set out to torture him in the cruelest manner possible," Goodwin said. Or he would go to the Situation Room at 3 a.m. because there would always be people there, Pentagon and intelligence officers who would have the latest news, and body counts.

"As Johnson was trying to wrestle through Vietnam," Jack Valenti said, "as it became a fungus on the face of the administration, Billy Graham was a warm, confiding human being. In that presence, Johnson felt comfortable. For those moments—and I don't know how long they lasted—they brought him a little peace. And some peace at a time of despair in a president's life is the coin of the realm. It helps him get through the sadness of the day.

"There's nothing more brutalizing," Valenti went on, "than to order men into battle and then pick up the phone from the Pentagon and find out how many were lost that day. I once asked Johnson, 'How do you stand it?' And he said it was like drinking carbolic acid every morning."

And it was not only Vietnam. It was that the war was seen as the wanton error of a vain and devious man. The Tet Offensive that winter, however costly to the North Vietnamese war machine, was fatal to Johnson's credibility. The surprisingly fierce offensive convinced millions of people that the president had been lying all along; support for him plummeted, the editorial pages mutinied, and Eugene McCarthy swept the New Hampshire primaries promising peace. Bobby Kennedy soon announced he was jumping in. Absent an insulating layer of loyal defenders, Johnson was easy prey for his critics, who compared him to Caesar, Caligula, and Mussolini. The ridicule was constant, vicious, violent. SNCC head H. Rap Brown suggested that the president and Lady Bird ought to be shot. "Lee Harvey Oswald, Where Are You Now?" read the protesters' signs.

On March 31, Johnson stood before the country, announced a bombing halt, laid out a path toward progress in Vietnam, and then declared, "There is division in the American house now. . . . With America's sons in fields far away, with America's future under challenge right here at home . . . I do not believe that I should devote an hour or a day of my time to any personal partisan causes. . . . Accordingly I shall not seek, and will not accept, the nomination of my party for another term as your president."

Much of the country may have been stunned at the announcement, but Graham, for one, was not. "At that point," he said, "he'd wrestled with it a long time, whether to run again." He had first raised the issue with Graham as much as a year before, long before his support collapsed. "It was in the family dining room as I remember, and he said, 'You know, Billy, I come from a family of short livers.'" If he ran again and won there was a good chance he wouldn't serve out his term. He'd even had a secret actuarial study done in 1967, to predict his life expectancy, and whether he'd be exposing the public to the death of another sitting president. "I may not live through this," he told Graham. "I've already had one heart attack. I don't think that's fair to the people or to my party."

There was great celebration the next day, as if the entire country had exhaled. Johnson himself, said Lady Bird, had the air of "a prisoner let free." That night, he skipped his bedtime reading. Thereafter he could appear in a city without provoking riots. "It was Lyndon Johnson's fate," columnist Tom Wicker wrote, recalling Johnson's heroic performance during those first unimaginable months in office, "that he moved us most at the first and the last, in those moments when he was able to set himself apart from the politics by which he has lived."

Graham was glad Johnson was out of it. He wrote to the president that "while the country desperately needs your leadership, yet I feel a great sense of relief that you will be leaving office early in January. I feel that another four years under this strain would be too much. I want to see you live to a ripe old age and enjoy a few years of well-deserved rest. . . . There

are very few men in our generation that I have come to personally love and
appreciate more than I have you."

JOHNSON IN TWILIGHT

E ven after Johnson left office, Graham continued to tend to him, for
his friendships with presidents did not end when they retired; in
many cases, they deepened. In Johnson's case, Graham understood what
the prospect of freedom and an end to duty would feel like to a man with
few inner resources and a primitive need for applause.

"I am sure that it has been a very difficult time for you after so many
years of public service to find yourself suddenly a private citizen," he wrote
to Johnson early in 1969. "Even in my small way I experience it from time
to time. I have often gone on three- to six-month crusades abroad in the
midst of a whirlwind of activity. I jet home to the quietness of this mountain, and for the first few days I hardly know what to do with myself. There
even come times of depression. However, that all soon passes."

Johnson was packing memories away to ship off to the ranch, and wrote
back of his gratitude for Graham's pastoral care. "As I read and reread your
wonderful letter of February 3, my mind went back to those lonely occasions at the White House when your prayers and your friendship helped to
sustain a President in an hour of trial.

"No one will ever fully know how you helped to lighten my load or how
much warmth you brought into our house. But I know."

In a remarkable witness to the passing of power, Graham would spend
the last weekend with the Johnsons in the White House, before offering
the invocation at Nixon's inauguration and returning as a guest for the new
president and his wife's first night. In later years he would remember little
other than praying for the old president, and the new one. But Luci Johnson recalled how he ministered to the retiring president at that moment.
"My father had a sense of relief, 'I've given all I can, I've done the best I can,
I gave my political life trying to get us closer to the peace table . . . but there
was so much more I wanted to do domestically than I was able to achieve.'
I just remember Reverend Graham offering a strong arm of empathy. Not
your cheerleader, ah, let me tell you you've been wonderful, let me tell you
what you want to hear, how great and fabulous you are. But just a lot of

respect for your feelings, a lot of strength and consolation." Graham told Julie Nixon Eisenhower that he had never seen Johnson so melancholy.

That weekend they all watched a movie together. As was his custom, Johnson fell asleep, but Graham walked back and asked the projectionist to save the film; it was *The Shoes of the Fisherman*, about a fantasy pope, played by Anthony Quinn, who tried to bring peace. He thought the Nixons would like it.

The Grahams and Johnsons went to church together Sunday morning, the nineteenth. A light snow was falling. Like magic, overnight, everything would change, the rugs rolled up, the pictures removed, walls painted, broken things fixed. The workmen were everywhere except the Oval Office; this they would not touch until the president was gone. During the inaugural ceremonies the next day, as the Johnson family left the platform, both Johnson daughters slipped out of the line, went over to Graham, and kissed him.

After that Graham saw Johnson mainly during visits to the ranch. Those may have meant more than any White House encounter. "Here's Johnson at the ranch," said Goodwin, "not easily able to go places because he can't appear without demonstrations, pretty much sequestered. It's a lonelier time for him. The fact that Billy Graham would come visit would be enormously important for him; he was not the center of power anymore, so anyone who came, he triply valued." One time, courtesy of President Nixon, Graham flew to Texas on Air Force One to speak at the dedication of the LBJ Library. They went back to the ranch afterward, and walked down to the northern bank of the Pedernales. Here, Johnson said, under the oaks next to his parents, was where he would be buried.

"Billy," Johnson said, very direct, "will I ever see my mother and father again?"

"Well, Mr. President, if you're a Christian, and they were Christians, then someday you'll have a great homecoming."

And now Johnson had one more favor to ask. Would Billy preach at his funeral? And make sure the message got through, because the world listens when a president dies. "Don't use any notes," he said, because the wind will just blow them away. And no fancy eulogizing either. "I want you to look in those cameras and just tell 'em what Christianity is all about. Tell 'em how they can be sure they can go to heaven. I want you to preach the gospel." And he paused. "But somewhere in there, you tell 'em a few things I did for this country."

Graham wrote to Johnson when he got home, saying he was honored that Johnson would even think of him. "I love you and your family so much that it would be one of the most difficult tasks I have ever performed," he wrote. "Yet in another sense, it will be a triumph: for I know that not only in your head but in your heart you have put your trust in Jesus Christ as your Lord and Savior. We are not saved because of our own accomplishments or good works; we are saved totally and completely because of what Christ did on the cross for us. . . . I am not going to Heaven because I have preached to great crowds or read the Bible many times—I'm going to Heaven just like the thief on the cross who said in that last moment: 'Lord, remember me.'"

In his last conversations with Doris Kearns Goodwin, before he died in January 1973, Johnson talked about the odds that history would remember him kindly—or at all. "I'd have been better off looking for immortality through my wife and children and their children in turn instead of seeking all that love and affection from the American people," he told her. "They're just too fickle."

Graham got word of Johnson's death fifteen minutes after he walked in the door at Montreat, having just returned from Nixon's second inaugural. There was an immense state funeral; then the body was flown down to Texas. Graham met Lady Bird in Austin and rode with them to the ranch two hours away. On the way out of the city, the roads were lined with people, some carrying signs. In one case two white students held one side, two black students the other. "Forgive Us Mr. President," it read.

"To him, the Great Society was not a wild dream. It was a realistic hope," Graham told the funeral congregation. "The thing nearest his heart was to harness the wealth and the knowledge and the greatness of the nation and help every poor and every oppressed person in the country and in the world. It was his destiny to be involved in a war he never wanted and search for a peace he didn't live to see achieved. As President Nixon said on Tuesday night, 'No one would have welcomed peace more than he.'"

SIXTEEN

The Return of Richard Nixon

The emphasis I tried to leave was love, that they need to have love for the people who were opposed to them.

—Graham on political warfare

I f Billy Graham was beloved in part because his own goodness disposed him to see the best in others, that generosity of spirit incurred a great cost in the case of Richard Nixon. Suspicion came as naturally to Nixon as love came to Graham, and if there were times when Graham made Nixon better, there were also times when Nixon made Graham worse.

Though many clergymen from many faiths passed through the Nixon White House, none came more often or were tied more publicly to the president than Graham. He was thrilled to see his friend build his presidency around spiritual themes, and thought it a basic duty, as both citizen and pastor, to help in any way possible. But some crippling combination of modesty and innocence and fascination prevented Graham from seeing what over time became so plain even to some who loved him best: in fact it was Senator Mark Hatfield—who perhaps came closest to Graham's ideal of a politician—who described the danger most clearly. As Nixon's reign was approaching its end and his sins, if not crimes, were becoming more apparent, Hatfield talked to the *Washington Post* about the dynamic he saw between Graham and Nixon.

The American people, Hatfield told the *Post*:

"'See a picture of Billy speaking in a great crusade. Everything is religious in this atmosphere—Billy speaking, Billy praying, Billy reading the Bible. Billy is one of the most admired and respected men in our country. Billy with the Pope, Billy with Madame Nehru, Billy with kings and queens, Billy,' and he lowered his voice, 'with the president.'"

"You begin to think—you say 'Gee Whiz, Billy's speaking at the White House. Billy's a friend of Nixon.'" The next step, Hatfield said, by the logic of civil religion, is for Christians at least to think: "Billy's close to God. Billy's close to Nixon. Therefore God must have ordained Nixon to be President and he's getting his messages through Billy." Other politicians, he added, "are very much aware of this and they want to be pictured with Billy and they want to be on the platform with Billy. It's the political thing to do."

By the time Graham grasped this truth, his image had been battered, his confidence shaken, and his ministry damaged; but the change that came over him as a result may also have helped save all three.

NIXON'S RESURRECTION

In 1962, Richard Nixon was a political corpse. After his disastrous California governor's race he told one interviewer, "I say, categorically, that I have no contemplation at all of being the candidate for anything in 1964, 1966, 1968 or 1972. . . . I have no political base. Anybody who thinks I could be a candidate for anything in any year is off his rocker." He could say it because it was quite true—at least until it became untrue.

Billy Graham, for one, was not convinced that his friend was dead and buried after 1962. "It would be very easy for you to become bitter, to draw up in a shell, and even to exclude those you love most," he wrote to him. "A man's true character is seen in the midst of disappointment and defeat." Graham warned that it would be "the greatest tragedy I can think of for you to turn to drink or any of these other escapisms. . . . Millions of Americans admire you as no other man of our time. You have a tremendous responsibility to live up to the confidence they have placed in you."

Graham went out to see him and they played a round of golf. "He was *so* dejected. I mean he just, his shoulders drooped and he was almost haggard. And I could see he was very discouraged. And I put my arm around him and I said, 'Dick,' I said, 'the American people will call on you again.'"

Fast-forward five years: to hear Nixon tell it, it was Graham who ultimately made him change his mind about his political future. All through 1967, as campaign season approached, Nixon said he had doubts about sinking back into the political swamps. He liked his private life; he had a "loser" image to shake; his mother had just died in September—Graham preached at her funeral, and upon leaving the church Nixon had collapsed in tears in his arms. Another failed campaign would be a disaster for his family. He'd lost some of his taste for combat, and hated the idea of having to be nice to reporters again.

After a long talk with his family on Christmas Day, Nixon left them and headed down to Key Biscayne to pursue his favorite hobby: beach-walking. He called Graham at home and asked if he could fly down to see him. Graham had been sick with pneumonia, so sick that his events had been canceled for the next four months. But he faithfully flew down to meet Nixon, they watched some football together, read the Bible, talked about politics, sports, and God. On New Year's Eve they walked more than a mile down the beach to an old Spanish lighthouse. By the time they were back at the hotel, Graham was weak. And Nixon was still unresolved.

The next day, New Year's Day, Graham was packing to leave. "Billy," Nixon said, "you still haven't told me positively whether I ought to run or not."

And Billy, of course, gave the blessing. "If you don't," he said, "you will always wonder whether you should have run and whether you could have won or not." The problems were worse now than in 1960, he said; Nixon had been denied his chance to lead then, but Providence was offering another chance. "I think it is your destiny to be President."

Or at least that is how Nixon remembered it, not just years later in his memoirs, but a few months later when the campaign was rolling and he was recounting his decision for *Good Housekeeping*. "In the end I decided that if they really wanted me, it would be worth all the hell," he told the magazine. "Billy Graham had a great deal to do with that decision." When his daughter Julie was campaigning in North Carolina she said the same: "I think his family and Billy Graham are the two forces that persuaded him to run," she told reporters.

But Graham was more equivocal; when reporters asked him about the visit, he praised Nixon's experience, but repeated that he was a registered Democrat who voted independently. Even after Nixon triumphed, Graham was not inclined to claim any credit. He told David Frost in 1969 that "I gave him the reasons why I thought any prominent American in whom many people had confidence ought to offer himself at a critical period of history—not specifically him, but any American. Whether that had any influence in his decision or not, I don't really know . . . because he's never told me." In his memoirs Graham flatly denied advising Nixon one way or the other, only promising to pray that God would guide him.

If some part of Nixon was undecided before that December walk with Graham, he had still hired staff and reserved rooms at the Miami Hilton Plaza, planned site of the GOP convention, before its construction was completed. This would not be the last time a walk on the beach with Billy Graham would offer a presidential candidate a mythic setting for a life-changing choice. Graham's power sometimes worked this way, after the fact, sanctifying a decision already made, whether it was Eisenhower deciding to run, or Johnson deciding not to, or, in years to come, George W. Bush mending his wayward ways. Political careers became higher callings, once Graham was there to bless them.

WAR, PEACE, AND POLITICS

Just because Nixon had never really stopped running doesn't explain why the country would welcome him back. To understand his return in 1968, it helps to look past the man to the times—which he made easy, as he set out to run the most unexciting, unemotional campaign possible. Let's all calm down, he seemed to say, enough with the drama, enough clamor, enough crisis. Vote for me and I'll put out the fire, leave you in peace.

Peace was everything, both at home and abroad. Vietnam was certainly the crushing issue of the day, challenging people's basic patriotism: how could one love one's country, honor its soldiers, but have no faith left in the wisdom of their mission? This was a new place to be politically and emotionally, and an awful, unnerving one. The City on a Hill was burning down, American power and goodness both turning to ashes. But no one, in either party, really had control over events; anything they said, any position they took, could lose votes at home or harm peace efforts abroad.

So it was the war at home that mattered, and 1968 was Armageddon, the country shuddering with each new bombing and riot and assassination and assault on everything that had once seemed certain. Inflation mocked the very notion of thrift; the culture viewed traditional values as quaint, even vulgar. The Supreme Court was busy defending freedom, which included protecting children from mandatory prayer in school, and criminals from police misconduct. In New York the murder rate jumped 21 percent in 1968 alone; murder swept away heroes, Bobby Kennedy, Martin Luther King, and the ideals they honored. Students occupied the classrooms they used to study in, or burned them. Inspirational black activists were crowded off the stage by a new generation of leaders appealing to anger, not conscience, and calling for violence as a form of justice. When Stokely Carmichael took over the SNCC, he talked of killing whites who were disrespectful, of street warfare, of a fight to the death.

These events inspired people to ask the kinds of questions Billy Graham had been asking from his pulpit for years. Where was all this violence coming from? Is this Evil, and had it burrowed somehow into the country's soul? His was still a congregation of Scout leaders pledging allegiance and homemakers wrestling with the grocery bill, who flew the flag without irony and spanked their kids when they cussed. They didn't hear many people in Washington, or New York, or Hollywood, speaking their language just now. Nixon would talk about the "quiet voice" of those forgotten Americans, "who did not indulge in violence, those who did not break the law, people who pay their taxes and go to work, who send their children to school, who go to their churches, people who are not haters, people who love this country." He might as well have added that they worshipped God and Billy Graham. During his crusades Graham clasped the same audience: "They are not out carrying placards and demonstrating. They are not vocal radicals. They don't believe in taking what they want by violence. But they're out there across the country . . . a great unheard-from group somewhere, both black and white, who are probably going to be heard from loudly at the polls."

Graham went into the 1968 race promising, as ever, neutrality in all things political. He informed the millions on his mailing list that he intended to heed the advice of his "friends Nixon and Johnson" and stay out of politics. He agreed to offer a prayer at both parties' conventions. But where 1964 had been relatively easy—he didn't really know Goldwater and didn't always agree with Johnson—this race was pure temptation. When Nixon's candidacy materialized in 1968, he admitted later, "it muffled those inner monitors that had warned me for years to stay out of partisan politics."

It was in Oregon in May, where Graham was holding a crusade and the candidates were holding a primary, that he first stepped onto the field. By this time you couldn't have a campaign without the columnists keeping a close eye on him. "Will Billy Graham Wield Influence to Help Nixon," asked the headline on Marianne Means's column. The biggest and most enthusiastic crowds in town, she observed, were not for Bobby Kennedy or Nixon fighting for their votes, but in the 20,000-seat coliseum where Graham was fighting for their souls. "Graham will probably get the biggest write-in vote," one local politician observed. One night Senator Hatfield was on the platform with him; within a few weeks Graham would be pushing him for vice president. He introduced Julie Nixon and David Eisenhower in the crusade audience, saying, "There is no American I admire more than Richard Nixon."

Graham told reporters that he was looking for a president who would set a religious example, as Ike and Johnson had. "This country is going through its greatest crisis since the Civil War," he said. "Many people who just don't know how to cast their vote might accept what I have to say." He wanted someone who could calm the waters, a "middle of the road" type. He planned to stay quiet until after the conventions had chosen their nominees. But if either party were to nominate someone he hadn't talked to in depth, he figured he knew enough people that it wouldn't take "me long to find out about the inner life of anybody." And he hoped to have a chance to examine the candidates personally. "There's an inner dependence upon God that I don't think you can detect through the mass media," he said. "That's a private thing, and I'd like to know a candidate had it before making any statement." The reason he felt so comfortable making statements about Nixon, of course, was because he'd had so much time to get to know him so well.

It was only a matter of days before Graham, and the country, had one less candidate to wonder about, and one more victim to mourn. When Bobby Kennedy was assassinated in Los Angeles in the early-morning hours of June 5, Graham declared that he would head to New York for the funeral, "even if I can't get into the church—even if I just stand on the sidewalk and weep for America as Jeremiah wept for Jerusalem." On the day after the funeral he stayed with Johnson at the White House and conducted a private service there for the first family.

Bobby's assassination threw the Democrats into complete turmoil, with Senator Eugene McCarthy rallying the antiwar vote and Vice President

Hubert Humphrey struggling to find his voice; they'd have been glad if Johnson, vowing to stay out of the fray, could chaperone Graham for the rest of the summer and fall, keep him out of trouble. As the Republican convention approached, Johnson's adviser James Rowe wrote to warn him that a group of southern Democrats were nervous: they'd heard that Graham was about to come out publicly for Nixon. "They say he was about to do this in 1960 when Joe Kennedy and Steve Smith talked him out of it," Rowe explained. "There was of course no problem in 1964 because of your close relationship with Graham. . . . I know and understand (and approve) of the rules you are operating under but there must be some way or suggestion you can make on how to prevent Billy Graham from doing this."

Handwritten at the bottom of Rowe's memo were Johnson's prophetic notes: "I can't control him." Nor, given Johnson's own doubts about Humphrey, did he necessarily want to try.

The Inner Sanctum

And so in the first week of August Graham was off to Miami Beach for the Republican convention. From his command post on the top five floors of the Hilton, Nixon led his army of short-haired men, serious, passionless, a group in no way resembling Goldwater's fervent crusaders four years ago or McCarthy's earnest disciples now. If these delegates were divided over Vietnam or civil rights, they would keep it to themselves.

Nixon could be fairly confident that neither Ronald Reagan nor Nelson Rockefeller nor anyone else had the support to deny him the prize; but just in case he had Graham among his team working the delegates. Congressman James Gardner, who was running for governor of North Carolina, led a key southern delegation; he personally assured Graham that he was strong for Nixon. So when at the last minute he switched and backed Reagan, Nixon's men were stunned. "It's okay to lie to another politician," said one. "It's okay to lie to the press. But you just don't lie to Billy Graham. That's going too far." That fall, in the final campaign against Gardner, North Carolina Democrats took out ads that read, "Would you vote for a man who lied to Billy Graham?" The outcome indicated that the answer was no.

Graham was rumored to have had a hand in picking Nixon's running mate, Spiro Agnew. By this time he was often cast as a kingmaker; columnists

Rowland Evans and Robert Novak had already that summer floated one delicious, if premature, rumor: "Evangelist Billy Graham," they wrote, "a keen judge of political talent, recently transmitted to his friend Richard Nixon an unusual suggestion: Rep. George Bush of Texas for Vice President."

But Graham was merely one of many who was consulted, and ultimately ignored. He and Nixon had dinner at Nixon's New York apartment a few weeks before the convention and talked about running mates. Nixon knew he had to weave his way between the southern conservatives who loved Reagan and the northern liberals who swooned for New York mayor John Lindsay. Graham recalled sitting in front of the fireplace as Nixon floated names. Graham offered Hatfield, a devout evangelical but from the liberal wing of the party. He'd be a loyal deputy, Graham argued. And "he certainly would appeal to the strong Christian vote, Catholic as well as Protestant."

The real veep debate took place on the night Nixon won the nomination; the power brokers on the convention floor were summoned to his suite once the balloting was finished. Goldwater was there, and Dewey and Gerald Ford and Strom Thurmond, about two dozen senators and governors and party chieftains sipping coffee and Cokes. Nixon invited Graham to sit in: "You'll enjoy this," he said. "This will be a little bit of history." The discussion went on past 5 a.m. Graham made one more pitch for Hatfield, who emerged as a finalist. "I believe in his spiritual commitment," Graham said. "I believe that he's a moderate liberal and that you need a balanced ticket because you are considered a conservative. You need the spiritual strength he could bring the country. The country needs it." Recalling the debate after Graham had left, one participant noted that the fact that Hatfield was so "square," didn't smoke or drink or have any apparent vices, was politically fatal. So was his near pacifism, given Nixon's position on the war.

In the morning the Secret Service was told to guard Lindsay, Reagan, Hatfield and Senator Charles Percy. Nixon called Graham, asking that he pray about the choice, which Graham said suited him better than sitting in a smoke-filled room. But in the end Nixon ruled them all out and chose Spiro Agnew, whose great virtue was that since no one knew him, no one hated him. He asked Graham to call Hatfield and break the news. Graham was disappointed. He thought Hatfield would have been a good moral influence. He had no idea how much Nixon would need one.

SEVENTEEN

The Courier

I often talked to both of them; both of them wanted to end the war; but Johnson thought the way to end it was to win it. Nixon wasn't sure he could win it.

—Graham on Vietnam

Richard Nixon was viewed as a man who would use just about anyone for any purpose. But there were limits to how he was willing to use Billy Graham. His recollections in his memoirs about how he always tried to protect Graham's ministry did in fact echo private conversations he had with his closest strategists. How much this was his genuine concern for Graham, how much a desire to maintain the evangelist's usefulness for the future, how much a recognition that there were things Graham couldn't, or wouldn't, do for him anyway, is impossible to know. But he certainly knew that both personally and politically, simply being his friend was the greatest gift Graham could bestow.

On the night Nixon accepted the nomination, he called his speech-writer William Safire to his room in the wee hours. They talked about how Graham could help as the fall campaign got under way. They were especially concerned about George Wallace running a third-party campaign that would drain votes from Nixon in the South. Any way Graham could pitch in there? Safire wanted to know. "No, that would hurt his ministry," Nixon said. "Maybe we could get a thing like 'The Dick Nixon I know' for a magazine, but nothing political, nothing hard." It was as though he imagined a do-over, one more chance to run that gushing *LIFE* story of 1960.

Graham gave the invocation at the Democratic convention in Chicago. He prayed that God would protect the Democratic nominees; he could not have known just how much protection they all would need in the next few days. He said that he felt a pall over the convention, "something that was darker than mere political pessimism."

Graham had already moved on to Pittsburgh to prepare for his next crusade when the protests in the Chicago streets landed on every television screen and front page. "The unreality of Chicago was beyond anything I have ever seen before," he said. "I never thought a president would have to be elected under these circumstances." But he called on reporters to balance their reporting. "It would not be as much of a news story to see 5000 young people carrying prayer books rather than tearing something down. In Chicago, there are millions of decent young people you don't hear about."

Humphrey limped out of Chicago fifteen points behind Nixon and trapped by Johnson. A vice president can't really attack his own administration, but Humphrey couldn't win if he didn't. How could he appease his liberal allies who wanted him to come out flat against the war, without angering Johnson, who said he would be endangering lives if he showed any opposition now?

Nixon meanwhile had left Miami and set out on a clandestine mission all his own. He flew to Johnson's Texas ranch, ostensibly for a national security briefing; but in this conversation he set in motion a strategy in which he would enlist Graham as his unwitting accomplice.

Nixon understood how helpful—or unhelpful—a sitting president can be when his vice president is looking to succeed him, as he had tried with Eisenhower in 1960. He also knew the war haunted Johnson; the desire to end it honorably consumed him. Peace talks were under way in Paris, where the parties were fighting over who got a seat at the table, even what shape the table should be. Johnson was adamant that the United States would not de-escalate without concessions from the North Vietnamese; anything else, he was sure, would send a signal of vulnerability and prolong the fighting rather than shorten it. Johnson had concluded that Humphrey was "weak," disloyal, looking for a way out.

Nixon saw a chance to make a secret deal. At the ranch, he promised that he would not criticize Johnson's conduct of the war, provided that Johnson didn't soften his negotiating position with the North Vietnamese—and thereby help Humphrey earn the mantle of peacemaker. Nixon, Johnson told his national security team afterward, saw things his way: "The GOP may be of more help to us than the Democrats in the next few months."

It was, said presidential historian Robert Dallek, "the prelude to a fall campaign that would produce as much skullduggery and hidden actions as any in American history."

Graham's Private Mission

Labor Day marks the official start of a presidential race: Graham invited both candidates to join him for his Pittsburgh crusade during that first week of September. Humphrey couldn't make it, but gamely sent a telegram expressing his admiration for the evangelist's work and congratulations for the crusade's great success, which Graham read to the audience.

Nixon did not miss the opportunity. On September 8, he and Pat were sitting in the VIP section of a crowd of forty thousand when Graham described their friendship as "one of the most cherished I have ever had." You can really learn a man's character when you play golf with him, he said, and praised Nixon for his "generosity, tremendous constraint of temper and his integrity in totaling his golf score." The crusade would end up being broadcast right before election day—a last-minute addition to Graham's television schedule.

Nixon called the crusade "one of the most moving religious experiences of my life." And Graham's sermon made a strong impression. He shot a memo afterward to his speechwriters: don't just give me quotes or jokes, he told them; give me stories, parables. "If any of you took the trouble to listen to Billy Graham's sermon you can see the effectiveness of the parable technique. With all the brilliant people we have working for us, I think they should be able to sit down, read some books, speeches etc. and get me a few more quotes of this type."

There was a private meeting that day as well, in Graham's room at the Hilton, at which Nixon told him that he had a confidential message he wanted him to deliver to President Johnson. Nixon dictated; Graham took notes. This was a role he liked to play, speaking to the best in people, in this case delivering what he believed to be a noble offer from one man of honor to another. Graham called the White House and asked to see Johnson as soon as possible. "Graham notes he never has asked for an appointment and that this is a matter of 'some importance,'" said Bob Faiss, the assistant who took the call.

Nixon, meanwhile, left Pittsburgh to campaign in North Carolina, where he stopped to pay a visit to Graham's mother, Morrow, in Charlotte. "He's homey and very easy to talk to," Morrow told reporters afterward, wearing a jeweled Nixon pin at her neck. Did he tell her any secrets? they wanted to know. "Well, yes he did," she said. "He said he was going to win in November, but not to tell the press."

Graham went to Washington to meet Johnson in the Oval Office on September 15. He brought his notes to be sure he didn't miss a point.

First, Graham told Johnson, Nixon promised that he "will never embarrass him [President Johnson] after the election. I respect him as a man and as the president. He is the hardest working and most dedicated president in 140 years." Second, Nixon said he wanted a working relationship with him, "and will seek his advice continually." Third, he wanted Johnson to go on special assignments after the election, including overseas. While it was inevitable that he would point out some of the weaknesses and failures of the administration, Nixon promised that it would never reflect on Johnson personally. And when Vietnam was settled, Nixon would give Johnson "a major share of credit—because you . . . deserve it."

Graham recorded that Johnson was "not only appreciative but I sensed he was touched by this gesture on Mr. Nixon's part. It was my private judgment that this might be unprecedented in history between two leaders of the Democratic and Republican parties in these particular circumstances. (!!!)"

Johnson asked Graham to read the points to him again; he took the notes from Graham's hand and tried to read them himself. "Let me give you answers point by point," he said. There was no way Johnson could come out against his own vice president. But "if Mr. Nixon becomes the President-elect," he told Graham, "I will do all in my power to cooperate with him."

Two days later, Graham was preaching at West Point when Nixon called to hear the outcome. Graham reported that the president was "deeply appreciative of his generous gesture." And indeed, Dallek argues in his biography *Flawed Giant*, Nixon's vow did influence Johnson's behavior, at least over the next few weeks. Johnson told Defense Secretary Clark M. Clifford that he doubted Humphrey had the ability to be president. He would have more respect for him, he said, "if he showed he had some balls." He tapped Humphrey's phones, to make sure he stayed in line. When he picked up word that military dictators in Greece were secretly funding Nixon to the tune of half a million dollars, Johnson declined to launch an investigation or leak the news. "Nixon's approach through Graham had, at least for the moment, neutralized LBJ in the campaign," Dallek concluded. It was a measure of the president's ego that he, so wily himself, did not realize how Nixon's courtship of him might be less a measure of respect than a cunning piece of political marksmanship.

Of course, if Johnson missed this, one reason was surely that the message was delivered by Graham, whose sincere belief in Nixon's sincerity made it easier for Johnson to trust them both. Nixon had sent the same message through other intermediaries as well, but Graham was certainly unique as a guided missile.

Nixon's operation was smoothly lethal; Humphrey's was a mess. On the trail with both, Theodore White wrote that "in 1960 correspondents left Nixon to join the Kennedy tour with a sense of returning home from the enemy camp; in 1968, one left the Nixon tour to join the Humphrey tour as if leaving a well-ordered and comfortable mansion for a gypsy encampment."

Among the costs of Nixon sidelining Johnson in September was a bare cupboard: flat broke, the Democratic Party did not run a single national ad for their ticket between the convention and late October. At one point when Humphrey made an appointment to mend fences with Johnson, he arrived late from a campaign rally and the president refused to see him. "That bastard Johnson," Humphrey said. But there was always plenty of free media, since it was Humphrey whom the protesters haunted, shouting him down at rallies, calling him a sellout, and making even sympathizers see him as a victim. Voters don't like to vote for victims.

They like to vote for gods—or at least that's what Nixon's men were saying. His speechwriter Ray Price wrote him a memo about the kind of image he needed to project, a challenge in which Graham was the natural ally. "Politics is much more emotional than it is rational, and this is particularly true of Presidential politics," Price told Nixon. "Potential presidents are measured against an ideal that's a combination of leading man, God, father, hero, pope, king, with maybe just a touch of the avenging furies thrown in. They want him to be larger than life, a living legend, and yet quintessentially human; someone to be held up to their children as a model; Reverence goes where the power is; it's no coincidence that there's such persistent confusion between love and fear in the whole history of man's relationship to his gods. Awe enters into it. . . . Selection of a president has to be an act of faith. . . . This faith isn't achieved by reason. It's achieved by charisma, by a *feeling* of trust."

Hence the immense value of having Graham at his side: if he vouched for Nixon's character, who was to disagree? Some of it was just making sure people knew of their friendship: the attendance at the Pittsburgh crusade, the visit to Graham's mother, the invitation to Graham to sit conspicuously in the audience when Nixon taped his town hall meetings.

Graham's neutrality was transparent, coy. He continued to uphold as his ideal an image of himself as being above partisanship. "I feel my role is that of spiritual advisor to men of all parties," he told *TIME*, "and the moment I start getting involved in partisan politics, it would greatly diminish my ministry." But to other reporters he admitted, "Naturally my convictions and sympathies are strong this year and it will be difficult to keep quiet when I feel so deeply!" He frequently noted that people were looking for "change," as in his "fellow citizens were looking for a change in the moral and spiritual direction of the nation and that the candidates for president should be aware of that fact." When outgoing UN ambassador George Ball attacked Nixon's integrity, Graham rose to his defense: "There's nothing 'tricky' about him," he declared. "I've known Richard Nixon intimately for 20 years. I can testify that he is a man of high moral principles. I do not intend publicly to endorse any political candidate as some clergymen are doing, but I maintain the right to help put the record straight when a friend is being smeared."

As October crackled along the race was tightening; by the middle of the month Humphrey had closed to within five points. The vice president had finally found a way to present himself as what he always was, a man desperate to make peace. He announced in Salt Lake City that he would risk a complete bombing halt and judge how the North Vietnamese reacted; maybe the gesture would help bring all sides to the table. Very soon he was showing a new energy. The heckling faded, the money flowed, even McCarthy's legions came on board. It was not a huge policy shift; but it was enough, especially since by now Johnson had reason to believe that he had been conned.

Among the characters Johnson was watching closely during that season was a woman known as the Dragon Lady, Anna Chennault, a legendary China lobby doyenne and Nixon fund-raiser. Johnson learned that she had been conducting her own secret diplomacy on Nixon's behalf, aimed at sabotaging the peace talks long enough to get Nixon elected. Johnson was closing in on a diplomatic breakthrough; Nixon, ever artful, announced that he thought there was no truth to the rumors that Johnson was desperately manipulating events abroad to help Humphrey in the home-stretch. On the Thursday evening before the election, Johnson savored the moment he had been waiting for all these months of crucifixion as a warmonger. He announced a complete bombing halt of North Vietnam, since an agreement had been struck that would allow for "productive, serious and intensive negotiations."

Humphrey's support immediately jumped; the doves flew home. In Nixonland they could practically feel the race slipping away. Pollster Lou Harris's last survey, out the day before the election, had Humphrey up by three points. He called it the wildest climax he'd ever seen.

The day after Johnson's triumphant speech, the *Dallas Times Herald* ran an exclusive interview: Billy Graham was voting by absentee ballot for Nixon. Did he consider an actual endorsement? "He was prepared to do it if necessary," said Harry Dent, the Baptist deacon who was organizing the South for Nixon. Consultant John Maddox called Graham "the second most revered man in the South among adult voters." Once the wires reported Graham's absentee vote, "that was all I needed," said Dent. "I used it in our TV commercials right to the end."

But the devastating blow to Humphrey came the next day, the Saturday before election day, as the aborning visions of peace just as suddenly collapsed. Was this Chennault's handiwork bearing fruit, by convincing the South Vietnamese they would get a better deal if Nixon were in the White House? By Saturday the headlines yanked people back to earth. "Saigon Opposes Paris Talk Plans, Says It Can't Attend Next Week," declared the *New York Times*.

It is almost impossible to imagine an election taking place amid such confusion. No one knew if peace was at hand or not, if Johnson, by now denied the benefit of the doubt on matters of war, had been playing games by declaring that all the parties had agreed to negotiate—or was it the South Vietnamese who were playing games? Alerted to the reports of possible Republican interference, Humphrey could have pulled back the curtain; a *Christian Science Monitor* reporter in Saigon was saying that it was guidance from the Nixon camp that had led the South Vietnamese to balk. Intelligence from a bug planted in the South Vietnamese presidential palace suggested the same thing.

Hearing of Johnson's rage, Nixon called him personally and denied having anything to do with Chennault's efforts. And such was Humphrey's nature that he could not quite believe Nixon himself could have possibly authorized what amounted to treason. If Nixon won but then came under suspicion of having broken the law, he feared, the country would be in even deeper trouble.

Everyone knew it would be close. Nixon invited Graham to be his guest at the Waldorf on election night, but Graham declined; this would be a very partisan, and emotional, night. But he did tell Nixon, "If you lose I will be ready to come over and have a prayer with you."

Nixon finally carried the day, winning almost as narrowly as he had lost the last time. Humphrey lost by .01 percent of the vote. Nixon did not win a mandate; he did not even win a majority: at 43.4 percent his margin was less than any president's since Woodrow Wilson in 1912. But he had won the presidency. And that was all that counted.

The next morning Nixon called Graham and asked if he would come have a prayer before he went down to meet with reporters. In the thirty-fifth-floor Waldorf suite, freshly pressed and shaven men and women in demure dresses sipped coffee and tea. Graham greeted them with a grin. "We did it," he said, as he headed into Nixon's room. He viewed this summons to prayer as a real breakthrough for a reserved Quaker. Graham, Pat, Dick, and the girls stood in a circle holding hands as Graham gave thanks for "God's plan for the country" and the spiritual heritage of Nixon's mother.

After the election Graham was in Toronto and called his old friend Charles Templeton, to see if they could have dinner. Templeton listened as Graham talked about his excitement at what lay ahead. "Billy has always been given to enthusiasms—as have I—but this was a greater one than usual," Templeton recalled. Graham talked about how well prepared Nixon was, what a good man he was, and eventually Templeton grew irritated, and a bit sad. "I wanted to take issue with some of his assertions but didn't want to cool his zeal or fall into confrontation. It was obvious as the evening wore on that the years had taken us to almost diametrically opposed viewpoints on many things." The evening ended early and Templeton drove Graham back to his hotel downtown.

Years later, Templeton would write about how they had traveled such different roads. "I think Billy is what he has to be. I disagree with him profoundly on his view of Christianity. . . . But there is no feigning in him: he believes what he believes with an invincible innocence. He is the only mass evangelist I would trust. And I miss him."

EIGHTEEN

White House of Worship

After Nixon was elected, he asked me to come and see him. He said, "Billy, what job do you want? I'll appoint you to any ambassadorship if you want it." I said, "Mr. President. I don't want anything." I said, "God called me to preach and I'm never gonna do anything but that." That's what I told him.
—Graham on political temptation

Nixon and Graham shared a pulpit on Inauguration Day 1969, the closest America ever comes to a national church service. Those trying to promote a sense of the sacred that January day had to contend with the protesters in macabre masks spitting obscenities, the bulletproof glass and armored trucks and anxious agents with machine guns, a cold north wind and a sky the color of cement. The Religious Observance Committee distributed ten thousand specially printed cards, to be put in store windows and public buildings, showing hands clasped: "Thanksgiving, blessing, rededication, guidance and [Nixon's campaign slogan] Forward Together." The ceremony included blessings from no fewer than five different ministers, led by Billy Graham, which according to a *Washington Post* columnist made Nixon "the most publicly prayed-over new President in the history of the republic."

Three days before, Nixon's chief of staff, Bob Haldeman, began to keep a diary, determined to create a raw record of a White House in action unlike any historians had ever seen. In that, he was completely successful.

He recorded the moment when Richard and Pat Nixon appeared at the top of the Capitol steps and the fanfare sounded. "Expression on his face was unforgettable, this was the time!" Haldeman wrote. "He had arrived, he was in full command, someone said he felt he saw rays coming from his eyes."

To say nothing of Graham himself: James Reston of the *New York Times* described Graham's long invocation as sounding like "almost a political document," his own inaugural address. The *Christian Century*, teeth bared, called it a "raucous harangue." Describing America as "a nation under God," Graham declared that "morality and faith are the pillars of our society," but they were being eroded by materialism and permissiveness. "O God, our new President needs Thee as no man ever needed Thee in leading a people! . . . In the lonely moments of decision grant him an uncompromising courage to do what is morally right." As for the country, "Help us this day to turn from our sins and to turn by simple faith to the One who said, 'Ye must be born again.'" He offered the prayer in the name of "the Prince of Peace who shed His blood on the Cross that men might have eternal life." This ensured that Nixon's inaugural prayer was, among other things, an evangelical call for the nation to come to Jesus for salvation. No less than for the individual, repentance and conversion were, in Graham's eyes, the necessary path for a nation as well.

Sworn in on two family Bibles, Nixon offered a sermon of his own. He urged that Americans "build a great cathedral of the spirit—each of us raising it one stone at a time, as he reaches out to his neighbor, helping, caring, doing." And he would lay his own foundation stone that very week, as he instituted a new tradition that Graham was the first to celebrate, literally and figuratively: the White House church service. This institution, which featured Graham as First Preacher, would take Eisenhower's civil religion to new heights—and the privately cynical use of religion to new depths.

Shortly after the election Graham had explained why Nixon seldom went to church: "He was always afraid that people would misinterpret his going to church as using religion to gain political strength." But now that he was elected he would need all the divine help he could get. Nixon had toyed with the idea of holding silent Friends meetings, Graham said, but the nearest meeting house, where Herbert Hoover had worshipped, was strongly antiwar, and given the open-mike structure of a Quaker meeting, there was no telling what would have been said in those days in the presence of the president. Besides, Nixon's temperament and the temperature of the times argued for something a little more contained. "In those years President Nixon, rightly or wrongly, thought that church was so important that you should emphasize it by having it in the White House," explained Barbara Bush, whose husband Nixon appointed as UN ambassador. "And of course it also, in all honesty, kept an awful lot of people from going to an awful lot of trouble. If you had church at the White House you didn't have to have the church sniffed and security all checked and eighty people have to do all that when the president moves."

The first service was held on Nixon's first Sunday in office, with Graham as the preacher. Nixon's aides Dwight Chapin and John Ehrlichman picked Graham's brain for how the service should work: Nixon would preside like a master of ceremonies, welcome the congregation, introduce the preacher, praise the visiting choir. So which preachers should they invite, should there be a denominational quota? Graham sent them a list that included Norman Vincent Peale, Graham's brother-in-law and surrogate Leighton Ford, his father-in-law L. Nelson Bell, National Council of Churches head Dr. R. H. Edwin Espy, *Christianity Today* editor Harold Lindsell, several prominent black preachers, and prominent Christian sports figures like Dallas Cowboys coach Tom Landry.

Having prayed at the inaugural and due to speak at the National Prayer Breakfast in a few days, Graham worried that preaching the first service would be pushing his involvement too far; but Nixon insisted. Graham brought Bev Shea with him to sing for the two hundred guests from the cabinet and staff. "I've never heard of anything like it happening here before," White House curator James Ketcham told *TIME*, which added that "Billy Graham has come on like a White House chaplain-in-residence." Before the service Billy and Ruth were in the private quarters with Nixon. "I'll never forget the President sitting down on the spur of the moment at an old, battered Steinway that they had there," Graham recalled years later, "playing the old hymn, 'He Will Hold Me Fast, for My Saviour Loves Me.' He will hold me fast."

There was nothing "political" about any of this, Graham insisted at the time. The president was just "trying mainly to pursue his religious commitment without becoming the center of attention at regular church service and a distraction to others in the congregation." Nixon's communications chief Herb Klein recalled it the same way: "We'd have cabinet officers, it was a social thing in many ways. And an opportunity to worship. It was never political in any aspect of the sermons or the service." Within weeks of those first services, however, unnamed Protestant clerics were telling the *New York Times* that "the president is trying to have God on his own terms." This brought rebuttals from both Peale and Graham. "The fact is that the apostles held divine services in their homes for more than a century before there were any churches," Graham argued. "So history and precedent would seem to be entirely on the side of the president." He suggested that critics were worried about the larger trend toward people worshipping at home, and were afraid of losing their congregations. "I know the President well enough to be entirely sure that the idea of having God on his own terms would never have occurred to him."

In this as in so many things, however, the memos and memories of the Nixon administration tell another story, a tale of two White Houses, one upright and earnest and staffed by good men like Klein, whom *TIME* once described as "a considerable chunk of Richard Nixon's better nature," the other subterranean and malignant. "Sure, we used the prayer breakfasts and church services for political ends," Nixon chief counsel Charles Colson said. "I was part of doing that." Whatever else they were, the services were a great opportunity for arm-twisting, fund-raising, loyalty-testing. Haldeman sent one of his action memos to Colson, passing along Nixon's request "that you develop a list of rich people with strong religious interest to be invited to the White House Church services." This would include top executives from AT&T, General Motors, PepsiCo, and many others. Another time Haldeman complained to his aide Alexander Butterfield about the guest list: "It isn't going to do one bit of good to have a member of a regulatory agency at the Church service or any other function," he argued. "If they are to be invited, please limit the invitations to the Chairman or to an appointee we were working on for a specific purpose." When a speechwriter praised Nixon's performances at two prayer breakfasts that very first week in office, he laughed it off: he'd just given them some "church stuff," he said. It was that side of him that inspired Norman Mailer to describe Nixon as "a church usher, of the variety who would twist a boy's ear after removing him from church."

Pastors who volunteered their services didn't get very far; but one Baptist preacher whose twin brother was running for governor in South Carolina was invited, and both brothers were photographed with Nixon on the White House steps afterward. The services were a perfect market-place for political favors: one candidate for the presidency of the Southern Baptist Convention should be invited, a memo urged, since that "would aid greatly in his campaign for this office, and if elected, Colson feels that [he] would be quite helpful to the President in 1972." Denominations varied but the theology was consistent: the White House generally picked preachers who, like Graham, focused on individual salvation more than social reform. Some who were invited declined; others who came knew to pull their punches, or were reminded in notes from White House staff members not to step out of line. One Minneapolis Lutheran, wrote *New York Times* religion editor Edward Fiske, had planned a sermon called "Let's Have More Radicals." He wound up preaching on "The Great Adventure" of the moon landing.

That accommodating impulse fed the horror felt by Nixon's and Graham's critics. Private chapels were the province of princes, who sought to equate their role with God's will; they had no place in a democracy, where the muscular faith of a diverse people was an essential check and balance on secular ambitions. "It's wonderful what a simple White House invitation will do to dull the critical faculties," argued Niebuhr in a lacerating essay, "The King's Chapel and the King's Court," published in the summer of 1969. Suggesting that all the country's problems were essentially spiritual, critics argued, simply gave the rich an excuse to ignore the poor, with a content-free, unchallenging, ratifying faith. It was as though the quiet concerns raised during the 1950s about complacent public religion had now ripened into a full rebellion. Because now the stakes were so much higher: not what pledge Americans say when they face the flag, but what wars they fight, what laws they make, what definition of justice they embrace.

Graham might have been on stronger ground promoting the White House worship services had they reflected his consistent desire to bring the gospel straight into the Oval Office. But the services were so liturgically casual that when rabbis were invited to preside they stood comfortably by during the singing of the Doxology. It was a faith, Nicholas von Hoffman observed in the *Washington Post*, that featured "an emasculated, non-denominational God, the state divinity of diffuse goodwill whose blessings are invoked at all important banquets and awards ceremonies by one priest, one minister and one rabbi."

Despite the attacks, Graham had few qualms about this aspect of his ministry. It was not just the idea of the nation's leaders setting an example by giving worship a central place in their lives. By now he had come to see the job of the president as too great a burden for any man to bear alone. "I've been fairly close to two or three presidents," he said in 1972, "so I know something of what they feel, and it's just really beyond a man to deal with."

"Graham was without question the principal spiritual influence on him," Charles Colson said. "He told me a couple of times that Nixon prayed like a man who believed his prayers." Except that Graham had seldom heard Nixon pray himself, other than grace at mealtime. Herb Klein described a unique dynamic between the two men during the first term. Graham, Klein said, "never went in with an agenda but to pray with the president and be helpful to him. I think Graham gave him a lot of personal comfort. He could talk about a lot of things with him without the president feeling there was a political aspect. And Nixon had no fear of reading about it in the *Washington Post*." The president could run ideas past Graham, Klein said, hear how they sounded without necessarily planning to carry them out, but feel better just for having talked them through. It suggested that there was indeed a pastoral element to the private conversations between the two men. Haldeman tried to enlist Graham occasionally in a pastoral role. After an especially grueling stretch, he worried that the president was going off the rails, pushing himself too hard. He tried to get him to take a break, but with no luck. "I talked to both Bebe [Rebozo] and Billy Graham and they said they'd work on him," he wrote in his diary, "but there's been no visible result to date."

Though he always characterized his dealings with Nixon as purely personal and spiritual, Graham occasionally used his access to pursue his own concerns. He received literally thousands of requests for some intervention or another, for jobs, pardons, for help getting a relative out of Russia. He called the White House just a few weeks into the first term, alarmed at news that young men working full-time for Campus Crusade for Christ were being drafted, rather than exempted like other clergy. Memos circulated in the West Wing recommending that they replace uncooperative members of the Review Board and instruct the new, more loyal members that Campus Crusade members should be treated like ordained clergy—especially since they were a rare good influence on many campuses, "to offset the bad influences now prevailing on many campuses."

Another time Graham asked for help penetrating the deep secular heart of French society. "I appreciate your willingness to try to arrange the appointment with Mr. Pompidou," he wrote to Dwight Chapin about the new French president. He had heard from French religious leaders that the time for revival was ripe, and thought maybe a meeting with Pompidou would create an opportunity.

After one long meeting between Graham and Nixon in the Oval Office, Haldeman wrote to Ehrlichman that "Billy Graham raised with the president today the point that postal rates for religious publications are being increased 400% while postal rates for poronography [*sic*] are only being increased 25%. Needless to say, the President was horrified . . . and wants to know what we are doing about it."

Certainly Graham's most ambitious initiative came during that first spring, when during a trip to the Far East he met for three days in Bangkok with his missionary contacts and produced his Confidential Missionary Plan for Ending the Vietnam War. In advance of the meeting the missionaries met nearly a dozen times with President Thieu and his government and received a full military briefing from Admiral John McCain, the U.S. commander in chief in the Pacific. They were generally hawks who had supported the war but felt the current strategy was a mess. The South Vietnamese were very pro-U.S., the missionaries argued, but terrified of being sold out at the Paris peace talks. American troop morale was falling; 40 percent were on drugs. The financial waste and corruption were breathtaking, like a poison: "We have the 'crud' of American society in these business firms," the missionaries said.

American policy was all wrong, they argued. Their advice matched closely what Nixon would unveil in November as "Vietnamization": not the quick withdrawal many Americans hoped for, but a process of turning responsibility for the fighting over to the South Vietnamese with much more discreet U.S. help, using Special Forces and guerrilla tactics more suited to the fight. They also suggested that the local television be used for propaganda, not showing American movies. In closing, Graham shared their argument: "The communists are desperately afraid of a well-armed South Vietnamese military power with an emphasis on guerilla warfare using Oriental methods," he wrote. "They look upon Americans as inferior. They look upon the other Vietnamese and Orientals as equals." Over the years, critics charged Graham with being too passive a bystander, having no idea he had weighed in with very specific policy recommendations for getting the United States out, only not ones his critics would have favored.

These efforts were innocent enough; but there were occasions when Graham's good intentions were easily twisted to other purposes. Graham was intent on opening lines between the White House and black clergy whom he saw as a vital positive force in their communities; Nixon, however, saw a chance to split the black vote. After Graham brought a group of prominent black pastors to meet with Nixon at the White House, Haldeman told Len Garment that Nixon was very eager to follow up on the meeting. "He feels, as does Graham, that this may be our best chance to make inroads into the Negro community."

Nixon was not at all satisfied with the White House's response. More than a month after the ministers' visit, Haldeman sent a confidential memo to Ehrlichman, saying that the president was annoyed. "He wants to see at least ONE of their projects approved and underway even if it means that the staff at OEO have to take up a collection from their own pockets to do it. He would like [director of the Office of Economic Opportunity Donald] Rumsfeld to get one of these projects cleared and done tomorrow. He points out that you can always find a way to do things for the people on the other side and that just for once he'd like to see us find a way to do something right for the people on our side."

Thanks to the White House intervention, the roadblocks came down and some of the projects received funding. Looking back, Graham believed he was building bridges: "I was aware of the risk at all times, political risk," he said. But what he was aware of and what was actually happening were often two very different things.

And there were times when Graham was offering more earthly advice and assistance. As he had with all the previous presidents, he guided the White House on how to handle conservative sensibilities. He told the *New York Times* that Nixon had not consulted him on the sensitive appointment of Henry Cabot Lodge as special envoy to the Vatican; this glossed over the question of whether Graham had weighed in anyway. Ten days earlier, Graham had privately warned Chapin that Southern Baptists were furious. He urged that Nixon invite SBC president Carl Bates to speak at a White House service. "Dr. Bates is conservative both theologically and politically," Graham advised, "and wields tremendous influence in religious circles."

THE PRESIDENT'S EYES AND EARS

Colson understood how Nixon's personal interest in Graham overlapped with a political one. "He had a very real affection for Billy," Colson said. But he was drawn to insights that ranged well past the spiritual. Nixon preferred southern Democrats to most Republicans, and had a special respect for his two favorites of this species, Graham and Connally, whom he viewed as "the best man in the country." He would instruct Haldeman to make sure to call both men at least every week or two to take their temperature, hear what was on their minds, and make sure they had the White House talking points. During his very first staff meeting, Nixon warned his team about getting trapped in the bubble: "The White House provides almost total isolation from the real world," he told them, so they needed to be careful of paying too much attention to what columnists were writing and not enough to "what moves and concerns the average guy."

Nixon saw in Graham the skill set of a top politician: he had, as Nixon told Graham's admiring biographer John Pollock, great administrative ability, decisiveness, a wide understanding of foreign affairs, the ability to absorb documents rapidly, near photographic memory, and where he was weak, the willingness to draw on the advice of others. "I could tell in my conversations with him," Nixon went on, "that he is a great student of history, and consequently he was able to evaluate current events with rare perspective and insight. This is one of the reasons his prediction of political trends usually proved to be strikingly accurate."

Hostile as he was to the press and elites, Nixon was constantly gathering information about what *TIME* in 1970 called "the mood of the majority." "He has gauged the popular feeling on inflation, the war and other issues with a sure instinct that has led some to wonder where he gets his information on the country's moods," the magazine observed, and quoted a Nixon aide observing that "every visitor to his office, every guest at his table is bringing in information on what the country is concerned about. When he talks to a business friend on the phone or plays golf with Billy Graham, he's finding out what people are thinking."

That was indeed where Graham came in. Graham "knew what was going on around the country . . . Nixon liked that," Colson said. "He liked the fact that Billy was in touch with groups that others were not . . . so they clicked. When Billy Graham called, his calls got through." Nixon "tended to reduce everything to a sociological examination. When he evaluated a religious leader, he wasn't looking at what they were saying, but how they were positioning themselves publicly," Colson said. Long before political operatives were paying close attention to religious trends, Nixon was keeping track. When he saw a Gallup poll in the spring of 1970 that showed a decline in religious activity and interest, he wanted Graham's reaction. Graham said he thought this was the backlash to the social activism in the main line. "[Seventy-two percent] of the membership of places of worship do not agree with their clergy when they become social activists." People, especially the young, wanted to hear about God, not man, Graham argued. "They want nurture for their spiritual welfare, not guidance as to what political or social posture they ought to assume." Plus, too many churches were locked into too formal a style, in music and liturgy. Young people were much more attracted to the gospel now than when he was a child, he said. They were fascinated by Jesus.

Graham was excited by the possibilities for revival; Nixon by the possibilities for power. The president saw how different voting blocs— ethnic urban Catholics, conservative Southern Baptists, devout black Americans—were defined by their religious beliefs, and how some traditionally Democratic constituencies were open to a Republican with the right social message, on issues newly resonant like school prayer and the strength of the family. Nixon was among the first to spot the power of the evangelical vote, which was one of the reasons why he installed Graham in so central a place in his White House. "The evangelical vote was the key to the southern strategy," Colson told William Martin, "so he began to invite evangelical leaders in. And one of my jobs in the White House was to romance religious leaders. We would bring [religious leaders] into the White House and they would be dazzled by the aura of the Oval Office, and I found them to be about the most pliable of any of the special interest groups that we worked with."

Eager as he was to enlist Nixon in the cause of revival, Graham was all but blind to any parallel agenda from the White House—and never more so than on the one occasion when a sitting president came and spoke at a Graham crusade.

NINETEEN

Summons for the Silent Majority

I was aware of the risk at all times, political risk.
—Graham on proximity to power

Nixon needed Graham's help in a much more public way in the spring of 1970. It had been a season of random violence and political fury in the streets. In March the radical Weathermen plotted to blow up an officers' dance at Fort Dix in what the conspirators intended to be "the most horrific hit that the United States government had ever suffered on its territory." Instead three people died when a brownstone in New York's West Village exploded; the Weathermen's bombmaking factory was in the basement.

Campuses everywhere were steaming with protests against the war. On April 29, Nixon called Graham at home in Montreat at one in the morning, on "a personal matter." He was going to be making a major speech the next night, he said, though he didn't get into specifics. "All I knew was that it would be a tough speech," Graham said, "and aimed at saving American lives."

The next night Nixon went on television to announce that the United States had invaded Cambodia—a neutral country he had been secretly bombing for a year—to root out North Vietnamese camps and break enemy supply lines. Rather than portray this as a regrettable but necessary move to protect U.S. troops, he was all righteous fervor. "If, when the chips are down," he said, "the world's most powerful nation, the United States of America, acts like a pitiful helpless giant, the forces of totalitarianism and anarchy will threaten free nations and institutions throughout the world. It is not our power but our will and character that is being tested tonight."

Such a sudden and defiant escalation of a war people had hoped would be over by now triggered a revolt among students, inspiring Nixon the next day to denounce "these bums blowing up campuses." But it was not just the radicals in a furor; kids who had never picked up a rock in their lives were now inflamed, and many professors and parents as well. When National Guardsmen shot and killed four unarmed students at Kent State University, virtually the entire system of higher education shuddered and stopped. Colleges from Yale to Berkeley shut down in a massive student strike; Democrats and editorial pages denounced Nixon's move; there was dissent within his cabinet; 250 State Department employees, including fifty Foreign Service Officers, signed a statement of protest; and some Peace Corps employees seized their building and flew a Viet Cong flag from it. The stock market had its worst week in forty years. "The very fabric of government," Henry Kissinger wrote, "was falling apart."

At that moment Nixon needed both Graham's private reassurance and public support; in the days to come he would call again. "He's very disturbed," Haldeman said of Nixon after the campus shootings. "Afraid his decision set it off . . . talked a lot about how we can get through to the students, turn this stuff off. . . . He's out there on a tough limb, and knows it."

Nixon went on television on the night of May 8 to defend the invasion as furthering the students' goal of peace. Afterward he was so troubled he couldn't sleep; nearly one hundred thousand protesters had converged on the White House that day, and there was talk of placing machine guns on the White House lawn. There were demonstrations all over the capital that night; students kept vigil at the Lincoln Memorial. Nixon called his daughter Tricia, called Haldeman seven times, Kissinger eight times. He called William Safire, Bebe Rebozo, Pat Moynihan, Thomas Dewey, Nelson Rockefeller . . . and Billy Graham. Kissinger thought the president was on the edge of a breakdown. At dawn Nixon set off with a clutch of Secret Service agents to the Lincoln Memorial and talked to the surprised and sleepy students there. "I know you want to get the war over," he said. "Sure you came here to demonstrate and shout your slogans on the ellipse. That's all right. Just keep it peaceful. Have a good time in Washington, and don't go away bitter."

Even before the uproar his team had been talking about his loss of momentum and leadership in the public eye. The image makers like Klein, Ron Ziegler, and Ehrlichman all saw a serious problem; but it was all a matter of theater: "They argue for more public presidential presentation, press conferences, speeches, review trips," Haldeman recorded in his diary, "demonstrate that P [the president] cares and is interested and will *try* to do something. Whole thrust is on need for appearance, not substance."

Nixon told his staff that he wanted to try an idea Graham had for a big pro-America rally, maybe for the Fourth of July. He thought they were all still too timid about mobilizing their Silent Majority. Nixon felt that "he should probably go out into country and draw crowds and show popular enthusiasm." It was easier to believe that the problem was one of slanted press coverage rather than broad public repudiation; he and Graham talked about this by phone, and afterward Nixon sent Haldeman a memo. Graham, he said, had observed how "CBS in its coverage of the [pro-administration] construction workers march gave approximately a minute of time to the 150,000 who demonstrated in New York and two to three minutes to the 1,000 left wing lawyers who came to Washington. The purpose of this memo is simply to be sure that you jog our watchdog group to see whether they needle CBS a bit for unbalanced coverage."

Above all Nixon had to do something about the roiling campuses—so it was irresistible when an opportunity presented itself. Graham was holding a crusade in the football stadium at the University of Tennessee in Knoxville, and invited Nixon not just to attend, as Johnson had in Houston in 1965, but to speak. It would be a chance for him to appear on a campus before tens of thousands of students—but friendly ones, in a friendly setting, in his first appearance outside the White House since the invasion. In fact it turned out to be the largest public meeting in the history of the state.

And so Nixon and his entourage flew down to Tennessee, and the president joined Graham on the platform. "I'm for change," Graham said in introducing Nixon to the congregation of eighty-eight thousand, "but the Bible teaches us to obey authority."

"Perhaps," Nixon declared, "America needs to know something about America's youth, and perhaps America's youth needs to know something about America." Dialing back now his remarks about student "bums," he waxed conciliatory. "I am proud to say that the great majority of America's young people do not approve of violence. The great majority do approve, as I do, of dissent."

People sat in the aisles and on the hills around the stadium. Several hundred demonstrators speckled the crowd, some with signs reading

"Thou Shalt Not Kill." Some shouted obscenities, one waved a Viet Cong flag, while others knelt on the field in memory of the war dead. One young man, "dressed in a Christ-like costume," according to the *New York Times*, was extracted from a group of demonstrators, taken to a passageway under the stadium, beaten by a policeman, and then arrested for disturbing a religious service.

But by and large the antiwar chants were buried by the cheers, and police hustled the protest ringleaders away. *TIME* pronounced it one of Nixon's more effective speeches, and even more so when it was televised later with the protests excised. As for the spiritual harvest, several dozen of the demonstrators responded to Graham's invitation, some to make mischief, some because they were genuinely moved; one even went on to become a minister.

When it was his turn, Graham referred to the agonizing decisions a president faces. "All Americans may not agree with the decision a president makes," he said, "but he is *our* president." When the offering plate was passed, Nixon had no money; Graham slipped him some bills, unseen. Four months later, Nixon sent a note, and repayment: "A number of presidents have looked to you for spiritual sustenance," he wrote, "but I suspect I was the first to hit you for a loan. . . . I only wish that all the money problems that confront me could be handled that efficiently."

Graham may have seen himself as a good and faithful servant; but the political sensors were all sounding that day, in part because among those present in Nixon's delegation was William Brock, the Republican challenger in a fierce fight to unseat the incumbent antiwar Democratic senator Al Gore Sr. Graham denied that the event was in any way like a political rally, in accordance with his conviction that presidents were not politicians anymore. "This is not a presidential election year. He is the President of all the people," he insisted. "There were no political implications. If I thought there were I would not have invited him." White House spokesman Ron Ziegler explained that Senator Gore had not been invited because he was not from "East Tennessee." Senator Gore went on to lose his race. Many years later his son was serving as vice president, and Graham told Al Gore Jr. he was sorry about the whole thing.

When it was over the Grahams drove with Nixon back to Air Force One in a long black bulletproof limo. Nixon left orders for the limousine to take the Grahams back to their hotel. Ruth recalled feeling "ridiculous" as they drove through town with a motorcycle escort, lights flashing.

She was feeling let down and admitted later that she'd had mixed feelings about the whole thing—especially after the president failed to give a spiritual message. "I think to have [presidents] come and sit in the audience is one thing," she told her biographer Patricia Cornwell. "To have them speak from the platform is another." Graham himself later agreed that "his remarks were not as forthright a witness for Christ as I had wished for, but I rationalized that he was extremely tired."

But Nixon's men couldn't have been more pleased. Kissinger, who had also attended, called Graham from San Clemente to tell him how glad Nixon was to have been there. "It was a good forum for the President," said Harry Dent, at that point a special counsel to Nixon and a key political adviser. "Billy is a good man to know. Many members of Congress would like to be associated with a man who has such a strong following."

HONOR AMERICA DAY

The next step was more ambitious by far, a revival of a whole other kind. This was to be a revival of hope, a celebration designed for those who saw the need for reform but not revolution. Graham, like Nixon, felt that moderate voices weren't being heard amid the shelling of the antiwar left and the hyperpatriot right. "We all know there's a need for change in the educational system, in social justice. We shouldn't have ghettoes in modern America," Graham said. But change had to come by working within the system, or else the United States risked anarchy, and worse. "If we destroy the system, a dictator is going to rise—either a right winger or a left winger."

The flag itself had become an argument: do you fly it or burn it, patch your pants with it? If the sight of burning villages inflamed the protesters, burning flags inflamed the Silent Majority. Graham wanted to reclaim the term "patriotism" from the far right, for he understood that there were many ways to express one's love of country: "I don't guess anybody loves the flag more than some of the people that are against the war," he told the *New York Times*.

Honor America Day was the entire era in gaudy miniature. It was born of a conversation between Graham and *Reader's Digest* president Hobart Lewis, and staged by Disney as an apolitical family picnic and national birthday party on the Washington Mall. Graham would handle the morning's worship service, Bob Hope the evening entertainment. "Let's keep it away from the war," Graham told Hope. "This is not pro-war or anti-war." This was to be a day of respite from rage. Nor was it only white evangelical Protestantism on parade: Bishop Fulton Sheen, Rabbi Marc Tanenbaum, and the prominent black pastor Dr. E. V. Hill of Mt. Zion Baptist Church in Los Angeles took part as well. "Only atheists and agnostics were not invited to participate in the service," Graham said, "because they don't believe in God." Johnson and Truman were both sponsors, as were the Republican and Democratic party chairs. If the event became partisan, Graham warned, he would pull out.

To those who charged that the whole thing was staged by Nixon's friends to wrap the war and the White House in a holy patriotic haze, Graham insisted that "this is not a political event. Let's sing a little, let's wave the flag, let's rejoice in all that's best in our country. We know America has its faults. But there are good things about America. It has not gone to the dogs. Let's be happy on our birthday."

Chapin sketched the plans for Haldeman, who scribbled in the margins, "All this is excellent!" but added that they need more "professional press/publicity work" and "some real, tough, nitty gritty crowd building. Most of all, we need a solid *cornball* program developer." Walter Smyth, Graham's director of planning, had decamped to Washington full-time; his team would use its vaunted mailing list to help build attendance, contacting churches up and down the eastern seaboard. Graham promoted the event on his *Hour of Decision* broadcasts and worked especially hard to get black churches involved.

On the night before, July 3, Graham did as Nixon had done a few weeks back; he went to the Mall and visited with several hundred kids camped around the Washington Monument. They offered to share their pot; he declined. They flashed a peace sign; he offered an index finger, the symbol for Christ as the One Way.

When the ninety-degree day dawned, people came by the thousands, lugging baskets and thermoses, flags and blankets and Bibles. "They gathered in front of the Lincoln Memorial, where so many others have assembled in protest," noted *TIME*, "to bear witness that it was their country too, a country more right than wrong."

The crowd for the worship service was not as big as organizers had hoped—maybe fifteen thousand—but the networks still preempted their regular programming. Pat Boone sang the national anthem, Apollo astronaut Frank Borman gave a prayer, Kate Smith sang "God Bless America," and Johnny Cash sang as well. "Real Peace is Jesus" read the lapel buttons. And Billy Graham called for people to come together, before it was too late.

Seven years after Martin Luther King's address, this was Graham's own "I Have a Dream" speech: he even called it "The Unfinished Dream." His vision focused less on justice, the pursuit of which divides people, than unity. "We have listened and watched while a relatively small extremist element both to the left and the right in our society have knocked our courts, desecrated our flag, disrupted our educational system, laughed at our religious heritage, and threatened to burn down our cities," he said. "The overwhelming majority of concerned Americans—white and black, hawks and doves, parents and students, Republicans and Democrats—who hate violence have stood by and viewed all this with mounting alarm. . . . Today we call upon all Americans to stop this polarization before it is too late." Honor the nation, he implored the crowd, then quoted Churchill's cry: "and as you move to do it, never give in. Never give in. Never! Never! Never! Never."

Hazel Gay from Memphis had waited since the wee hours. "We were there early to hear Dr. Graham," she said. "It nearly broke me up. I could feel victory. Like we all felt victory and a united feeling at the end of World War II. Remember? I felt a spiritual uplift. When they raised that big flag I got goose bumps." Jack Benny, Red Skelton, Dinah Shore all joined Bob Hope that evening. Hubert Humphrey was there, and Senator George McGovern, and 350,000 other people.

It was in all a peaceful, celebratory day compared to all that had gone before. When people talked politics and policy, the rebukes were gentle, there was room for doubt, uncertainty, civility; some who said they supported Nixon admitted that they did so not because they liked him, but because he was president. It was a day designed to lower the volume, let people find something in common, even if it was just a longing for the kind of Fourth of July they had had when they were kids.

But there was no escaping the battle completely. Some protesters demanded the right to plant Viet Cong flags on the Ellipse behind the White House, where Boy Scouts and others set out a field of American flags like poppies. Yippies held a pot party on the Mall featuring red, white, and blue joints, and went skinny-dipping in the Reflecting Pool. Some protesters threw rocks at the police; tear gas was fired. Elsewhere the placards read "God, Guts and Gunpowder Maintains Liberty" and "America Will Survive Traitors, Trash and Pantywaist Politicians." One group of Mennonites brought a banner directly confronting Graham for his entwining of church and state: "Hour of Decision," it read. "God or Country?"

But the front page of every paper showed crowds reaching to a horizon speared by the Washington Monument, and a headline, "Billy Graham Is Cheered as He Speaks from Steps of Lincoln Memorial." His fame, his place as the evangelist of national unity and the preeminent preacher of patriotism, was now at its height. And it left some people who watched him to wonder—what would Jesus have made of such a scene, such an embrace by the popular heralds of the day?

The president himself never did appear; he sent a telegram of congratulations instead from San Clemente. But he didn't need to be there—in fact it was better that he wasn't. It was already a bit suspect that the event was chaired by hotel magnate J. Willard Marriott, who had organized the Nixon inaugural and employed Nixon's brother Donald as a vice president. And at the same time that these public events were occurring, at the very time that Graham was trying to restore faith in the American government and institutions, Nixon and his men were engaged in an enterprise that, when revealed three years later, would have precisely the opposite effect. It would be something like an act of heresy, if a democracy can admit of such a thing.

During those early summer weeks of 1970, there circulated through the White House a very different kind of proposal to address Nixon's concerns about domestic dissenters. The "Huston plan" would have effectively suspended whatever laws interfered with a president's protection of national security. It would have allowed him to wiretap anyone, read any mail, search any home, through a kind of clandestine superpolice system under the direction of a twenty-nine-year-old named Tom Huston. There was in Huston's circle talk of creating camps for detaining antiwar radicals if ever the need arose.

Nixon ended up revoking the Huston plan shortly after he approved it in mid-July, largely because of the objections of J. Edgar Hoover; but not before various members of his guard had gotten the message: do what you need to do to stop leaks, track down traitors, punish enemies, and ensure domestic tranquillity.

Character Witness

G raham knew nothing of this, of course. All he knew was that he was trying to help his friend and the very good men around him to do a very difficult job. He would recall the thousand ways Nixon showed his appreciation. He told the story of the time he was playing golf in France, where he rented an old set of clubs. "I played one of the best games I've ever played and I wanted to buy those clubs," Graham said. "The golf pro would not sell them to me. So when I got home and was playing golf with Mr. Nixon in California one day, I told him about this and didn't think anything more of it. And did you know I got those golf clubs for Christmas. He had sent over there and gotten them. He was just always kind, courteous and thoughtful. I never felt he was using me—*ever*."

It seemed at times as though Graham had made it his particular mission to make over Nixon's image, humanize him to the voters who may have respected him without particularly liking him. Public affection came so easily to Graham, he experienced adoration in such abundance, it couldn't do any harm to share it. On New Year's Day 1971, when he was to be grand marshal of the Tournament of Roses parade, he called the White House in the morning: "He thought it would be appropriate to talk to you this morning on the telephone," stated a memo to the president, "so that he could mention the conversation publicly as opportunities presented themselves throughout the day."

His defense could go to lengths that tortured both logic and faith. That spring of 1971, as the country wrestled with its moral bearings after the conviction of Lieutenant William Calley for the massacre of old men, women, and children at My Lai, Graham wrote a Good Friday op-ed in the *New York Times*. "Perhaps it is a good time for each of us to re-evaluate our life," he proposed, suggesting a kind of moral equivalence that would make it impossible to hold anyone accountable for anything. "We have all had our My Lais in one way or another, perhaps not with guns, but we have hurt others with a thoughtless word, an arrogant act or a selfish deed. . . . 'Let him who is without sin cast the first stone.'" He would return again and again to this theme as Nixon's misdeeds became known, inviting his critics to charge that his moral judgment was selective and calls for mercy too politically convenient.

His testimony on behalf of the president extended all around the world: just as Nixon had found in him the perfect messenger to Lyndon Johnson in 1968, he continued to deploy Graham as an off-the-books diplomat engaging with the many world leaders he had come to know during the course of his crusades. If ever Nixon's methods or motives came under suspicion, Graham was a powerful antiseptic.

When Nixon announced the historic change in U.S. policy toward China and his intention to visit Peking, Taiwanese president Chiang Kai-shek worried that his most powerful ally was abandoning him. Haldeman wrote to Kissinger in November 1971 that Chiang and his wife had invited Graham to Taipei to talk about what was happening. "They have told him that they are deeply troubled and that Billy Graham is the one person from this country that they will listen to and would like to meet with." Nixon approved a trip for early December, and Kissinger prepared a briefing, so that Graham was clear on what he should and should not say.

Kissinger's confidential talking points emphasized Nixon's admiration for Chiang, his desire for stability in the region, and his continued commitment to Taiwan's security. Kissinger warned Graham against being drawn into details of military assistance. "We are acutely conscious of the deep and fundamental differences between ourselves and the leadership in Peking," Graham was told to say. "These will remain after the president's trip. The trip is not being undertaken with an aura of naivete which in any way misjudges or underestimates the differences that divide Peking and Washington." There were no preconditions or secret deals attached. "We will not sacrifice our friends or renege on our commitments as a price for improved relations with our adversaries." On other occasions Nixon would use Graham to send and receive messages from Indira Gandhi, Golda Meir, and other world leaders.

If Graham offered Nixon a kind of blanket benediction that the president was a good man guided in all things by his better angels, Nixon, his nature less angelic, returned the favor with the various tools at his disposal. One memo from Alexander Butterfield to Herb Klein reported, "The president wants to know which of the Washington Post's society section reporters wrote the extremely critical, slashing attack on Billy Graham. . . . Please provide a report as soon as you have the information." The culprit had called Graham America's court preacher: "In him we can see . . . the working partnership between God and Caesar, not rendering to each other so much as washing each other's hands." Klein investigated, and reported back that "his comments are on my list of criticisms which I will take up with the editor of the Wash Post next week."

When John Connally mentioned to Nixon that Graham was being audited by the IRS, Nixon was livid. He wanted to know why the auditors were hounding the administration's friends rather than focusing on its enemies. Nixon was particularly irate at the news about Graham and wanted to know why the IRS wasn't looking into the major Democratic donors.

"You call [John] Mitchell," Nixon told Haldeman, referring to his attorney general. "Mitchell can stick his nose into this. Tell him about Graham. Say now, Goddammit, are we going after some of the Democrats or not?" The next day he picked up the subject again in an Oval Office meeting. "What about the rich Jews?" he asked Haldeman. "The IRS is full of Jews, Bob." That's why they were going after Graham. Haldeman proposed looking for some anti-Semitic IRS agents to focus on auditing Jews, especially major Democratic donors. "What we ought to do is get a zealot who dislikes those people just as much as a zealot who dislikes Billy Graham is working on his file."

"Go after 'em like a son of a bitch," Nixon said.

And so in ways he himself never really knew, Graham became a de facto member of the first-term Nixon White House, with all the privileges and protections that entailed. When Nixon came under fire from the right, Haldeman suggested recruiting Graham as a counterinsurgent. He proposed creating a committee of "Conservatives for the President," including Lewis of *Reader's Digest*, *National Review* editor Jeff Hart, Clare Boothe Luce, and Billy Graham, that would "support the president down the line from a conservative viewpoint. They could develop letter-writing activities, etc. to counterbalance the offensive now being launched in other directions by some of the conservative publications."

To the public, and perhaps to himself, Graham had not crossed any bright lines. In fact, he thought he had closed the door on playing any role other than a spiritual one. "After Nixon was elected, he asked me to come and see him," Graham recalled. "He said, 'Billy, what job do you want? I'll appoint you to any ambassadorship if you want it.' I said, 'Mr. President. I don't want anything.' He said, 'You mean you don't want anything?' And I said nothing. I said, 'God called me to preach and I'm never gonna do anything but that. I'm gonna preach the gospel.' That's what I told him." And that's what he believed. But the coming of Nixon's 1972 reelection campaign would change everything.

TWENTY

1972: The Race to the Bottom

I don't understand it. I can't even remember it. . . . I never felt that way. I never thought that way and I was just trying to agree with what he said or something. I don't know.

—Graham on his Oval Office meeting with Nixon in which
they discussed what the Jews were "doing to America"

It's impossible to pinpoint a single moment when Graham became an unofficial but invaluable consultant to Nixon's 1972 reelection campaign. But one August night in 1971 he joined the president's inner circle for dinner on the presidential yacht *Sequoia*. Kissinger was there, and Attorney General John Mitchell, Haldeman, and Ehrlichman, a cast that, according to the *Washington Post* the next day, "suggested the dinner may have had political overtones."

As Haldeman remembered the night, Nixon was in an expansive mood, waxing sociological once more as he explained his theory of decadent leadership. The country's real problem, he argued, was not with the kids, the hippies, but with the leadership class, the clergy (other than Graham and his kin), the professors and academics, the business leaders. "He thinks they've all become soft and that this is where the problem lies."

Graham agreed with Nixon's premise but took it further: what the country needed was a strong challenge from the president, a call for work and sacrifice such as Kennedy had offered rhetorically but not substantively. Haldeman noted that Graham felt such an effort, "plus a recognition of the importance of the spiritual side of things and the growing interest in spirituality, would be extremely effective and popular. Graham also expanded on his firm belief that it was absolutely imperative that the P be reelected next year, or there wouldn't be any hope for him and his movement or the country." His faith in Nixon had reached the point that he even helped talk his friend and model Mark Hatfield, now an outspoken war critic, out of challenging Nixon for the nomination.

If Graham was truly convinced that the future of evangelism and the fate of the United States depended on Nixon's remaining in office—this was before anyone knew who the Democratic opponent would be—it still goes only part of the way toward explaining what happened next. For the story of 1972 is the story of Graham's deepest descent into partisan waters. It was not that he did so much, but that so much of what he did is hard to explain given the rules he had set for himself. Years later, when he had put aside his memories of those years, his biographer William Martin presented him with the evidence, so many meetings and memos, reflecting how useful the Nixon White House had found their preacher friend. Graham felt, he told Martin then, "like a sheep led to the slaughter."

Graham, of course, was not treated like a sheep or a servant by the Nixon White House: he was treated like a king. His calls were returned, his favors granted, his stature respected in ways he would never have noticed or cared much about. That night on the *Sequoia*, the president's party returned by helicopter to the South Lawn, and the next day Haldeman fired a rocket at a White House underling. He deplored the "awkward incident" that his own car had been waiting in line ahead of Graham's: when such a guest was present, Haldeman wrote, his car should be first.

The approach of the campaign moved Graham deeper into the White House orbit, and particularly into Haldeman's gravitational pull. Recalling his response to Nixon when the president asked him if he had any advice as he launched his reelection campaign, he said, "I said 'Yes. Let others run your campaign and you just keep on being a good president.' In hindsight I wonder if it was good advice."

It was Haldeman, the J. Walter Thompson ad man turned advance man extraordinaire, who was charged with maintaining regular contact with Graham. Graham saw in Haldeman a crew-cut, straight-arrow Christian Scientist who didn't smoke or drink or approve of people who did. He wielded immense power because he controlled access to the president and had taken to heart the advice Eisenhower and Johnson both gave him before Nixon took office: keep Nixon away from the day-to-day trivia so he can concentrate on a few overwhelming issues. "Dick says that there have to be a few SOBs in any organization," Haldeman liked to say, "and I'm his."

It is the Haldeman records, his memos and diary entries, that cast Graham deep into the shadows of the administration's political efforts. Graham later expressed concern that as Christian Scientists, Haldeman and Ehrlichman did not believe in the reality of sin or human depravity. "Perhaps that caused Haldeman, later in his published diary, to give a negative slant to some of the comments he claimed I made, many of which I never did." But tapes can't slant, and Graham would find himself among many friends and members of the administration to have his private conversations explicitly exposed.

A year before the reelection campaign was even under way, Haldeman wrote himself a memo: "Graham wants to be helpful next year . . . point him in areas where do most good. He thinks there are real stirrings in religious directions, especially re young people. I call him and set up date. No other level—can't have leak."

This is not to say that the president wanted to keep his friendship with Graham a secret—only the political partnership. When Charles Crutchfield, the eager and enterprising chair of the Charlotte Chamber of Commerce, proposed to Graham that the city mark Billy Graham Day to honor its favorite son, the evangelist demurred; he had been honored plenty already, thank you. He had, if anything, too high a profile: he'd had to install fencing around the Montreat house, which was now patrolled by three guard dogs who responded only to commands in German. In one week alone, there were five attempts by intruders. For all the precautions, Graham told Nixon that if terrorists or radicals kidnapped him, "Don't ransom me—don't try to save my life."

Besides, Graham worried that an event in his honor would be an irresistible target for war protesters looking to embarrass the president. That turned out to be exactly the prospect the White House most savored: their man, persecuted by his enemies as he sought to laud Billy Graham. Nixon called Graham himself, urging that he agree; he'd come himself to honor their friendship. Obediently, Graham said yes.

The city of Charlotte threw a huge party: October 15, 1971, was Billy Graham Day. Schools and stores and courts closed like it was the sabbath; crowds lined the street to greet the president's motorcade. Nixon and Graham rode together, lights flashing; Nixon showed him the best way to wave. Graham called it one of "the most wonderful things" that had ever happened to him. "All this for a preacher—and an evangelist at that." He worried that the celebration might be thought to have political overtones, since they were heading into an election year. But Nixon reassured him: the White House had asked people to take down political signs along the motorcade route, and Nixon said he had turned away the local Republicans who wanted to visit with him at the airport. "He said to me 'No, this is your day,'" Graham recalled, "'and I'm not going to let politics spoil it.'"

But of course the whole occasion fairly hummed with politics. Connally's presence in the president's traveling party was attributed less to his long friendship with Graham than to rumors that Nixon was hoping to drop Agnew from the ticket next year and swap Connally in as his running mate. By this time Graham might have started to see the warnings: among the signs in the crowds was one declaring "Jesus and Caesar weren't best friends." Even the hometown paper sent up a flare. "Notwithstanding the genuineness of their admiration, the President and the Chambers of Commerce draw honor to themselves by honoring Mr. Graham. He in turn moves closer to the places of power, anointing those who are there," read an editorial in the *Charlotte Observer*. "Together they represent an American phenomenon akin to that of old Europe, with its alliances of crown and cross. Good can come of that, or bad."

At the Coliseum, before a crowd of two thousand, the Third Army Band played Ruffles and Flourishes as the two men reached the stage. Famous friends who could not be there sent telegrams: there were tributes from Bob Hope, Prince Rainier, Roy Rogers, Arnold Palmer, General Westmoreland, Pat Boone, Pearl Bailey, Ronald Reagan. The two men stood together in the warm October sun, Nixon in a sober dark Quaker suit, Graham in an especially psychedelic blue checked suit with bell bottoms that he'd bought specially for the occasion, not realizing quite how vibrant it would look in the sunlight. He presented his friend as a man of such moral strength that expediency and compromise were alien to his nature: "I remember once when I made a suggestion to him. He looked me in the eye and said 'Billy, that would not be morally right.' When I thought it through, I realized he was right. . . . At that moment I felt that he were the preacher and I was the sinner."

Graham took the occasion to comment on social issues; his view of the War on Poverty appeared to have changed since defending it in 1967, and his own biography was roughed up as well. "We also wrestled with poverty," he said of his childhood, "that is, if you go by today's standards, except we did not know we were poor. We did not have sociologists, educators and newscasters reminding us how poor we were." And, he said, "We also had the problem of rats. The only difference between then and now is we did not call upon the federal government to come and kill our rats."

Nixon devoted the bulk of his remarks to a review of the nation's challenges and strengths; it was a Graham tribute in name, a campaign speech in every other way. But eventually he returned the homage: "You have contributed to America and the world one of the greatest leaders of our time," he said. He praised Graham's contribution to the strength of American faith, but described that faith in the most flavorless terms. "I have faith in [America] not because we are the strongest nation in the world, which we are, and not because we are the richest nation in the world, which we are; but because there is still, in the heartland of this country, and the heartland of America is in every State of America, there is still a strong religious faith, a morality, a spiritual quality which makes the American people not just a rich people or a strong people, but makes the American people a people with that faith which enables them to meet the challenge of greatness."

A reporter asked Graham if he thought the president was sounding more like an evangelist. "Maybe," Graham replied, "I'm sounding more like him."

The warmth inside the Coliseum was in some contrast with the scene outside. Protesters who tried to get into the event were stopped by marshals who tore up their tickets; officials said they had warnings that the demonstrators were plotting to unfurl banners and disrupt the proceedings. The sixteen-year-old daughter of a superior court judge was denied admission, along with her little brother. One woman and her fourth-grade son were told they could not get in after they stopped and talked to some demonstrators. "I'm just a nice, greyhaired, everyday mother," she told local reporters. "He thought he was coming down here to be saved, and he just got kicked out." Also barred was a group of children from a Quaker Sunday school class. Even the Democratic governor of North Carolina, Robert Scott, protested his treatment by the Secret Service; he was ordered not to fly the state flag from his car, and blocked from saying good-bye to the president's delegation at the airport. Fourteen people would end up suing over their treatment. Afterward when Graham was asked about it, he said, "If the Secret Service was keeping anyone out because of long hair they would have kept out my son, because he has long hair." The incident was unfortunate, he said, but surely not deliberate. "Anyways you can't blame it on the president."

Actually, you could. It would be another two years, when the Watergate hearings laid bare all the grease and grime introduced into the electoral machinery, before the full story of Billy Graham Day emerged. Federal agents had been on the scene in Charlotte for weeks in advance, scouting the local campuses, looking for radical groups that might use the occasion to confront the president. The day before the ceremony, Haldeman received a memo from advance man Ronald Walker, who had the assessments about potential demonstrations. "They will be violent; they will have extremely *obscene* signs as has been indicated by their handbills. It will not only be directed toward the president, but *also toward Billy Graham.* They will have smoke bombs, and have every intention of disrupting the arrival and trying to blitz the Coliseum in order to disrupt the dedication ceremony." In the margins of the memo, Haldeman wrote "Good" at the prospect of obscene signs, and then underlined that they would target Graham as well. "Great," he wrote. It would serve the president nicely to be martyred by profane protesters, with Billy Graham right there at his side.

When the memo surfaced during the Watergate hearings in August 1973, Connecticut senator Lowell Weicker pronounced the whole episode "a disgrace." "What mentality," he wanted to know, "indicates 'good' when the words obscenity and violence are mentioned. How in any way can that be good?" Haldeman replied that reporters tended to underplay the protests, and that this showed how well planned and profane they actually were.

But in the fall of 1971, Nixon got from Billy Graham Day just what he wanted. A story in the *Chicago Daily News* began, "If Evangelist Billy Graham's millions of religious followers also take his political advice, the result should be an electoral bonanza for President Nixon."

THE WORST MEETING EVER

Three months later, on January 31, 1972, Haldeman took notes at a staff meeting: he knew Graham was in town for the prayer breakfast the next day and planned to see Nixon afterward. "Get Billy Graham in re politics today w/some of us," Haldeman noted, "then see P later."

At the prayer breakfast, Graham read the gospel for thirty-one hundred lawmakers and Supreme Court justices and foreign dignitaries, while Nixon talked about the challenge of his forthcoming trip to China, and the possibilities of peace. Afterward Graham went back to the White House and spent a long time with Nixon in the Oval Office. The tape recording of that meeting contains a number of long gaps, which make it impossible to be certain of all that was said and intended. But Haldeman was there and took his own notes, and by any measure, it was a conversation Graham never should have had.

He told Nixon how well he'd done. "There were a lot of people in tears when you finished this morning," he said. They talked about Graham's schedule in the coming months, according to Haldeman's notes, "and of the states in which it would be most helpful for him to be active during the balance of this year." They agreed that time spent in Pennsylvania, Ohio, Illinois, and New York could all be useful for the president, since he had California and Texas already covered.

It was agreed that Graham would be given political and foreign policy briefings, and after the China and Russia trips should "invite his elite group in for a Kissinger briefing," meaning the key religious leaders whom Graham thought should hear directly from the White House. "There was a great deal of general discussion on political outlook, and the opportunity that Graham feels he has to be helpful, which he indicates he will do in every possible way."

But that was not the worst of it, the pretense of neutrality abandoned. In his diary Haldeman noted one more topic that he did not include in his official memo of that long meeting. "There was considerable discussion of the terrible problem arising from the total Jewish domination of the media, and agreement that this was something that would have to be dealt with."

And indeed in this longest of all his Oval Office meetings, at this critical moment in both men's careers, something poisonous was in the air, and Graham was lost in the toxic fumes. He mentioned that he'd been invited to have lunch with the editors at *TIME*—the first he'd heard from them since Luce's death five years before. "You meet with all their editors, you better take your Jewish beanie," Haldeman said. "Is that right?" Graham remarked, noting that he no longer knew any of the editors. This inspired Nixon to complain about how much of the press was "totally dominated by the Jews." Since it could be said of Nixon that some of his best friends were Jews, he qualified this by saying he didn't mean that all the Jews were bad; in fact the Israeli Jews were the best ones, he said. The distinction he was making was more political than religious. The left-wing American Jews were the problem, especially the younger ones, Nixon said. They didn't understand the threat the country faced, and were for peace at any price in Vietnam.

"And they're the ones putting out the pornographic stuff," Graham added. There is a long gap in the tape at this point, but when it picked up again Graham was talking about how "this stranglehold has got to be broken or the country's going to go down the drain."

"Do you believe that?" Nixon asked.

"Yes, sir," Graham said.

"Boy," Nixon said, "I can't ever tell you, but I believe it."

"If you get elected a second time, then we might be able to do some-thing," Graham responded, and then went on to talk about how careful he had been to stay out of the news since Nixon took office. "I had to be quiet on just about everything that would make news," he said, "due to the fact that I didn't want to look like I was critical of some policy of yours. Or being interpreted as political and so forth." He'd had to watch what he said as never before. "Even when Eisenhower was president," he noted, "I spoke out against the way we were giving to India; Mr. [John Foster] Dulles called me up to his home to explain it to me, and I would talk out against this or that or the other thing . . . and it would make news. But with you as president, I feel like, you know, I can't do that."

Nixon talked at length about the balance of power, and his belief that the United States still had enough influence to broker a lasting peace; he even talked about how "the millennium will come some day . . . when everybody may want peace for the right reasons." But for now, there had never been a time when it was so important to have someone in the Oval Office who really understood the communists, and what it would take to make peace possible. This was what his enemies couldn't understand, the professors especially: "I think 90% of them are atheists or worse. They have no confidence in themselves. They have no faith in this country."

"So they are undermining the country," Graham said.

Graham suggested that he was even more conservative than Nixon was; but he had learned to "*lean* a little bit," cover up his feelings when he was with liberals. "A lot of the Jews are great friends of mine," he said. "They swarm around me, are friendly to me, because they know I am friendly to Israel and so forth. They don't know how I really feel about what they're doing to this country."

"You must not let them know," Nixon said.

It's hard to pick the worst part of the long, ghastly meeting, one of the rare occasions when Graham met a president in the Oval Office, and with other aides present. This was not ministry; it was the moment of greatest temptation, the high-water mark of Graham's political power, when the president of the United States invited him deep into his inner circle and enlisted him in his cause. It didn't matter that Graham's entire career refuted the charge of anti-Semitism, that Golda Meir had inscribed a Bible to him as "a great teacher and . . . a true friend of Israel." When the tape of the meeting became public thirty years later it did more damage to Graham's reputation than any incident, any comment, any action of his nearly sixty years in public life. And it was not only because of what he said but because of what he did not: here was a chance to make a moral witness, to remind Nixon of what the Jews had suffered and the nature of those who persecuted them. If the whole point of maintaining his access to the Oval Office was to bring the gospel in with him, then surely that required that he return evil with good. But in this case, he didn't. One Nixon aide likened it to locker-room talk, with Graham joining in. And when it all became public, "I went to a meeting with Jewish leaders and I told them I would crawl to them to ask their forgiveness."

"I don't understand it," Graham said of his conduct. "I can't even remember it. I mean I remember I guess the meeting. But I can't remember what I said because I never felt that way. I never thought that way and I was just trying to agree with what he said or something. I don't know."

Graham wrote to thank Nixon later, and promised that "I will try to follow through faithfully on each point we discussed."

Thus began an election-year reconnaissance between Nixon and Haldeman and their key sensors, particularly Connally and Graham. In the conversations back and forth, the memos and messages, one can sense the White House's respect for Graham's political connections and acumen, and his pleasure at being on the inside of a great game.

It was an alliance that required a light touch: "Billy was, I have to say, very careful in my dealings with him," Charles Colson recalled. "We asked him for his mailing list, so we could contact them. And he said no. It was all handled through channels but the word came back, no thanks."

Haldeman prepared a weekly talking paper to guide his calls to Graham, listing questions to ask and themes to raise. He called a week or so after the Oval Office visit with some general questions on the political temperature, a heads-up that there would be a new attorney general arriving as John Mitchell shifted to the campaign full-time, and advance word of the new FBI chief, Patrick Gray. Nixon had just revealed his secret eight-point peace plan for Vietnam: Haldeman wanted to know what Graham thought of it, and of presidential hopeful Edmund Muskie's response. Haldeman's next talking points for Graham included the notion that "one line that is being pushed is that Muskie's statements on the war disqualify him from being considered for President because he has put partisanship above peace." And by the way, did Graham have any suggestions for the Kennedy Center board?

Nixon kept on top of Haldeman's outreach: he sent a memo as the China trip approached, looking for ways to defuse the hostility of conservatives against his trip. "I assume that the meeting with Billy Graham's religious leaders is going forward," he wrote. "If it is not being done this week, be sure it is done the week after Henry [Kissinger] gets back from his vacation. I do not believe the problem is potentially too great a one, but it could become one in the event the extremists get to them before Henry has a chance to put the record straight."

Valuable as Graham was, Nixon was also careful about how he was handled—and by whom. Was it a protective impulse, or a preference to keep their conversations cleaner somehow, that inspired Nixon to tell Haldeman to handle the nitty-gritty political issues himself? "With further regard to Graham," Nixon instructed, "would you be sure to place a call to him about every two weeks to discuss the political situation. I would prefer not to get into these matters as directly with him, but I do want a continuing contact kept with him so that he doesn't feel that we are not interested in the support of his group in those key states where they can be helpful."

This Haldeman did dutifully; each week brought some other story on which he wanted to gauge Graham's reaction, and by extension the mood of those he spoke for. "Can McGovern really be nominated?" Haldeman wanted to know in April. "Will Wallace just get stronger or has he reached a peak?" On school busing, "Do people understand the President's position? What should we be doing in this area?" And on Vietnam, "What is your reaction to Kissinger's secret trip? Does the public accept this type of secret negotiation?" In another call Haldeman asked, "Do you believe the recent attacks on certain members of the media are hitting the mark?"

In mid-June, as the planning for the Watergate burglary was in its final stage, Graham was in Dallas for Explo 72, a vast gathering of young people to sing and pray and witness, a kind of "religious Woodstock." It wouldn't be bad for Nixon to send a congratulatory telegram to Explo, Graham told Haldeman aide Lawrence Higby, which Graham could read onstage. (Higby had speechwriter Ray Price draft one, which he would clear with Graham before sending it on for Graham to deliver.) "He wanted to mention to you the fact that if McGovern is nominated, religion will be an issue this year, that the National Council of Churches will probably go all out for McGovern," Higby told Haldeman. "He pointed out that McGovern is the son of, and a former pastor, and that many church people will think the idea of having a former pastor in the White House is a good idea."

The Watergate break-in occurred on June 16; Nixon had just returned from his triumphant trip to Moscow with an arms control treaty in hand. It was called the most important superpower summit since Potsdam in 1945, and had followed his historic trip to China in February. He was having an extraordinary run of statesmanship; he had taken multiple, immense strategic gambles, and they had worked. The Democrats, meanwhile, were already gnawing on one another in their fight over the nomination. So when Haldeman called Nixon in San Clemente two days after the arrests at the Democratic Party Headquarters at the Watergate, both men appeared more annoyed than alarmed at the gambit.

The next day Nixon and Graham talked—but not about Watergate. It was about how to keep George Wallace from threatening Nixon's reelection by running as an independent. "Graham has a line through to Wallace through Mrs. Wallace, who has become a Christian," Haldeman recorded. "Billy will talk to Wallace whenever we want him to. The P feels our strategy must be to keep Wallace in the Democratic Party. . . . So immediately after the Democratic conventions, I'm supposed to call Graham and Graham should put the pressure on Wallace to decide whether he's going to be used as a spoiler, which would surely elect McGovern."

After their talk Nixon fired off an action memo of his own: "I need to meet with Graham when he's available regarding his role and his people's." The next day Haldeman's talking paper explored what Graham thought was the smart response to McGovern. "Should he be hit now or after the Democratic Convention? How can we counter his appeal to ministers and church leaders due to his background?"

Two weeks later on July 11, as the Democrats were gathering to nominate McGovern, Graham called to offer names of Christian youth leaders who might be enlisted. He would stay behind the scenes, but could put the campaign in touch with the fifty major Christian youth groups and their immense mailing lists. Haldeman noted with satisfaction that one of Graham's best organization men, Harry Williams, would be among those taking leave from their jobs to work full-time for the president's reelection committee. Graham also did some matchmaking between Nixon and Oral Roberts: thanks to the success of Oral Roberts University and its basketball team, "Roberts has close identification with clean-cut youth, as well as conservative folk in general," Harry Dent told Nixon. He did note that Roberts had prayed at the Democratic convention, but added that he "has indicated to me he wants to help your re-election." Nixon was eager to pursue the relationship, even though Haldeman thought it was "a terrible idea."

Graham was now operating on multiple fronts at once. He and Connally, as faithful southern Democrats, were the natural agents to assign to both Wallace and Lyndon Johnson. Wallace was still recuperating from the assassination attempt in May that had left him partially paralyzed. Graham called him after he had surgery to wish him well, and reported afterward to Haldeman that he concluded there was almost no chance that Wallace would run. "Wallace asked whether he would take more votes from the P, and Graham said he would take at least 75%. Wallace said he would never turn one hand to help McGovern and that he didn't have the physical strength to run and that he's 99% sure he won't do it."

JUST BETWEEN US PRESIDENTS

As the Republican convention approached, Graham was home in Montreat, getting ready to swing down to see Johnson at his ranch. He had scheduled no crusades in the United States that summer: "It's difficult

Graham at the 1949 Los Angeles crusade, which cast him into the national spotlight. [GETTY IMAGES]

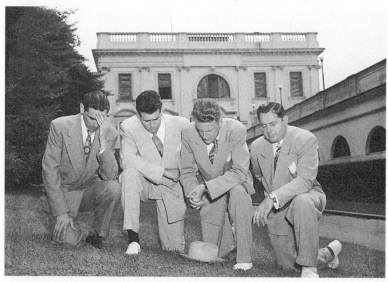

Graham and his team (from left, Jerry Beaven, Cliff Barrows, Graham, and Grady Wilson) pray outside the White House after meeting with President Truman in 1950. [BETTMANN/CORBIS]

Graham's 1952 Washington crusade attracted dozens of senators and congressmen every night, but Truman steadfastly refused to attend, despite the urgings of many in his party.
[UPI Bettmann/CORBIS]

Graham visits with the Reagans at a movie exhibitors' meeting in June 1952. Within days Hollywood was buzzing with rumors of a movie about Graham's life...starring Reagan. [Squire Haskins/University of Texas at Arlington Library]

In August 1952, Graham gave Eisenhover a Bible marked with his margin notes, which the president kept by his bedside. [Courtesy of Billy Graham Evangelistic Association]

Graham became close to Nixon when the latter was vice president and frequently sent him Bible passages to read. [Bettmann/CORBIS]

On July 20, 1957, more than 100,000 came to hear Graham at Yankee Stadium. On the platform, Nixon witnessed firsthand Graham's power over his
audience. [Courtesy of Billy Graham Evangelistic Association]

A few days before his inauguration, Kennedy invited Graham to play golf in Palm Beach and join him at a press conference afterward. Florida senator George Smathers (far right) arranged the meeting. [Bettmann/CORBIS]

Graham saw Kennedy only a few times, including at the annual presidential prayer breakfasts. [Courtesy of Billy Graham Evangelistic Association]

Johnson and Graham at a public prayer breakfast in 1966. Johnson invited the evangelist to stay at the White House more often than did any other president. [COURTESY OF BILLY GRAHAM EVANGELISTIC ASSOCIATION]

Particularly as Vietnam consumed both him and his presidency, Johnson wanted Graham at his side. He would often call him into his bedroom to pray in the middle of the night. [Bettmann/CORBIS]

In 1968 Graham visited Truman at home in Independence, Missouri, and got a tour of his library. [Courtesy of Billy Graham Evangelistic Association]

Nixon's 1969 inauguration: Graham was so close to both men that he stayed in the White House for Johnson's last weekend and on Nixon's first night. [BETTMANN/ CORBIS]

As California governor, Reagan and his wife join Graham at the 1969 Anaheim crusade. [COURTESY OF BILLY GRAHAM EVANGELISTIC ASSOCIATION]

In May 1970, when Nixon came under fire for bombing Cambodia, Graham invited him to speak to an audience of friendly students at his Knoxville crusade. [BETTMANN/CORBIS]

Nixon and Graham greet the crowds on Billy Graham Day in Charlotte, North Carolina, October 15, 1971. [BETTMANN/CORBIS]

Just months before Ford ascended to the presidency in 1974, he and Graham enjoyed a game of golf in Charlotte, at the Kemper Pro-Am. [BETTMANN/ CORBIS]

Graham had more in common theologically with Jimmy Carter than with any other president, but the two men were never close. Here, after the 1980 election, Graham, Carter, and Vice President-elect George Bush meet outside a church in Washington where Graham had preached. [AP]

Vice President Bush and Graham share the platform at the Southern Baptist Convention in 1982. As Bush began his quest for the 1988 GOP nomination, Graham featured him prominently in the telecast of his 1986 Washington crusade. [Bettmann/CORBIS]

Reagan and Graham appear together in Washington in 1983, a few days after the president awarded the evangelist the Medal of Freedom. [Getty Images]

The Grahams with George W. Bush and his twin daughters at Walker's Point in 1983. [George Bush Presidential Library]

As Arkansas governor, Clinton joins Graham at the Little Rock crusade in 1989. Clinton secretly contributed to Graham's ministry when he was thirteen. [Courtesy of Billy Graham Evangelistic Association]

The Grahams visited the Bushes regularly at their summer home in Kennebunkport, Maine; the president's mother, Dorothy Bush, is seated at right. [Courtesy
of Billy Graham Evangelistic Association]

Graham with Hillary and Bill Clinton during a national prayer breakfast in the early 1990s. [IMAGE © WALLY McNAMEE/CORBIS]

Graham with Nixon at the funeral of his wife, Pat, at the Nixon Library on June 26, 1993. He also preached at the funeral of Nixon's mother, Hannah. [REUTERS/CORBIS]

Former President Carter and Graham meet privately during the 1994 Atlanta crusade. [COURTESY OF BILLY GRAHAM EVANGELISTIC ASSOCIATION]

Clinton embraces Graham after the luncheon at his second inaugural in 1997. A year later the evangelist would come to the president's defense and preach forgiveness as the impeachment scandal erupted. [AFP/GETTY IMAGES]

Graham declares his support for George W. Bush in Jacksonville, Florida, two days before the 2000 election. [AFP/GETTY IMAGES]

to stay out of politics when you're in the limelight like that," he said. But he did come out and admit that he was planning on voting for Nixon. In this case there was no point in feigning neutrality.

Nor could he pretend that his actions didn't matter. That month, a book called *Religion and the New Majority: Billy Graham, Middle America and the Politics of the 70s* argued that the candidate whose values most closely matched Graham's would stand the best chance of winning. Graham was now much more than a great revivalist or mere White House chaplain, said authors Lowell Streiker and Gerald Strober. "Graham is today the leader of the politically decisive majority, the man who more consistently than anyone else articulates the aspirations and fears of the bulk of his fellow citizens." And they noted Nixon's assiduous effort to be as closely associated as possible.

Graham had remained devoted to Johnson since he'd left office, and had helped persuade the Nixon White House to treat the former president well. Graham had suggested how much Johnson would love to be present at the launch of the Apollo mission to the moon; Nixon called Johnson personally to invite him. Nixon celebrated Johnson's sixty-first birthday in the summer of 1969 by dedicating the Lady Bird Johnson Grove in Redwoods National Park, praising the former president's courage and service, with Graham in happy attendance.

So Johnson was already soft on Nixon, and his distaste for McGovern was no secret. He thought the South Dakota senator was a loser, out of touch on the war and outside the mainstream on matters at home. Johnson called him "the most inept politician, inept presidential candidate . . . in all of history. . . . I didn't know they MADE presidential candidates that dumb." The Democrats seemed to return the feeling, as though by distancing themselves from Johnson they could erase the sour taste he had left behind. Their convention hall in Miami was hung along one wall with fifteen giant portraits of Democratic heroes, past presidents and candidates. Johnson's image was nowhere to be seen. You had to look at the other end in a hidden little annex where there were pictures of congressional leaders to find one of him. Johnson had told friends in Texas that he would probably go fishing instead of campaign anywhere if McGovern got the nomination.

Nixon had used Graham to neutralize Johnson four years before to great effect; now he ran that play again. Just before Graham's weekend with Johnson, Nixon and Connally met to talk about how Graham could help—maybe persuade Johnson to keep his endorsement of McGovern as cool as possible, explain that Johnson's friends wouldn't understand it if he suddenly played the loyal Democrat and helped the nominee. This Graham faithfully did; he and Johnson had a good visit. Grady Wilson was there too, and they all piled into Johnson's convertible and rode all around the ranch with the dogs. The visit happened to coincide with the Grahams' twenty-ninth wedding anniversary. When Billy called Ruth that night, Johnson picked up on the other phone: "I surely do want to thank you for letting us have Billy today," he told her. "But I needed him more than you did."

When he got back, Graham told Haldeman that he had helped tone down whatever Johnson would say publicly about McGovern. Johnson wouldn't attack Democrats who were defecting to Nixon. And he had a message to deliver to Nixon as well. The president, Johnson said, should just ignore McGovern. The best thing Nixon could do was "go all out and identify with people, to ball games, factories and so on. [Johnson] thinks the McGovern people will defeat themselves. He feels very strongly anti-McGovern. Says the P should not do much campaigning, stay above it, as Johnson did with Goldwater." When Graham raised Watergate with Johnson, who knew something about wiretapping the enemy, he just laughed. "Hell," Johnson said, "that's not going to hurt him a bit."

Graham and Haldeman went on to talk about Nixon's acceptance speech. It was only natural that Graham would see these major speeches as a chance for the president to witness, to raise the tone. It is also possible that Haldeman used his reports of his conversations with Graham to add weight to arguments of his own. "Billy feels it should not be like four years ago, because he's now P. He doesn't need the flamboyance of the challenger. What will appeal is a high road, illuminate the accomplishments. Look to the future, what can be done. . . . Hit the socialistic welfare state vs. America where you can start at the bottom and work to the top. The only way McGovern's plan would work is under a dictatorship." And please, Graham added, don't forget to bring God into the picture.

"He believes that you will be making a serious mistake if you do not include a spiritual note in the speech," Haldeman told Nixon the next day, passing along Graham's advice. "Many of our hard core supporters have a strong belief in God and will be looking for a spiritual note." Graham had proposed several Bible passages from Psalms 20 and 33 and Proverbs 14. The best, the evangelist suggested, might be from Joshua 24, which would appeal to both Christians and Jews. Graham's advice notwithstanding, in his speech Nixon went after the Democrats hard; he did quote Lincoln's aspiration to "be on God's side," but there was no scripture and no prayers.

While Nixon and the Republicans launched an election drive that all indications suggested would be a blowout to match any in history, McGovern and Shriver made their scheduled visit to Johnson's ranch. Johnson would not allow reporters in; but once he had McGovern and Shriver alone, he let them have it. He told McGovern he thought he was "crazy as hell" on the war, so they should change the subject. Talk about how Republicans only care about rich people; they'll "always sell you out to Wall Street." And don't expect Johnson to lift a finger for him.

As they were leaving, Johnson picked up the phone and called Graham in Montreat. McGovern and Shriver were just now heading out of the gate, he said. "They are trying to get me to play a part in the campaign. But I'm not gonna do it." Johnson was furious that they could treat him so shabbily at the convention and then come and try to enlist him in their cause. He said he had told McGovern he was associating with amateurs, that the candidate ought to shake up half his staff and he ought to stand up and say what a wonderful place America is. And, he added, he was grateful for all the kind things Nixon had done for him and his family since he left office. Graham immediately called Haldeman with the good news: Johnson, Haldeman recorded, "made it clear to Graham that he would be happy to see Nixon if he wants to come and visit him."

Graham did start to get a little worried in the fall, and told Haldeman so, sensing perhaps in what he was reading that winning reelection might not be the greatest of Nixon's challenges. In September he still agreed with Johnson about Watergate: the *Washington Post* was chipping away at the notion of a conspiracy around the break-in, but Graham still thought it wasn't hurting Nixon. "It's too clouded, people think the Democrats placed it themselves, and that they've overplayed it," Haldeman recorded in his diary. "He thinks that the P is finally succeeding in creating an Eisenhower father image for himself, there's no one else, and he should stay above partisanship."

But the FBI investigations traced the break-in further up the chain of command, including toward Haldeman. By mid-October the *Post* revealed that the investigators had concluded that Watergate was just one part of a much larger scheme of White House political spying and sabotage of opponents; hundreds of thousands of dollars had been spent to discredit the strongest potential Democratic challengers. Graham felt it was all casting at least the president's men if not Nixon himself as unscrupulous characters. He told Haldeman that "he'd be most happy to make a statement on my behalf, or Dwight [Chapin's], on our character and so forth. That we shouldn't let them get away with the whole thing."

In the end of course it wasn't much of a race. The Religion News Service reported that "most evangelical Protestants will 'probably follow the lead of evangelist Billy Graham' and vote for President Nixon, according to a *Christianity Today* analysis of the 'religious campaign.'" *Christianity Today* editor Barrie Doyle noted that "Graham insists he's not campaigning for Nixon but allows that the California Quaker will probably go down in history as one of the country's greatest presidents."

Haldeman wrote an action paper on October 30. "We need to prepare a phone list for Presidential calls to be made election night. . . . On the calls for the President to make, we should set very high priorities, Connally, Billy Graham, Rockefeller, Reagan, John Mitchell, Maury Stans, Clark MacGregor, Bob Dole, three or four key labor people, not very many contributors or old friends—just a few of the top ones." By then his talking points with Graham were already looking down the road. "How should the president handle McGovern in his acceptance speech? How can we best keep the present support for the President after the election?"

And once again come November, the Associated Press reported that Graham had cast his absentee vote for Nixon, a man who was, he said, "born to be president." To McGovern's charges that Nixon was corrupt, Graham said he was "desperate, and he is tired. I know the president as well as anyone outside his immediate family. I have known him since 1950 and I have great confidence in his personal honesty. I voted for him because I know what he is made of."

TWENTY-ONE

The Reckoning

I could sense that something was bothering him. I didn't know what it was.
—Graham on Nixon at the start of his second term

And so the unloved and unlovable Richard Nixon won in an enormous landslide. He would have won even if his side hadn't cheated. Nixon had promised peace; Kissinger declared that it was at hand scarcely a week before election day. He had passed historic environmental policies, fattened the cities with revenue sharing, the draft was disappearing. Most of the Congress couldn't stand him, nor the press or even many in his own party; but eighteen million more people voted for him than for McGovern, thereby bestowing on him both their trust and, by virtue of its scale, the curse of the landslide victory.

The election laid a kind of curse on Graham as well. Though the vast majority of their conversations and memos were private, Graham's embrace of the Nixon administration had reached such a point that it was a matter of rising public debate in evangelical circles. The greatest hero the movement had ever known seemed to be challenging a tradition of clerical distance from politics that dated to colonial days. Had Graham been less of an icon, the relationship might not have cost him so much. But the more embedded he seemed to be in Nixon's operation, and the more often he defended the president in public, the bigger a target he became. Even some who were devoted to him now feared that he was compromised by his closeness to power, telling the king what he wanted to hear.

One of the first shots had come from two well-known southern clergymen in an open letter to Graham published in *Katallagete*, a liberal journal sponsored by the Committee of Southern Churchmen. Graham, they said, had become "a false court prophet" and a "cop-out" to the truth. "You are our Baptist brother, and we love you," they wrote. Over the years they had defended Graham against those who "early in your career, haughtily and with snickers barred you from their common rooms and chapels. We opposed them at the time because we thought . . . that you were a man preaching more Jesus than culture, more Gospel than law. And so maybe now we are a little hurt and peeved to see a man we once tried to stand up for become more and more the man of tremendous power and influence. Maybe it's the use of that power and influence, in Christ's name, to become a court prophet . . . whether in the semi-secrecy of a political convention corridor or on the golf course or at the East Room of the White House."

"Graham's White House Role Has Protestants in Quandary," read the headline in the *Charlotte Observer*. "Not only does he counsel privately with President Nixon, he pronounces public blessing on the policies of the Nixon administration," wrote Louis Cassels, the well-known religion reporter for UPI. In the article, Louis Benes, editor of the Reformed Church in America's *Church Herald*, made the counterargument. Protestants should be grateful, he argued, that a president was consulting someone like Graham. "Who else would we want there in the role of confidential White House advisor? Some God is Dead theologian or a Playboy philosopher?" Graham's own *Christianity Today* was cautiously encouraged: "We grant there is risk involved when a clergyman becomes a confidant of powerful figures in the secular world," read an editorial. "But is not the risk far outweighed by the opportunity? Have not evangelicals long prayed for an entrée without compromise into the affairs of state?" While the Bible warned of false prophets, there was to date "no evidence" that Graham had "watered down his convictions to gain access to the White House."

To the extent that Graham was prepared to answer the critics, it was with a combination of modesty and mystery. He didn't always agree with the president, he told the *Observer*, "but I also know there are facts available to a president, especially in foreign affairs, that simply aren't available to you and me." And those who were inclined to challenge Graham faced the same limitation: "People have no idea what I say to the president," he said. "If I ever publicized what I say, I'd never have this entry again. And it is an unusual entry . . . an opportunity for me to discuss with him my views on matters. I don't call it being a prophet, because I'm not a prophet. I've tried to keep the relationship on spiritual matters." Years later, when at least some of those private conversations became public with the declassification of the Nixon tapes, Graham sounded shocked, and certainly contrite, about the occasions when he had not followed his own rules.

Ruth was as devoted to Nixon as her husband was, and she swatted away the critics as well. "Do we want a president in the White House who is not free to call on a clergyman if he feels the need of one? Well, that's what it will boil down to if clergymen are driven to the position some members of the press have tried to drive Bill to. Christianity is above ideology. It's for Democrats and Republicans alike. It's for sinners, and I think the press would be the first to admit there are sinners in politics."

The real test did not come until after Nixon's reelection triumph. For all the relief at the October announcement of a breakthrough in the Paris talks, the negotiations with Hanoi had broken down again by December. Nixon overruled the objections of his air force and began the Christmas bombing of North Vietnam. It was unprecedented in its scale, fifteen thousand tons of bombs falling in a matter of days. "It was perhaps the most painful, the most difficult, and certainly the most lonely decision" Nixon had made in office, Kissinger claimed in a television interview a few weeks later. The president didn't explain; he didn't defend it. "The more difficult Hanoi was, the more rigid Saigon grew," Kissinger said, "and we could see a prospect where we would be caught between the two contending parties." Only another round of brutal bombings, Nixon concluded, would dislodge them and yield a settlement—except that it ended up being the same settlement they could have had in October.

In the meantime, the country was on the verge of a nervous breakdown.

Someone had to do something. Someone had to tell the president that this was wrong, indefensible. Three days before Christmas, a group of ten Chicago clergymen publicly called on Graham to "implore President Nixon to stop the bombing of North Vietnam in the name of the Christmas Christ.

"Bombing any time is despicable," they wrote in a telegram, "but to renew bombing when 'peace is at hand' and to beat Vietnamese to their knees and to kill thousands in the name of peace just so that we can have our way is outrageous. In the name of the Prince of Peace, Jesus Christ, our Lord and Saviour, do something to stop it."

At the same time forty-one religious leaders, including the chiefs of four national religious bodies, Catholic, Protestant, and Jewish, sent Nixon a pastoral letter deploring the bombing and accusing the White House of "betraying the duty of peace." On New Year's Eve war protesters assembled in New York and heard Ernest Campbell of Riverside Church preach a sermon titled "An Open Letter to Billy Graham," challenging the evangelist to respond to the pastors' appeal. "As one of the 'near voices' within hearing distance of the throne, you surely bear a responsibility to critique government policy as well as bless it."

Graham was hearing from pastors in private as well, scorching denunciations from men he had joined in crusades in their cities, men who had honored and aided his ministry over the years. Hundreds of letters and telegrams poured in; some were less fair than others. One minister who had met Graham more than a decade earlier through a crusade had always been an admirer and defender. "Years ago when friends attacked you for oversimplifying issues and dodging problems of global ethics, I spoke of your 'sincerity' and the 'good' you were doing," he wrote. "I was wrong." He said he had always defended Graham when others ridiculed his "hunger for the spotlight and . . . lust for famous friends. I suggested that you were doubtless using such opportunities to advance the cause of Christ. I was wrong." He pleaded that Graham would use his chance to witness. "Forgive the harshness of some of the above, but history is involved—millions of lives are involved—and your unique position in public affairs will continue to play a decisive role in the 20th century story of mankind."

Graham had made it a policy not to answer his critics, to turn the other cheek. And in this case he did not fire back. In fact he embraced the criticism, put himself in the writer's place. "I can easily understand the harshness and outrage of your letter," he wrote. "I accept your rebuke with all the humility I can muster. If I were in your place and from your vantage point I might have written a stronger letter."

However, Graham went on, it was impossible for anyone to know the true nature of his relationship with Nixon or any other president. "You may not believe it but I deplore the continuation of the war in Vietnam as much as you do." He noted that he had just spent time with the new head of the World Council of Churches, and had inquired why his organization didn't speak out as forcefully about injustice behind the Iron Curtain as in the West. "He gave a remarkable answer. He said it was for tactical reasons so that they could have the greater influence when genuine crises arose. I would ask of you, beloved friend, to give me just a little of that same privilege."

It was hard for anyone who had not been in Graham's position—and no one had ever been in Graham's position—to understand the line he was walking. He was as depressed as everyone else about the Christmas bombing; but it was out of his nature to storm into the White House, question Nixon's judgment, and then come out and talk about it publicly. His critics suggested that all he was risking was his access: anger a president and you won't be invited back. But to Graham that didn't just represent no more cruises on the *Sequoia*. It meant no more chance to preach the gospel to the most powerful man on earth. As for his prophetic or pastoral obligations, Graham issued a statement the first week of January 1973: "I am convinced that God has called me to be a New Testament evangelist, not an Old Testament prophet! While some may interpret an evangelist to be primarily a social reformer or political activist, I do not! My primary goal is to proclaim the good news of the Gospel of Jesus Christ. The basic problem of man is within his own heart."

Everyone knew of his long alliance with Nixon—but he rejected the idea that he had any influence on policy. He was no more some kind of "White House Chaplain," he said, than Cardinal Cushing was during Kennedy's term. "I'm not one of [Nixon's] advisors. I'm just a personal friend, that's all."

"The President doesn't call me up and say 'Billy, shall we do this or that?'" he told the *Charlotte News*, drawing a distinction between a president asking "shall we do this?" and asking "what would people think if we did this?" "In no way would he ask me military strategy. He's never even discussed it with me. If I have something to say to President Nixon, I'll do it privately, and I won't announce it from the housetops with a lot of publicity."

And yet, while declaring his public "neutrality," Graham did not want the White House to think he was disloyal: on January 8, 1973, Dwight Chapin sent Haldeman a memo saying Graham was "very disturbed by some press reports which quote him as saying the war is deplorable," and wanted to be sure the president saw the full text of his statement.

Looking back on those hard days many years later, Graham said that most of the time, when people called on him to deliver some message to the president, he didn't do it. "But I did on that occasion," he said. "I was getting a little bit depressed about it." But in no case would he say anything publicly that might suggest the president did not have his support.

On the night before Nixon's second inauguration Graham was cochair of a celebratory black-tie concert at the Kennedy Center, where they heard a triumphant *1812 Overture*. In mournful counterpoint across town, Francis Sayre, dean at Washington National Cathedral, presided over a free concert, featuring Haydn's *Mass in Time of War*. Nixon was grumpy, distracted, quite unlike a conquering hero, and later Graham would suggest that this was when he first glimpsed the gathering storms. The Nixons were seated directly in front of the Grahams at the concert, Graham recalled. "I saw that he didn't have a program so I handed him my program and he knocked it out of my hand. And Pat leaned over and spoke to him, I don't know what she said but he reached and picked it up and turned around and apologized to me."

On Inauguration Day, Graham was a special guest of Governor and Mrs. Ronald Reagan at the California ball. But his sensitivity about his role was such that he also took time to sit down once again with Edward B. Fiske, religion editor at the *New York Times*, to try to clarify his position. Calling the war the "judgment of God on America," he said he had had grave questions about it from the start—which was fair, given things he had been saying privately back in 1965. "I doubted from the beginning over sending American troops anywhere without the will to win," he said. "We entered the war almost deliberately to lose it." When the Russians stormed into Czechoslovakia, he observed, they used such overwhelming force that there were fewer casualties in the end. And then in an especially gruesome image, he noted, "I don't think we should ever fight these long, drawn-out, half-hearted wars. It's like cutting a cat's tail off a half-inch at a time." Now he worried about whether America would end up destroying what she had gone in to save. "I think it will take 25 years," he said, "to know whether America was right in making this commitment."

What about the Christmas bombing? Fiske asked. "I'll be honest with you. I felt gloomy," Graham said. "Like all Americans, I thought a ceasefire was imminent. I think that this was what caused the reaction across the nation." But as he always did on so many issues, from racial hatred, to war, to, eventually, Watergate, Graham returned to his basic biblical message: human sin is everywhere; tragedy is with us always, a mark of our fallen nature, and to focus on one sin or sorrow over another is to miss the larger point that we are all in need of grace. It amounted to a grand spiritual absolution of any public folly. "I deplore the suffering and the killing in this war, and I pray it can be ended as soon as possible, but we also have to realize there are hundreds of thousands of deaths attributed to smoking. . . . A thousand people are killed every week on the American highways and half of those are attributed to alcohol. Where are the demonstrations against alcohol?"

In one sense Graham was being consistent, and true to his faith, in his refusal to judge his public friends on the grounds that it was God's province to do so, not his. But here he neglected the difference between democracy and theocracy. Voters are called to judge their leaders for their public acts, and hold them accountable. To declare that all men are sinners is a spiritual truth but not a political one; citizens may personally forgive politicians for their failings, but the system of checks and balances was designed to sanction them as well.

He insisted once again that contrary to popular opinion, he had never taken a public position on the war. But that surely should have been a signal to him of the role he had come to play; if a majority of people *believed* that he had taken a position, what responsibility did he bear for that, and what lesson might he have learned about the symbolic weight of his presidential friendships? Silence on a controversial issue can send a loud message as well.

And so can proximity. Preaching at the White House church service the next day, Graham talked about the need to work for peace; but he warned that "we can only patch and help and promote peace and justice in the world. Perfect peace," he said, "awaits that day when we will have a perfect world ruler, the Messiah that both the Jew and the Christian look forward to coming." And then he returned home, to be greeted by word of the death of Lyndon Johnson the next day, and flew to Austin for the funeral of his friend.

The crisis over the war receded as fast as it arose; by the second week of January the North Vietnamese had come back to the negotiating table, and soon the deal was done, prisoners of war were coming off the airplanes to giddy parades, the stock market hit an all-time high, and Richard Nixon was a hero, with a 68 percent approval rating.

Nixon wrote to thank Graham for everything, and the letter had a valedictory tinge. Maybe it was just the perfunctory note of a victorious candidate with many people to thank, but it also hinted that the relationship was about to change. "This gives me an opportunity to put in writing what I have often said to you personally," Nixon wrote. "I shall be eternally grateful for your friendship and your support and your prayers over the years."

And Graham's response was every bit as much a farewell, as though his own term had ended. At least the war might now be behind them: on January 27, 1973, the day the Paris peace accords were signed, Graham told Nixon that "by your persistence, determination, courage and faith," he had rescued the United States from the "quagmire. Some of the liberal commentators seem to be disappointed that you were able to do it!"

So maybe everyone could move on now. "If there is any way that I can serve you this year," Graham wrote, "please do not hesitate to call."

TWENTY-TWO

The Man He Never Knew

I did misjudge him. It was a side to him that I never knew, yet I'd been with him so many times. He was just like a whole new person. I talked to Julie about that and she felt that about her own father. I almost felt as if a demon had come into the White House, and had entered his presidency, because it seemed to be sort of supernatural, I mean it was so ugly and so terrible, especially the cover-up and the language and all that. It was just something I never knew.

—Graham on Nixon

Graham could preach as many sermons in the East Room as he liked, take Nixon's late-night calls, reassure him about both his own loyalty and God's unconditional love during the hardest times. But that was all occurring as the White House evolved as a vast criminal operation—and not the kind seen in every political generation, not Teapot Dome, not Truman and the fur coats, Sherman Adams and the oriental rug. This was not about greed and graft and influence peddling. Those were earthly crimes of a low order. At their worst Nixon's were mortal democratic sins, committed by blindly righteous men. Graham himself referred to their "magnificent obsession," by which he meant the protection of Richard Nixon at all costs. Many of Nixon's men were true believers, so convinced that their enemies—the radicals, the nihilists, the bleeding hearts and America-haters—were immoral and dangerous that whatever they did to stop them was justified by a higher calling, a deeper need. Nixon himself captured the ethos he instilled when he told David Frost that "when the president does it, that means that it is not illegal." If war protesters could break the law in the cause of peace, then why should the White House not do whatever was necessary in the same pursuit: plug leaks, crush opponents, defend the man who would make peace possible? "The whole hopes of the whole Goddamn world of peace, Ron, you know where they meet?" Nixon asked his press secretary, Ron Ziegler, as Watergate was exploding. "They rest right here in this damn chair." Whatever the president's men did was by its nature good because they were good men, the last patriots, with the country's best interests at heart.

And Graham was complicit in this. He had no idea about what Attorney General John Mitchell called the "White House horrors," no idea of the secret funds set up for political intelligence, the enemies lists, the wiretaps, the bribes and threats. Like many of Nixon's stalwart defenders, he didn't know the president had approved the cover-up of crimes committed in his name. But he did defend both Nixon's greatness and goodness. The president couldn't have had anything to do with Watergate, Graham explained when the scandal broke, because "his moral and ethical principles wouldn't allow him to do anything illegal like that. I've known him a long time and he has a very strong sense of integrity."

Nixon was fully aware of how much people's faith in his morality protected him, and he preyed on that faith. "We'll survive," he said in one of his last calls to Haldeman before telling him to resign. "Despite all the polls and all the rest, I think there's still a hell of a lot of people out there . . . you know, they want to believe, that's the point, isn't it?"

Billy Graham was certainly one of them.

As 1973 unfolded and the dark forces in the White House cringed at the daylight that soon streamed in, from investigating committees and dogged reporters and unflinching public servants in both parties intent on learning the truth about Watergate, Nixon stopped calling Graham. Some thought he was trying to protect the evangelist: that's what Graham was told, and he was inclined to believe it because of all the times Nixon had talked about shielding him. "He told his staff to have nothing to do with me," Graham said. "He didn't want me to be tarnished by Watergate, when it started blowing up. I tried to get to him a few times but they wouldn't let me talk to him." But Nixon may also have been trying to protect himself, when it just became too painful to be around his preacher friend. It was perhaps a testimony to what remained of Nixon's conscience: he could lie to anyone but Billy Graham.

All through the summer of 1972 and the fall campaign, then during the winter of 1973 as he finally declared victory in Vietnam, Nixon continued to talk in a way that presumed his own innocence, and Graham in a way that assumed the break-in was no big deal. But in the spring of 1973 came the revelations of a conspiracy in what Nixon's press secretary had tried to dismiss as a "third rate burglary." Nixon might have made his confession and, falling into the proven compassion of the American public, perhaps even found a saving grace. His approval rating in February, after the signing of the peace accords, had been close to 70 percent. But lacking whatever faith he needed, in himself, in the people, and aware of just how much there was to hide, he began the long string of human sacrifices that delayed his own departure for another sixteen months.

Graham had been holding historic integrated crusades in South Africa that spring, the first big interracial gatherings in that nation's history; Nixon wired his congratulations. Graham wrote back that "I have marveled at your restraint as the rumors fly about Watergate," and pointed him to scripture for strength. "King David had the same experience. He said: 'They accuse me of things I have never heard about. I do them good but they return me harm.'"

Nixon, however, was no King David, and by the time Graham got back to the United States, the world had changed. The Senate had voted unanimously to create its Watergate Committee, chaired by Graham's old friend and home-state senator Sam Ervin. "This is his great moment of glory," Graham told Nixon when the president called, noting that Ervin had been a neighbor all his life.

"Sure," Nixon said. "Well, we'll let him have it," and the two men laughed. "He'll dig away," Nixon went on, "and he'll make a lot of headlines, and he'll irritate a lot, but those things also pass." And then came the warm, wicked reassurance: "The main thing about those, of course, as you know, the campaign people—I can assure you nobody in the White House is in, but campaign people, they sometimes do silly things."

Billy Graham could no more imagine that the president of the United States, his friend of twenty years, might be flatly lying to him than that cars could fly.

But it was all starting to unravel, with the reports that the Watergate burglars who had just pleaded guilty had been pressured and paid off and perjured themselves on orders from above. Until then the president had the benefit of the doubt: before the election, the charges unfolding in the *Post* were dismissed as "political garbage" by GOP chair Bob Dole. Now Dole was calling publicly for the resignation of Haldeman and Ehrlichman and saying "the credibility of the administration is zilch, zero." White House counsel John Dean was ready to pull back the curtain for the Watergate prosecutors and implicate the president's inner circle.

Graham called for the punishment of everyone connected with Watergate—while insisting that this could not possibly include the president. "Of course I have been mystified and confused and sick about the whole thing as I think every American is," he said, and he called on the president to appoint an independent investigator and clean up the mess. "I personally do not think he knew about it," Graham said of Nixon on the *Today* show. "It was a stupid blunder to begin with, and he's too smart for that. . . . Secondly, I think his moral and ethical principles wouldn't allow him to do anything illegal like that. I've known him a long time and he has a very strong sense of integrity."

Even that was enough to make Nixon anxious. He talked to Ziegler: "This is a time for strong men, Ron," he said. "Don't you get panicky." And he reminded Ziegler to keep repeating that he wanted to get to the bottom of it. "I was rather sorry to see Billy Graham join the chorus of saying do something, you know," Nixon said. "I was really surprised to see him say that. . . . But I suppose that's just a straw in the wind. He's probably jumping ship, don't you think?" Because, Nixon admitted, it was too late now to "do something. . . . The grand jury's too far along the line, and they're going to indict."

Two days later, on April 30, 1973, Nixon fired Dean; Haldeman and Ehrlichman, the two men who had served him most faithfully, resigned. It amounted to the complete collapse of the command structure that had surrounded and protected him, carried out his will through the first term. "You're a strong man, goddamn it, and I love you," Nixon told Haldeman over the phone after the announcement. "I love you, as you know. . . . Like my brother."

"O.K." was all Haldeman could say.

Nixon never lost faith in his ability to look into a TV camera and make the truth wince. He went on the air that night to pledge his determination to uncover the whole truth of this "sordid affair." "There can be no whitewash at the White House," he said, and promised to purge the system of any abuse or misconduct. And he asked for people's prayers, that his presidency would be worthy of their hopes for it.

Graham seemed desperate to believe Nixon's story, if only because the alternative was unthinkable. He told reporters after the speech that Watergate was a symptom of a permissive American culture. Nixon had demonstrated "a commendable humility" in his address to the country: "He asked for our prayers, and he has mine."

Nixon called Graham that night at 10:20. "I had to tell Haldeman and Ehrlichman to resign, which they wouldn't do voluntarily, and that was tough," he said.

"Well, your sincerity, your humility, your asking for prayer, all of that, had a tremendous impact," Graham replied.

"You really think so, Billy?"

"I really, I'm telling you the truth, and I'm not trying to just encourage you. I know you get all that. But I really mean it."

"Well, that's good of you, Billy. You've been a friend, and, and—" The tape then cuts off.

That night Haldeman wrote in his diary one final entry. Among the calls he had made that day was one to Graham. "He seemed to feel it was the right thing to do, said he didn't believe that in government he had met two finer men than Ehrlichman and me, that we have his full support—he feels we've been caught in a web of evil that will ultimately be defeated. He has great affection and love for me as a man, that I should count on him as a friend, and that what I'm doing is going to help the P."

Two days later Graham tried to get through to Nixon; Haldeman's assistant Lawrence Higby took the call. "He feels that people are finally starting to realize that this whole Watergate situation is overblown and unfair," Higby reported to Nixon. "He wanted to pass on to you his suggestion that whenever possible we create picture situations such as the one yesterday with you and [West German chancellor] Willy Brandt. This causes the public to focus on the fact that the president is not bogged down on one issue. . . . The American people need to be diverted from Watergate and pictures such as the one yesterday with you and Brandt do this. He emphasized that speeches are not necessary now, in fact, they may not be productive."

But even as he was coaching the White House on how to change the subject and move on, Graham was arguing publicly for some deep national soul-searching. That Sunday, the end of the wrenching week of revelations, he wrote an op-ed for the *New York Times* titled "Watergate and Its Lessons of Morality," in which, once again, there was plenty of blame for everyone. Watergate was indeed a "sordid" affair, he said, but "no political party can claim the title of Mr. Clean."

He called for the punishment of those found guilty while reminding people of the presumption of innocence. But then he cast his net wider. "The time is overdue for Americans to engage in some deep soul-searching about the underpinnings of our society and our goals as a nation." He called for revival and repentance; America, he said, was always driven to God in a crisis. And the reporters who had broken the scandal open should now, he suggested, do some penance of their own. "They could render constructive service to the nation at this critical moment . . . if they joined hands with the churches and synagogues and used their vast powers to fan the dying embers of the moral and spiritual life of the nation."

This brought Graham back into the line of fire; coming within months of the Christmas bombing furor, the response to Graham's response on Watergate was nearly as hostile. He was called to account not only by fellow clergy, but also by fellow opinion leaders. It was untenable, many felt, that he should have gone to such lengths to support and defend Nixon and now, as the president's perfidy became clear, cast it into the larger shadows of original sin and shared human weakness. "This is the larger cover-up," wrote James Reston of the *Times*, "the cover-up of the true feelings of many men and women who know they have influence but they don't want to commit themselves in public on the moral issues."

The *Washington Post* was next: "Graham is Silent about Watergate" ran the *Post* headline on June 15, 1973. It recounted Graham's remarks to the General Assembly of the Presbyterian Church in the U.S. (Southern), where he was criticized for not speaking out against the president. Graham came to the meeting escorted by eight armed guards, said to have been hired for "crowd control." "I still have confidence in President Nixon," Graham declared. He was waiting until all the facts were in—but noted that he had no special insight into the situation. "The President has never discussed Watergate with me; he has had no private conversation with me in 18 months," which was not exactly true given the phone calls. But he still honored his pastoral obligations. "I think what we ought to do is pray for all our leaders . . . if McGovern had been President I would be praying for him and supporting him as much as I could."

Less than a month later the headlines suggested the pressure he was feeling. "Billy Graham to Abandon Crusades," announced the *Post*. In Minneapolis for a ten-day crusade, Graham told a press conference that this might be one of his last. He might have to retreat to more mass media, a less demanding schedule, because he felt he was "physically unable" to continue.

All through this period, Graham wasn't talking to Nixon much; the calls wouldn't go through. And with one exception, the invitations stopped coming. The Sunday services had essentially been suspended. Nixon was neither going to church nor seeking spiritual counsel. "I tried to get in touch with him a number of times, to assure him of my prayers and urge him to seek the Lord's guidance in a very difficult situation," Graham said. And then he gave a clue about the sense of spiritual distance he had come to feel: he said he saw the president as a friend, not a parishioner: "I seriously doubt if he looked upon me as his pastor. . . . There was little I could do for him except pray."

Nixon's withdrawal was entirely characteristic; he had conducted much of his presidency from an emotional bunker. But Colson, for one, who had left the White House in March 1973, was surprised that Nixon shut Graham out. "Nixon I would have thought would have leaned on Graham through that. Sometimes, when Nixon was just melancholy, he would just pick up the phone and call Graham. It's hard for me to see how he could go through Watergate [without that]."

In October came Agnew's indictment and resignation, and the Saturday Night Massacre, when Nixon ordered his attorney general, Elliot Richardson, to fire Watergate special prosecutor Archibald Cox; Richardson resigned instead, as did his deputy, and the constitutional crisis that loomed inspired *TIME* to publish its first editorial ever, calling for Nixon to resign.

Asked in November whether the president should resign or be impeached, Graham concluded, "Democracy must have a moral basis. If a criminal act has taken place and he is guilty, then he should be impeached. . . . I pray for the President. I cry for him. If he asked me for spiritual advice, I'd give it to him. But he hasn't." He offered Nixon some Thanksgiving encouragement in a public statement, but it was muted compared to past defenses. The "tragic events," he said, would "probably make him a stronger man and a better president. I do not always agree with the judgment and policies of his Administration. But President Nixon has my support and prayers." Given that he would likely stay in the White House for another three years, "I think he should have the prayers of all Americans." It wasn't much, but it was enough to prompt Nixon to call him at home and thank him.

Graham's misgivings were growing as he glimpsed sides to his friend that bore no resemblance to the president he knew. In December Nixon's tax returns as president revealed just how tightly clutched a soul he was. Nineteen seventy was the only year his charitable gifts approached the average for his income level. That year the largest gift by far, $4,500, more than half of his total giving, was to the BGEA. His total income since he'd been in office approached $3 million, his charitable giving scarcely $10,000 during those years. Of reports that Nixon had used federal funds to upgrade his estates in San Clemente and Key Biscayne, Graham said that this set a bad example: "It seems to me these expenses ought to have been called personal," he told the *Washington Post*, whose story noted that Graham himself gave between 10 and 15 percent of his gross income to charity.

By that time, Nixon was a prisoner of the White House. The gas crisis meant that travel was restricted, and Nixon could not very well jet off to Key Biscayne or San Clemente. He was sleepless, cornered. He gathered his friends around him and got drunk at a cozy dinner with his family, his secretary Rosemary Woods, and Barry Goldwater on December 21. Then Pat Nixon called Billy Graham, who was at a planning meeting for the coming World Evangelization conference in Switzerland, and asked him to come back to preach.

Graham realized the political stakes. By now some pastors were passing petitions around their churches on Sunday mornings calling for impeachment, as were a number of national church bodies. But he would always view a White House invitation as a spiritual opportunity, as he explained to *Christianity Today* in a way that suggested what hostile territory the West Wing had become. "I have said for many years that I will go anywhere to preach the Gospel, whether to the Vatican, the Kremlin or the White House, if there are no strings attached on what I am to say." The idea that by going he would be offering a benediction on all that was going on in the White House was "ridiculous." That charge amounted to McCarthyism, he said, a kind of guilt by association. "It is quite obvious that I do not agree with everything the Nixon Administration does."

Ruth and Billy stayed at the White House the weekend before Christmas—and ministered at various times to the whole family. "I was feeling the strain of over six months of Watergate," Julie Nixon Eisenhower recalled, "and more important, I was facing the fact that after years of searching I still did not have a deep spiritual base in my life." She and Ruth sat for a long time in a little sitting room, talking about how to study the scriptures; she marveled at Ruth's Bible, so worn and under-lined, with notes in every margin. "She led the kind of life I wanted to lead," Julie said, and Ruth Graham put her in touch with a congressman's wife who could include her in their weekly Bible study.

Graham preached Sunday morning about repentance, and justice for the poor and dispossessed. He introduced himself to the congregation, which included Vice President Ford and Senator Edward Kennedy, as "just a North Carolina country preacher" who was in "the most distinguished company I've ever been in at Christmastime." He sounded like a man in retreat, back to the safety of his symbolic perch—since the one thing he had never been in his life was just a North Carolina country preacher.

After the service, Graham and Nixon talked privately about Watergate for the first time; he told reporters it was the first real conversation he had had with Nixon in two years. He wrote to Nixon afterward: "I was delighted to see you looking so well and chipper in spite of all the difficul-ties you faced during the past year. Certainly the Lord has sustained you in a remarkable way. Lesser men would have folded long ago."

But he also had some explaining to do. The *Christianity Today* inter-view was by far the fullest exploration of his views of Watergate and the Nixon presidency; it was picked up by the major papers the week after the White House visit, with headlines like "Graham Criticizes Nixon, Old Friend, on Judgment." He was hard on Nixon, harder than he had been before. Even his affirmation of his "complete faith in the President's integrity" was, this time, qualified: "until there is more proof to the con-trary." Though Nixon had been charged with no crime yet, "mistakes and blunders have been made. Some of them involved moral and ethical ques-tions, but at this point, if I have anything to say to the President, it will be in private."

Asked whether Nixon had used him as a tool to win respectability, Graham was sharp: "That's foolish. If Mr. Nixon wanted to make me a tool, why has it been so long since he invited me to the White House? During the period when he might have needed a person like me the most he didn't invite me."

What about those men around Nixon, the ones who had seemed so upright, so dedicated? "These Nixon aides thought his reelection was the most important thing in the world," Graham said. "They thought that future peace depended on him. I think most of them were very sincere, but they began to rationalize that the 'end' justified the 'means,' even if it meant taking liberties with law and the truth." But if he was right, he added, the culture of the times bore some of the blame. "They had heard people call for all kinds of civil disobedience. They felt that their 'cause' was just as great as peace in Vietnam and civil rights. In fact they felt peace in Vietnam could only be achieved by the reelection of Richard Nixon." He offered the contagion of "situational ethics" as an explanation, not an excuse. "Some of the men involved in Watergate practiced that kind of ethics. If God is, then what God says must be absolute—man must have moral boundaries. He cannot devise his own morals to fit his own situation."

It was clear as Graham explored what had happened that the wounds were deep, and that his call for repentance applied to himself as well. "Throughout the years," he confessed, "I have said things to various Presidents that could be construed as political advice. I'm not so quick anymore to make political judgments." He wouldn't comment on Nixon's infuriating and stubborn self-righteousness. But he did say that "I have personally found that when you've made a mistake it's far better to admit it. . . . I've had to admit errors in judgment, and I've found Christian people more than generous in understanding my faults."

The blistering criticism of the past year had left him worrying that he was even harming the larger cause of evangelism itself—and that was a terrifying prospect. "I sometimes put my foot in my mouth," he said. "I've made many statements I wish I could recall. I am an erring, fallible disciple of our Lord Jesus Christ, and am subject to all the temptations, human frailties, and errors of other disciples of the Lord."

Graham tried to make amends with Nixon after the critical newspaper stories appeared. "Unfortunately some of the news media carried only the negative aspects," he said. "Again I want to reaffirm my personal affection for you as a man, my appreciation for our long friendship and my complete confidence in your personal integrity."

But Nixon's most staunch defenders were not mollified. Graham's critics from the left were typically the more public and outspoken, but the ones on the right were furious now; one angry letter writer likened him to a rat deserting a sinking ship. Norman Vincent Peale let Graham know how disgusted he was, and copied Nixon on the correspondence. "I was saddened by your recent reported statements about President Nixon. It appeared that you were trying to get out from under and were not standing by the man for whom you have professed abiding friendship.

"As for me, I am sticking with President Nixon one hundred percent, all the way. I believe in him absolutely and have been totally unaffected by the vicious attacks on him."

Graham still believed in confession and forgiveness, and he worked hard to persuade his friend of the possibility of mercy. The prayer breakfast loomed once more, and Graham sent two proposals of what Nixon could say, one short, one much longer and more confessional: it was all Graham's hopes for Nixon's spiritual journey wrestled onto the page, an expression of what he desperately hoped the president was thinking. "I hope I shall not be judged as hiding behind religion when I say that I have, like many of my predecessors before me, been driven to my knees in prayer." Graham's draft ended with Nixon saying, "I want to take this opportunity today to rededicate myself to the God that I first learned about at my mother's knee."

Nixon's new chief of staff, Alexander Haig, passed Graham's draft along to Nixon, noting that the longer version "is replete with Watergate mea culpa and is totally unacceptable from my point of view."

Graham accompanied Nixon to and from the prayer breakfast—and went back home a troubled man. He could vouch for the president's spiritual life all he wanted, but in private he was never so sure, as became clear in the letter he wrote from Montreat. It was as close to a rebuke as Graham would allow himself in writing to a president.

"It was nice that you talked about Lincoln's spiritual life," Graham wrote to Nixon. But then he pushed. "I had rather hoped that you would go from the wonderful expression about Lincoln's dependence on the Lord in times of crisis, to your own personal experience. I think everyone was waiting for it and expecting it. As one Senator said to me afterward, 'he went to the brink and backed away.' . . . While I know you have a personal and private commitment, yet at some point many are hoping and praying that you will state it publicly."

Then Graham brought it all together, the whole point of his presidential ministry, if only he could get through this time. "To be President is a great and thrilling attainment," he wrote. "However there is one thing far greater than being President—and that is being a committed child of God. There is a thrill, a joy, an adventure, an excitement, a satisfaction awaiting you in that direction, no matter what the circumstances around you, that is indescribable." Graham's sermons, whether to a congregation of a hundred thousand or an audience of one, were always urgent and eager at the same time, a warning and a welcome to a new hope. But this letter especially, given its tone and timing, revealed just how lost he thought Nixon was, if after twenty years together he still felt he needed to persuade him of the thrill of being a child of God. Wherever Nixon was at that moment, it was someplace much more complex, a pit of tragedy that Graham could not begin to fathom.

As the months passed and the worst White House sins became public, Graham had to face the possibility that he had been fooled, or fooled himself, about his friend all these years. He had known Eisenhower was a lapsed Christian, and so had witnessed; he had known Johnson was no angel, and so prayed with him. But Nixon's piety and pedigree he had not questioned. "I remember how many times he quoted his mother," Graham said. "He saw her with a Bible often in his thinking . . . and I think that influenced my thinking." That very first time they'd met and played golf, "we talked a great deal about the Lord and I just assumed . . ." And his voice trailed off. Surely, they were kindred spirits; until it became clear that they were nothing of the kind

The revelations of the spring of 1974 were among the most excruciating experiences of Graham's life. After reading the transcripts of Oval Office conversations in the privacy of his study, he became physically sick. His family worried for him. "I wanted to believe the best about him for as long as I could," he said. "When the worst came out, it was nearly unbearable for me."

He was now forced to explain himself publicly. "Those tapes revealed a man that I never knew," he said. That alone was a kind of personal crisis of faith. But his association with Nixon made him a target as well. Pat Robertson charged that Christians had been victims of a cruel hoax: "We were led to believe that the man who appeared as a confidant of Billy Graham . . . was in truth a man of personal piety. We can surmise that Dr. Billy Graham has been used for political image-building."

With Nixon's immolation, Graham's personal and pastoral priorities were at odds with his public and political self-interest. To his credit, he chose to be a pastor, no matter how hard Nixon made that for him. Nixon was his friend, he said, and while he could not defend what he did, he would not kick him when he was down. He tried to reach the president, but couldn't get through. So he was left to pray for him.

"There was something spiritual about the whole thing," he said as he looked back years later. "An evil spirit had somehow come upon him."

"I wonder," Graham wrote in his memoirs, "whether I might have exaggerated his spirituality in my own mind. . . . Where religion was concerned with him, it was not always easy to tell the difference between the spiritual and the sentimental. In retrospect, whenever he spoke about the Lord, it was in pretty general terms."

TWENTY-THREE

Ford and Forgiveness

I never was sure that it really hurt [Ford], but maybe it did.
—Graham on Ford's pardon of Nixon

At the very moment that Graham's political world was crumbling, the evangelical world was gathering at his feet. In July, after years of careful planning, he assembled 2,400 church leaders from 150 countries at a massive conference in Lausanne, Switzerland, to debate and then decide nothing less than the future of evangelism. Graham organized a half dozen world evangelism convocations over the course of his ministry, and each was built around a different challenge confronting the fast-growing evangelical universe.

The Lausanne meeting was more of a battle cry than a battle: evangelism, Graham worried, was being sidetracked from its paramount purpose of saving souls to more temporal tasks of improving the welfare of men and women while still on earth. Who was doing the sidetracking? The decidedly more liberal World Council of Churches, which Graham and many other conservative American evangelicals believed had lost sight of evangelism's chief goal of preaching the gospel. In its dispatch from Lausanne, *TIME* put it pointedly: "Some of the World Council's advocates of ecumenism increasingly have questioned whether Christians even have the right—let alone the duty—to disturb the honest faith of a Buddhist, a Hindu or a Jew." Graham told *TIME*'s Richard Ostling that the Council had "gradually moved further and further from orthodox ties. The gulf between it and the Evangelicals has deepened."

In Lausanne, Graham wasn't just picking a fight about the future of evangelism; he was doing so in the Council's backyard: the Council is headquartered in Geneva, just a few dozen miles down Lake Leman from Lausanne.

The conference wrapped up its work the same week that two other gatherings in Washington—one legislative, another judicial—wrapped up theirs. After a seven-month investigation, the House Judiciary Committee voted 27 to 11 to approve a single article of impeachment: "Wherefore Richard M. Nixon, by such conduct, warrants impeachment and trial and removal from office." The same week, the U.S. Supreme Court issued a unanimous opinion that, in effect, ordered Richard Nixon to turn over tapes and other records of sixty-four White House conversations to special Watergate prosecutor Leon Jaworski.

And so at the very moment that Billy Graham stood atop the evangelical world, redirecting a vast flock toward the fundamental task of saving souls worldwide, one of his best-known sheep was apparently lost. He had triumphed dramatically in the Kingdom of God—but played a poorer hand in the Kingdom of Man.

Even when surrounded in Lausanne by his admiring peers, Graham did not hide from the criticism at home. In his keynote address on the first day, he said it was a mistake "to identify the Gospel with any political program or culture. I confess tonight that this has been one of my own dangers in my ministry." And in his closing remarks, he added, "You know what God has been saying for these last ten days. I know what he has convicted me of and what I must do."

But it may be that what he was advising in private was as important as what he was confessing in public. Sometime during the ten-day meeting, Graham requested a meeting with a Lausanne conference attendee named Billy Zeoli, a producer of religious films who had been having private Bible study with Vice President Gerald Ford for months. Graham and Zeoli had known each other since 1955, when they had met on the Wheaton College campus the year Zeoli was graduating. Two years later, Zeoli joined a committee of local preachers to plan the 1959 Indianapolis crusade. During that twenty-eight-day event, Zeoli sat with Graham onstage nearly every night. In the early 1960s Zeoli moved to Grand Rapids and decided one day to meet his congressman. He dropped in on Ford and gave the lawmaker a Bible. Over the next few years, the two men became close. And now Jerry Ford was about to become the thirty-eighth president of the United States.

Zeoli reported to Graham's office at Lausanne and was ushered in by an aide. "Whoever brought me in left," Zeoli recalled. "When that happened, I knew it was important." Speaking in a tone that was both thoughtful and tender, Graham told him that he now had a responsibility "to share the Word with the next President. When you get to the White House, don't play golf with him. Don't go on the *Sequoia* with him. Don't make it a social event. Be yourself. You have to try to ground him in scripture."

Graham was passing on some lessons learned the hard way. He had not been called to be a politician, Graham admitted. God had called him to do one thing—preach the gospel. Zeoli should do the same. It was, said Zeoli later, a "very serious" lesson in what "not to do." Before the conversation ended, the two men read scripture and then prayed together.

Graham was passing the torch—perhaps not forever, but certainly for a while.

ANOTHER BILLY IN THE WHITE HOUSE

A week after Lausanne, as Graham had suggested, Zeoli telephoned Ford from Germany. Ford was by then in the final days of his vice presidency and was fully aware of what was about to take place. "I suggested we pray together when I returned to the States," Zeoli recalled telling him. "But Jerry said, 'You can pray there now and I can pray here now.'" And so the two men prayed telephonically for wisdom and guidance.

Gerald Rudolph Ford hailed from Grand Rapids, Michigan, a center of Dutch Calvinism so strict that even in the late 1950s, some residents argued about whether it was appropriate to read the newspaper on the sabbath. Ford's own upbringing was never that austere—his mother and stepfather attended an Episcopal church, which observed a more relaxed attitude toward Sunday afternoons. "Sometimes," Ford recalled, "I'd just go out and play baseball. Of course, some of my Dutch friends weren't allowed to do that."

Grand Rapids was the site for the very first of Graham's citywide crusades in 1947. The two men met sometime in the 1950s—neither can recall exactly—when Ford was a rising Republican in Congress. Ford attended a weekly late-morning prayer session with several colleagues: John Rhodes of Arizona, Mel Laird of Wisconsin, and Al Quie of Minnesota. He described those weekly gatherings, which began in 1967 and continued off and on through 1975, as a "very quiet, much off the record group." He never elaborated, a friend later said, because "many people get the idea that if you say you have religious beliefs, you somehow think you're perfect."

Zeoli, meanwhile, had created a ministry for professional athletes whose travel schedules precluded regular church attendance. It was at a pregame "football chapel" sometime in the early 1970s, Zeoli says, that Ford reaffirmed his personal commitment to Christ. Zeoli was holding a service at a Washington, D.C.–area hotel for the Dallas Cowboys, who were in town to play the Redskins. Ford, the all–Big Ten Michigan center who had gone on to become House minority leader, sat in the front row to hear his friend preach on "God's Game Plan." Ford was especially moved by the sermon and hung around to talk privately afterward about Christ and forgiveness and what it all meant. The inquiry felt real and raw: was that the moment Ford committed himself to Christ? "It's hard to say when a man does that," Zeoli explained. "That's a God thing. But I think that day is the day he looked back to as an extremely important day of knowing Christ."

When Ford became vice president in late 1973, Zeoli began sending him a weekly devotional message that began with a verse or two of scripture and concluded with a prayer. Zeoli mailed his messages on Friday afternoons so they would be on Ford's desk in Washington by Monday morning. Over the next three years, Zeoli sent Ford 146 devotionals. "Not only were they profound in their meaning and judicious in their selection," Ford said, "I believe they were also divinely inspired. Billy Zeoli was the instrument."

After the imperial Nixon era, everything about Ford's initial days as president seemed shockingly, wonderfully normal. The Fords spent the first ten days still living in their four-bedroom home in Alexandria, Virginia. On his second day in office, the president opened his front door wearing baby blue short pajamas to retrieve the morning newspaper. He was driven to work on the capital's clogged commuting routes along with Washington's other government workers. Much was made of the fact that he toasted his own English muffins. Two days after Ford was sworn in, Betty Ford wrote in her diary, "There aren't going to be any more private services in the East Room for a select few."

Graham knew Ford was a different creature than his predecessor.

He told the *Washington Post* in mid-August 1974 that the new president would be more spiritual than the old. "He'll probably talk more about the Bible, God and the need for prayer than Nixon. President Nixon didn't like it; I never knew why." In fact, Ford began each day in the White House by quietly repeating the same verses from Proverbs that his mother had taught him years earlier for help in times of trouble: "Trust in the Lord with all thine heart; and lean not unto thine own understanding. In all thy ways acknowledge him, and he shall direct thy paths." It was the same verses he had thought of as he clung to the side of an aircraft carrier in a December 1944 typhoon in the Pacific. And it was the passage he and Betty cited in their prayers the night before he became president.

Zeoli became something of an unofficial White House chaplain, visiting Ford twenty times in the thirty months he was president, usually for a private breakfast or for dinner and conversation in the evening. But just as Graham had advised, he and Ford rarely discussed politics. They would meet every month or so to read the Bible and pray, either in the Oval Office or the family quarters upstairs. The *Washington Post* noted the change in spiritual staffing when it ran a story called "And Now Playing at the White House . . . Another Reverend Billy." Worried that such stories might sting in Montreat, Zeoli called Graham to make sure that Graham knew he had not made the stories happen. Graham told Zeoli to "be thankful that neither of us came off looking worse."

"MY FRIENDSHIP CAME BACK TO ME"

Barely a month into Ford's presidency, Graham reemerged to plead for a pardon for his friend Richard Nixon. Ford said Graham did not make the difference in his decision to pardon the former president. But his timing, as usual, was excellent.

In late August 1974, both Graham and Nixon were in California: Nixon in seclusion at Casa Pacifica in San Clemente and Graham and his wife in their Pauma Valley vacation home, about an hour away. Graham was keen to reach Nixon, but the disgraced former president had gone to ground, refusing to take his calls. Worried about Nixon's health, Graham began to call former Nixon aides—Bob Finch and Herbert Klein—to try and break the radio silence. He doubted his old friend would survive a trial if, as many expected, Watergate came to that. A pardon was an obvious solution—an argument Nixon's son-in-law, David Eisenhower, was making as well. Graham also believed, less plausibly, that a pardon would be good for Ford's presidency. When Graham finally reached Klein, by then a San Diego newspaper executive, he made his case for a pardon. Klein urged Graham to call Ford directly.

Graham tried a different approach: he called Ford adviser Anne Armstrong, a Nixon holdover who worked briefly for Ford. She relayed Graham's view to General Alexander Haig, another Nixon holdover, who telephoned Graham and said Ford would soon be in touch.

By this time, Ford was already thinking about a pardon. At his first press conference a few days earlier, he had been dismayed to discover that eleven of twenty-nine questions were about Nixon and Watergate, and he was less than adroit in handling them. After reviewing the transcript of his performance, he told his aides that the matter would dog his presidency for months unless he could set it aside. Most of his personal aides were horrified when he proposed the idea in a private Oval Office meeting on August 30. "We sat mute," Counselor Robert Hartmann would later write. "The President's logic was unassailable, yet I felt as if I was watching someone commit hara-kiri." That same day, Ford asked Phil Buchen, his old law partner from Grand Rapids, to spend Labor Day weekend researching whether, and how, a pardon could be done. Buchen urged Ford to win from Nixon some statement of contrition in exchange for the pardon, but even at this stage Ford did not see a confession as a condition. After the meeting broke up, both Hartmann and longtime Ford ally John Marsh tried to talk the president out of his decision—or at least into postponing it.

On Saturday, August 31, Ford had mercy on his mind. Hoping to bind the wounds left over from Watergate, he spent the morning discussing a plan for granting some kind of amnesty to Vietnam draft resisters and evaders. The long session with aides from the Departments of Justice and Defense centered on how to craft a plan that gave appropriate measures of punishment and clemency to young men who had resisted in different ways. When the clemency meeting ended, Ford returned to the Oval Office and, just as Haig had promised, telephoned Graham in California.

The call was less than fifteen minutes long and appears to have caught Ford very near the tipping point. "I told him how I felt," Graham said, recalling how he went over his conversations with Finch and Klein and then reported to Ford that Nixon was "very low." Graham said he was worried about "this tremendous possibility that [Nixon] would be tried and [sent] to prison. I suppose, at that point, my friendship came back to me. I just couldn't see that. And I told President Ford that."

If Ford had decided by this point to pardon Nixon, he did not disclose it to Graham. Ford, Graham said, told him merely that he was working through the prospect of a pardon and its implications. Ford asked Graham for his prayers. The two men concluded their call with a prayer.

In an interview in 2006, when Ford was ninety-two, the former president was quite firm that the conversation took place after he had decided to pardon Nixon. "I didn't talk to him in advance," Ford insisted. "But when I made the decision, totally on my own, he was very supportive."

On Sunday, September 8, Ford went to St. John's Episcopal Church, directly across Lafayette Square from the White House. With about fifty worshippers, he took communion and knelt in prayer. He returned to the Oval Office, read the pardoning statement aloud twice, added a line noting his concern about Nixon's health, and then moved to a smaller adjoining office to alert congressional leaders of his plans. At 11:05, he announced the pardon. In his brief statement, Ford invoked God's name six times. "The Constitution is the supreme law of our land and it governs our actions as citizens. Only the laws of God, who governs our consciences, are superior to it. . . . I do believe, with all my heart and mind and spirit, that I, not as President but as a humble servant of God, will receive Justice without mercy if I fail to show mercy."

It was a profoundly Christian statement coming at a moment when the nation was not in a very forgiving mood. Graham watched Ford's announcement on television, he recalled, because he had been alerted to Ford's plans in advance by a White House aide. Someone in the White House had valued the preacher's counsel enough to give him notice before the rest of the nation learned of the president's decision.

The reaction was blistering. It quickly became clear that the country might not forgive Ford for forgiving Nixon. Graham, who was one of the few public figures who backed the pardon, took a longer view. "I never was sure that it really hurt [Ford], but maybe it did." And yet once again, quite apart from Graham's personal views on Nixon's fate, he had played a supporting role in what was easily the most important—and fateful—

decision of the Ford presidency. Ford told reporters in 1999 that he was glad the preacher was on his side during that difficult first month in 1974. "To have Reverend Graham contact me and reassure me it was the proper thing to do," he said, "was very, very important in my own reconciliation of the controversies that followed."

Graham's worries about Nixon did not abate. That fall, after Nixon was admitted to a hospital with phlebitis, Ruth Graham appealed to a friend to hire a private plane and troll back and forth above the hospital, pulling a banner that read, "Nixon—God Loves You and So Do We." Nixon saw it from his hospital window, but did not know its source until later. "We would like to think it was an encouragement," Graham said. The two men had dinner together in San Clemente and settled into the kind of quiet, postpresidency friendship Graham had maintained with Eisenhower and Johnson; certainly a less intense relationship than when they were in office, but a sustained and supportive one nonetheless. In 1993 he would preach at Pat Nixon's funeral, and at her husband's the following year.

For the most part, Graham watched the Ford presidency from a distance. In May 1975, Billy and Ruth went to hear him speak in Charlotte, sitting in a special section at the front of the crowd. When a shirtless and barefoot demonstrator moved adjacent to Ruth in the aisle, holding up a sign that read, "Eat the Rich," and apparently blocked her view, Ruth grabbed the sign and placed it under her feet. When he asked for it back, she refused. Later, when he sued her, she vowed to go to jail rather than pay a fine. (The case was dismissed after a forty-five-minute hearing, but Ruth caught up with her accuser afterward and presented him with a Bible.) As she said later, "The man had every right to his opinion. But when the president of the United State is speaking, it is definitely not the place to express his opinion. I am the mother of five children and disrespect has never been tolerated." Ford sent Billy a note of thanks, in which he urged Ruth to "leave the demonstrators to the police. . . . But it's wonderful to have such good friends—willing to support me even physically!"

And yet a Ford-Graham visit would be difficult to arrange. That may have been in part the result of bruised feelings: in August, after Betty Ford said that she probably would have tried marijuana if it had been popular when she was young, Graham said he was "disappointed that she said it," and then added, "I know on many occasions I had put my own foot in my mouth and wished I could retract a statement, and I think maybe she does, too." But several veterans of the Ford administration recalled that, in addition to Graham's remarks, it was also true that some in the Ford White House simply did not want Graham around, trailing Nixon's ghost behind him. "There was a deliberate effort," said Jim Cannon, "to move away from anything that was reminiscent of Nixon." There is also some evidence that Ford was personally frustrated by his inability to get Graham in for a chat. In September 1975, Ford dashed off a note to Dick Cheney, reminding his deputy chief of staff that he had already asked once about arranging a meeting with Graham. But nothing had happened.

"Dick," it began, "a week ago, I talked with Billy Graham and he indicated willingness to come up for visit to WH. I wrote note to you . . . What is story?"

Cheney got the message. After some back-and-forth that autumn, a meeting was finally scheduled for December. But at the last minute, Ruth called to apologize and say Billy would not be able to make it.

Their reunion would have to wait until 1976.

TWENTY-FOUR

The Campaign That Changed Everything

Carter was very serious-minded. I didn't see him much.
—Graham on his relations with Carter

American politics changed forever one night in March 1976, when Jimmy Carter stood on a platform in a backyard patio in North Carolina and began talking about his relationship with God.

It was a cool spring evening in Winston-Salem, a few days before the North Carolina primary. Carter was just beginning to take questions from the crowd of seventy-five supporters who had gathered to hear him when someone asked the candidate if he was a born-again Christian. "And I said, 'Yes,'" Carter recalled. "This has been a natural answer since I was a young adult."

If this testimony had come from anyone else born and raised in southwest Georgia, it would have hardly been noteworthy. Nearly half of southern Protestants considered themselves born again in the mid-1970s. But this was no private, church-basement testimony and this was not just anyone doing the speaking: Jimmy Carter was running for president as the first strong contender from the Deep South in decades. And despite what he would imply years later about his comments that night, he wasn't talking about his personal profession of faith at age eleven in the Plains Baptist Church. He was talking about his decision in 1967, at the age of forty-two, to recommit his life to Christ following a particularly difficult year. "I recognized for the first time," he told the group gathered on the patio, "that I had lacked something very precious—a complete commitment to

Christ, a presence of the Holy Spirit in my life in a more profound and personal way. And since then I've had an inner peace and inner conviction and assurance that transformed my life for the better."

This was—there is no other way to describe it—a new kind of stump speech: a candidate who was putting his faith at the center of his bid for the presidency. And it was no improvisation. Stuart Eizenstat, who was one of Carter's earliest campaign aides, recalled that whenever Carter sat down to make a list of his strengths as a candidate to be included in a basic stump speech, he routinely listed his Christian faith among his assets. Attempts by Eizenstat, who doubled as a sometime speechwriter, to remove that detail from Carter's standard campaign remarks kept going nowhere: "I kept striking that out in every draft and he kept putting it back in every draft. He obviously had an intention—which I was unaware of at the time—of making that a fairly central focus in terms of appealing to some of the rural southern white voters. I don't think it was a totally political decision. I think it's something he very deeply believed in. But in my previous discussions and conversations with him, he certainly didn't advertise that to me."

Carter had already given several strong hints of his deep religious faith in newspaper interviews. His campaign autobiography, *Why Not the Best?*—published six months earlier by a division of the Southern Baptist Convention—included just enough heavenly praise to signal to evangelicals that he spoke their language, but stopped short of saying anything so pious that it would scare off secular Democrats who might regard deep faith as a disqualifier. Before Winston-Salem, Carter had rarely hinted at his faith on the stump. But now, as the 1976 primary campaign moved into the Bible Belt, Carter was bringing his personal faith story out in the open.

In case anyone had missed the message, Carter held a press conference the morning after the backyard confession to explain further. His decision to come to Christ had been gradual, he said, not a bolt out of the blue. It had come after an unprecedented setback in his life, and out of the meditation and mission work that followed. "It wasn't a voice of God from heaven," he said. "It wasn't mysterious. It might have been the same kind of experience as millions of people have who do become Christians in a deeply personal way."

It was certainly true that nothing had rocked Jimmy Carter's world like his 1966 defeat in a long-shot bid for governor. The race had been unlikely from the start; the campaign struck his wife, Rosalynn, as "unbelievable" simply because no one outside of Sumter County had ever heard of him. And yet when defeat came, Carter was stunned. In the space of just a few months, he had gone $66,000 into debt, dropped twenty-two pounds, and wound up losing to an Atlanta restaurateur named Lester Maddox who was known for greeting black would-be patrons of his café with an ax handle in his hand. When he learned he had placed last in a three-way Democratic primary race, he quietly packed his bags in Atlanta and went home to Plains at midnight. He didn't bother to tell his aides. Carter went into a profound personal and spiritual funk. "I was really distressed," he told us. "It was the first time in my life I had a major goal fail. I kind of turned away from my faith and myself and from God. I thought I should have been made governor, and if I wasn't, it shouldn't have been someone who imposed racism on our state."

When Ruth Carter Stapleton learned of her older brother's condition following the 1966 election, she drove down to Plains from North Carolina to talk to him. Ruth was a well-known regional evangelist who mixed new age psychology and Christian faith into a freelance ministry. As they walked around the Carter place in Plains in 1966, Ruth at first tried to console her brother with scripture. "She quoted some passages in the book of James that said that disappointment or failure or sorrow or loss could be an opening to patience and self-assessment and strengthening of one's faith for greater success in the future," he recalled. "I won't tell you my exact phrase but I thought it was a bunch of crap." Carter went on, "And she said, 'Well, Jimmy, you've gone to the Naval Academy, you've been a navy officer, state senator, you've run for governor, you've got a good business established, you've been on the Sumter County school board. Why don't you put that aside and devote yourself to God and see what happens?'"

And then, that summer, something unexpected came along. "There was a call that went out from Billy Graham's headquarters to my county for someone to head up a Billy Graham crusade," he recalled. "And I volunteered to do it. And I guess, in retrospect, a weak moment.'"

Why was this "a weak moment"? Carter had no sooner stopped running for governor in 1966 than he began running again. He would soon learn, to his surprise, that Graham's organization required racially integrated crusades, as well as integrated planning sessions. As Carter put it, "You know, I was an up-and-coming politician and still had hopes of being governor. And I'd already lost once. And so becoming the leader of an integrated religious crusade was not something that was designed to get me additional votes in a segregated state."

At first, Carter could not find any place that would allow him to hold a mixed-race planning session. (He settled on the basement of an abandoned school building.) His next challenge was finding a venue to hold the crusade itself. In small towns like Americus, the Graham operation sent out crusade films and asked organizers to simply screen the movie, make the invitation, collect the names, and send along the results. "Billy couldn't come to a little dinky place like ours," Carter explained. He finally prevailed upon the owner of a local movie theater to screen the film, and hundreds turned out to see it. After each of a half dozen showings, Carter himself stepped to the front of the theater to lead the invitation. One account reported that 565 people came forward. "Everyone was startled," Carter said, "because [there were] black and white people walking down the aisles, together, in front of the theater, to place their faith in Christ. Together."

For Carter, the Graham crusade was one of several steps down a new spiritual road. He volunteered to run a handful of statewide service organizations and began filling in for vacationing preachers in his area. Later that year, he joined six other Baptist laymen on a mission to Lock Haven, Pennsylvania. Their goal: to build a church, family by family. (The trip was part of a larger effort by Southern Baptists in the 1960s and 1970s to establish beachhead congregations in the northern half of the United States—a factor that would help Carter politically in later years.) Carter arrived in Lock Haven, checked into the YWCA, and was given a hundred notecards, each marked with the name and address of one of Lock Haven's unchurched families. He was paired with another sojourning businessman from Texas who had done this sort of work before. But Carter quickly discovered that he wasn't as natural a door-to-door preacher as his partner. One problem, he explained, was that "I realized very quickly I didn't have much testimony to give.

"It was very difficult for me," he said, to climb the steps of each home, knock on the door, and make his pitch for Jesus. "We would kneel down on the sidewalk and pray that God would guide us and the Holy Spirit would be in charge and that we would do the best we could to plant the idea of salvation and we wouldn't worry about the consequences." By the time he and his partner had worked their way through the list of a hundred names, they had recruited forty-eight locals to the new church. For Carter, the Lock Haven mission was the first time that he had given everything he had to God without a single hour of distraction—no strings attached, he said. He later wrote to one of his Lock Haven families that the days he spent there left him the "closest to Christ" he had ever felt. Sister Ruth had been right. The experience, Carter said, changed his life. It also gave him his testimony, a compelling story to tell about setback and renewal—how he wrestled with his faith, went into the wilderness, did his questing, was lost and found.

ROLLING IT ALL TOGETHER

By the time Carter emerged as the Democratic front-runner in the spring of 1976, he was weaving his faith and his politics so tightly that it was hard to tell them apart. He made it clear repeatedly that summer that he regarded politics as God's extension service, the most important rescue mission after the saving of one's own soul. For the lead epigraph of his book, he chose Niebuhr's observation that the "sad duty of politics is to establish justice in a sinful world." Asked to distill his campaign message into one word, Carter said, "faith."

There was even an element of crusade to Carter's campaign. He would repair on many Sundays back to Plains, where he would attend Plains Baptist and open his Sunday school class to reporters. He would sometimes preach in local churches when he was out of town on Sunday, and made himself available to religious cable programs and did interviews with religion writers. Sister Ruth wrote letters to the faithful around the country; her list of six thousand Iowans who followed her ministry formed the backbone of her brother's come-from-nowhere finish there. She set up shop in the back of her brother's campaign plane, where she held impromptu counseling sessions with traveling reporters who wanted to talk about their personal problems.

Carter's politics-as-ministry wasn't designed to marshal the nation behind some great purpose, as Eisenhower had done. But it had great popular appeal in the aftermath of Vietnam, Watergate, and a presidential resignation—and at a time when a huge spiritual rebirth was under way around the country. As political strategy, faith had many advantages—and many audiences. The first was white, southern, and not automatically Democratic anymore. Southern whites had abandoned the Democratic Party in huge numbers for George Wallace in 1968 and to a lesser degree in 1972. Carter needed to win them back in order to prevail in 1976, and if he could not find common ground with them on policy, he might find it on cultural terms. "When Jimmy Carter speaks," the theologian Michael Novak wrote in April 1976, "millions of Protestant Americans experience a sudden smack of recognition. He's for real. He's them in their idealized selves. . . . Carter seems to understand very well, perhaps too well . . . what most Americans want primarily (though not solely) in a President is a person they can look to and say, 'He represents me. He is us.'"

If Carter's invocation of his faith was aimed at southern whites, his incantation of his own humility was aimed at liberals and black Americans, who had reason to distrust him. No major party had nominated a presidential candidate from the Deep South in 128 years for one reason: race. Most of the southerners who had climbed to the top of their party organizations by 1970 hailed from a racist political culture, and Carter was no exception. He had served on a segregationist school board during the late 1950s and early 1960s. In his race for governor in 1970, he spoke favorably of Alabama governor George Wallace and employed tactics that made some of his own aides wince years later. He had run hard to the right to beat Carl Sanders, a popular liberal, to become governor that year. Carter tried to wipe the slate clean when the race was over: he pronounced in his inaugural address that the era of segregation was over.

The astonishing thing about Carter's religious messaging in 1976 was that he was deploying it to reassure southern conservatives, blacks, and liberals that he shared their values—all at the same time. He was able to unwrap his faith to remind one set of voters that he was not that different from George Wallace, while using some of the same language to reassure another set that he wasn't like Wallace at all. Faith was the coin of both realms and the coin had two very different faces. "Carter," said one old friend, "was clever enough to roll all this together."

Whatever calculations it may have carried, Carter's faith-based crusade had one overriding virtue: Carter himself. Few could doubt that he was a genuine Christian who lived by the Bible. And that virtue dovetailed with what most Americans felt was needed most in Washington in the post-Watergate moment: authenticity. Carter never had much of a platform and he never advanced anything like a detailed agenda. He promised simply never to lie to the public and to restore a federal government "as good as the people" it served. Whatever else people made of Carter's positions, most could see that his faith was for real.

The relationship between Jimmy Carter and Billy Graham is the most contradictory of all those profiled in this book. No president was closer to Graham theologically or spiritually; but no president save Kennedy was as distant personally from him, either. Carter alone among the presidents studied here taught the Bible throughout his life, wrote books of religious meditations, and needed no help with scripture or its challenges. Carter alone personally led a Billy Graham crusade; he and his wife actually read the Bible in Spanish one year.

And yet Jimmy Carter uniquely did not need Billy Graham—and for most of his time in the Oval Office, he more or less ignored him.

In another time, perhaps, they might have bonded: here was Carter, a devout Christian, a southerner who attended church every week; a deacon in his local Baptist church; a man who had led Bible study in the torpedo room of his nuclear submarine; who had at one time offered himself as a stand-in preacher around Georgia; who could hold forth about the meaning and lessons of all sorts of passages in both testaments; who had organized one Graham crusade and been honorary chairman of a second; and to whom prayer was, as he said, "almost like breathing."

But it was not to be. Some of the distance between Graham and Carter may stem from how they met. The preacher met the future president at a White House reception Richard Nixon was giving for new governors. An ever-alert Graham, aware of Carter's work on the Sumter County crusade, quickly picked him out from the crowd and motioned him over to say hello. "He saw me," Carter recalled. "I think one of his aides told him who I was. And he called out my name, which was a great compliment to me, and he asked me to come forward. He said he wanted to thank me for conducting the crusade in Sumter County."

Even as he told the story of meeting Graham and Nixon thirty-five years later, a huge grin stole across Carter's face. The memory still pleased him. Graham was something of an idol for Carter as he came of age, someone who among Southern Baptists "personified success," Carter would explain. When asked in 2005 who had the most influence on him spiritually, he pointed to Graham. "He's been constant. He's been broadminded. He's been forgiving. He's been humble in his treatment of others, he's reached out equally for opportunities to serve God, Christ, to men and women, as the Bible says, to Greek and Hebrew, to masters and slave, without distinction."

And yet the two men did not click. Carter was so thoroughly grounded in conventional church life that he hardly needed a drop-in presidential pastor like Graham. And even if he did, it was certainly not going to be Richard Nixon's personal pastor. When Carter did reach out to clergy, he was far more interested in winning over two members of a new generation of evangelical preachers: Jim Bakker, the Charlotte host of *The PTL Club*; and Pat Robertson, who anchored *The 700 Club* out of Virginia Beach. Carter courted both men hard: he appeared on Robertson's network in 1976 and talked about how he prayed. By midyear, evangelical leaders were in an unmistakable thrall: before speaking to the Southern Baptist Convention in June, Carter was introduced to the crowd of eighteen thousand by an enthusiastic Oklahoma pastor who noted the Georgian was the one man who was running for president, was born again, and whose "initials are JC!"

The other reason Carter didn't need Billy Graham is that he didn't seem to need *anybody*. He was an intensely private man. Friends of nearly forty years would reflect that Carter, as far as they could see, was not close to anyone apart from Rosalynn, never confided personal thoughts even to those he had known for decades. Carter had a zone of privacy so closely guarded that not even Graham was likely to be given a passkey. "Carter was very serious-minded," Graham recalled later. "I didn't see him much." While other commanders in chief would turn out to be friends, Graham added, Carter was not to be in that category. "I looked on Carter," said Graham, "as the president."

And so through what was easily the most spiritually soaked campaign since 1960, Graham and Carter struggled to maintain an uneasy truce. It didn't last long: trying to calm American Jews who had begun to fear that Carter was perhaps a bit too New Testament for their tastes, campaign aide Jerry Rafshoon said in June, "We're reassuring people Jimmy won't turn the White House into a Billy Graham Bible Class." If that comment stung Graham, the preacher nonetheless echoed it a few weeks later when he said to reporters, "I don't think there should be any more

White House Sunday services of the kind held in the East Room during the Nixon Administration. The problem was not so much what went on there on Sunday, but what we found out was going on . . . the other six days of the week."

Graham was trying to reduce tensions. When two rising stars of the Republican Party's Christian wing—Bill Bright, the highly influential leader of Campus Crusade for Christ, and John Conlan, a conservative Arizona congressman—announced in July that they were trying to organize American evangelicals into a voting bloc, Graham told the *New York Times* that he was opposed to such a move. "I learned my lesson the hard way," he said. "Bright has been using me and my name for 20 years. But now I'm concerned about the political direction he seems to be taking." Graham said he was going to "have it out straight" with Bright in a meeting the following week.

Then, just before the Republican convention, Graham slipped. Arriving in San Diego for a weeklong crusade (and a pastoral drop-by at the Nixon home in San Clemente), he said, "I would rather have a man in office who is highly qualified to be President who didn't make much of a religious profession than to have a man who had no qualifications but who made a religious profession." Graham predicted that religion would not be a factor in the upcoming election because, as he put it, "I would say there wouldn't be a hair's difference between what Jimmy Carter, Gerald Ford and Reagan believe religiously." Given how much Carter had talked about his faith on the stump, it was easy to interpret at least some of what Graham said as an implicit hurrah for the Republican candidates.

Certainly Ford's aides noticed the remark. They knew that Carter was poised to drain perhaps half the southern white vote from whatever remained of Nixon's sturdy "Silent Majority." But Ford refused to take the hint and make Jesus his running mate. He had a good faith story and a solid religious background. But his reserved Dutch ways made it unlikely he would ever discuss it in public. Privately, Billy Zeoli pressed him to loosen up a bit and talk about his faith in public. Zeoli asked Ford to permit him to lend his name to committees working on the president's behalf. And he volunteered to write a book describing Ford's faith in some detail. Ford declined both requests. "He wasn't willing to use God to get elected," said Zeoli. As Ford explained later, "Throughout the campaign, Carter had talked about his religious convictions in a way I found discomfiting.

I have always felt a closeness to God and have looked to a higher being for guidance and support, but I didn't think it was appropriate to advertise my religious beliefs."

By Labor Day, with the situation for Ford looking grim, the White House prepared to recall Graham to duty. On September 3, White House personnel director Richard Brannon, a Baptist minister who also served as a kind of informal adviser to Ford on religious matters, urged the president to reach out to Graham for help. Ford had been pressing aides during 1975 to get Graham to the White House, but the meeting could never be arranged. Now the push was on: "Graham plans to remain neutral in the election this year. Privately, Bill, his wife Ruth and most of his staff are going to vote for President Ford." Brannon urged Ford to call Graham and seek his advice about "what he thinks about the election this year and ask if he has any suggestions to offer." The memo included Graham's home telephone number.

Ford placed the call the next day, Saturday, September 4. Graham was ready to suit up once more if Ford's notes of the chat are any indication. "Excellent conversation," Ford wrote in a note to Dick Cheney, now chief of staff, following the call. "Will help in many ways + has. He is putting on a Crusade in Michigan at the new Pontiac Stadium about Oct. 10th. He wonders if it would be helpful + appropriate for Betty and me to attend. I asked him to stop by here. Very willing—free in about 10 days. Talk with me."

A week later, Graham fleshed out his proposal for inviting Ford to the Pontiac crusade. "The committee that invited me to Michigan has already had a discussion about what would happen if either you or Governor Carter came to the Crusade. They have left it up to me to make the decision. Of course you and Betty are cordially invited. Because it would be so close to the election, it would be impossible to ask you to speak. I think the backlash would not only hurt our ministry but would hurt you as people would think you were 'using' me. However, if you came and sat in whatever area the Secret Service would decide is best and were recognized from the platform I am sure you would get a rousing reception. . . . Of course, since I am maintaining a public neutral position—as I always try to do in politics—I will also extend a similar invitation to Governor Carter. When Mr. Nixon was campaigning in '68 he sat out in the audience in our Pittsburgh Crusade. I extended the same invitation to the then

Vice President Humphrey, who was unable to attend the Crusade. In the meantime, I am praying that God's will shall be done on November 2 and that the man of God's choice will be elected."

Once again, the call had gone out from president to preacher, and the preacher stepped forward to help. Then, on September 20, Carter gave Ford a gift. In an interview with *Playboy* released that day, Carter acknowledged that, while he had never committed adultery, he had "looked on a lot of women with lust. I've committed adultery in my heart many times. . . . Christ says don't consider yourself better than someone else because one guy screws a whole bunch of women, while the other guy is loyal to his wife." The *Playboy* interview was designed to reach out to voters who, as one longtime aide put it, thought of Carter "as a narrow minded Baptist." Carter had so leaned to the pious and proper side of things during the campaign that some secular voters were beginning to wonder if he wasn't too straitlaced for their taste. But in trying to adjust his appeal ever so slightly, he overdid it.

Bible believers were horrified that Carter had deigned to speak to a magazine like *Playboy*; secular voters Carter was trying to woo were put off by his direct quotation of the Sermon on the Mount. Carter was theologically correct about the sin of lust, something some ministers pointed out. But that fine point of Christian doctrine was lost in the general oddity of the thing: the interview struck just about everyone as showing poor taste and poorer judgment, especially from a presidential candidate. The result gave everyone something to complain about. As one adviser put it, "It came off as goofy, contributed to this 'weirdo factor' and almost cost us the election." Some evangelical leaders who had trumpeted Carter's innate piety cooled at record speed on the Georgian. "Like many, I am quite disillusioned," Jerry Falwell said in late September. "Four months ago, the majority of people I knew were pro-Carter. Today, that has totally reversed." A few days after the interview was published, Graham appeared with Ford at a diplomatic event in Washington.

On September 29, Carter's twenty-four-year-old son Jeff was asked on a Tulsa radio program about a comment by Graham that politicians shouldn't flaunt their religion. "I hate to talk about religion to tell you the truth," Jeff Carter replied. "I think that the thing the people should watch out for are people like Billy Graham who go around telling them how to live. That's my personal opinion." The next day, young Carter went a step further, falsely charging that Graham had received a doctorate degree for a few dollars through the mail. "I think that religion should stay out of politics," he added. When it was pointed out that his father had certainly conflated the two in his campaign, Carter's son replied, "Sure he has. But that's different from religious leaders picking politicians."

This was becoming, as these things go, a range war, and both sides moved to calm things down. Jeff Carter retreated on his diploma comment a day later. Rosalynn Carter telephoned Graham to make amends, and Graham told reporters later, "I told her to give Jeff a big hug. I have two sons and I understand." Carter telephoned Graham as well. The awkward back-and-forth ended Graham's dabbling in the campaign.

The cease-fire held, but only barely, and it appeared that both men were simply choosing not to get along. Following the dustup with his son, candidate Carter told reporters in Plains that Graham had sent word to the Democratic nominee that he "wanted to do everything he could to support my campaign . . . not in preference to President Ford but not to do anything detrimental to (the campaign)." A day or two later, Graham let it be known that Carter had overread his suit for peace. "The last part of that is correct," he told reporters, but the first part "might be misunderstood."

Neither Ford nor Carter made it to the Pontiac crusade later that month, though Robert Dole, Ford's running mate, dropped by a week before the election. The final vote was closer than had been expected: Carter won by less than two million votes out of more than eighty million cast. He had nonetheless pulled off a stunning reversal, taking just over half the evangelical vote—a mark that would not be matched by a Democrat for another twenty years. But the most foreboding result for Carter's party, widely missed at the time, was the number of Catholic voters who pulled the lever for Ford. Put off by Carter's Protestant persona, his slippery stand on abortion, or both, Catholics turned out for Ford in places like Pittsburgh, Cleveland, and St. Louis. Religion had again played a role in a presidential campaign, first by helping Carter win, and then in making it close.

When it was over, Graham tried to soften the blow. In a typewritten letter to Ford three weeks after the vote, he wrote from Montreat, "During the election period I prayed constantly that 'God's will' be done. This was the prayer of Jesus the night before the cross. He said, 'not my will but Thine be done.' For some mysterious reason unknown to us, Mr. Carter won. . . . You and your associates put on a whale of a campaign. With the low Republican registration in the country I think Mr. Carter should be asking himself how he came so close to losing.

"I believe that you will go down in history as one of America's great Presidents. You took the leadership of the country at one of the most ominous and precarious periods in our two hundred year history. . . . I am eternally grateful that you were willing to be the right man at the right time to lead this nation . . . you are loved, admired and appreciated." Ford replied two weeks later: "It certainly was kind and thoughtful of you to write so warmly and I appreciate your wonderful understanding as well as your prayers." He promised to find time in the future to get together with Graham again—and saved his letter for his personal scrapbook.

After the election, Graham explained just how much influence he would have in the new White House. "Probably not very much," he said. "We're friends, and I've spent several nights with him . . . and I'm very much for him." Many years later, Graham said he approved of Carter's startling new amalgam of politics and religion. "Jimmy Carter did not present himself as perfect or pious. . . . Neither did he compromise his understanding of the Gospel by verbal dodging or double talk. He took a political risk by being so forthright about his faith, in the end though, I believe his candor worked in his favor. After the disillusionment of Watergate, the American people were attracted by Carter's summons to a moral revival."

Carter insisted in 2005 that he never intended to talk about his faith during the 1976 campaign—which seems implausible—and that it involved considerable political risk. "Back then it was not attractive, ostentatiously professing to be a born-again Christian. It was not looked upon as a wise political statement." If Carter had regrets about his decision, it is more likely because he helped activate a massive army of politically minded evangelicals in the elections that followed—most of whom have voted for Republicans ever since. "I had watched with great attention the fallout that had attended John Kennedy with his Catholicism," he told us. "During the campaign, it was my original plan not to talk about my religion at all. I tried to refrain from that public espousal of my religion after that. But you might say that the ice had been broken or the damage had been done. And I've been identified ever since with having injected my faith in 1976.

"After that," he added, "it became the thing to do."

TWENTY-FIVE

The Next Great Awakening

I looked at them as personal friends, not presidents, most of the time. I looked on Carter as the president.
                    —Graham on his unusual relationship with Carter

It was a measure of Jimmy Carter's political radar that when he finally turned to Billy Graham for help in 1979, it was not for advice about reelection.

It was for help with an arms control treaty.

Graham was not the first evangelical leader to put his name and moral authority behind arms control in the late 1970s. He was merely the most important. More than a hundred other church leaders pledged in 1978 in stark and uncompromising terms to resist all research, development, and deployment of nuclear arms "in the name of Jesus Christ." The Southern Baptists passed a resolution urging the government to negotiate arms control agreements and beat its swords into plowshares. The National Association of Evangelicals joined the chorus as well. But it was Graham who caught everyone's notice, in part because he made his declaration two weeks before Easter in the most public fashion possible for the age: on the *CBS Evening News* with Walter Cronkite. "I'm in favor of disarmament and I'm in favor of trust," he said. "I'm in favor of having agreements not only to reduce but to eliminate. Why should any nation have atomic bombs?"

Graham was thinking anew. After years of calling on American politicians to match the Soviet threat with a trinity of prayer, sacrifice, and unmatched military spending, he was the first to admit that he was undergoing a profound change of heart. His crusades in Hungary in 1977 and

Poland in 1978 taught him that Americans had become "complacent" about "the destruction and disruption that war brings." He had seen that churches overseas were wrestling with the deployment of nuclear weapons much closer to population centers. But what really sparked his new approach was a visit to Auschwitz, where he witnessed the horrors of the Holocaust and imagined paying that price again—or many times over—in a nuclear exchange.

In 1979, Graham told *Sojourners* magazine, a Christian journal that reports on social justice issues, that he saw strong theological grounds for his new teaching. "I know God is sovereign and sometimes he permits things to happen which are evil. . . . But I cannot see any way in which nuclear war could be branded as being God's will. . . . I have come to the conviction, and this has been a rather late conviction of mine, I didn't—I didn't really give it the thought that I should have given it in my earlier years. But I've come to the conviction that this is the teaching of the Bible."

Jim Wallis, the liberal evangelist who edited *Sojourners*, said the pivot on arms control was the direct result of preaching overseas. "Any good preacher, any good evangelist, in order to speak to people, you have to fall in love with your congregation. So he's speaking to these huge crowds in Eastern Europe and he realizes, 'My country has nuclear weapons targeted on these people with whom I'm falling in love, who I want to bring to Jesus Christ, and I have a problem with that.' I don't think he ever had questions about nuclear policy until he went to the Eastern bloc. He always supported the president because the president knows more than we do. But now he has the experience of contact with people behind the Iron Curtain, he loves them. His heart goes out to them and he becomes protective of them regarding nuclear weapons, and Auschwitz just triggers this."

There was another factor: Graham was getting older. He had turned sixty in 1978, already had more than a dozen grandchildren, and openly admitted that he was concerned about where the world was heading. "I guess I would have to admit that the older I get the more aware I am of the kind of world my generation has helped shape, and more concerned I am about doing what I can to give the next generation at least some hope for peace." And as other American evangelists such as Jerry Falwell and Pat Robertson began playing larger roles in public life, Graham may have also seen a chance to take the lead on a moral—as opposed to a simply religious or spiritual—issue. "There was a time when evangelicals were in the vanguard of some of the great social movements," he told *Sojourners*. "I think of the fight against the slave trade, for example. Then, in some respects, we lost sight of our responsibilities to fight social evils. We said that the world would never be reformed completely anyway until Christ came, so why bother?"

Graham was not calling for unilateral disarmament; instead, he said the West should reduce its arsenal only when it was certain that the Soviets would do the same. But he was also looking over the horizon, hopscotching past every credible arms control proposal at the time and calling for a complete *elimination* of weapons of mass destruction. He attracted considerable attention for his departure. The story line was irresistible: the leading American evangelist, having spent five years in the political wilderness for getting too close to the ultimate cold warrior, had emerged reenergized and had refocused a part of his ministry on the future of mankind. Graham's statement caught the notice of Rosalynn Carter just as her husband began an uphill fight to push the SALT treaty through the Senate.

Fortunately, the lines of communication between the White House and Montreat had not all gone down after the 1976 campaign. There were the perfunctory exchanges of letters and Christmas cards; Ruth and Billy sent a fruitcake one year; at several points, the Grahams sent books about Asia and more topical issues. Graham came to Carter's aid early in 1977 when the president announced that he would serve wine at state dinners, despite the belief in some Baptist congregations that the born-again president should avoid such temptations. Wine was okay, Graham ruled, because "Jesus drank wine." Citing the wedding miracle at Cana, where Christ transformed six jugs of water into wine (John 2:1–11), Graham said, "That wasn't grape juice, as some of [the teetotalers] try to claim."

Carter also supported Graham's breakthrough trip to Hungary in 1977. "Some people suggested that he wait until the country was free," Carter later recalled. "I advised him that he should go." The Hungary trip was strictly limited in scope; there was little advance notice of Graham's visit, and his meetings were not permitted to be large. But that it occurred at all was due in part to Graham's perceived ties to the White House. Graham spoke with Carter before departing, and the president authorized the preacher to convey his personal greetings to Hungarian Christians, particularly his fellow Baptists. John Akers, Graham's top foreign policy adviser, believes this verbal greeting was more important than it appeared. "It signaled to the Hungarian government that Graham had been in touch with the president before coming, and that the president would be watching how the trip went." Hungary's interest was hardly evangelical, Akers pointed out; Budapest wanted closer relations with Washington and particularly most favored nation trading status. But in what was surely a substantive as well as political blunder, Carter's aides made only minimal effort to connect the two men when Graham returned that autumn to discuss the seven-day trip. Instead, Carter aides directed Graham to an aide to Vice President Walter Mondale, who did later see him. This handling may have bruised Graham after years of routine Oval Office visits, but it could not have surprised him very much. Relations between the Carter White House and Montreat were still no better than arm's length—by mutual agreement. Graham himself told *People* magazine a few years later that "I just didn't hang around the White House any more after Nixon. . . . Watergate changed me a little bit along that line."

So did other challenges. Graham had spent the middle of 1977 defending himself against allegations of financial mismanagement—the only such charges in his lifetime of ministering. Graham is a frugal man: he never built a church, he never lived extravagantly; his log home in Montreat, though on a large parcel of well-protected land, is in every other way unassuming. And his organization's fund-raising has over its sixty-year life been low-key compared to others. But in early 1977, after doing a thorough examination of the Graham organization's books, the *Charlotte Observer* reported that the BGEA had amassed a $23 million charitable reserve fund, held mostly in stocks and real estate. The account, which was funded and overseen by the BGEA board, raised a stir because Graham officials had not previously disclosed it to the *Observer* despite a long series of interviews about the Graham operation in general. Graham spent many weeks that year explaining his outfit's handling of the reserve fund. He opened his books, and would go on to form an association of clergymen dedicated to financial transparency—in part because the charges about his team came at a time when other evangelicals were undergoing scrutiny of their finances for more substantive reasons. The reserve fund would eventually provide the money for a thousand-acre laymen's training center outside of Asheville called The Cove. But the tempest over Graham and his outfit's finances kept him on the defensive for some of 1977.

Carter, meanwhile, was facing a sea of troubles in his own political base, but was slow to grasp its depth. The Bible-quoting, born-again president backed by half of all evangelical voters in 1976 turned out to be, of all things, a genuine Democrat. Carter was a religious man, yes, but in his heart too was a commonplace, classical Southern Baptist faith in the strict separation of church and state. Though he could preach the Bible with the best of them, he had no intention of governing with one in his hand. Evangelical voters fell out of love with him in 1977 almost as quickly as they had fallen into a swoon the year before. But more than that—and sparked in part by Carter's example—they were becoming politicized for the first time in two generations, activated by his stand on abortion, by what they regarded as his uncertain hand at foreign policy, and by their widespread belief that federal officials were harassing Protestant day schools. Instead of pulling back from politics after their dalliance with Carter in 1976, they were becoming more involved, stoked by hundreds of religious radio, television, and cable TV outlets and an exploding number of conservative political groups organized around every imaginable social issue. By the middle of 1978, the Southern Baptist Convention did not even ask Carter to speak at its annual convention, and friends inside that group had to organize a special event afterward to give him a venue to speak. "I referred to it as Christians coming out of the closet," said Texas evangelist James Robison. "We had a civic responsibility to take a stand. And that caught on."

Rosalynn Carter was the first to sense her husband's vulnerabilities. On a reconnaissance mission in Georgia in late 1978, she heard from friends that her husband had lost the confidence of many of his longtime supporters. She began pressing him to bring a Baptist pastor from Georgia named Robert Maddox to Washington to be a White House liaison to religious groups. Carter at first was resistant and some of his aides later dragged their feet. But Rosalynn eventually prevailed over all the skeptics. When Maddox was finally hired, he came aboard as a speechwriter in May 1979. It was the same month that Jerry Falwell founded the Moral Majority. Maddox was behind from the start.

That month, Carter sent Graham a telex asking for his support on the SALT treaty and inviting Graham to the White House for a "briefing and discussion." Compared to other presidential messages to Graham, the form letter was perhaps as impersonal as any the evangelist had ever received. Not long afterward, Graham wired his regrets from Australia, explaining that he was "in the middle of our Sydney . . . crusade and cannot possibly attend." Then in August, Graham told the *Milwaukee Journal* that his contact with presidents had been overstated and he would no longer "get close enough to any president or presidential candidate for people even to suspect who I am for." Early that month, Graham's lengthy pro–arms control interview with *Sojourners* was released.

At Rosalynn's suggestion, Maddox flew down to North Carolina on August 29, and was met by Graham's longtime aide T. W. Wilson. The two men drove up to the mountaintop home in Montreat. Maddox was hoping to win from Graham an agreement to testify before the Senate Foreign Relations Committee on the SALT treaty's behalf. It became quickly apparent to Maddox that the session was only nominally about arms control. Graham seemed quick to set aside any bad feelings that lingered from 1976; he recalled Carter's service during the Americus crusade more than twelve years earlier and also mentioned Carter's service as honorary chairman of an Atlanta crusade in 1973. Graham also sought to play down his criticism of Carter during the 1976 campaign and restate his comments of that period in a fashion that, Maddox reported, was "not at all critical of Jimmy Carter."

But Maddox didn't get very far on SALT. In a memo written to Carter afterward, Maddox reported that Graham promised to "use every public platform at his disposal" to talk about the arms treaty, but declined Maddox's invitation to testify before the Senate. "It would give Dr. Graham pleasure to be of service to the President," the memo noted. "He would especially welcome private time with him for conversation. Dr. Graham does not care to be a highly visible figure at the White House." So once more, an American president reached out to Graham, but this time, the preacher resisted. Graham was still in recovery from Watergate and avoiding any public role, at least on SALT ratification.

The two men moved on quickly to other political issues. Graham told Maddox that he saw no problem with just-installed Pope John Paul II visiting the White House as long as it was "handled with due regard to church/state separation." Graham turned down an invitation, presented by Maddox on behalf of Lynda Johnson Robb, to make a public endorsement of the Equal Rights Amendment. "He quickly, with nervous laughter, declined, though I got the impression that he himself has no problem with the amendment," Maddox wrote. Graham invited the president to attend a conference on the family in New York later that month—something Rosalynn later considered but then was unable to attend. Though the election was still more than a year off, there is little doubt that Graham grasped Carter's perilous political standing. "The conservative right, fundamentalist evangelical political coalitions are a definite factor in American life," Maddox reported. "Dr. Graham urged the President to take careful note of this group."

Maddox included one final note: "He was glad I came. He was delighted to be back in touch with the President. Dinner at the White House, most any time, would please him." At the top of the memo, a handwritten notation from Carter to his wife reads, "Ros—Set this up." As he often did, the note was signed simply, "J."

But shortly after hosting Maddox in Montreat, Graham gathered twelve fellow preachers at a Dallas hotel to talk and pray about the future of the country. Graham didn't merely attend the early-October session; he organized it and composed the guest list, according to Dallas evangelist James Robison. Attending were many of the nation's regional, if not national, evangelical powerhouses. Among them: Robison, televangelist Rex Humbard, and Adrian Rogers, who had just led a conservative theological takeover of the Southern Baptist Convention that was to alter the character and direction of the SBC. Joining them were Charles Stanley and Jimmy Draper, who had played key roles in Rogers's SBC election, as well as Clayton Bell, Graham's brother-in-law. The men took over the entire floor of a hotel near the Dallas airport. These men were not part of the new breed of preachers who had one foot in the pulpit and another in the Republican National Committee. They were older and, at least in public, far less partisan. None was buying, as Falwell's Moral Majority soon would, millions of dollars in radio spots across the South to defeat Carter. But each was a conservative Christian, who had by 1979 given up on the notion that Carter was a partner worth keeping.

Graham asked his colleagues to gather in Dallas for what Robison described as a "special time of prayer." But it was understood, Robison recalled, that the men were there to talk about whether the country needed new leadership. "It really was Billy's meeting," Robison said. "What he wanted us to do was pray together for a couple of days and to understand something very significant had to happen." Graham told his fellow preachers that the security and freedom of Americans were in jeopardy in the face of rising Soviet aggression in Africa, Central and South America, and the Middle East. In this regard, Graham was on target: the

Dallas meeting took place just three months before the Soviet invasion of Afghanistan. But Graham saw the spread of communism not only as a threat to religious freedom around the globe but as an encroaching evil that could only be stopped by a leader who saw it in those terms. Recalled Robison, "Billy said, I can well remember, that we only had a thousand days, three years, of freedom if something significant didn't occur. We had to have a change of direction." Robison added, "We did not see Carter as the necessary strong leader in the face of a grave threat." And he said, "No one was talking about Jimmy Carter's faith. It was his ability to lead."

What Graham and his friends were now looking for, said Robison, was "a very effective communicator who had convictions. There was a consensus in the room that if former California governor Ronald Reagan had the convictions that he appeared to have, he certainly had the ability to communicate them." And though Graham organized the session, had a role in choosing the participants, and was the first to speak when they gathered, he made it very clear to his guests that he did not want—and could not play—a public role. He said he had been hurt and misunderstood by simply counseling and praying with previous presidents, and that he could be seen only as a person of prayer. He told his colleagues he would not be able to, as Robison put it, "say some of the things that need to be said. . . . Graham could not afford the damage."

When the meeting broke up, the group assigned Robison the task of making contact with the Reagan camp and arranging a meeting to determine if the former California governor was both serious about a race and sufficiently deep in his convictions. Most of the pastors attending, Robison said, did not know Reagan and wanted to learn more about the actor turned politician. Of course, by this time in 1979, Reagan was no longer just thinking about making his third bid for the presidency. He was well into it. And Graham by then had known him for more than twenty-five years.

Graham flew to Nova Scotia in the second half of October for a five-day crusade; by the time those meetings concluded on October 26, Graham and Carter aides had agreed on a long-awaited White House meeting for their bosses. At first the invitation was for dinner; but at some point in the final preparations, Rosalynn encouraged the Grahams to spend the night. Before Graham arrived, Maddox and White House liaison chief Anne Wexler urged both the president and the First Lady to take a look at *The Emerging Order*, a new book on the growing political power and orthodox theological direction of American evangelicals. "Conversation on the basis of this book should be most stimulating," they advised Carter in a memo. And they suggested that Carter again try and win from Graham a new statement endorsing SALT.

On November 1, the Grahams arrived at the White House. Graham recalled the evening fondly. "For several hours, we reminisced about our southern backgrounds and talked about national affairs," he said. "Little Amy Carter sat quietly watching the television set. Much of the time that evening, however, we shared our mutual faith in Jesus Christ and discussed some of the issues that sometimes divide sincere Christians." The two couples prayed together before turning in for the night. The next morning, the Grahams said good-bye to the Carters in the Oval Office.

How did Graham justify organizing the prayer session in Dallas in early October and then just weeks later accepting an invitation to a White House sleepover with Carter and his family? One explanation is his kaleidoscopic view of his role as pastor to the presidents. Graham wore many hats: as a counselor to mortals, as a minister to presidents, as a preacher to the nation as a whole. Whatever he may have felt about Carter personally or politically, he was not going to decline an invitation to meet and talk, much less an opportunity to pray, with the most powerful man on the planet, whatever his party. He obviously had not given up dabbling in politics, whatever he may have been saying to himself and others. But he would never, whatever his political bent, turn down any president who needed his help or asked him to dinner.

A few days later, Ruth sent the Carters a handwritten thank-you note, dictated by Billy. "Ruth and I came away with a new insight into the dedication of both of you to the cause of not only peace and justice in the world, but your evangelistic urgency. We are deeply grateful for your spiritual leadership and boldness in witnessing for Christ. We have vowed to pray for you more often that God will continue to give you wisdom, courage, faith and guidance in the months ahead." Ruth then added a note in her distinctive hand: "Bill had to dictate this over the phone as he was leaving for Paris, Oxford and Cambridge. He regrets not being able to write it by hand but it's a good thing as you'd never be able to read it. Thank you for an unforgettable evening. We pray for you."

By the time the note arrived, the Carters needed it more than ever. Two days after the Grahams departed, on November 4, students in Tehran took sixty-six American diplomats hostage and showed no sign of giving them up. The Iranian government, such as it was, was either unable or unwilling to step in. It was, Rosalynn wrote later, "the beginning of the end."

Early in 1980, Carter invited to breakfast some of the nation's most popular televangelists, who were in Washington for a convention. Bob Maddox urged the president to acknowledge the "political and moral power of the evangelicals" in his speech to the group and let them "feel his identification with them as a Christian believer while still communicating that he is president of all the people." But when the time for the breakfast arrived, Carter declined to actually join his guests for the meal. When he did arrive, each visitor was allowed one question—which Maddox had approved in advance. The resulting atmosphere was, he admitted, a little stilted. And that was just the reception from those who came to breakfast. Pat Robertson, who had backed Carter in 1976, declined to attend. Two months later, Robertson boasted, "We have enough votes to run the country. And when the people say, 'We've had enough,' we are going to take over."

For Carter, the rest of 1980 went from bad to worse: the hostages remained in custody. He had to fight off a challenge for the nomination from Senator Edward Kennedy and the Democratic Party's left wing; the April attempt to rescue the hostages in Iran ended in a tragic failure. Mount St. Helens blew in May. The SALT treaty stalled in the Senate and was shortly thereafter withdrawn. Reagan beat a field of Republicans for the nomination and then tapped another Graham friend, former CIA director George Herbert Walker Bush, to be his running mate at the convention in Detroit. Graham was on hand to deliver the opening invocation. Team Reagan-Bush enjoyed the strongest association with Graham since Nixon; both candidates' family ties to the evangelist dated to the early 1950s. In case anyone missed the connection, Graham spent a weekend at the Bush family compound in Kennebunkport, Maine, two weeks after the GOP convention.

In November, Reagan and Bush won easily, sweeping Carter out of office and the Senate Democrats out of power in a historic landslide victory. The extent of the rout surprised even Falwell, who sat listening to the returns in his truck in Lynchburg, Virginia. The next morning, Falwell was greeted by his supporters at Liberty Baptist College to the tune of "Hail to the Chief."

A few weeks after the election, with his presidency in its final days, the hostages still in custody, and a Republican revolution already under way in Washington, the president and First Lady asked Maddox and his wife over to the residence for a quiet dinner, just the four of them. Rosalynn met them coming off the elevator and, with what Maddox later described as a look of utter earnestness, asked him, "I want to know where the will of God is in this?"

TWENTY-SIX

The Road to Moscow

The more I prayed about it, the more I thought about it, the more I thought this might open up a whole new chapter for the gospel in Eastern Europe and Russia. So I finally decided to go.

—Graham on his 1982 trip to Moscow

Hollywood glimpsed the destinies of Ronald Reagan and Billy Graham long before anyone else.

A group of conservative Texas cinema owners, their theaters slowly dying, organized a three-day meeting in Dallas to discuss the advent of television and tacky movie content. They invited a Hollywood actor whose career was in a holding pattern, a studio producer whose films were exactly the kind that audiences once flocked to see, and an up-and-coming preacher who, among other things, liked to rail against sin and communism and the breakdown in traditional values.

Which is how in June of 1952, Ronald Reagan met Billy Graham. Reagan, forty-one, was newly married (for the second time), already famous, and on tour for studio owners to promote the motion picture industry. Graham, thirty-four, was reviving the very idea of revival, a young evangelical phenom who drew huge crowds, dabbled in politics, and was the subject of almost constant media attention. Rounding out the conversation in Dallas was David O. Selznick, the producer of *Gone with the Wind*. Graham remembered Reagan as a forceful presence in that first meeting: he marveled at how Reagan convinced a local fundamentalist pastor to let his flock see a movie from time to time. But it was Graham who had the most to say that day: "As the most powerful single factor for molding and shaping public opinion, America needs you more than she has ever needed you," he told the studio heads, "to put old fashioned Americanism on the screens, to promote racial tolerance, honesty in government . . . to make every kid proud of the American flag, to pull the wraps off communism and show it for what it really is. . . . Take sex and crime out of the movies. We've had so much sex in this country until we're sick of it. That's why people stay away. Decent people are ashamed."

A week later, *TIME* correspondent Willard Rappleye wired his editors in New York that Hollywood had watched the overnight rushes of the three-day event and came away convinced of what it had to do next: "Plans are being discussed," Rappleye cabled, "about a movie on the life of Billy Graham and wife, to be played by Ronald Reagan and his wife."

Graham and Reagan were both young, handsome, charismatic, talkative, fascinated by politics—and visionary innocents in a world of hard-boiled sharpies. They shared supernatural gifts as communicators who could reduce complex problems to instinctive and clear solutions. Both men invoked images of an idealized America when they talked, relying heavily on their roots in Illinois and North Carolina. Each man would become larger than life: mythic to their admirers, simplistic to their detractors—and a bit unknowable to their biographers. Both wanted to show "communism for what it really is," and both thought Christianity could play a big part in the showdown.

Partly because of the sheer breadth of what Reagan tried to accomplish as president, historians have tended to dismiss his faith and its impact on his presidency. It's easy to do: Reagan came out of a permissive Hollywood culture where piety tended to perform incognito. He rarely went to church as commander in chief and his excuses for not going were unconvincing. It was commonplace among reporters in the 1980s to write off Reagan's faith as a convenient story cooked up by his handlers to mollify the cultural conservatives who worshipped him. But with a depth of field of nearly twenty years since his presidency came to a close, Reagan's faith seems a more integral part of both the man and his time in office than was realized in the 1980s.

Like so many presidents before him, Reagan was raised by a woman who would be called an evangelical today. His daughter, Maureen, described Nelle Reagan as "a Bible thumper of the first order." Noting that her grandmother had undergone a brush with accidental death earlier in life, Maureen wrote that "Gramsie came away from the experience thinking that her work here on this earth wasn't finished and that she had been called back because she was needed to preach the Gospel." It was in a Dixon, Illinois, church, where Nelle staged religious skits, that young Reagan got his first taste of greasepaint. It was also a refuge from a home where Reagan's father, distant, troubled, and sometimes drunk, never provided much security or stability. Nelle passed her faith on to her boys, and much later, Reagan's wife, Nancy, recalled how her husband used his faith to try to sustain her in difficult moments. "He often wrote to me of what was important to him in spiritual terms, and I admired his faith, although I did not share the firmness of his convictions."

Reagan made regular demonstrations of his faith as he began his climb to the top. In a conversation with David Frost in 1968, the year he mounted his first bid for the Republican presidential nomination, Reagan put Jesus at the top of the list of historical figures he most admired. Reagan and his wife opened Graham's 1969 crusade in Anaheim, where the governor said that "I'm sure there will be those who will question my participation here tonight. People have become so concerned with church-state separation that we have interpreted freedom of religion [as] freedom from religion." (Graham responded to Reagan's welcome by saying, "No matter whether you agree with what he says or does, he's got political courage.") He told stories about substituting prayer for antacids during his first term as California governor and invited Graham to address the state assembly in 1971 about faith's role in politics. He capped his 1980 acceptance speech in Detroit with a silent prayer, noting he was almost scared to do it. (Graham had given the convention's invocation.) As president, Reagan would often, before an important speech or meeting, tell his chief of staff, James Baker, "I need a minute." Baker would turn and see Reagan saying a silent prayer in preparation. "Faith was a part of him and always was," said Deputy Chief of Staff Michael Deaver, who began working for Reagan in 1966. "Whenever there was a disappointment or a setback, his response was always, 'There's a reason for this and we'll find out someday what it is. But it's all a part of God's plan.' He wasn't sappy about it. He was almost matter-of-fact."

But his intense interest in religious freedom in the Soviet Union was something of an obsession. His letters were sprinkled with sad mentions to friends about the Soviet people's inability to pray openly when their loved ones passed away. He saw the steady reintroduction of faith as one of the keys to breaking the communist empire. Jerry Falwell recalled that Reagan brought up the topic in their first meeting in 1980, during a car ride together. "He felt that the people of faith and particularly Christians in the Soviet bloc nations were of such a large number that if ever the release came, they would spring forward and create great ministries in all those nations." As president, he worked this agenda behind the scenes: he met nearly two dozen times with a Russian cultural expert and discussed the pace of religious freedom in the Soviet Union. National Security Adviser Frank Carlucci recalls being astonished to learn that Reagan had devoted a large part of one summit with Mikhail Gorbachev to criticizing the Soviet leader for his slowness in opening church doors. "He was fascinated by that," said Carlucci. "He beat up Gorbachev on freedom of religion in the Soviet Union." Graham said Reagan's interest in the spiritual lives of the Slavic peoples was always "part of the conversation."

His instincts in this campaign had only been fortified by the assassination attempt in 1981—which Reagan interpreted, just as Nelle would have done, as part of a larger plan. It had been a very close call—closer than most people would know for months. On Good Friday, eighteen days after the shooting, Reagan asked Deaver to find a minister for him to speak to. Deaver telephoned Terence Cardinal Cooke in New York City and invited the priest to the White House. The two men huddled in the Yellow Room on the second floor of the White House, speaking in what Deaver later described as "deep, hushed conversations." But Deaver caught some of what Reagan was saying: "I have decided that whatever time I may have left is left for Him." Reagan believed he had been spared for a purpose—to help reduce the risk of a nuclear conflict. "Perhaps having come so close to death," Reagan later wrote, "made me feel I should do whatever I could in the years God has given me to reduce the threat of nuclear war; perhaps there was a reason I had been spared." He would share this idea with a few people, including his family, the pope, and Billy Graham.

Graham's road to Moscow followed a different course. He had stopped briefly in Red Square in 1959 and prayed that he would someday be able to return to preach in public. Like Reagan, he worried for two decades about Moscow's designs on the West, fearful it would spread its antireligious culture across the globe. But by the late 1970s, Graham had seen firsthand that the people who lived under Soviet domination did not share that ideology. And so he decided to push directly into Russia. If he could somehow wrangle an offer to preach there, he reasoned, he could expect offers to preach throughout the Soviet bloc.

The invitation that arrived from Moscow in late 1981 was not exactly the one he had been hoping for. He was invited by the Russian Orthodox Church to something called the "World Conference of Religious Workers for Saving the Sacred Gift of Life from Nuclear Catastrophe." Amid one of the greatest buildups of arms ever, the Soviets invited Graham to a peace conference.

The Moscow conference was timed, organized, and pitched entirely to the Soviets' public relations advantage. Some twenty Protestant denominations in the United States had called for a nuclear freeze by the spring of 1982 and large rallies had taken place around the country as well. Voices like that of John Cardinal Krol, a conservative leader of the Philadelphia archdiocese, labeled Washington's nuclear buildup "irrational and suicidal" at a peace rally of fifteen thousand in the City of Brotherly Love. Activists were planning massive demonstrations in Europe that summer, including protests at the planned NATO missile deployment sites in Germany and Italy. The May conference in Moscow was designed to amplify that view—and turn European public opinion against the coming U.S. deployment.

Graham knew the conference was a barely disguised Soviet propaganda effort, but he hoped his participation would amount to a foot in a long-closed door. Those who did not share his belief in the gospel's power to change hearts, and history, would try to talk him out of the trip. Some members of his own board opposed the journey, while others he trusted for advice, including Richard Nixon and Henry Kissinger, urged him to go. But the Reagan administration was full of hard-liners who favored a no-quarter attitude toward Moscow. The trip would put Graham at odds with much of his own government throughout the spring of 1982—but not at odds with Ronald Reagan. It would also show just how far Graham was willing to push Washington when he saw a chance to break new spiritual frontiers.

On February 3, Graham aides John Akers and Walter Smyth met with National Security Council (NSC) official James Nance to review plans for the journey. Nance wrote Reagan and National Security Adviser William Clark a memo noting that Akers and Smyth "say they know they are playing a 'dice game' and that the Soviets will try to use them for propaganda purposes. However, Billy is going to leave before any possible communiqué can come out of this meeting. In addition, he will alert other western church leaders to be careful they are not entrapped by some Soviet propaganda campaign. In general, I believe they are going in there with their eyes open and their guard up for any possible Soviet actions."

Graham was betting that the value of preaching the gospel—both in Russia and in the Eastern bloc countries that would follow—far outweighed any compromises he would have to make or any criticism he would endure. Nance hinted at this trade-off in his memo: "I asked Akers and Smyth why Billy goes to Russia and Eastern European countries. They said they knew they were being exploited in some fashion because the communist countries always try to show the world that things were better off than they really are and that their countries are not anti-religious. However, Billy feels the good he gets from the great religious gatherings that he holds far outweighs the uses the Soviets and Eastern Europeans make of the visit. He may be correct."

But just a week later, other NSC officials grew more concerned about the Graham trip when a confidential, six-page cable arrived from Moscow that suggested, without saying so directly, that Graham was in way over his head. The cable's author, Deputy Chief of Mission Warren Zimmerman, argued that Graham was being used by Soviet officials for political purposes. Distributed to embassies worldwide, the Zimmerman cable urged all recipients to "make the obvious propaganda objectives of this conference clear to potential attendees." The top American officials in Moscow were asking Washington, in the diplomatic equivalent of a fire alarm, to get Graham to change his mind. The next day, William Stearman, a naval officer on loan to the NSC, wrote Clark a confidential memo, based on Zimmerman's cable, warning that the Russians had convinced Graham to attend a conference designed principally to condemn U.S. arms control positions. "Since the conference will be rigged from the beginning—the final communiqué is already in draft—any religious leaders attending will perforce be entrapped by a Soviet propaganda campaign.

"Billy," Stearman concluded, "has been had already."

If the White House never asked Graham to abandon his plans directly, it certainly tried to make him think twice about going. Vice President

Bush telephoned him in London in early March and passed along the Moscow embassy's reservations. One report stated that Bush urged Graham not to go during this conversation but Graham said later Bush passed along the reservations of others but did not take a position himself. When *Newsweek* broke the story about Graham's plans on March 15, the evangelist made it clear that he would not let international politics stop him. "If I go to Moscow, I will only preach the Gospel," he pledged. This was a perfectly good enough answer on his own terms—and not nearly good enough for those with more secular concerns.

On March 19, two other NSC officials, Robert Linhard and Sven Kraemer, met with Graham aide Akers again at the White House. Akers spent most of the hourlong session in the Situation Room explaining why Graham would go forward with the trip—whatever the downsides. A cancellation would only delay a return by Graham to the Soviet bloc nations he had begun to visit in the late 1970s. Akers told the two officials that Graham had already discussed the trip generally with Vice President Bush and that only the State Department seemed opposed. The NSC men assured Akers that the White House shared State's concerns and warned again that the Soviets would "do their best to use Graham's visit to legitimize their own purposes." Rather than offer a greeting from an American president for Graham to read, they urged Graham to consider making a statement or a "sermon focusing on the need for reducing armaments (rather than freezing them), for supporting free expression of religious conscience on issues of war and peace in all countries and for eliminating the walls and curtains that divide men." Akers offered to run a draft of such a statement by the White House in advance.

It is clear that White House officials would have preferred that Graham skip the trip. But by late March it was also increasingly apparent that he would not be turned. "The more I prayed about it, the more I thought about it, the more I thought this might open up a whole new chapter for the gospel in Eastern Europe and Russia," he said. "So I finally decided to go."

So U.S. officials decided to try to bend the trip to their own design, help Graham maintain a distance from the worst of the propaganda, and then get out of the way in case things went sour. After that, an unofficial blessing was not long in coming: in late March, Graham joined George and Barbara Bush for lunch at the Naval Observatory in Washington. Famous for making spur-of-the-moment social invitations, Bush invited the Reagans to join the party. The Reagans drove over, and during lunch Reagan pulled Graham aside and privately gave him the green light to attend. "I'll be praying for you every step of the way," he said.

If Graham showed himself willing, for the first time in his now thirty years of public life, to defy the official guidance of the national security establishment, it reflected a conviction that the man he cared about most seemed to understand best what he was trying to do. However skeptical the State Department and NSC officials were about what an evangelist might accomplish as a strategic player, Reagan himself showed no such doubts. In fact, Reagan and Graham had more conversations in April 1982 than at any other time during Reagan's presidency. White House telephone records indicate the two men talked several times on one day that month. Graham spent much of the second half of April on an eight-city swing through New England college campuses, where he preached on the growing danger of nuclear Armageddon and the need to eliminate weapons of mass destruction. On April 26, responding to a letter Graham had written a month earlier, Reagan underscored his support for the journey. "Dear Billy . . . Please know that I have complete confidence in your decision about the Soviet trip. God does work in wondrous ways, and he'll show the way on this."

Whatever anyone else may have thought, Graham now had a written blessing from Reagan himself. The rest of the government fell quickly into line. In mid-April, after clearing the move with Clark, Bush cabled Moscow with an official endorsement of the trip. "After doing all we could to present Billy the ideas you articulated for me, he remained adamant. The President and I felt it would be counterproductive to insist Billy Graham not go to Moscow or to not be helpful to him."

Graham's six-day Russian odyssey would prove to be both fair and foul: as promising for future evangelical missions behind the Iron Curtain as Graham had hoped—and as costly in public relations terms as some had feared. He was outmaneuvered by the Soviets almost from the minute he arrived. On his first full day in Russia, the storied Soviet Americanologist Georgi Arbatov captured him for conversations about bilateral relations for more than three hours—twice as long as planned. Carefully laid plans to preach twice the next day, the lone Sunday of his trip—first at an Orthodox cathedral and then at Moscow's only Baptist church—were rewritten by his hosts, reversed in their order, collapsed into a tight, two-hour window, and so restricted in who could attend that Graham was, for the most part, muffled as a preacher. After his thirty-minute sermon at the Baptist church, attended by a thousand carefully selected ticket holders, plainclothes officers escorted a woman out of the church for unfurling a banner that noted, "We have more than 150 prisoners for the work of the Gospel." Asked about that incident later, Graham said that he had not noticed the incident and chose instead to defend the government's clumsy move. "We detain people in the United States if we catch people doing things wrong."

After the church services, Graham's handlers whisked their guest off for an exhaustive and time-wasting four-hour tour of a Russian Orthodox Church publishing facility. A man of Graham's appeal was not someone the Soviets could afford to permit unstructured time. Graham, who was shepherded from meeting to meeting in a black, chauffeur-driven Chaika limousine, was polite almost to a fault. He marveled at his treatment later on in the trip. "In the US, only a millionaire could afford caviar," he said, "and here I have caviar with every meal."

When the time came for Graham to address the "peace conference," the meeting was already collapsing under the weight of its own heavy-handed propaganda. Other American clerics who had traveled to Moscow complained that the meetings had taken on an absurd anti-American tilt. That made it easier for Graham to try and level the playing field. "No nation, large or small, is exempt from blame for the present state of international affairs," he said. He inserted into his remarks a passage, however vaguely addressed, that was obviously aimed at the Kremlin. "I urge all governments to respect the rights of religious believers outlined in the [United Nations] Universal Declaration of Human Rights. We must hope that someday all nations will recognize and respect the freedom of the individual to profess and practice, alone or in community with others, religion or belief acting in accordance with the dictates of her own conscience."

But a few days later he remarked to reporters that "I think there is a lot more freedom here than has been given the impression in the United States." He compounded the error by noting that Russian church attendance on Saturday nights seemed higher to him than it might be in the United States. "They were jammed to capacity," he said. "You never get that in Charlotte [North Carolina]."

Graham would spend the next several weeks on the defensive; he insisted that his remarks were taken out of context and misinterpreted, and there is some truth in that. But his efforts to clarify and correct the record were ragged, and only served to deepen the impression that he had been duped by his hosts. He appeared from London on ABC's *This Week with David Brinkley* the following Sunday, backtracking only slightly from his earlier assessments. The next day, William Safire spat out a withering column about Graham's consortium with the devil, headlined "All Things to All Men." In it, Safire accused Graham, "in his zeal to make a deal to spread the Word," of bearing false witness. "The person who purposes to represent Truth with a Capital T has a special responsibility to bear the embarrassing burden of truth and to turn no blind eye to the reality and extent of religious persecution." The criticisms Graham endured from the right echoed the attacks he had endured from the left for his refusal to criticize LBJ and Nixon over Vietnam. Few media outlets of any kind came to his defense. One exception was the liberal *Christian Century*, a steady Graham tormentor. "To his credit, Billy Graham has come to realize the basic immorality of nuclear arms and he has used his prestige to announce his opposition to the arms race."

His problems did not abate when he returned to the United States. Graham quipped upon landing in New York that "I am not a Communist and I have not joined the Communist party." A few days later, at a press conference in the New York Hilton, he was still groping for solid ground. "I'm told that anyone who can find and get into a house of worship is free to worship. There is a bit more freedom in the Soviet Union than I had anticipated. There is freedom of worship, but not of religion." That same day, to protest Graham's comments about Soviet religious freedoms, more than a dozen members of the Jewish Defense League invaded an office of the World Council of Churches on Riverside Drive in Manhattan. The protesters demanded that the Council censure Graham "for giving absolution to the Soviet regime."

Back in Washington, it is easy to imagine Reagan administration hardliners sharing knowing looks as Graham's sloppy finish unfolded across several continents and almost as many weeks. In its public comments, however, the White House was careful to be circumspect—and shrewd enough to take the long view. "I don't think we need to get into that," said Larry Speakes, Bush's spokesman, when asked repeatedly about Graham's trip. And, in a larger sense, Graham was soon vindicated. Within just a few months, he received invitations to preach in the nations that were then known as Czechoslovakia and East Germany—trips that would turn out to be genuine crusades in countries desperate for Christian ministry. It had not been easy to watch, but Graham had wedged his foot in the door. And he would help kick it wide open over the next few years.

When the invitation came for Graham to return to the Soviet Union two years later in 1984, he would get the chance to lead a crusade through four cities and twenty-three sermons in twelve days. By then, he knew how to order his steps. He consulted personally with senior Reagan officials in preparation for the second trip rather than send aides to make the arrangements with Washington. And when he arrived in Moscow, he was more candid about the balancing act he was performing, no longer in denial about the line he was walking. Asked again if the Soviets might exploit his appearance to their advantage, Graham replied, "I'm sure that there is some element of truth in that. But I think it's worth taking a risk for peace in the world, worth taking a risk to preach the Gospel."

Within minutes of his return to Soviet soil, Graham was confronted by a party religious affairs officer who began to lecture him on U.S. military posture. Erik Amfitheatrof, a *TIME* correspondent in Moscow, filed this dispatch to his editors in New York about what happened next: "The fellow began pouring out the Soviet line on peace and what an important part church leaders could play in the struggle . . . while Graham's eyes glazed over and he stood waiting for the official to take a breath. When that moment finally came, Graham smiled and said in his deep, mellow baritone . . . 'You must trust in the Lord.' The party official gazed after Graham, a bit crestfallen, and protested, 'But I am an atheist.'"

Without missing a beat, Graham got into his limousine and yelled out, "Well, you would have made a fine preacher!"

TWENTY-SEVEN

The Secret Agent

I turned him down several times. But he took it real well. . . . I had a lot of those experiences with different presidents.

—Graham on Reagan's requests for political help

It took the Christian right a little while to realize that the religious agenda Reagan brought with him to the White House had as much to do with the people of the Soviet Union as it did with the people of the United States. Reagan paid lip service to social conservative positions on abortion, school prayer, gay rights, and sex education, but he often stopped short of rewriting the regulations and laws that governed those practices. Meanwhile, he was privately cheering on the efforts of Graham and Pope John Paul II to energize the latent Christian masses in Eastern Europe. Reagan would turn to Billy Graham for help in a variety of ways, not least of which was as a counterweight to the other religious force that helped get him elected but whose political agenda he did not always share.

Nor could the leaders of the Christian right have missed the ways Graham continued to keep his distance from them, both in the positions he took (or sometimes did not take) and the more independent role he played. Ten days after Reagan was sworn in, Graham told *Parade* magazine that "evangelicals can't be closely identified with any particular party or person. We have to stand in the middle, to preach to all the people, right and left. I haven't been faithful to my own advice in the past. I will in the future." He even telephoned Jerry Falwell, he said, and urged the Virginia Baptist to stay out of politics. "I told him to preach the Gospel—that's our calling," Graham said. "The hard right has no interest in religion except to manipulate it." Just a week later, Graham received only tepid applause when he told a group of religious broadcasters in Washington that the United States could not be indifferent to the spectacle of millions "who live on the brink of starvation each year, while the nations of the world spend $550 billion each year on weapons." Graham warned the broadcasters to beware their own complacency. "We dare not sit around patting ourselves on the back when the world's despair without Christ is becoming increasingly evident around us."

At times, Graham took on the Moral Majority directly. In 1981, for example, he personally lobbied U.S. senators at Reagan's request to help build Senate support for the controversial sale of AWACS early-warning planes to Saudi Arabia. Israel had strongly objected to the sale, and its formidable U.S. lobbying arm, which included elements of the Moral Majority, mobilized to halt the sale. Graham nonetheless pitched in on Reagan's side, calling a few key senators. Graham would eventually say that Falwell and the Moral Majority too often got "sidetracked" on issues that undercut the message of the gospel. "I think where political issues invade moral situations, spiritual leaders have to speak out. But I do not intend to use what little influence I may have on secular, non moral, non religious issues like the Panama Canal."

Graham was again stepping out—and in a different direction. He wrote a story for *TV Guide* in March 1983 warning that some televangelists had subordinated the gospel to fund-raising on their programs. "Money is a means," he wrote. "It must never be the message."

In the spring of 1983, Graham performed a covert political reconnaissance mission for William Clark, who at that time was serving as Reagan's national security adviser. Clark had asked him to survey evangelical leaders and gauge their reaction to the possibility that Washington might grant full diplomatic status to the Vatican, an idea Graham had discussed since the Truman administration. Reagan was looking for a way to link arms with the Polish pope in the West's battle with Moscow and needed to anticipate problems at home the move would create.

Graham's seven-page survey on Clark's behalf is almost as interesting for who he polled as for what they said. He checked in with at least a dozen evangelical and religious experts either directly or through cut-outs, to gauge the expected reaction: Gilbert Beers, the editor of *Christianity Today*; Dr. J. Richard Chase, the president of Wheaton College in Illinois;

Dr. James Dunn, the executive secretary of the Baptist Joint Committee on Public Affairs; Dr. David Hubbard, president of the Fuller Theological Seminary; and Dr. Billy Melvin. Graham also made contact with, among others, both Pat Robertson and Jerry Falwell, noting that he and Akers had made their inquiries without mentioning that they were "being made at the request of the White House." Graham also sounded out two senior U.S.-based Roman Catholic officials—including one in the Apostolic Delegate's office—about a new diplomatic arrangement.

Graham's informal poll turned up a mixed bag. Pat Robertson was, Graham reported, the most supportive of the idea, noting it could bring what Graham called "positive diplomatic and intelligence gains to the US." Several experts said that moderate evangelicals would barely notice the shift. But most of those Graham and Akers polled ranged from luke-warm to downright hostile: Dunn vowed to oppose the move publicly; Melvin said most of the National Association of Evangelicals members would take formal stands against it; and several said Jerry Falwell would be sure to oppose it. Graham did not reach Falwell, but a go-between reported that Falwell "is against it."

Graham stopped short of offering his own advice about whether to recognize Rome. Indeed, there was an echo between the candor the White House paid to Graham on his Moscow trip in 1982 and the candor Graham paid to the White House on Vatican relations a year later. "I honestly don't know what I personally would recommend that the President do," he wrote Clark. Instead, he limited his counsel to suggesting, in the event the president decided to go forward, how likely critics might be handled and how the new arrangement might be sold publicly. Reagan, advised Graham, "would need to cover his political bases, so to speak, and be sure he brought people into the picture who might cause him trouble (Jews, Bishops Committee, National Council, etc). It may also be that some people (like Jerry Falwell) could be persuaded to keep silent on the issue." Helpfully, he offered a suggestion designed to reduce the impression that Washington would ally itself not only with the Vatican itself but the Roman Catholic Church in the United States. He urged Clark to consider splitting into two the job of representing the United States: one for religious issues and another for political matters. "Maybe that would underline the fact that the US was recognizing the Vatican as a political state only," he wrote.

Graham also suggested that the White House not limit consideration of candidates for ambassador to Roman Catholics, presumably to draw no special distinction to the relationship. Still, he seemed on balance to be for the diplomatic gesture, noting for Clark that his own 1980 visit to the Vatican generated far less controversy from evangelicals than he had expected. "We actually were surprised by how little vocal opposition there was," he wrote.

Graham sent his memo to Clark in late April; it was not until December that word of the White House initiative leaked. The reaction from evangelicals was much as Graham had predicted: Falwell immediately described the proposed move as a serious mistake and a violation of the establishment clause. Other groups, including several in Graham's memo, went further and briefly tried to stop the diplomatic initiative in the courts. By and large, moderate evangelicals did not react to the news at all. The muted response also owed something to a new political alignment in the United States: the coalition between southern Baptists and northern Roman Catholics for Reagan that emerged in the 1970s. Though the two factions had been separated by a theological divide for decades, they began to join forces after the 1973 Supreme Court decision legalizing abortion. They would stay more or less aligned on some social issues for the next several decades.

Graham noted that every president had asked him to perform minor political tasks but none responded as graciously as Reagan when he declined to help. "I turned him down several times," Graham said. "But he took it real well." In 1980, he declined a request by Reagan to put in a favorable word to North Carolina primary voters, saying it would harm his ministry. On another occasion he turned down a request by Reagan aide Edwin Meese to join the candidate on what Graham perceived as a political appearance. "He said Reagan wanted me to. And I told him I just couldn't do it." Ruth and Billy spent a night in the White House in July 1981, when Reagan was still in recuperation from the March gunshot wound, and again in September 1982, on the occasion of a state dinner for the Marcoses of the Philippines. In February 1983, Reagan bestowed on Graham the Presidential Medal of Freedom. Graham would again come to Reagan's aid in September 1984 after Reagan, while practicing for a nationwide radio address, had joked into an open microphone, "My fellow Americans, I'm pleased to tell you that I've signed legislation that will outlaw Russia forever. We begin bombing in five minutes." While preaching in Estonia a month later, Graham called the remark "unfortunate" but added, "You have to remember that he was a film actor." Actors, he said, are "used to little jokes they don't mean."

And if Graham was occasionally willing to take on a mission for Reagan, the president was happy to repay the favor. On June 30, 1986, Graham wrote Nancy Reagan saying, "I have a request to make and I apologize for making it!" He noted that he was about to embark on a weeklong crusade in Paris, dubbed Mission: France. He noted with characteristic modesty in his note to Mrs. Reagan that though he was well-known in France after World War II, "I am virtually unknown now." He expressed a concern, as he often did before many crusades, that no one would attend the sessions. "For the French Christians, where church attendance is almost zero," he wrote, "it is a tremendous undertaking. It has been strongly suggested that I be received by either President [François] Mitterrand or Prime Minister [Jacques] Chirac. The Ambassador and I both feel it would be a great help if your husband could mention to Mr. Mitterrand that our Ambassador will be approaching him about an appointment— that I am a longtime friend—and that he hopes Mr. Mitterrand will receive me."

Graham was betting that a photo opportunity with the French leader would generate nationwide publicity for his visit—and thus bring more people to the crusade. It was a version of what his organization had done for decades in the United States and elsewhere: issued a routine invitation to all the local and statewide officials wherever a crusade was planned. A week later, on June 7, Reagan handwrote a note to Mitterrand. Reagan thanked the French president for attending the hundredth anniversary celebration of the Statue of Liberty over the previous Fourth of July weekend. He then added, "May I impose on you further? One of our most prestigious religious figures, the world-renowned Reverend Billy Graham, is holding a crusade this September in Paris in the new Bercy Sports Stadium. We have been close friends for many years. Our Ambassador Rodgers will be speaking to you about a possible appointment with Reverend Graham while he is there. I would be most grateful if you could find time to see him."

But most of Graham's letters to Reagan are pastoral in nature, offering words of support, promises of prayer, and above all scripture. In December

1986, Graham cabled Reagan with Isaiah 43:2: "When thou passest through the waters, I will be with thee; and through the rivers, they shall not overflow thee: when thou walkest through the fire, thou shalt not be burned; neither shall the flame kindle upon thee." Reagan replied, "Believe me, it helped and was, and is, most comforting." In March 1987, Graham wrote a letter praising a speech, as he did Eisenhower's first big foreign policy speech in 1953, reporting that he had prayed for Reagan throughout his delivery and likening his style and technique to that of Jesus on the mount. "The thought that comes to me from Scripture is Jeremiah 32:17—there is nothing too hard for God. You don't face a problem but what God can help you solve it." Reagan replied a few days later—"just a line, but a heartfelt line"—thanking Graham for his prayers. Throughout Reagan's years in office, Graham regularly supplied the president and his speechwriters with ideas for homilies and prayers for the National Prayer Breakfast in January of each year. But most of the letters reveal a pastor simply asking God to look out for his friend in the Oval Office. A few days before his time in office ended, Reagan wrote both Graham and his wife a letter of thanks for all their help over the previous eight years. "Thank you for your prayers. I know they have been answered, and to steal Lincoln's words, I have had help from One Who is stronger and wiser than all others."

Graham has said repeatedly that his relationship with Reagan was chiefly a private one, and it is true that many of the visits and telephone calls were never made public. "I have been there many nights," Graham said in 1984. "We're just more quiet about it now." Reagan called Graham often, Graham reported, simply to discuss various topics in the news. Reagan would see an article in the newspaper, for example, and telephone Graham for his reaction to it. But there remained an element of mystery to the relationship, even to Graham, who described Reagan as the president he was closest to—and the one he would have liked to have known better. Nancy Reagan said her husband's relationship with Graham deepened when he became president. "Their relationship was beyond political," she said in 2006. "Billy would keep in touch with Ronnie on all levels. He told him that he thought that Russia had more of a spiritual revolution going on there than people realized and Ronnie thought that too. They talked about that. Then of course, he would write after speeches that he heard Ronnie give. Or after a difficult period that we were going through, he would write. And, really, a lot of that was on a personal level but some of it was pastoral, too.

"However close Billy got to anybody," Nancy Reagan said, "it was because that person was able, and wanted, to have that kind of relationship. Ronnie was just that kind of a person. I think if they are open to [a spiritual conversation], it can be helpful. But they have to be open to it. Billy was Billy and he brought another dimension into it—and it was one that Ronnie believed in." Added Michael Reagan, the president's oldest son, "Billy came to pray with my father, sit with my father. Dad always had great respect for him. He knew he was a person he could pray with and ask advice of and do it confident that it would remain in confidence. Billy is one of those people you can go to, and talk to, without worrying that it would show up the next day in *TIME* magazine."

Graham sent Reagan off into private life with a letter that praised him for "making America strong" and reviving "our national spirit. You made us stand tall and become proud that we are Americans. You gave us a sense of self-confidence. You have inspired people as no other president since Roosevelt and that is a tremendous achievement in itself." Graham touched on some topics that he and Reagan had been talking about for nearly thirty years, including the Second Coming of Christ. "Not all the problems of America and the world have been solved. Some are frightening. Some of them indicate that this present age is drawing to a close and that the coming of Christ cannot be far off—things such as poison gas, the greenhouse effect, etc., just to name a couple. These seem beyond the control of mankind."

But the bulk of the letter is devoted to Graham's dissection of Reagan's success in office. "You had a philosophy of government and life that did not change, no matter what the circumstances. You believed America could be great. . . . Secondly, your strong faith in God and your willingness to talk about it publicly, no matter what the critics might say. . . . Thirdly, you have a compassion for people. God gave you a marvelous charisma that did not come just from your Hollywood days as some would like to assert. It came from something God gave you. No matter how bad the circumstances or how harsh the questions from the reporters were, you always had a smile, you had a way of saying the right thing. I doubt if America will ever see another Ronald Reagan."

And following Reagan's return to California, Graham telephoned often and never failed to drop by whenever he was in Los Angeles. "When he was still able to travel," Nancy recalled, "Billy would always come to Los Angeles and this was the first stop he would make." Reagan kept in touch as well. "Nancy comes home from Paris today," Reagan wrote Graham in May 1990 in a "Dear Billy" note. "She's been over there helping her publisher who has plans for printing a French version of her book. I told her of your illness in a phone call and she gave me orders to tell you to take care of yourself."

Graham was one of the very few people outside the immediate family who was permitted to call on Reagan in his final years. Graham, for his part, recalls visiting Reagan one time in the 1990s, talking with Nancy before going outside in the backyard to sit with the former president. Reagan, whose Alzheimer's was by then in an advanced stage, pressed his guest to hold off on prayer until Billy Graham arrived. "Billy's relationship with presidents was not just to be there when they were president," said Michael Reagan, "but 24-7."

In 1998, Graham wrote Nancy to steady the former First Lady as she cared for her husband. "My thoughts and prayers are with you and Ronnie daily. I love you both and wish there was something I could do more than I have done. But when we come before the Lord in humble prayer, that's the *most* we can do."

Both Reagans asked Graham to preach at the president's funeral, but when the time came, Graham was too frail from a pelvis injury to make the trip.

When Reagan passed away, the first call that Nancy placed outside the family was to her husband's old friend in the hills above Montreat.

TWENTY-EIGHT

The Family Pastor

We went to Kennebunkport every summer for a while.
—Graham on his invitations from George and Barbara Bush

There were a great many reasons why Ronald Reagan was one of the harder acts to follow in American politics. He was a movie star who knew how to take the stage, knew what to say once he got there, and knew how to make an exit. He had all the sales skills a president could want, too: charm, timing, a sense of humor, a gift for storytelling, and a handful of clear, simple convictions that did not blot out his belief in compromise. All of that would create a huge challenge for whoever came next. But Reagan's successor would have an added disadvantage: the evangelical voters who swarmed to the GOP in 1980 were by 1985 feeling burned once more. If Jimmy Carter had turned out to be a liberal Democrat who did not share their views, Reagan had proved to be an even more complicated partner: someone who shared their values but did little to advance them. Bound by an Eleventh Commandment to refrain from speaking ill of any Republican, leaders of the religious right had no plans to abandon the party of Reagan as the 1988 campaign opened. But nor did they intend to blindly transfer their loyalties to the man next in line for the nomination. Vice President George Herbert Walker Bush would have to win them over.

Bush had an unusual pedigree: he hailed from the tony New York suburb of Greenwich, Connecticut, and graduated from Andover and Yale; but then he had struck out on his own, moving to Midland, Texas, during the postwar oil boom to make his fortune. He was a dazzling political success story too: he had campaigned for Barry Goldwater, befriended Lyndon Johnson, worked for Richard Nixon and Gerald Ford, and then served as the trusty viceroy to Ronald Reagan. He was a decorated World War II veteran, a self-made businessman, the son of a senator, the head of a large family, a vestry-man at two Episcopal churches, and a longtime friend of Billy Graham.

He also had no clue about how to talk to evangelical Christians.

In February 1985, Bush walked from his suite in the Old Executive Office Building down a long marble hall to see Pete Teeley, his press sec-retary. When he arrived, he could see that Teeley already had company: Doug Wead, a thirty-eight-year-old author of religious and inspirational books. Teeley explained to the vice president that his guest was a born-again Christian. This intrigued Bush, who asked Wead questions about his faith. Wead ticked off the names of other White House officials who shared his convictions, and before long, Bush had invited Wead to ride with him to the National Religious Broadcasters' convention, where the vice president was to speak that day. On the way, Bush showed Wead his prepared remarks, and almost immediately Wead proposed a few changes to the text. It was clear to Wead that Bush had a fuzzy understanding of the right things to say to the religious leaders and broadcasters he was about to address. But help had arrived. "It was," Wead said, "like water falling on dry ground."

Wead was a controversial but pivotal player in the dance between Republican politicians and evangelical voters between 1980 and 2000. He worked for Bush from 1985 until 1990, when he resigned from the White House staff in a minor scandal. A motivational speaker by trade, he had an easy manner that enabled him to move between two worlds—one political, the other evangelical. He began to work as Bush's official liaison between camps, interpreting the language of the evangelists for the pols who spoke a different tongue altogether.

Bush was not the first to identify Wead's unusual value: an aide to Jimmy Carter consulted with him and invited him to roundtables in 1979 at the White House in an effort to help shore up Carter's support among religious leaders. Not long after, Reagan aides asked Wead to write a fast book about Reagan and his religious background. In late 1979, they invited him to Pacific Palisades in California for dinner and conversation with the Repub-lican hopeful and his wife. When Wead's book on Reagan was published six months later, it sold more than half a million copies. Because of his work for Amway in the 1970s and 1980s, Wead had extensive contacts around the United States and unparalleled knowledge of the flora and fauna of the various evangelical factions and their leaders. By 1985, he had interviewed Ford, Carter, and Reagan and many of their aides about their experiences discussing faith on the campaign trail. As a link between two very different worlds, Wead looked invaluable to the Bush team.

Over the next three years, Wead helped Bush meet or speak to more than a thousand evangelical leaders, put the vice president's name and face before millions of churchgoers, and set the standard for evangelical politicking by Republican presidential candidates for the next two decades. Under Wead's guidance, Bush would court evangelical voters aggressively in 1985 and 1986 as part of a deliberate campaign to lock them up early, long before anyone was paying much attention—or asking many questions. Bush's eldest son, George Walker Bush, would play a key role in this little-known campaign-within-the-campaign, serving as the vice president's lead surrogate speaker and working at Wead's side for close to two years. The son's role in the 1988 campaign was not restricted to evangelical outreach. But that sideline provided the younger Bush a chance to learn firsthand how to woo and win this pivotal bloc of Republican voters. The apprenticeship would prove useful later on.

Within days of accompanying Bush to his NRB speech in January 1985, Wead became a part-time consultant to the Fund for America's Future, the Bush exploratory committee. Working from his home in Springfield, Missouri, Wead spent the next several months writing a strategy for wooing evangelical voters. He showed a draft to a few evangelical leaders for accuracy before turning it over to Teeley. His first draft ran to more than 160 pages; Bush aides twice asked him to cut it down. The final result was a fifty-seven-page step-by-step plan for winning the nation's growing evangelical voting bloc. The memo detailed the growing size and number of evangelicals, where they lived, what they believed, and then divided and subdivided them by denomination and leadership. It distinguished fundamentalists from charismatics, Pentecostals from Southern Baptists. It provided Bush with thumbnail sketches of most of the evangelical leaders and explained how Ronald Reagan had quietly wooed those leaders in the late 1970s without paying a price for doing so among more secular voters.

Wead made dozens of recommendations. He proposed that the vice president learn as much as possible about the evangelical movement, get to know its leaders, find ways to talk to them regularly, and hire a consultant (i.e., Wead) to serve as a liaison. He proposed White House meetings and discreet get-togethers with local preachers when Bush was traveling around the country for other reasons. Wead urged that Bush find ways to stay in touch with the leaders by card or telephone, sharing news about various goings-on in the religious world. His core recommendation, however, was that Bush send "an early signal" about the depth of his Christian faith when publicity would be relatively small and therefore would present "less risk of any backlash." Wead's conclusion: "The Vice President would not be well served to ignore the special needs and concerns of this large segment of America. He is in a position to inherit from President Reagan the support of this constituency, but the President has had a long and carefully established relationship with evangelicals dating back to his California Governorship. . . . There is no guarantee that the Vice President will automatically have this support."

Wead knew that if Bush planned to meet several hundred leading evangelicals over the next two years, he would need a clear formulation about his relationship to Jesus. Wead spent a few pages tutoring the vice president on the definition of being "born again" and how to answer questions about whether he was, in fact, saved. There was some confusion in Wead's mind about the state of Bush's personal faith and so, hoping to tease it out of him, he conducted a sort of seminar on personal salvation. One section posed the question, "Can a person be born again without a crisis experience?" (Answer: Yes.) Another asked, "Can a person be born again without knowing it?" (Answer: Yes again.) And so forth. Wead knew the veep had to get it right: Bush had not done well in the informal oral exams with evangelicals when he ran for president as a dark horse in 1980. Bush had met that year with a group of pastors convened by Dr. James Kennedy at Chicago's O'Hare Airport Hilton. During the session, the preachers asked Bush what he would say to Saint Peter when he arrived at the gates of heaven. Bush botched the answer, replying that he would say he had tried his best to follow God's teachings while he had been on earth. When asked point-blank if he was born again, Bush said he was not. Reagan, by comparison, aced the exam (which in his case had taken place at a hotel in Washington, D.C.), telling the pastors that he didn't have to plead his case to Saint Peter besides saying that Jesus had died for his sins. It would be important for Bush to get the answers right the second time around, particularly in a primary contest that looked, at least to Wead, like it might pit Bush against televangelist Pat Robertson. And after that, his formulation could not change.

While almost every other religious leader mentioned in the paper was treated as ripe for recruitment and open to courtship, Graham was clearly in a different category. The Montreat preacher, wrote Wead, "is considered by many . . . the father of the evangelical movement. He is its most respected and influential institution. . . . Dr. Graham, in spite of a decade of self-imposed silence on political issues and a comparatively low key public image, has the highest name recognition of any other evangelical figure." The strong suggestion in the memo was that Graham could not, and should not, be wooed. Instead, the paper made only one suggestion when it came to the most famous evangelical of all: it called for "maintaining the friendship he already has with Billy Graham."

By that point, Billy Graham's friendship with the Bush family was three decades old. Graham had known Bush's mother since the mid-1950s; he had played golf with his father; he had vacationed with the vice president and his wife; he had ministered to his children. By the mid-1980s, Billy Graham was firmly established as the Bush family's unofficial pastor. All of which created a different kind of temptation for politician and preacher: in the months leading up to the 1988 campaign, Bush was under considerable pressure from aides to spotlight his relationship with America's most admired man. When aides gently nudged him to bring his relationship with Graham front and center, in an effort to curry favor with evangelical voters who did not instinctively trust him, the vice president resisted, but only to a point. Bush was a man of uncommon courtesy and kindness, capable of spectacular sensitivity to people he barely knew. He was also plenty calculating when he needed to be. Both Bush and Graham would struggle with the boundaries between friendship and politics in a contest where evangelical voters were playing a pivotal role. And when the moment came that Graham could offer a blessing to his friend, he was happy to do so.

Teeley delivered Wead's memo to his boss just before Bush departed for his annual August retreat to Kennebunkport—where two of the many houseguests at the old family compound would be Ruth and Billy Graham.

OLD FRIENDS

M aintaining his ties with Graham would not be difficult for Bush— if anything, the trick would be to keep what was a genuine friendship from looking like another predictable marriage of convenience. Bush and Graham had known each other for years—indeed, longer than Bush had known most of his aides. Dorothy Walker Bush, the wife of a Republican senator from Connecticut, invited Graham sometime in the mid-1950s to address her Florida Bible study group. "She invited me to come and speak, to answer questions from the ladies who had gathered in her home," Graham said. "So I did." After the Bible lesson, Senator Prescott Bush told Graham he was heading out to play golf and asked the preacher to come along. That, too, was a good pairing: "I do know that in those days," George H. W. Bush recalled, "Billy was a good golfer and I know my father, a one- or two-handicap player in those days, enjoyed playing with Billy."

Dorothy Walker Bush was a formidable Christian who held regular Bible readings at the breakfast table when the five Bush kids were growing up—and then again at night with her husband. She taught her son to be polite, generous, competitive, and, above all, modest. She enforced a no-tolerance policy on self-importance and kept a watchful eye out for any lapse in manners well into her son's presidency. A sturdy Episcopalian, she was tough but she was also spirited: she told her children to wear bright colors to their father's funeral to celebrate his arrival in heaven. She liked to say that one never stops growing spiritually; late in life, she visited Francis Schaeffer's retreat in Switzerland and met the theological evangelist's wife. During another summer, Dorothy invited Graham to join her for breakfast in her own bungalow on the Walker's Point compound. "The two of them sat quietly and read some Bible passages and Billy said a prayer," her son later wrote. "Later that day, Mother said to me, 'that was the most glorious time of my life.' She loved the man."

Bush could not recall when he met Graham for the first time. Neither could Graham. Both men had a hunch it came in the mid-1960s, when Bush spent four years in the House of Representatives as a member from Texas. Graham touted a forty-four-year-old Bush to be Nixon's running mate in 1968, though the Texas congressman had, as syndicated columnists Rowland Evans and Robert Novak noted at the time, "neither a national reputation nor a block of delegates to offer Nixon." Certainly the two men were friends by 1970, when Bush gave up his safe House seat and made an unsuccessful bid for the Senate. They ran into each other at White House functions in the early 1970s, when Bush was named by Nixon to several high-level government posts. In the late 1970s, when Bush began his first campaign for the presidency, the relationship with Graham began to deepen. Almost by accident, the Grahams and the Bushes began to vacation together—a pattern that would continue off and on for the next fifteen years. It began in 1979, when both men were in Acapulco to address a group of young executives. The two couples went boating together one morning—Graham borrowed a pair of white swimming trunks from Bush for the occasion—and shared a picnic lunch on an empty beach. When the meal was done, Graham opted to walk back to the hotel rather than swim back to the boat anchored offshore. And walk he did, right onto a Mexican naval base, where he was briefly detained for trespassing and told to walk barefoot down a hot sidewalk. Adding to his discomfort was that he had been detained on a bench still wet with fresh green paint, thus forever marking Bush's borrowed white trunks with two green stripes. The Acapulco trip was the first time, George Bush believes, that "we were around Billy in a rather informal setting. . . . I remember the awe in which people held Billy when they would see him there in Acapulco." Barbara would joke that the swimsuit story proved that "unfortunate things happen even to God's chosen people."

The easy, informal connection forged during the Mexican getaway led the Bushes to tighten their links to the evangelist. The Naval Observatory became Graham's routine overnight hostel when he was in town for the annual prayer breakfast. And it wasn't long before the Bushes invited the Grahams to their summer home in Kennebunkport. By accepting these offers, Graham would become more entwined with the Bush family than with any other presidential clan.

The seaside visits were not public, but they were not exactly private either. Graham became a fixture at the Bush family compound in late August— the time when all the Bush kids tried to make it back to Maine for a week. "We went to Kennebunkport every summer for a while," Graham recalled. "Maybe four or five times, maybe more than that. They invited me every time, but I couldn't go a lot of times." But a lot of times he did. The visits usually took place over weekends—which meant the Bushes and Grahams went to church on Sundays together. The two men were seen, and photographed, leaving church, and on some occasions doing so twice: first at St. Ann's Episcopal Church and later at the First Congregational Church. Graham would occasionally be asked to preach; sometimes, Bush would give the homily. Then it was back to the Point for lunch, horseshoes, tennis, bike rides, fishing, and speedboating—all manner of what Bush would have only half-jokingly called mano-a-mano showdowns.

The Kennebunkport summers bonded the two men—and more closely knit their wives as well. Barbara Bush and Ruth Graham shared an extensive correspondence over the years and a great deal more: both were strong-willed and outspoken women who married young and found themselves responsible for large families while their husbands moved in ever-widening circles around the world. Both women also looked out for their sometimes too-trusting spouses. And each could unholster a wicked sense of humor when she needed it. In 2006 Barbara noted that Ruth had once been asked whether, as a Christian, she had ever contemplated divorce. "Her answer," Barbara explained, "was, 'Divorce? No. Murder? Yes.'" Added Barbara, "I could understand that."

The Grahams' 1985 visit to Kennebunkport came at the very moment when Bush was gearing up for his second presidential bid—and when his oldest son, George W. Bush, was looking for a new direction in life. At thirty-nine, George W. Bush had struggled in the shadow of his peerless dad. It was during the August visit that the vice president asked Ruth Graham whether her husband would mind speaking to the Bush kids one night after dinner. Ruth replied that a question-and-answer session might be a better format. And so one evening, the five Bush kids, along with a cousin or two, gathered in the family room to hear Graham talk about what Bush called "the real meaning of life, and about Jesus. And heaven and sin. And wonder." There were questions and answers, conversations that followed, and the first session was so successful that it led to a second a year later. "Billy was very generous in sitting down with kids and grandkids to talk about faith and his belief in Christ," Bush said later. "Everyone left those meetings in awe of the Nation's Pastor." Doro Bush Koch, in her mid-twenties at the time, recalled that Graham's message "of Good News was clear that night, and what made the difference was how humbly he spoke about it and his life of service." He would also make a lasting impact on George W. Bush.

"Signalling Early"

If the multiple thank-you notes to Wead are any indication, Bush returned from Kennebunkport in September 1985 with evangelical voters on his mind. One card from Bush, handwritten on September 14 on Air Force Two, thanked Wead for "that fascinating study on the Evangelical Movement" and went on to say, "'Signalling Early' (p 26) makes sense—a lot of sense." Ten days later, in a second note, Bush asked Wead to come to Washington. "I have now read, re-read and studied the paper you sent me. It is outstanding and very helpful, I would welcome a chance to sit down with you at my house to go over this material."

By then, Wead was bombarding Bush's many aides with memos, often several times a week, and with intelligence reports of rivals prospecting for votes among other evangelical leaders. Wead was ringing the alarm bells almost constantly, worrying about Jack Kemp, fretting about Pat Robertson, fearful that the vice president was squandering the chance to make an early and clear pronouncement of his faith. Wead's output that fall betrays a novice's enthusiasm, but clarity of vision, too: in November, he sent his campaign chiefs a revised edition of his initial June memo; the second edition was more hard-hitting and far more specific in outlining the steps Bush should take. The vice president, Wead argued, should read C. S. Lewis's *Mere Christianity*, so that he could quote passages in key speeches as Ronald Reagan had done. Bush, Wead wrote, should study some works by Francis Schaeffer. (Jack Kemp, Wead noted, was quoting Schaeffer's work in his meetings with preachers.) Finally, the memo noted, the Reverend Pat Robertson was picking up steam—just as Wead had predicted in June. Bush was going to face a genuine preacher in the race, a man who might have thousands of backers across the country already keyed up and ready to go.

For months, the Robertson candidacy struck the Bush high command as incredible—even comical. Bush, who had a tendency to handicap the field like potential tennis partners, was far more concerned about New York lawmaker Jack Kemp. The vice president and his aides believed that Kemp, the handsome former NFL quarterback and Buffalo congressman, could emerge as many conservatives' preferred tax-cutting legatee to Ronald Reagan. And so while Bush read Wead's memos, he at times ignored his advice about the Christian right. Bush wrote Wead in November 1985 thanking him for his latest efforts but signaling that he'd never give as convincing testimony as other Christians. Bush knew his strengths—and his weaknesses—and was careful about diving headlong into waters he knew he couldn't navigate. "I am no good at the breast beating bit, Doug, but I know what's in my heart—and I think it's what our interlocutors have in their hearts. I can't compete with Kemp's more public more flamboyant scripture quoting—nor will I try. Keep sending me ideas."

Wead obliged. In December 1985, he sent a third paper to the Bush high command, titled "Targets: The Vice President and Evangelical Leaders of Influence." This document listed more than 150 evangelical leaders in order of importance—and included specific instructions on how to woo the most important twenty or so. At the top of the list—and far ahead of all the others—was Graham.

While urging the vice president to strengthen his ties to Graham in a public way, Wead went on to note the extremely complex—even risky—signals such a move would engender. "While Graham's prestige as an evangelical would be enhanced by stories of a friendship with Bush, he would presumably use such prestige to caution evangelicals from politicizing their faith. The Vice President, however, would probably have no problem with this, since it is likely his own view." It was an interesting argument: the very strength of the personal bond between Bush and Graham, Wead proposed, would immunize them from any suggestion that they were pairing up simply to bolster Bush's credentials among evangelicals.

Bush's ground game for God unfolded at high speed. On March 7, 1986, his top aides met in Craig Fuller's office to coordinate the vice president's appeal to evangelicals. According to a memo from campaign aide Bill Phillips to Wead, Fuller, and Lee Atwater, Bush would appear by videotape on Robert Schuller's *Hour of Power* broadcast later that year; Wead would develop a generic videotape to be used on other religious networks and programs. He would compile a list of top evangelical leaders around the country and work with others to get them on the vice president's schedule; articles, written largely by Wead, would be placed in a variety of religious publications. These strategy meetings would recur regularly throughout 1986—another indication that the "early signal" strategy proposed by Wead and seconded by Bush had been adopted by the high command. "We concluded it was right to do it in a low-key way,"

Fuller recalled later. "[Bush] was a little uncomfortable, but he realized he had to do it."

It quickly became a matter of some urgency. In the spring of 1986, Robertson backers in Michigan mobilized in huge numbers to take control of that state's arcane delegate selection process for the GOP convention. Normally, a front-running presidential candidate like Bush could oversee that process with one or two well-organized operatives and a network of several hundred supporters. Robertson's army, however, got an early start and counted its supporters in the thousands. His followers were turning up everywhere in the state—in Flint, Grand Rapids, Battle Creek, according to Wead's field reports. The troubling development was that these voters were newcomers, people who had until that time been off the political grid, had avoided politics, and were thus largely unknown to the vice president's network of Republican activists. "They have the numbers to take over the party," Wead warned in April, "if they ever figure out how to do it." Bush could not afford to ignore the Michigan maneuvers: just eight years before, he had won the Michigan primary, beating Ronald Reagan by a two-to-one margin. The state party that warmed to Bush in '80 had disappeared. In its place was a new party devoted to the Virginia Beach televangelist. The evangelical giant that had been awakened by Jimmy Carter in 1976—and jumped ship for Reagan in 1980—was now shaking up Republican *primary* politics.

Inside the Bush camp, holding the state's delegates became a crisis of almost primal anxiety. And then an opportunity to even the score presented itself right in the vice president's backyard. Billy Graham was set to begin an eight-day crusade in Washington, D.C., in late April 1986. Bush's operatives had known about the crusade for months; Wead had been urging Bush to make plans to attend since the previous December, but could not win from the high command an agreement to go. On April 16, Wead sent Fuller and press secretary Marlin Fitzwater a memo that seemed to sweeten the deal: Wead claimed to his superiors that Roger Flessing, a leading Graham communications assistant, had assured Wead in advance that the Graham TV producers would put an isolated camera on Bush for much of the opening session at the old Washington Convention Center and include some of the resulting footage in the nationally televised specials that normally follow a big-city crusade. Wead wrote that the resulting video would catch Bush "laughing, bowing his head solemnly," and displaying other emotions. Those moments would be interspersed, wrote Wead, in appropriate fashion throughout the show. Because that subsequent TV audience would "consist of millions of evangelicals," Wead argued in his memo, "it would be an excellent time for the Vice President to 'be seen' with a key leader of the movement." Wead even told his bosses that Flessing offered to let the vice president's aides edit the tape themselves.

Flessing, in an interview in 2006, flatly denied making any such offers and claimed instead that Wead had approached him and asked for the isolated camera treatment first. Flessing insisted that he never promised the Bush team any special camera coverage or any access to any editing facilities, and that it was standard operating procedure for the Graham organization to splice pictures of VIPs into crusade videos. All decisions about those things, he added, were made by senior BGEA officials.

Perhaps more important than who promised what was how Bush responded to the idea. Wead recalled in several interviews that Bush wanted to attend the crusade, but was reluctant to permit any special attention—in the form of using footage for a political advertisement later—to be given to his role. And the suggestion of leveraging the political value of a visit to Graham's crusade made the vice president uncomfortable, even angry, Wead recalled. Bush was clearly torn about attending the crusade: he wanted to go, but he didn't want to make his visit seem like a political pit stop.

Bush told us he did not remember any such discussion of his role at a Graham crusade in 1986; Wead does not recall being told by campaign aides to shut down negotiations with the Graham team over how any footage might be used. Which may explain why one Bush campaign veteran who did recall the conversations about the event described it years later as "a situation where the leaders in a campaign want good things to flow from an event, we just did not want to be too involved in how they came about or who made them happen." Not long afterward, the crusade was added to Bush's schedule.

More than twenty thousand people turned out for the first meeting in the Washington Convention Center. Bush, flanked by Secret Service agents, escorted Graham to the speaker's platform inside the center's cavernous main hall. Graham asked Bush to greet the audience, and the vice president set the tone for the occasion. "In this nation, we do believe in separation of church and state," Bush said. "But we also believe that when all is said and done, we are indeed one nation under God." Graham preached for an hour. That afternoon, 1,309 people in the audience answered his invitation to receive Christ in their lives.

Two weeks later, Wead sent Bush aide Ron Kaufman a memo reporting that the vice president's remarks would be featured in the first ten minutes of the post-crusade TV special. The voice-over in the opening sequence of the program, which can be heard while many panoramic pictures of Washington's monuments are pictured, intoned, "And in a few moments, you'll hear from the vice president of the United States, George Bush." Wead told his superiors that images of Bush speaking would come near the start of the video and that the show itself would appear on "more than 230 television stations" in prime time in June. The Nielsen ratings of just one of Graham's crusade videos, Wead added, were equivalent to "six months of viewers" on Pat Robertson's *700 Club*. "The vice president has been so very kind and careful not to politicize his relationship with the Grahams and yet this couldn't come at a more needed time," Wead wrote.

It is clear that both Graham and Bush were sensitive about the intimate nature of their relationship—and the sometimes arbitrary way the line between friendship and politics was drawn through it. Though neither Bush nor Graham could recall how the Washington crusade event came together exactly, both could vividly recall how another meeting between them a few months later did not come to pass at all. Returning to D.C. from someplace in the Midwest that fall, Bush was scheduled to make a stop in North Carolina. The plan called for him to drop by Graham's place in Montreat, spend some time on the patio enjoying the view, maybe taking a walk around the deep woods that surround the Grahams' hilltop home. But Bush called and canceled, telling the preacher that he would only cause an awkward scene if he brought his vice presidential retinue to Montreat. Graham retold the story in his autobiography in 1997, and Bush recalled it in 2006: "I did not want to appear to be 'using' him in any way, and that might have been seen to be the case had I asked to call on him at Montreat."

Bush put Graham in a different category from all other religious figures—indeed, from nearly everyone else except his own immediate family. He would often refer to his conversations with Graham in his meetings with lesser evangelical figures, Craig Fuller explained, both as a way to underscore his credentials as a Christian and also to hint to those with whom he might not be comfortable discussing his faith that there was, at least, someone with whom he was. "George Bush was not someone who would, at least before he became president, spend a lot of time talking about this stuff," said Fuller. "We could put five religious leaders in five states on the schedule and [Bush] would do them. But what emerged from these conversations is that the only person he really trusted was Billy Graham. He would tell people that he knew Graham and that he had discussed a lot of these things with Graham. And when he talked to us, everyone he met in this area he compared to Graham. It made me think that Billy Graham was the one person he was communicating with, and talking to, about his faith. My own guess—and it's only a guess—is that Graham was one of the few people who could get George Bush to confront his spiritual feelings or beliefs."

Graham returned to Kennebunkport in the summer of 1986—again, during late August, and again he engaged Bush's children in conversations about God. He would return again in 1987. But by then Bush had cleared most of the evangelical hurdles Wead had laid out on the track two years before. He had sent his early signal. He had impressed a group of evangelical leaders at a meeting in Atlanta in 1986—so much so that the question of his faith hardly came up again. With the campaign's encouragement and cooperation, Wead published a fawning book about Bush in 1987, titled *Man of Integrity*, that included long quotes by Bush praising various evangelical leaders and settled for good the born-again question by letting the vice president rephrase the query: "If by 'born again' one is asking, 'Do you accept Jesus Christ as your personal Savior?' then I could answer a clear-cut 'Yes.' No hesitancy, no awkwardness. But if one is asking, 'Has there been one single moment, above any others, in which your life has been instantly changed?' then I can't say that this has happened, since there have been many moments." *Man of Integrity* included a long passage in which Bush talked about his relationship with Graham and his desire not to "let it become politicized."

By the time *Man of Integrity* was published, Wead's work was done. Robertson gave Bush a scare in the Iowa caucuses but then faded quickly. As for Graham, he was careful during the election year to keep one foot planted on each side of the partisan divide. He made the short trip from Montreat to Atlanta in July 1988 to deliver the prime-time invocation at the Democratic convention. At the time, Massachusetts governor Michael Dukakis was running a dozen points ahead of Bush in the polls. "People do get the impression that if you're an evangelical Christian, you're a conservative Republican," Graham said. "I do feel that that idea should be dissipated." In an effort to do his fair part in this rebalancing, Graham skipped the festivities at Kennebunkport that summer.

After a brutal fall campaign, Bush prevailed easily, winning forty states, 53.4 percent of the popular vote, and 426 electoral votes. Along the way, he picked up a record-setting 81 percent of the evangelical vote—a testament to more than three years of largely behind-the-scenes work. A few weeks later, Bush telephoned Graham and asked him to handle the inaugural prayer duties. In early December, Graham made a quiet trip to Florida to see the president-elect's mother. When he got to her house, Mrs. Bush had assembled a few dozen of her friends, much as she had thirty years earlier when she first met the evangelist. As he explained to the president-elect in a letter in mid-December, "I arrived there with the thought of staying five or ten minutes and found the house full of guests she had invited and they expected me to conduct a Bible study. Naturally, I was overwhelmed, but terribly unprepared."

But by January 20, he was ready for the big show: Graham gave both the invocation and the benediction at the inauguration. He did not linger for all the public festivities. Instead, he spent most of the afternoon of Inauguration Day upstairs at the White House, watching the parade with Dorothy Walker Bush from the warmth of the Queen's Bedroom. Mrs. Bush, then eighty-seven years old, was sitting up in bed when Graham came in. They had prayer together, Graham asking God "to lead, guide and protect George in the years ahead."

When he finished, Graham later recalled, Mrs. Bush "had tears in her eyes and spoke in a whisper, 'He'll need it.'"

TWENTY-NINE

"It Was Billy I Reached Out To"

He told me he wanted me to speak the next morning. So I went to my room and decided what I should say. And I decided to talk on peace.

—Graham on his night at the White House before the Gulf War

George Bush and Billy Graham exchanged gifts when Bush became the forty-first president of the United States. Graham gave Bush a portable massage table—a wooden-and-cotton-batting platform for the relief of everyday aches and pains. Bush sent Graham a note thanking him a few days later. "That is something not only needed, but very special indeed," he wrote. Bush gave Graham something nearly as soothing: more direct personal access to a commander in chief than at any time since Richard Nixon had occupied the Oval Office. Graham would not flaunt it this time; nor would Bush let the relationship ever become too public. But when it came to Graham, Bush did not need, and would not tolerate, middlemen.

Wead, who had been installed by Bush as White House liaison with the religious community, learned this lesson early. He told Graham by telephone in the first few weeks of 1989 that Bush wanted Graham to introduce him at the prayer breakfast later that month. Coming after Bush's personal invitation to conduct the inaugural prayer, Graham understandably found the second-hand offer a bit odd. According to a memo from Bush to Chief of Staff John Sununu, Graham called Bush to double-check it. Bush's hand-typed message to Sununu revealed that Wead had indeed been freelancing—as well as the special care the new president reserved for one of his treasured friends. "Bill, close friend that he is, felt funny that the invite had come in like this—in fact, Weed [*sic*] had never mentioned this to me. I told Billy: a. I will see to it that people don't invoke my name . . . b. I would love to have you introduce me at that meeting. He will introduce me and he is sending over to Patty [Presock, Bush's executive assistant] some material that he thinks might be helpful. He used to write a lot of RR's prayer breakfast speeches and offered to help me on this as well. . . . Maybe a gentle word to the well intentioned Doug . . . would be in order. . . . All's well, though!!!!"

Both Bush and Graham had, over the years, developed an almost constant awareness of the other man's whereabouts. In late May 1989, Graham wrote to let the president know that he would be in London "for the next five weeks," a period which overlapped a short stop by Bush at the end of his NATO summit trip that spring. The correspondence that followed lays out the extraordinary courtesy each man paid the other—as well as the delicate maneuvers each made to stay in the other's orbit. Graham moved first: "I wanted you to know that because of your heavy schedule and trying to adjust to jet lag in preparation for the European conference, I certainly will not be expecting to see you. However, perhaps we can say hello to each other on the telephone." In reply, Bush promised to call when he got there and added that he hoped "I will be seeing you somewhere along the way, but from your letter I can tell you are very busy." In separate memos, Bush then made sure his advance team had all of Graham's telephone numbers and arranged to have Graham invited to the American embassy for a visit as well.

Several different epoxies now cemented the Bush-Graham bond. First, Graham had ministered to two of the most important people in Bush's life—his mother and his eldest son—and thus it was practically unthinkable for him to trust anyone else more in the area of spiritual counseling. But another factor was Graham's agenda: he had none. It was often said of Bush that he prized loyalty, and that was true. But what he prized as much, if not more, were friends who had no agenda. "To George Bush, the person without an agenda had greater standing than someone who has one," said Craig Fuller. Bush himself underscored this: "I never felt Billy Graham had 'an agenda,'" he said. "He came to us as a pastor and friend. He gave us comfort. I think he knew that neither Barbara nor I would ever try to abuse the friendship we revered."

Graham, in part because he was nearly Bush's peer in age, was one of the very few people to whom the president would admit his innermost worries and fears. Bush was, after all, a WASP of the old school, far from unemotional but hardly confiding, someone who resisted "climbing onto the couch," as he put it. Graham, he said, helped him maintain his balance under pressure. "A president needs to keep current matters in perspective and needs to have a reaffirmation of faith," Bush explained in 2006. "I can recall no specific 'topic of faith' that Billy and I talked about, but I know that having him at my side, with absolutely no politics involved, meant a great deal to me. I am a Christian and his teaching and his faith gave me strength."

In return, Graham issued what amounted to regular reports from the residence, and sometimes they were a little over the top. Near the beginning of Bush's second year in office, Graham told *TIME* that "Bush is easy to talk to about spiritual things, easier than other presidents I have met. He says straight out that he has received Christ as his savior, that he is a born-again believer, and that he reads the Bible daily, and so forth. He has the highest moral standards of almost anybody that I have known. He and his wife have such a relationship, it is just unbelievable. If you are with them in private, you know, they are just like lovers. When I would go and spend the night, as I did many times when he was vice president, the room that I stayed in was right across the hall from theirs and they always kept the door open. And there they were, you know, in bed, holding hands, or reading a newspaper, or reading a book."

Graham returned to Kennebunkport in summers of 1989 and 1990. August 1989 was an idyll of fishing and barbecues and spontaneous presidential jaunts around the seaside village. But by August 1990, Bush was distracted by events in the Persian Gulf. Saddam Hussein's invasion of Kuwait in early August caught the United States by surprise, as did Bush's decision, announced on the South Lawn just a few days later, that he intended to reverse it. "This will not stand," he said. Bush launched a breathtaking, half-year-long campaign on the diplomatic and military fronts. First, he quietly repositioned much of America's land, air, and sea forces for a counterinvasion at the earliest date. Then he mounted a diplomatic effort to keep allies on board and neutralize possible opponents, using a Rolodex of contacts overseas he had collected during nearly three decades in government service. The combination was a presidential tour de force, marked by energy, imagination, and patience that has not been matched since.

And yet, as carefully as Bush had proceeded overseas, the looming war remained unpopular in liberal Protestant circles at home. Edmond L. Browning, the presiding bishop of the Bushes' own Episcopal Church, met with Bush on December 20 to express his opposition. The next day, nineteen church leaders, many of whom had just returned from a pilgrimage to the Middle East, signed a statement opposing the war.

Graham was an exception. On January 6, he telephoned Bush and offered the president a quote from a James Russell Lowell poem (and well-known hymn): "Once to every man and nation comes the moment to decide and the choice goes by forever twixt the darkness and that light." Bush copied the passage in his diary and added, "It does hit me pretty hard—That moment's upon us." Bush added that Graham "wants to speak out in any way he can, and that would indeed be helpful." The next day, a full-page advertisement in the *New York Times*, signed by the nineteen religious leaders, proclaimed that "War Is Not the Answer."

A few days later, Graham went public on Bush's behalf: "No sane person wants war," he said on January 10. "At the same time, it has been well said that there is an ethical responsibility that goes with power, and sometimes it becomes necessary to fight the strong in order to protect the weak."

Bush set a deadline for Saddam to withdraw from Kuwait by January 15. When that deadline came and went, war was inevitable, though the exact timing of the attack was uncertain. Whatever he might have been hearing from military and intelligence officials on January 16, Bush spent a lot of time that day talking to clergymen: he spoke to the pope, Browning, Graham, the Senate chaplain, as well as Bill Bright and Cardinal Bernard Law. Only one was invited to the White House the next day.

Graham arrived about ninety minutes before the bombs started to drop. The fact that the Bushes called Graham to the White House on the eve of the war appeared, on one level, to be an effort to deflect criticism from religious figures who opposed the conflict. Americans want to believe that wars are just and righteous, waged in defense of principles and not merely interests. Many religious leaders, including some from Bush's own denomination, were not cooperating, and so Graham's presence would certainly have had an inoculating effect. But it is also true that there is nothing a president does that is more personally punishing than sending soldiers into battle—and thus few times when they are more in need of pastoral support. If Graham, as Craig Fuller believed, was the only preacher the president was likely to ever truly confide in, then it made sense on a pastoral level to have him there as well. Both Bush and his wife insisted in their subsequent memoirs that they did not tell Graham that war was imminent when they invited him—an after-the-fact exoneration of any political collusion.

So was Graham's visit about prayers or pictures? Since presidents are public figures with private needs, it is never either/or. It is typically both.

Around dinnertime that evening, Barbara Bush, sitting in a wheel-chair following a sledding accident, knocked on the door of the Queen's Bedroom and asked Graham if he wouldn't mind "rolling me up to the Blue Room to watch some TV?" Bush joined them ten minutes later, and the three sat there together, Graham recalled, "watching as lights were blacked out all over Baghdad." The three had prayer at dinner, and then again later in the evening. Prayers were held a third time that night a few minutes before Bush addressed the nation from the Oval Office.

Before retiring, Bush asked Graham to join him the following day at nearby Fort Myer in Virginia for a military prayer service. "He told me he wanted me to speak the next morning. So I went to my room and decided what I should say," said Graham. "And I decided to talk on peace." The next morning, Graham preached a seventeen-minute sermon on peace, echoing Abraham Lincoln's prayer that the country was on God's side and not the other way around. "There come times," Graham said, "when we have to fight for peace."

Many years later, in 2006, Bush explained his summoning of Graham this way: "We wanted Billy Graham by our side principally because the toughest decision a president makes is when he sends someone else's sons or daughters into harm's way. We did not know how the battle would go, but we did know that in times of difficulty and crisis, one needs to reach out to those whose faith is unshakable and, through that, are able to give strength to others."

"A Living, Breathing Human Being"

Despite his stirring performance in the Gulf War, Bush never poured the same kind of energy and creativity into domestic affairs. One year after his triumph in Kuwait, his presidency came grinding to its effective end. The economy was in a brief, two-quarter recession, his domestic policy cupboard was empty, the conservatives he had won over in 1988 were in full rebellion over a tax increase, and Bush had no clear agenda for winning. At Christmas-time 1991, he tried to rally the country by heading off to a mall not far from Camp David to buy socks—a gesture that seemed to only underline his ineffec-tiveness. Conservative TV commentator Patrick Buchanan, who had worked for Richard Nixon, challenged the sitting president and won 37 percent in the

New Hampshire primary, paving the way for Texas industrialist Ross Perot to jump into the race as an independent and attack Bush from the center-right. Religious conservatives watched this meltdown mostly from the sidelines—and Bush, rather than keeping his distance in the general election as he had done in 1988, was forced to court them right to the very end, venturing to Jerry Falwell's Liberty University in the final days of the campaign.

Bush could neither win evangelicals back in the numbers he needed, nor, in trying so ardently to do so, avoid alienating more secular voters he had once impressed as well. And yet when Bill Clinton defeated him 42 to 37 percent, with the balance of the vote going to Perot, most of the inner Bush circle was stunned that the nation had turned to someone with so checkered a past rather than a certified war hero. Though he kept his feelings to himself, the president took the outcome very hard.

When it came time to decide how to spend their last night in the White House, George and Barbara Bush knew whom to call. Years later, he explained why: "Billy's presence always helped me put things in perspective," Bush said about that night. "In many instances [Billy] helped me realize that life would go on. I don't recall whether he mentioned that 'the Lord works in mysterious ways,' but if he did, he was sure correct because my life is a very happy one."

On January 19, 1993, Billy and Ruth Graham sat down to a dinner of shellfish soup with their old friends. If Graham found the outgoing commander in chief subdued, he did not let on. "He just talked about the next period in his life and the next period in America's life. I don't think he had any regrets. If you know him as *TIME* magazine said, he's almost too decent to be president." After dinner, the two couples strolled around the White House lawn, but Graham declined an invitation to spend the night. "I told him," he said later, "'tomorrow morning you're going to have to get up so early and I'm weary and have my own responsibilities tomorrow.'" The Bushes would be welcoming the Clintons to the White House in the morning, and Graham would be busy too: he was leading the prayers at the inauguration not long after that.

As he had with other presidents in retirement, Graham remained in close touch with the Bush family. He led the inaugural prayer for George W. Bush's gubernatorial inaugural in 1995. In 1997, he gave the invocation at the Bush Library opening in College Station, attended by Presidents Clinton, Carter, and Ford, as well as Lady Bird Johnson and Nancy Reagan. He also led the prayers at Jeb Bush's inaugural on a cold morning in Tallahassee in January 1999.

In April 2006 Graham flew to College Station, Texas, and accepted the George Bush Award for Excellence in Public Service—an award previously bestowed on statesmen like Mikhail Gorbachev. Several thousand people filled Texas A&M's Rudder Auditorium for the occasion. Four huge color photographs of Graham hung from the cyclorama: two with Bush at Kennebunkport, another of Graham with Barbara Bush on a speedboat, and another of Graham on the back patio. Texas luminaries dotted the audience: Robert Gates, who was then the president of A&M, action-movie star Chuck Norris, Houston televangelists Joel and Victoria Osteen. It was a crusade in miniature: Christian singer Michael W. Smith performed two songs. During a short video on Graham's life, the evangelist was shown at the side of several commanders in chief, including Bush, and was quoted as saying, "I wouldn't trade places with any president." The evening had an intimate, informal, and genuine feel to it. Barbara Bush kissed Graham when he walked onstage. When the former president turned the microphone over to his wife with a cursory introduction of "Now here's the Silver Fox," she quipped, "I cannot believe that introduction. I've been married sixty-one years. It just feels like sixty-two."

Barbara paid homage to Ruth Graham and said the couple's "impact on America and the world is a life force, a spiritual force that cannot possibly ever be measured."

The former president's comments were the shortest of all—by design. The other guests had been called in to speak because, he said, "if I knew the task fell to me to try to explain why we are honoring Billy tonight, I could not get through it. What he has meant to me and to my family is too personal, and too emotional," he said, his voice cracking. Recalling Abraham Lincoln, he noted that every president was driven to his knees by the demands of the job. He followed suit, he said, driven by need and "the conviction that I had nowhere else to go."

Then he added, "But sometimes even that is not enough. No matter how deep one's faith is, sometimes you need the guidance and comfort of a living, breathing human being. For me, and for so many other Oval Office occupants, that person was Billy Graham. When my soul was troubled, it was Billy I reached out to, for advice, for comfort, for prayer." It was a powerful and personal moment, and Bush could barely finish.

Later he told us, "I choke up very easily at this stage in my life . . . if I had gotten up there to say what was in my heart about Billy, I would have broken down and shamelessly wept."

THIRTY

Bill and Hillary

I loved those two people.
—Graham on the Clintons

A month before the inauguration of Bill Clinton as the forty-second president of the United States, forty antiabortion leaders wrote a letter to Graham urging the evangelist to skip the swearing in.

Graham's presence, they wrote, would be "taken as a positive endorsement of Mr. Clinton's anti-Christian agenda. The last thing we need is for a prominent and respected Christian leader to appear with [Clinton] to seemingly endorse his agenda. Never in recent history has a presidential candidate with such an explicitly unbiblical platform been elected to our highest office."

Facing his seventh presidential inaugural at the age of seventy-four, Graham was long past taking advice from anyone about whom he should or shouldn't pray for as commander in chief. He had never been exclusive, least of all about prayer, especially when it came to presidents, and he wasn't about to start now. Besides, he would explain, he had the Bible on his side. "No president stands outside the need for God's constant help and guidance," he later wrote. "Furthermore, the Scripture commands us to pray for all those in authority, that we may live peaceful and quiet lives in all godliness and holiness."

By 1992, Graham had known Clinton well for seven years, years dotted with letters, private conversations, and telephone calls long before Clinton was elected. Clinton had attended three Graham crusades in three different decades; the last he helped to organize. And the evangelist simply liked him. Graham saw something else he admired in Clinton that surely would have surprised some liberals and galled many conservatives: his wife, Hillary. And he had never been shy about saying what he made of them as a pair: "He's the easiest guy to get to know [and] has a brilliant wife who can be of help to him."

All presidents need forgiveness. But no president needed as much as Bill Clinton would as commander in chief. And in the long pageant of forgiveness that played out in 1998, few played as big a role in helping one member of the Clinton family forgive another as did Billy Graham.

The Secret Tither

Hearing Graham at age thirteen, Clinton once said, helped launch his political career. "It had a lot to do with how I wound up in public life, I think."

William Jefferson Clinton was the first president to encounter Billy Graham as a child—a junior high school student in Hot Springs, Arkansas. He knew what an evangelist was: his grandmother, who had helped raise him, used to tell her talkative young charge that if he were not so much trouble he might make a great preacher. But Clinton met Graham in a context that was at least as political as it was spiritual. In September 1959, Graham was about to begin a crusade in Little Rock. Though two years had passed since Governor Orval Faubus had prevented nine black students from enrolling in Central High School, the Arkansas capital was still on edge. Members of the White Citizens Council had proposed that Graham hold a whites-only crusade to avoid racial violence. "A lot of business people in Little Rock were worried about some sort of great encounter," Clinton recalled later, "because racial tensions were very high. And they asked Billy Graham to agree to give this crusade to a segregated audience. And he said if they insisted on that he would not come, that they were all children of God, he wanted to lead everyone to Christ. He would not do it."

In the end, the bigots backed down and Graham preached for two nights, giving Arkansas the chance to witness hundreds of people of both races rise out of their seats, stream down to the field together, and answer his invitation to receive Christ. Clinton was there to see it, too: his Sunday school teacher drove him and several other boys up from Hot Springs to hear Graham. "It was," Clinton said, "a powerful counterpoint to the racist politics sweeping across the South. I loved Billy Graham for doing that."

Graham's move left a deep impression on the young adolescent. "It really touched me," he would recall, "because my grandparents, who had no education particularly and were very modest people, were among the few white people I knew who supported school integration. And all of a sudden to have Billy Graham validating this, based on his Christian witness, had a profound impact on me. And it got me to think at that very early age about the relationship between your faith and your work."

It was a powerful story, and like so many encounters between Graham and the presidents, it was a politically useful one, too. In retelling it countless times, Clinton managed to honor the values of both white evangelicals and black civil rights leaders in one parable. But there was other early evidence of Clinton's devotion to Graham: for a time after the Little Rock crusade ended, Clinton sent Graham a portion of his allowance. He kept those donations a secret from his financially strapped parents, slipping out the front door of his house in order to mail the letters to Graham's organization without his stepfather noticing. "You know, I'm still on somebody's list somewhere for giving him next to no money," Clinton joked later, "but it was a pretty good chunk of what I had."

Twelve years passed before Clinton saw Graham in person again—and again it was from a long distance. The husky boy from Hot Springs had been on a tear since 1959: he had graduated from high school, shaken the hand of John F. Kennedy in the Rose Garden, been trained by Jesuits at Georgetown, won a Rhodes Scholarship to Oxford, and completed the first of three years at Yale Law School. He was, at age twenty-five, already planning a political career. But it was not the only thing he was planning: Clinton was in love. And he was almost surprised to find himself spending the summer of 1971 in Berkeley, California, trying to win the affections of a law school classmate named Hillary Rodham. He had followed his heart that summer, not his ambitions, giving up a chance to work on the fledgling presidential campaign of Senator George McGovern in order to keep Hillary from getting away. The Chicago-born Rodham had so bedazzled Clinton in New Haven that he had gone, somewhat sheepishly, to McGovern campaign manager Gary Hart early that summer to explain that he had found something more important to do.

And so, with Berkeley as the couple's home base, Clinton explored San Francisco by day while Hillary worked at an Oakland law firm. They went to movies and concerts and, one night, attended the Oakland crusade. "I wanted her to see Billy," Clinton said in 2007.

Fourteen more years passed before the two men finally met face-to-face. In the interim, Clinton had earned a law degree, married Hillary, been defeated in a race for Congress, elected governor of Arkansas, defeated two years later for reelection, and then reelected two years after that. Now, in the summer of 1985, both men were in Boise for the National Governors Convention. Clinton sought Graham out during the meeting, asked for time to talk, and the two spent several hours sitting outside in lawn chairs getting to know each other. "His quick mind and warm personality impressed me immediately," Graham wrote later.

Soon, Graham was providing aid and comfort to the rising star of the Democratic South. In 1988, Clinton was lampooned when he let his prime-time speech at the party's convention in Atlanta go on too long, for some thirty-two minutes. He quickly owned up to the blunder and appeared on late-night television to make fun of himself. Graham wrote Clinton not long after, congratulating him on how well he handled the mistake. "After your appearance on the Johnny Carson Show, and other events, you have come back stronger than ever," Graham wrote. "I think the thing that has gone over so well has been your sportsmanship. You are now a favorite with the press and media, which is extremely important for your future." "It did all work out for the best," Clinton wrote back, praising Graham as "a man of God who tried to live by his stated convictions. None of us can do it all the time, of course, but all of us must try."

In 1988, after flirting with an early run at the White House, Clinton joined a number of other Arkansas notables in urging Graham to come back to the state and preach a full, weeklong crusade in Little Rock. Clinton knew that such an event would have special resonance in the state thirty years after Graham had helped break down color barriers. He also needed some help: he had made reforming the state's backward education system a top priority in his first six years in office, but he continually ran into problems with teenage drug use. (His own brother, Roger, had been arrested for cocaine possession.) Clinton needed Graham's help to move his state forward.

And so, partly at Clinton's urging, Graham returned in September 1989 for an eight-day run at Little Rock's War Memorial Stadium. Clinton's prepping paid off: in a telephone call a few weeks before arriving, Graham told an Arkansas newspaper that he would make drugs a top priority in his sermons and said the time had come for the nation's religious and elected leaders to join forces in the war on drugs. And, in an unmistakable echo of the chords he struck in 1959, Graham reached out to another oppressed minority in the weeks leading up to the crusade. "I have friends who are homosexuals," he said, adding that they would be welcome at the Little Rock meetings too.

On the third night of the crusade, Clinton joined Graham onstage and spoke first. He had asked Graham to come back, he said, because Arkansas was divided again, "not by race but by the scourge of drugs . . . this is not a problem that politicians can solve, it is not a problem for which there is a program. For all the efforts on the outside in the world will not cure the poverty of spirit that is within each heart that drives people off the brink and into that sort of destruction. And so we welcome Billy Graham here tonight because we need him, yes, but more we need the word of God that he brings."

Yet it may have been what Graham did in his private time that week that won him Clinton's gratitude all over again. In the middle of the week, Clinton invited Graham to accompany him to the Little Rock home of Worley Oscar Vaught, an old Graham friend who had helped sponsor the 1959 crusade and who was, by 1989, dying of cancer. Clinton would consult many spiritual advisers during his life, but Vaught was the most important. Clinton had joined Vaught's Immanuel Baptist Church in 1980 and began singing in the choir not long afterward. A year later, both Bill and Hillary traveled with Vaught on a pilgrimage to Israel, where they visited the Western Wall, the Dome of the Rock, the Sea of Galilee, and Masada. Vaught had been visiting the Holy Land regularly since 1938, but for Clinton it was "the beginning of an obsession to see all the children of Abraham reconciled on the holy ground on which our three faiths came to life." Vaught often visited Clinton at the Governor's Mansion and helped him work through his support of both abortion and the death penalty and once told Clinton that if he ever became president, he must never abandon Israel.

Clinton drove Graham out to the house himself and they were quickly shown by Mrs. Vaught into the pastor's bedroom. "W.O.," said Graham, upon seeing his old friend, "we're certainly praying for you." Though he was a hundred pounds lighter than Graham remembered him, Vaught was propped up in bed, his Scofield Bible open, ready to go to work. "I have something to say to you boys," Vaught replied. "Sit down." Vaught then conducted a thirty-minute Bible lesson for Graham and Clinton on the Second Coming and the promise of heaven. When he finished, Vaught asked for prayers for the crusade and each man prayed in turn. Clinton and Graham got down on their knees by Vaught's bed. Clinton prayed first, then Graham followed, and Vaught wrapped it up. When Clinton and Graham rose to leave, Graham reached for Vaught's hand and said, "W.O., it won't be long now for both of us. I'll see you soon, just outside the Eastern Gate." As Graham recalled, "Bill Clinton and I felt that we had received far more encouragement from our visit than we ever could have given to his pastor." The experience sealed the bond between Clinton and Graham: "It made me feel close to him because he was good and generous to a man I loved," Clinton said, "and because he was honest enough to admit he was a little afraid of dying."

"I Need Your Help on Korea . . ."

Conservative clergymen did not wait until Clinton's inauguration as president to savage him. Jerry Falwell talked about obtaining a Clinton sex tape within a week of Clinton's election in 1992, and while he would not play it on his *Old Time Gospel Hour*, he assured his television audience that "it makes it a little hard for me, having heard him . . . uh, to respect him." Dr. James Kennedy, of the 8,000-member Coral Ridge Presbyterian Church in Fort Lauderdale, repeated the story of Clinton's dalliance with Gennifer Flowers in 1992 that had surfaced a year earlier. "If his wife cannot rely upon him to keep his vows of fidelity to her in marriage," Kennedy said, "then why should the country be expected to believe that he would keep his vows made in the assumption of his office."

Graham's agenda was different. He was soon helping Clinton.

Two weeks after he had confounded some conservatives by delivering the benediction at Clinton's inauguration, Graham and Ruth returned to Washington to spend the night with the Clintons in the White House. They sat down to dinner that night—Billy with Hillary and Ruth next to

Clinton—along with the governor of Hawaii, who spent part of the evening talking to Hillary about health care. The next morning, a few hours before the prayer breakfast was to begin, Clinton and Graham rose early and had a long conversation. White House aides realized that there was more to the relationship than they had imagined. "When Clinton talked about Graham, even his tone changed," recalled Dee Dee Myers, his first press secretary. "It made me sit up and say, 'I'd better rethink who this guy is.' Every time I heard Clinton talk about him, it was clear he was in a different category, like a beloved father figure."

The Clinton White House gained a reputation early on for being a rowdy hybrid of college dorm and think tank. Pizza boxes piled up next to PowerBooks amid nonstop, all-night sessions on how to rewire everything from welfare to health care to crime policy. Clinton's ability to cite scripture in public was sometimes underappreciated by his own aides. "He was the only recent national Democrat who understood the connection between evangelism and politics, because he came from a faith-professing tradition," said one of his spokesmen, Mike McCurry. "But we had to deal with White House people who just didn't get it. We were so secular, so in our own stuff." People of faith on his staff tended to keep it to themselves, and were surprised to discover the fellow believers among them.

By his second year in office, Clinton faced a bewildering set of challenges on the Korean peninsula. Early in 1994, Pyongyang backed out of the nuclear nonproliferation treaty and began stalling whenever UN inspectors came calling. The American efforts to open the door were often undercut by South Korean reluctance to threaten a stronger military presence if North Korea didn't come along. Amid all the maneuvering, U.S. officials remained concerned that North Korean leader Kim Il Sung was not getting a clear picture of Washington's willingness to offer economic aid in return for renouncing nuclear weapons and agreeing to inspections. So when Graham informed Washington in January 1994 that he would be visiting North Korea, Clinton officials seized the chance to communicate directly with the Great Leader.

Prior to departing, Graham dispatched aide John Akers to confer with Clinton officials. Graham offered to carry a message from Clinton to Kim—a notion that had come from the North Koreans but for which there was ample precedent. (Graham had carried a similar message from President Bush to Kim during a visit to Pyongyang in 1992.) Now, two years later, National Security Adviser Tony Lake was for the idea. "We were never sure how far up the food chain our views were communicated," National Security Council aide Dan Poneman explained. "So we were interested in any direct contact we could get." The Graham family's roots to North Korea were considerable: Ruth had lived in Pyongyang as a teenager, and one of their sons had visited North Korea in 1993. Kim, whose mother had taught him about Christianity when he was growing up, had a soft spot for Graham, and Clinton's team knew he would get at least a few moments with him alone.

Before departing for Asia, Graham himself telephoned Clinton for last-minute guidance, but the call was hardly limited to geopolitics. Poneman recalled sitting in the Oval Office during the call and realizing almost instantly that this was no normal West Wing conversation. Clinton and Graham were chatting intimately about everything, about Hillary, about her Whitewater troubles, about Chelsea—and most of all about how Clinton was holding up. Poneman had never heard a presidential conversation like it. "Everything around the Oval Office is scripted," he said, "except in *this* space. I realized that there was this tiny, very thin veneer of people who could talk to this guy without talking points and vice versa. It was the only time I saw it in my life. There was no urgency on either side. Clinton seemed to have all the time in the world. No hurry. No agenda."

When Graham arrived in Beijing, U.S. ambassador to China Stapleton Roy conveyed to the evangelist the explicit oral message Clinton wanted him to deliver to Kim: straightforward wishes from Washington that the two countries could work together to resolve the standoff in the new year. Its chief value was less its content than the fact that it was a privileged signal from one leader to another—the kind of signal that Kim would value. When Graham finally sat down privately with Kim in Pyongyang forty-eight hours later, the North Korean leader wanted to discuss the nuclear situation. Graham delivered Clinton's message, just as Roy had asked, and did so several times through an interpreter to ensure that it was understood. Then the two men had lunch—a meal that Kim began by asking Graham to say a prayer. When Graham finished praying, Kim responded with an emphatic "Amen."

Afterward, Graham handed Kim a letter of his own that, unbeknownst to the White House, included much of the language Roy had given Graham in Beijing. He did this to be sure the right message was conveyed, but then, freelancing just a bit, Graham told Kim he believed that a meeting between the two leaders might be arranged if the nuclear standoff could be settled peacefully. Kim replied that North Korea did not want nuclear weapons and pressed the evangelist to help arrange a summit between himself and Clinton. Graham departed North Korea and arrived in Hong Kong the next day. At a press conference, he disclosed that he was carrying a message to Clinton from Kim—a message Akers delivered in Washington twenty-four hours later. Graham's secret diplomatic mission did not produce a breakthrough, and some in South Korea were not pleased with his amateur diplomacy. But no one in Washington shared that view. "He went a little beyond his script but it was no big deal," said Poneman. "He followed our guidance and he understood the limits."

Graham performed well enough in Clinton's eyes that, a few weeks later, when the game of cat and mouse again approached a boiling point, Clinton turned to him once more as a back channel. The president telephoned Graham in mid-March. "I need your help on Korea. . . . Would you be willing to convey a short oral message to Kim Il Sung on the phone?" Clinton wanted Graham to tell Kim that the United States preferred to avoid war and find a negotiated solution to the inspections standoff. And in this call, Clinton himself held out the promise of better relations and even a high-level meeting—just as Graham had done a month before. Of course, Graham accepted the challenge, trying to reach Kim by phone and by letter. "This could be your finest hour," Graham wrote. But this time, not even Graham could get through to Kim.

By now, it was difficult to tell where one conversation between Graham and Clinton ended and another began. Graham was in New York a month later at a dinner with North Korean diplomats when he received word from his son Ned that Richard Nixon had suffered a stroke. After failing to reach either of Nixon's daughters, Graham called the White House, but neither the switchboard operators nor the president's secretary knew Nixon's whereabouts. Graham then asked to speak to Clinton. When Clinton came on the line, Graham told the president that he would go to see the ailing Nixon as soon as he could figure out which hospital was caring for his old friend. Clinton telephoned the evangelist back a few minutes later with the address. When Nixon died not long afterward,

Clinton telephoned Graham and asked if he would check with the Nixon family to see if the former president's daughter would think it appropriate for Clinton and his wife to attend the funeral. Graham reported back, after checking with Julie Eisenhower, that the family would welcome the Clintons' attendance. This was surely a formality, but the two men were now working on all fronts: personal, presidential, diplomatic.

If Republicans in Congress resented the Democratic president's uncommonly close relationship with an evangelist they once called their own, they did not show it. In the spring of 1996, with a presidential election looming, Republican lawmakers passed a bill conferring the Congressional Gold Medal on Graham with the explicit stipulation that the medal would be presented by Speaker of the House Newt Gingrich, who had led the revolution that had swept the Democrats from power after a forty-year run. It was the first time in six years that a president was not called upon to confer the award, and the sponsors of the bill made no attempt to hide their intention to snub him.

Graham knew that he was a pawn in a partisan game and didn't wait long to signal that he knew it. Just a few weeks later, he told Larry King on his CNN show that the day had unfolded a little differently than his hosts might have preferred. Almost immediately after the medal ceremony concluded, a White House car whisked Graham to tea with the Clintons. Graham spent an hour and fifteen minutes with the president and Mrs. Clinton that afternoon; that evening, Clinton picked up Graham from his hotel and swept him to a second event. As Graham explained to King, "I was with him almost as much as I was with my hosts."

But Graham did not stop there. When King asked whether Clinton would have made a good "Bible minister," Graham conferred upon him the ultimate blessing a preacher can give a president: "I thought that when he left the White House he ought to become a minister and become an evangelist because he's got all the gifts that an evangelist should have. And he believes the Bible. He believes in God. He believes in Christ. He believes—he believes that he has been born again. And he has all these things that he would need to be an evangelist." Clinton was, Graham told King, "one of the most charismatic people I've ever met." This was hardly the testimony the Republicans had been looking for from the Congressional Gold Medal winner.

Given how both parties once again seemed to be fighting over who had bragging rights to Graham, it was no surprise that he kept his nose out of the 1996 race. He pronounced himself deadlocked: "Bill Clinton has been a friend, he claims, since he was 7 years old," Graham said. "The Doles have been guests in our home. We've known Mrs. Dole since she was a girl. Bob Dole, I've known him for, I don't know how long. We think a lot of them and we think a lot of the Clintons. And we're going to stay absolutely neutral."

Though the Christian Coalition, founded by Pat Robertson and run by Ralph Reed, was working actively on Dole's behalf, Graham declined to join the scrum. "I try to stay out of those things," he said, "although many of those people are friends of mine. I think Christians should vote. Whether they're voting Republican or Democrat, I don't think I have a right to tell them who to vote for."

When the time came for Clinton to be inaugurated a second time, he turned to Graham once more to give the prayer. During the preparation for the swearing in, a Clinton aide made a snide remark about Graham with the president in the room. Clinton tore into the aide, delivering a withering dressing-down in front of a handful of White House officials. "Clinton really jumped on him," said Mike McCurry, the president's press secretary.

On January 20, 1997, Billy Graham attended his eighth—and probably last—presidential inauguration. His words were prophetic: "Where there's been failure, forgive us. Where's there's been progress, confirm; where there's been success, give us humility and teach us to follow your instructions more closely as we enter the next century."

THIRTY-ONE

Mending the Breach

I said one word—"forgiveness."
—Graham on his prompt pardon of Clinton

O ne of the recurring features of Billy Graham's White House ministry is that he was often as close to the First Ladies as he was to the
presidents. There was as much mercy as method in this: they knew better
than anyone the extraordinary strain on their husbands; they also knew
the best passageways around all the worriers and doorkeepers. By the time
Hillary Clinton was First Lady, Graham had been working those back
doors for decades: though Jackie Kennedy never much cared for him, Lady
Bird Johnson stayed in touch well into her nineties, sometimes telephoning
to talk about the old days. Graham preached at Pat Nixon's funeral, and
it was Rosalynn Carter who repeatedly tried to bring him back into the
presidential fold in 1979. Nancy Reagan's mother first pressed Graham to
meet her new son-in-law back in 1952; more than fifty years later, Nancy
still talked about the big stack of letters Graham had written to her in the
years since her husband died.

Graham also had an admirer in Hillary Rodham Clinton. Gifted as
Bill was at preaching, and as inspired as he was after a night at an Afri-
can American church, Hillary was as committed if not as expressive. Her
faith was mixed from the start with a healthy dose of social justice. Fresh
out of seminary, her Park Ridge, Illinois, Methodist youth group leader,
Reverend Don Jones, had held a series of teenage think sessions he called
"the University of Life," in which he introduced Hillary and her peers to
John Wesley, Paul Tillich, Dietrich Bonhoeffer, and Reinhold Niebuhr.

Jones taught Bonhoeffer's belief that, as Hillary recalled it, "the role of a Christian was a moral one of total engagement in the world with the promotion of human development." There was, thereafter, a deep current of service that ran through Hillary's faith.

Hillary had watched Graham on television growing up, but she did not meet the preacher until just before the Little Rock crusade of 1989, at a reception for the evangelist. "I said, 'Oh, I would just love to talk to you sometime, maybe we could have lunch,'" she recalled. But Graham politely declined, explaining to the governor's wife that he did not dine alone with women—be they single or married. "Oh, well, I'm sorry," Hillary said. "Maybe we could have a lot of people there." Graham replied that he would think about it. "Word came back that I could have lunch with him and three of his colleagues," she recalled.

And so five people sat down at a round table in Little Rock's ornate Capitol Hotel that fall. Hillary's recollections of that first encounter are similar to the way George W. Bush described his first conversation with Graham. "We had the best conversation. I just really felt a great sense of calm and love. I had such a positive feeling about him."

Hillary recalled that Graham helped her on a matter that would be politically sensitive for years to come—the occasional difficulty of being a strong female partner to a man in power. "He was very supportive of me," she said. "He would say, 'I have a strong wife, you know, people don't realize how strong Ruth is.' He was very sweet about that and very kind to draw those parallels." There is little doubt they hit it off: when more than thirty-five thousand people attended the first night of the 1989 crusade, it was Hillary, not Bill, who was there to welcome them. She asked God to bless all who attended the crusade and prayed for a great spiritual rebirth all over Arkansas.

Hillary's transition from governor's wife to First Lady was a difficult one to watch; her first year in the White House was nothing short of ghastly—even Hillary called that season "pitiless." Her father died; she lost her friend Vince Foster, who committed suicide when he found life in Washington unbearable and unforgiving; a White House inquiry into the messy firing of seven travel office employees laid much of the blame at her door. She had an office in the West Wing, but the reach of what came to be known as "Hillaryland" was far greater than that of any First Lady in memory. The scarring, nonstop left-right tugs-of-war inside the

Clinton White House set her at odds with people like Vice President Al Gore and numerous members of Clinton's economic team. Hillary took refuge in her work—a huge overhaul of the nation's health care delivery system—and then got lost in it. When the First Lady's health care initiative was unveiled in early 1994, after more than a year's work, it was received politely, picked apart within weeks, and then dismissed as too risky, too large, and generally bewildering. By the time the murky details of a decade-old land deal began to dog the Clintons and provoke calls for a special prosecutor, she had become a touchstone for her share, though by no means all, of the missteps of the Clintons' first year in office.

Her faith was one place where she touched the ground. It was in the first six months that she joined a bipartisan prayer group; a circle of friends took turns praying for her that spring and throughout her time in the White House. When she traveled out of town, she carried a handmade scrapbook of sayings and scriptures that raised her spirits when they needed a boost. Coming off a two-week vigil at her father's bedside in April, she gave a speech at the University of Texas in which she claimed that Americans "lack, at some core level, meaning in our individual lives and meaning collectively." She went on to call for "a new ethos of individual responsibility and caring." While the themes she touched on would eventually connect to form the spine of the Clinton approach to the pressures of economic globalization, the response was lacerating. The *New York Times Magazine* published a cover story on the First Lady shortly after, depicting her as an angel and bearing the skeptical headline "Saint Hillary?"

The hostile reaction to the "politics of meaning" led Clinton to be more guarded in public about her spiritual instincts—and surely made her private conversations on faith even more important. She noted later that Graham understood better than most pastors the pressure public figures faced no matter what they did or said—and how difficult it was to find someone trustworthy enough to confide in. Graham's own celebrity had helped him connect with presidents and their spouses over many decades. "He had such a charismatic presence and you know, people who are president do too, different kinds, but still it's an element of who they are. I think there was a recognition there, and a comfort, with dealing with someone who was a public person, who had to put up with what's wonderful about being in the public eye and what's kind of a drag."

Plus, in some ways, being a world-famous preacher and being a U.S.

president weren't all that different. Graham "liked politics," she recalled. "And therefore he liked politicians. He could talk their language. He was always very interested in what you were doing, what the elections were like. He loved elections. Because he knew that you had to have a narrative, you had to tell a story, you had to connect with people, all the things we talk about in politics. And so he was interested in how people did it and different styles of leadership." But that wasn't all they talked about. In 1997, at the dedication of the George Herbert Walker Bush Presidential Library in College Station, Hillary and Graham huddled while the rest of the presidential party, and parade of former presidents, went on a tour of the facility. Graham recalled, "She was going to go and I was not going to go, couldn't do it physically. And she pulled me over and said, 'How about sitting here and talking with me?'" They talked, Graham said, about her husband. "She grabbed my head in her hands and held it there like that and looked right into my eyes and said, 'I want to tell you about Bill.'"

When it became clear that Bill Clinton might have lied under oath in a sexual harassment suit about his relationship with a twenty-one-year-old White House intern, two imperatives became instantly clear. First, the Republican-controlled Congress would try to impeach him. And second, the president's defenders would mount a counterattack, launched first by Hillary herself, on the grounds that the Clintons were the victims of what she called "a vast right-wing conspiracy."

On one hand, Hillary was right: the yearlong fight over Clinton's conduct would quickly become a political battle to undo an election by the president's enemies—with the president himself often lending his enemies a hand. But on another level, Clinton's actions pitched the nation into a moral battle over the sin of adultery. As a national moral pageant, Clinton was being called to account by a crusading independent counsel for his sins not as a politician but as a man. Hillary's alliances in these two very different fights were not identical: politically, she was fully aligned with her husband against those who were trying to toss out a president. But her alliances were more complex on the moral question: if her husband had in fact sinned, he had sinned against her. And though she would be at his side in the political fight, she could not share a foxhole with him on the moral battle. She would need to find some way to forgive him for that.

Unlike some other religious leaders, Billy Graham stayed out of the first fight. But he came to Hillary's aid in the second.

Though the issues were very different, Graham was as quick to forgive Clinton as he had been to forgive Nixon a generation before. Less than two months after the scandal broke, Graham appeared on the *Today* show and said, "I forgive him. I know how hard it is, and especially a strong, vigorous young man like he is; he has such a tremendous personality. I think the ladies just go wild over him." Graham's remarks caused an uproar in the evangelical community. "I said one word—'forgiveness,'" Graham said later. "I got all kinds of ugly letters about that. That's how I felt and still feel. I think a lot of the Clintons, both of 'em." Graham was consistent: a few weeks later he conveyed the message again at the seventy-fifth anniversary dinner for *TIME* magazine in New York. A crowd of more than a thousand had gathered for the event, featuring almost everyone alive who had been on the cover of *TIME*. Graham was to sit at a different table than Clinton. But when former Yankee great Joe DiMaggio declined to sit with the embattled president, Graham volunteered to take his place, telling a *TIME* editor that the move would be seen as a quiet signal of support for the president. This was trademark Graham: the more trouble a president was in—Johnson over Vietnam, Nixon over Watergate, Clinton over Monica—the more prepared Graham was to stand publicly by his side.

Not that Clinton really deserved it. The president denied the relationship from the start, launching a breathtakingly cynical strategy: he would lie to his wife and daughter, if only to buy himself time to sell the country on the idea that while a lie about a sexual affair was wrong, inappropriate, and immoral, it was hardly an impeachable offense. Then, when the time came to admit his offense to the prosecutors, the public anger would have cooled and he would have only his marriage to save. He was helped in his plan by Ken Starr, whose zealous prosecutors took seven months to cut an immunity deal with their star witness, Monica Lewinsky. By then, two-thirds of the country had concluded that Clinton had indeed acted inappropriately but did not deserve to be kicked out of his job for it.

The Clintons' critics were sure Hillary had been in on the charade from the start. For months, the White House staff divided into two camps: those who believed Clinton simply because he had insisted so dramatically that the charges were false, and those who feared he might be lying anyway. No one in either camp was much inclined to confront the Clintons about alternative explanations: many of the believers were already spending thousands of dollars on lawyers; the doubters kept their distance. Through much of 1998, the president and his wife were both isolated and alone, removed at some level even from each other. The president was left with his worries and his guilt and his calculations; Hillary was left to cling to her trust in him at all costs. It was an irony for the first baby boom First Lady: armed with a law degree and a longer résumé than any presidential spouse in history, she was never less popular than when she was helping to make policy, never more popular than when she was standing by her man.

Americans watched her closely as she picked her way through both the political and moral wreckage piling up at her feet. She was her husband's strongest supporter in the political trench warfare. For much of the year, her approval ratings hovered near 60 percent. Unlike the public, which had merely hired Clinton and could just as easily fire him, she had married him, signing on for better or worse. And so the question loomed: if the stories were true, would she forgive him once more—or dump him once and for all? She had always been the strongest of the entire Clinton team in the clutch, the one who almost alone had the clarity and courage in the worst moments to pick herself off the ground, rally the troops, get them fired up again. Could she do it now? And would she?

One morning before he was to testify before the grand jury, Clinton woke up his wife and confessed to her that his relationship with Lewinsky had been sexual. Hurt and angry, crying and incredulous, she descended into despair. Her spokeswoman told reporters the next day, "This is not a good day in Mrs. Clinton's life. This is a time that she relies on her strong religious faith." On vacation the next week in Martha's Vineyard, the Clintons slept in separate rooms and barely spoke. Clinton's early attempts at public apology revealed a man who was wrestling with the idea that he needed to apologize in public. He told a church gathering that August, "All of you know I'm having to become quite an expert in this business of asking forgiveness. It gets a little easier the more you do it. And if you have a family, an administration, and Congress and a whole country to ask, you're going to get a lot of practice. But I have to tell you that, in these last days, it has come home to me, again, something I first learned as

President, but it wasn't burned in my bones, and that is that in order to get it, you have to be willing to give it."

If Clinton had to ask for forgiveness from many, Hillary had to grant it only to one. An eclectic collection of voices nudged her in that direction. Don Jones, her youth minister, summoned for her the words of Tillich, who argued that grace and sin come as one; Jones urged Hillary to pass the idea along to her husband. As Hillary explained later, both Clintons took some courage from the model of Nelson Mandela, whom she had met earlier that summer and had found a way to forgive his tormentors despite decades of imprisonment in South Africa. And then there was Graham, who counseled her to find some way to forgive her husband as well. The two men, she said, "were sort of the secular saint and the religious saint in the firmament at that time [who] were both really outspoken in their support for both of us and in their understanding. They both have lived long enough and seen enough of human frailty and the challenges that people face. And it meant the world to me."

When the Clintons returned to Washington, the president went through a series of rolling apologies, first to his staff, then his cabinet, each one a little stronger than the next, yet none like a full-throated "I'm sorry." Outside his circle of supporters, his position was getting more precarious: Jerry Falwell called on Clinton to resign. So did Paige Patterson, president of the Southern Baptist Convention. Focus on the Family founder James Dobson sent letters to more than two million homes urging occupants to make their outrage known. Franklin Graham was harsher. "For the sake of the country, the best thing he can do is quietly resign," the younger Graham told the *Charlotte Observer*. Rex Horne, the pastor of Clinton's church in Little Rock, said the president's actions were "indefensible, but not unforgivable."

Finally, in mid-September, Clinton gathered a group of religious leaders in the East Room to apologize one more time. The prayer breakfast itself became political. The National Council of Churches sent a representative; the National Association of Evangelicals declined. The White House distributed talking points to aides who needed help fielding questions from friends and reporters about how they were coping with the need to forgive. But even in the staged setting of the East Room, surrounded by the ministers most likely to support him, and even after a night where he stayed up late trying to get it down on paper, Clinton could not finally pull the trigger. "I've been on quite a journey these last few weeks to get to the end of this, to the rock bottom truth of where I am and where we all are. I agree with those who have said that, in my first statement after I testified, I was not contrite enough. I don't think there is a fancy way to say that I have sinned. It is important to me that everybody who has been hurt know that the sorrow I feel is genuine, first and most important my family, also my friends, my staff, my Cabinet, Monica Lewinsky and her family and the American people."

In an interview in January 2007, on the eve of her announcement that she was running for president, Hillary Clinton stated that Graham was a critical voice in helping her forgive her husband. Clinton recalled that Graham was "incredibly supportive to me personally. And he was very strong in saying, 'I really understand what you're doing and I support you.' He was just very *personally there* for me. I remember it very vividly, on a couple of different occasions."

She continued, "The entire world was judging my decisions and my actions and there weren't very many people who, frankly, were understanding. And he was. He said, 'You know, forgiveness is the hardest thing that we're called upon to do. And we all face it at some point in our lives, and I'm just really proud of you for taking it on.' And he was so kind about Bill, he said, 'You know, Bill's a good man, a wonderful person.' It was very touching and reassuring and supportive."

Hillary Clinton left the White House with her husband in 2000, moving down Pennsylvania Avenue to become a senator and eventually contemplate a return as president herself. As the junior senator from New York, she appeared onstage at Graham's New York City crusade in 2005. "She held my hand the whole time in our private time," Graham recalled. "And she was just so sweet. She is different from the Hillary you see in the media. There is a warm side to her . . . and a spiritual one." By then, Hillary had learned a great deal about the role faith plays in public as opposed to private life—knowledge she would need as she calculated what forces could carry her back to the White House. She still felt the sting of being mocked for her attempts to anchor her public vision in a personal faith. But much had changed since those days, and she thought that maybe the rules for candidates had changed as well. "I think that everybody has to make his or her own decision about what they want to talk about. I talked about my faith years ago and was pilloried for it by the press. When

I talked about the politics of meaning and spirituality and faith, this was in '93 and '94, the press was saying, 'What right does she have to do this, this is really a step too far, this doesn't belong.' Well, maybe times have changed so that you can actually be yourself . . . which would be a nice thing. If you have a deeply held faith or you're comfortable expressing your religious feelings, do it. But if you're not, don't. The Constitution explicitly says [there is] no religious test for officeholding. So maybe we're getting back to where people can *be who they are*. And if that's an element of who you legitimately, authentically are, great. But don't make it up, don't use it, don't beat people over the head with it."

Neither party, she said, had a monopoly on cynicism. "You can have hypocrisy on both sides of the aisle," she said, "and the use of it on both sides of the aisle." But maybe, she proposed, candidates have learned something from the bruising battles of recent years. "I really think that maybe we could bring it to an end because there's no political gain in being something you're not, or playing the religion card just like people used to play the race card." And if the rules are different, if the field is open for people to say what they want about what they believe, she thought Graham had made that easier at a time when other religious leaders had not. "Part of what Billy Graham did was to evolve into a much more important religious figure in a way because he was a healer, he was someone who did understand, he tried to reach across all kinds of boundaries. So we'll see."

THIRTY-TWO

The Mustard Seed

I can see him sitting back there now. He's not yet governor. He's not even in politics.

—Graham on his first weekend with George W. Bush

Billy Graham does not brag. But only about fifteen minutes into our first conversation in January 2006, he told us that President George W. Bush had telephoned just the week before. "He called me this past Tuesday," said Graham. "He said he wanted me to come and have lunch with him or dinner." Graham was reluctant to meet Bush in Washington, he told us. "I said, 'Mr. President, I tried to reach you when you were in Crawford.' I said, 'That's my kind of life.' I want to go down there sometime. He said, 'You're invited anytime.'"

Graham had a singularly formative impact on George W. Bush. Other presidents wove Graham into their political biographies—their decisions to run, their inaugural prayers, their most difficult hours in office, the wins and the losses. George W. Bush did more than that: he gave Billy Graham credit *for changing his life*. It was Graham who led the man who would grow up to be the forty-third president of the United States to a deeper faith at exactly the moment in Bush's life when he needed direction and purpose.

Revelation is a mystery, more often a journey than a sudden jolt. It was that way for Graham as a teenager: no lightning strike brought him to Jesus, rather a series of encounters that sparked his decision to search for God's purpose for him. So it was for Bush, whose midlife course correction had many coaches, Graham not even first among them. But he was the most important.

Bush unveiled his Billy Graham story slowly, a little slice at a time. He told part of the story when his father ran for president in 1988 and a little more when he first ran for governor of Texas in 1994. He saved the biggest piece for his own race for the White House, when he would bring Graham onstage in part to introduce himself to the nation—and then again in the final forty-eight hours of the tightest and most contested race in U.S. history.

THE WALK ON THE BEACH

What do you do with a son like George? Married and the father of twins, the CEO of his own oil company in West Texas, and the namesake of the vice president of the United States, Bush's M.O. inside the family compound at Kennebunkport was anything but boardroom. He was the most kinetic member of the entire extended family, fun, full of energy, larger than life, coolly resistant to authority, outrageous at times, always the leader of a mostly male pack. When they were all younger, George would whistle up his brothers like soldiers in a ragtag platoon— "Line up, you little wieners!" he'd say—and then he would shoot them with his air gun and they would all flail and pretend to die—"and it really hurt," one family member said years later, "but we'd just get up and do it all over again."

He was to the manor born, but he did not always act like it: he'd sneak away from Walker's Point to smoke cigarettes with friends or drive golf balls off the roof of the nearby Nonantum Hotel and hit the cars on the coast road. His favorite movie was *Cool Hand Luke*, the story of a charming, stubborn, and clever prison convict. Where his dad's nickname as a kid was "Have-Half" for his habit of offering part of his Hershey bar to whomever was nearby, Junior was "a mild form of John Belushi," said a cousin. "He had a very broad personality, but he always kept just within the lines of truly offensive. The parents would roll their eyes and say, 'Oh my God, you didn't!' But there was some appreciative eye rolling in that."

Being the first child and bearing his father's name meant he carried burdens the other siblings didn't feel. And one extra burden, too: he was the one marked by death from leukemia of his little sister Robin when he was six—a lifelong motivation to live in the moment and never take anything or anyone too seriously. And yet flippancy was never the Bush family way. "When they were growing up, everything fell on George," one family member said. "He felt the old man's disappointment the most. The others almost felt, 'That's W's job. We don't have to measure up. We're just living our lives here.'" After college, Bush followed the family recipe for success and service: make your money first and get into politics later. But the recipe had lost some of its heat by the late 1960s. He carefully traced his father's footsteps—to Andover, to Yale, to flight training in Texas, to the oil patch—but each time emerged with less to show for it. By the time those personal and professional pressures had decanted into a full-fledged drinking problem, Bush was almost forty.

A casual attitude about drinking took an early political toll, during his first run for office. In 1978, in a tight race for Congress against Democratic state senator Kent Hance, Bush aides took out an ad in the Texas Tech newspaper offering beer for free at a "Bush Bash." Hance operatives immediately fired off four thousand letters to Church of Christ members in the district explaining the Bush campaign tactic. "Mr. Bush used some of his vast sums of money in an attempt, evidently, to persuade young college students to vote for, and support him by offering free alcohol to them," said the letter. There were other issues in the race; namely, Bush's outsider status and the financial help he received from his father's vast network of friends. But Bush had no smart response for the culturally conservative targets of Hance's mailing, and when the election was held a few weeks later, he lost by 7 percent. He had been, as the political consultants say, outchurched.

But there is no evidence that Bush's religious awakening a few years later was a matter of political expediency. His journey covered several years in the mid-1980s, well before anyone imagined that he might become governor—much less president. It began in the spring of 1984, when he sought the help of an itinerant preacher best known for dragging a twelve-foot wooden cross across the country and much of the world. His name, intriguingly enough, was Arthur Blessit. During one of Blessit's swings through Midland, where he was slated to speak each night for a week at the Chaparral Center, Bush heard him on the radio and, through a friend, arranged a visit with Blessit privately at his hotel. The men prayed together and, according to a lengthy account by Blessit, the preacher led Bush to Jesus that day. "We talked for a while more about following Jesus," Blessit wrote on his Web site. "I encouraged him to tell his wife and friends what happened in his heart. I told him he needed now to grow in the Lord and study the Word of God and be open in his testimony. I told him I would not get up and announce in the meeting about him being saved." But the two men did not keep in touch, and there is no evidence Bush followed up on his lessons that day.

By 1985, Bush was thirty-nine and marking time—"on the road to nowhere at 40," said a cousin. His father was about to begin a three-year odyssey for the biggest prize of all and Junior would again be expected to, at the very least, keep his flamboyancy in check. In August of that year, the Bush tribe gathered in Kennebunkport for the annual family reunion and the usual array of competitive sports. The clan always hosted special guests—visiting governors, friends from Texas, aging tennis pros, long-time golfing buddies who could reliably be called upon to act as ringers in any foursome, loyal campaign aides from way back, the occasional ambassador or foreign leader as well as a nonstop array of friends and political allies. Some stayed in hotels in town or came up for the day at the Point; others brought their entire families. Special guests stayed with the Bushes. The VIPs had Dorothy Bush's cottage to themselves.

Billy Graham and Ruth spent a few days in Kennebunkport in August 1985. Though they had five kids of their own, they found the experience completely hectic and utterly normal. Still a golfer, Graham was game for rounds at the Cape Arundel Club a few minutes' drive from the Point. He recalled walking up to the family's court to watch various pairings of Bushes take each other on at tennis in ferocious tests of will. He went swimming one day with George W. Bush and remembered only that Bush's son was young, that the water was cold, and that they talked while they swam. "It was just two people," he recalled. "That was our beginning."

One night, the Bush kids gathered to hear Graham speak. Graham recalled that first fireside chat: "I remember that one of the questions came from [George W. Bush]: 'How do you become a real Christian? Explain it to us.' Which I did as best I could. I can see him sitting back there now. He's not yet governor. He's not even in politics."

The next day, George W. and Graham took a private walk around the compound. According to Bush, it was in this second conversation that Graham pressed him directly about his faith. "They had a conversation about the Almighty," said Karl Rove, "and it inspired [Bush] to seek a stronger relationship with God." And so Graham gave Bush, as he had for so many people, more fuel for his journey.

The first time Bush talked in public about the weekend with Graham was three years later, in 1988, when he was helping Doug Wead write *Man of Integrity*, the laudatory campaign biography about his father aimed at Christian voters. In a series of interviews with Wead, the younger Bush talked about his family's faith in general, his father's spiritual side, and the night in 1985 when Billy Graham held Bible study for the extended Bush family. "It was one of the most exciting nights I have ever spent in my life," the future forty-third president told Wead. "The man is powerful and humble. That combination of wisdom and humility was so inspiring to me individually that I took up the Bible in a more serious and meaning-ful way. As you know, one's walk in life is full of all kinds of little blind alleys. Sometimes life isn't easy and so Billy redirected my way of thinking in a very positive way. He answered questions of all types."

There was no mention in the Wead book of the walk on the beach, but that was the son's story, after all, not the father's. It would be another eleven years, at the start of his own presidential campaign in 1999, before Bush talked about the oceanside encounter and its effect on him.

Bush left the job of detailing his conversation with Graham to several friends, and each put a slightly different spin on the encounter. Don Evans, Bush's close Midland prayer buddy and later commerce secretary, reported that Bush asked Graham if some sins were worse than others. Graham, according to Evans, replied, "Sin is sin." Karl Rove relayed that Bush was most affected by how closely the evangelist seemed to be measuring his character. "It was the wonderment of Graham's watching him," Rove told David Aikman, a veteran *TIME* correspondent who interviewed Graham many times. "Billy Graham was watching the interplay of [GWB] and his family and he asked, 'Do you have the right relationship with God?'"

Graham's memory of the walk is fuzzy, but he confirms that it occurred. "I don't remember what we talked about," he said. "There's not much of a beach there. Mostly rocks. Some people have written—or maybe he has said, I don't know—that it had an effect, our walk on the beach. I don't remember. I do remember a walk on the beach."

There is nothing surprising in the fact that Graham does not recall the details of the chat and that Bush was moved by the experience. Graham had similar conversations with thousands of people, and simply being in his presence can be unforgettable. In any case, there is no question that Bush turned his life around in the year that followed his conversations with Graham. He got out of the oil business (which was on the skids by late 1985) and began concentrating on politics. He woke up, hungover and disgusted, during a fortieth birthday celebration in Colorado Springs in 1986 and quit booze cold. Early in 1987, he moved his wife and twin daughters to Washington and began working full-time on his father's campaign. He would be a surrogate speaker around the country for his namesake, acting as the family's eyes and ears inside the highly charged campaign headquarters. And he would take a special interest in one group of voters that was particularly vexing for the vice president and would someday prove pivotal for the younger Bush as well: evangelical Republicans.

In late summer 1986, Graham returned to Kennebunkport. Once more, Graham took questions from the entire family, and once more, the preacher and the prodigal son carved out time alone. "He made it a point to call me aside and ask how things were going," Bush recalled later. "He took a real interest in me . . . and for that I am forever grateful. It's an example of one man's impact on another person's life. And it was a very strong impact."

"Get Me Billy Graham"

Bush did not talk about his encounter with Graham as he moved around the country in 1987 and 1988, meeting with evangelical leaders on his father's behalf—perhaps because his meetings with Graham continued.

In an interview with the *Houston Post* in 1993, Bush told a story about Graham as he was launching his own campaign to become governor of Texas. According to Barbara Bush, the story dated to the late 1980s, when Bush's father was still vice president. Bush had been talking with his mother about who could and could not get into heaven. The son said only born-again Christians could get past Saint Peter; Barbara Bush replied that her son's reading of the Bible was incorrect. "Mother and I were arguing—not arguing, having a discussion—and discussing who goes to Heaven. . . . I said, 'Mom, here's what the New Testament says.' And she said, 'OK,' and she picks up the phone and calls Billy Graham. She says to the White House operator, 'Get me Billy Graham.'"

As the son retold the story in 1993, it took a few minutes for White House operators to find the evangelist. "Billy came on the line . . . and he said, 'Look, I happen to agree with what George says about the interpretation of the New Testament,' but he added, 'I want to remind both of you never play God.'" Asked about this incident in 2007, Bush remarked that no one can play God and quoted, from memory, Matthew 7:3–5: "Why do you look at the speck of sawdust in your brother's eye and pay no attention to the plank in your own eye? . . . You hypocrite, first take the plank out of your own eye, and then you will see clearly to remove the speck from your brother's eye."

Bush unwrapped this story as he started his gubernatorial campaign in part to signal to voters in Texas that, while he was a born-again Christian, he had learned from the master not to be judgmental of those who were not. The audience for this tale, therefore, was vast: both deep believers and those suspicious of the faithful. (Even so, the campaign of Ann Richards placed an ad in a Jewish newspaper in Texas to draw attention to Bush's original notion about heaven's selective admissions policy.) He didn't need to tell the rest of his Graham story yet: he ran unopposed in the primary in 1994 and most of the evangelical voters in the state were Republicans anyway. Bush won the race, and Graham was on hand to do the prayer at his inauguration in 1995.

In 1999, Bush asked his old friend Doug Wead to send him thoughts on how to woo evangelicals in the coming 2000 presidential race. In one respect, the resulting document was a virtual carbon copy of the report Wead had written for Bush's father fourteen years earlier. Once again, it argued for signaling an alliance with Christian voters early in the primary process. Once again, it identified Billy Graham as the single most important religious figure in the universe of priests, ministers, and clerics. Once again, it urged the candidate to hire a special liaison with the religious bloc, publish a book that explained his faith history, place targeted articles in religious periodicals, and meet as many leaders as possible as quickly as it could be arranged.

Wead also urged Bush to tell his faith story to Richard Ostling, who by then was with the Associated Press. "It gets the story of the governor's faith out there early. It is free. It does not showcase prominent, controversial, religious figures. Only Billy Graham figures in the story. It is hidden away on the religion page. If it pops out into a one night story, so what?

A man's personal faith is not the same as hobnobbing with the religious right and patronizing them on the issues. But there is a very good possibility that it will slip right by evangelical antagonists and only be appreciated by those who read it." Wead promised at the end of the memo to send Bush "a number of one-liners and paragraphs that would have appeal to evangelicals."

But, unlike his father, Bush declined much of Wead's advice. He organized only a few meetings with evangelical leaders, and decided against a yearlong campaign to brand himself as a true believer with Christians. It simply wasn't necessary: he had already established plenty of bona fides with the pivotal faction of the Texas Republican Party. As governor, Bush had made faith-based programs a feature in a variety of state government practices, from prisons to education. According to Karl Rove, evangelicals in Texas simply spread the word about Bush's heart to friends in other states. Rove recalled that during a fund-raising trip to California in 1997, Bush encountered evangelical voters who would approach the governor and report what great things they were hearing about him from their friends in the Lone Star State.

Besides, Bush had something more alluring to evangelical voters than a strategy: he had a story. And he gathered it together—the one about going from aimless oilman to Bible-studying public man—in *A Charge to Keep*, his campaign autobiography, released in late 1999 and transparently ghostwritten by aide Karen Hughes.

Though he is mentioned on the book's very first page, Graham does not play a large part in the book, only a few paragraphs. But his role is pivotal. This time, Bush included not only the family question-and-answer session with Graham in 1985, but also the private walk on the beach. He credited Graham for sparking his turnaround during the stroll they took together. "The next day we walked and talked at Walker's Point, and I knew I was in the presence of a great man. He was like a magnet. I felt drawn to seek something different. He didn't lecture or admonish; he shared warmth and concern. Billy Graham didn't make you feel guilty; he made you feel loved. Over the course of that weekend, Reverend Graham planted a mustard seed in my soul, a seed that grew over the next year. He led me to the path and I began walking."

The story of his journey—joining the men's Bible study group, reading the Bible regularly, visiting the Holy Land, and giving up booze—won him the notice, and then the confidence, of evangelical voters outside of Texas. It was a pitch-perfect tale of discipline saving a prodigal son, of faith overcoming doubt. It was quietly retailed in a way that nonbelievers could have missed it and the faithful could not ignore it. Like Jimmy Carter's tale of loss and discovery following his 1966 campaign defeat, it told the story of someone who had been lost and found—and it had the virtue of being true. Omitted was any mention of Arthur Blessit; as far as most people knew, Bush had been set on a straighter path by Graham, evangelism's icon. Bush let loose a few more details about his time with Graham that spring in magazine interviews as he prepared to run for president. "I asked him a lot of questions about God and Jesus Christ—the skeptic's questions," Bush told Fred Barnes of the *Weekly Standard* in March 1999. "Billy Graham's presence is such that he can melt a skeptic. . . . When you are dealing with a skeptic, it takes a while for the message to sink in."

Bush was careful not to overplay the Graham card, partly out of deference to Graham, who needed to keep some distance from partisan politics, and partly out of deference to his father, who had been so painstaking himself about when and how to bring Graham onstage. After Bush told a debate audience in Iowa in December 1999 that Christ was the philosopher who had the most impact on his life, Graham said, "it was a wonderful answer." A few days later, he explained to the *Washington Post* that the accounts of Bush's formative years in some profiles were overdrawn. "They think he's a man of little substance, but that's not true. I think that he's a man of tremendous moral character to begin with, and what they have written about his earlier years could be true of nearly all of us."

It had to be a small source of pride for Graham, as he reached his eightieth year, that one of the men who would be the next president would turn out to be an acolyte. Otherwise, for much of 2000, Graham's reaction to Bush's candidacy was one of almost complete silence. And Bush, for much of the 2000 campaign, returned the favor.

Brian Jacobs, a "church growth consultant" in Texas who started his own church in Fort Worth after Graham held a crusade there in 2002, was not content to leave it at that. Jacobs had been a volunteer at nearly every Graham crusade in the United States since 1988, and when 2000 rolled around, he was keen to get Bush and Graham together, onstage, for voters to see. To Jacobs, the story of Graham's role in Bush's midlife rebirth struck a powerful and resonant chord—powerful enough to make or break the election, he believed. "If the American people, if the Christian public, knew more about that story, it would stir people to come out to vote," he said in 2006. "That was my whole purpose."

During the summer of 2000, Jacobs began sending faxes to Karl Rove in Austin, as well as Graham's office in Montreat, urging a rendezvous at the Jacksonville crusade in late October. Jacobs even volunteered to give testimony about George W. Bush's conversion at Graham's hands if Bush declined to attend. "It was a perfect PR event to really stir the evangelical right to the polls and vote." Jacobs recalled that both Graham and Bush were interested in the idea—but neither would agree to participate. "No one was willing to touch it." And so Jacobs finally gave up his search for an earthly solution. One morning, he got down on his knees and prayed to God that if He wanted Graham and Bush to be together, He would find a way to get it done.

Jacobs only imagined he was alone. In fact, he had been counseled in this process by none other than Wead, who was acting as a kind of free agent on behalf of his old friend the Texas governor. Though Bush had declined some of Wead's advice about how to woo the evangelical voters, he authorized him to perform a number of small missions under the radar during the campaign. Wead, in return, showered Bush with memos, most faxed to Bush's private fax machine in the Governor's Mansion in Austin. The two men also spent enough time on the telephone that Wead was able to tape-record nearly nine hours of conversations with Bush during the campaign. (Wead never told Bush he was recording him and was banished from the family circle when some of the tapes' contents became public in 2004.) But while Jacobs pressed the Bush team from the outside, Wead worked the inside track with Austin. He wrote Bush a memo on October 25, 2000. The last part was headlined "Talk to Billy Graham!"

Until now, Bush and Graham were keeping their distance because neither stood to gain much from a more visible relationship. Bush would in no way benefit from courting evangelical voters or their leaders in the final days of a general election campaign. Graham, meanwhile, had to preserve the appearance of political independence. But Wead decided to step in at this point and try to nudge things along. Wead told Bush in his October 25 message that he had secondhand reports that Graham wanted to speak to Bush privately.

The memo's evidence for this was thin, but that didn't stop Wead from pushing ahead: he suggested that Bush contact Graham and quietly table the idea of coming to the crusade. "If you call Graham to say that friends have been pushing you to attend the Jacksonville crusade but you haven't responded because of your deep love and affection and respect for him and you wouldn't ever allow him to be politicized, etc. etc., who knows? Lightning might strike and he may just say you would be entirely welcome to come to his crusade." He added: "This is one call that might bring helpful dividends. Battleground poll shows evangelical women way below the numbers you could have."

It is not known whether Bush read Wead's memo or, if he did, whether he acted on it. But a week later, as the Jacksonville crusade got under way, the questions plaguing the candidate were not about his spiritual past. They were about his drinking past.

On November 2, a Fox television affiliate in Maine reported that Bush had been arrested over Labor Day weekend in 1976 for driving under the influence of alcohol. Bush, who was thirty at the time, paid a fine and had his driving privileges suspended. The Bush campaign quickly confirmed the report that evening at a press conference, but this reminder of the governor's prodigal past sent shivers through his campaign and its supporters for the next few days. There were suspicions that the disclosure was part of a timed political hit—but it more immediately laid bare the fact that Bush had been trying to keep the arrest secret for years.

The news raised a number of questions about Bush's character and candor: whether he misled a Texas court when he was asked on a jury duty questionnaire about previous arrests and whether he had been straight with reporters who had tried to pin him down on such questions before. Bush had often deflected inquiries about his salad days by issuing a blanket confession: "When I was young and irresponsible, I was young and irresponsible." But in the final days of a presidential campaign, he tried to turn his past mistakes into a future strength. Appearing Friday morning at a religious college near Grand Rapids, Bush said, "It has become clear to America over the course of this campaign that I've made mistakes in my life. But I'm proud to tell you, I've learned from those mistakes. That's the role of a leader—to share wisdom, to share experience with people who are looking for somebody to lead."

By Saturday night, two days after the story broke, the DUI story was beginning to take its toll in voter surveys: polls in some states were shifting in Gore's favor. Bush aides, hoping to change the focus as quickly as possible, pressed reporters to look into who, or what, might have caused the story to appear at such a crucial hour. Late that evening, Bush's chartered jet touched down in Jacksonville, where seventy thousand had heard Graham preach that day. And his campaign chiefs had decided to slip a quick meeting with Billy Graham into the schedule on the final Sunday of the campaign.

The next morning, Bush attended a multidenominational church service led by five Jacksonville-area ministers. He then returned to his hotel, where he and his wife, Laura, joined Graham and son Franklin for a private breakfast. Afterward, in a tiny room a few steps away, the four appeared before a small group of reporters and cameramen to make brief statements. "It's comforting," said Bush, "to be with a close friend and to have coffee and prayer as we begin the final stretch of the campaign to be the president." Graham, he added, had been "a major influence on my life."

Reporters wanted to know why Graham was breaking his long-standing vow against personal involvement in campaigns to appear with Bush. "I don't endorse candidates," Graham said. "But I've come as close to it, I guess, now as any time in my life, because I think it's extremely important. We have in our state absentee voting. I've already voted. I'll just let you guess who I voted for. And my family—the same way." He continued, "We believe there's going to be a tremendous victory and change by Tuesday night in the direction of the country—putting it in good hands. I believe in the integrity of this man. I've known him as a boy. I've known him as a young man. And we're very proud of him." Gesturing to the governor and his wife, Graham added, "If they, by God's will, win, I'm going to do everything in my power to help them make it a successful presidency."

This was, at the very least, a moment of almost willful naïveté on Graham's part. At worst, he had lost sight of the difference between a personal friendship and a public blessing. As for Bush, it was a window on what he made of the gifts faith can offer to public figures in crisis. He had escorted Graham out for one last turn on the stage, a chance to polish his character in the reflection of a man Americans regarded as above reproach.

Karl Rove said that the eleventh-hour Graham-Bush meeting was purely serendipitous. "They happened to be in Jacksonville at the same time," said Rove. "When the governor found out he was there, he just arranged for a personal visit." There was never, he added, any plan to attend the crusade or seek an endorsement. "The governor had things to do and Mr. Graham had things to do."

Whether or not the meeting with Graham was purely coincidental—and it's difficult to believe that it was—there is no doubt that the Bush camp fully understood its redeeming power. Later that morning, *Face the Nation* host Bob Schieffer reported to his guest, Florida governor Jeb Bush, that, just the day before, Vice President Al Gore had told a Memphis prayer breakfast that "good overcomes evil if we choose that outcome, and I feel it coming." When Schieffer asked Jeb Bush for his reaction, Jeb replied, "If the implication is that my brother is evil, then I'll tell you what. My brother is having breakfast—had breakfast this morning in Jacksonville with Dr. Billy Graham and I'm confident that Dr. Graham will be able to purge all that evilness from my brother's soul."

Bush and his brother then departed on a four-stop swing around the Sunshine State. Graham wrapped up his Jacksonville crusade that afternoon, after more than a quarter million people had come to hear him over four days.

And less than forty-eight hours later, polls opened across the state of Florida and the rest of the nation. After they closed, Larry King asked Bush spokesman Ari Fleischer on CNN if Graham's appearance in the final days made a difference. "In a close race," he said, "every little bit counts."

It would be another thirty-seven days before anyone knew the outcome of the election.

Lessons of a Lifetime

For all the invitations on television and in newspapers—Come, come hear him one last time—invitations wrapped around lampposts and in the papers and on bus shelters, for all the summonses to come see history and hear from heaven, there were also plenty of warnings as well.

Highway signs on roads from north and south of New York City warned of traffic chaos: "Take Mass Transit." The temperature was heading toward ninety-five, the air like broth, too hot to breathe deep. "Ozone Alert" glowed the sign over the toll plaza. But of course they still came, in cars and mini-vans with fish stickers on the bumper, swarms of rattling school buses, and then thousands upon thousands of pilgrims on the Number 7 train from midtown Manhattan, or on foot from all around Flushing, where they say a hundred languages are spoken in a single zip code. The firemen stationed around the great lawns of Corona Park sprayed their hoses from the tops of their trucks to make a cooling baptismal fountain for children to run through; there were sweet breezes blowing across expanses of chairs. And you wondered how, even with hundreds of crusades over so many years of practice, did the Graham crusade operation manage to air-condition all ninety-three acres of the summer Cathedral of Queens?

This was where Billy Graham came in the summer of 2005 for what everyone was calling his last crusade. It was the world in concentrate form, gathered beneath the great steel globe from the 1964 World's Fair: seven hundred journalists from all over the world got credentials to attend; every network was there, all the anchormen had sat down for reverential interviews. There were reporters like Richard Ostling of the Associated Press who had covered Graham for decades; and there were newcomers who, for all the hoopla, couldn't fathom why so many people had come to hear this old man preach. It was ever thus. One veteran chronicler of the crusades recalled going into a new city and sitting the first night next to a new reporter who would watch the crowds press into whatever arena it was, packing stadiums that the biggest rock bands, the hottest sports teams, couldn't fill.

"I just don't get it," the rookie reporter would muse.

"You're not the first," the veteran would reply.

The immense boom cameras swept over the heads of the crowd like some skeletal dinosaur grazing on souls. They alone could capture the scale of the crowd: police and event organizers called it the most multinational, multicultural gathering they had ever witnessed: close to a quarter of a million people over three days, families spread out on picnic blankets in the overflow fields, whole congregations from fourteen hundred host churches in rows of seventy thousand chairs—it required four companies, including one from St. Louis, to get that many folding chairs to New York—plus the VIPs, New York mayor Michael Bloomberg, Senator Charles Schumer, business leaders, all listening to the Christian rock band Jars of Clay, and waiting.

When at last it was time for the main event, Graham emerged, shuffling softly with a walker, his son Franklin by his side. He was in a dark jacket and vest, moving carefully after having broken a hip, then his pelvis, and fearing another fall. Behind him stood the Clintons, come to pay homage to their old friend. And when the Lion moved to the podium, it was the crowd that rose and roared; Bill Clinton stood there, his lip thrust forward and up, his hands raised, clapping, and his eyes wet.

In his welcome, he greeted the Clintons as his "wonderful friends of many years." "I told him," Graham said of Clinton, "when he left the presidency, he should become an evangelist, because he had all the gifts." And he paused, his eyes twinkling. "And he could leave his wife to run the country."

Some things never change—including the judgment that Graham was just not judgmental enough. That remark unleashed a wave of letters and furious columns blasting Graham for endorsing Hillary for president; eventually Franklin Graham had to call the *Charlotte Observer* and explain that the line was a joke.

Clinton was not joking when he got up to respond. "This man I love," he said, "who I have followed, is about the only person I have ever known who has never failed to live his faith."

Clinton sat down and Graham began his sermon, quoting scripture and Mick Jagger, on the hollowness of a life without Jesus: "I can't get no satisfaction, though I try, and I try, and I try." Always trying to find his audience where they lived, he talked about the message of the new *Star Wars* movie, the meaning of events in the news, but in the end the message always came home. "You want to be loved," he said, "and the Bible says, God loves you." And every word was sent out like an arrow. "God . . . loves . . . you."

It ended where it always did, with the invitation for everyone, churched and unchurched, young and old, to come forward and accept Jesus into their hearts. The choir sang its invitation—"Just as I am, without one plea . . ."—and Graham stood quietly with a gentle smile, his eyes sometimes closed as though he was willing people to come toward him, and all across the immense field they came streaming down every aisle, some heading toward the men and women holding signs offering a message in Spanish, Korean, Armenian, Tamil, Arabic, Portuguese, Mandarin, Punjabi.

A reporter watching from the rows of cameras and laptops came forward, removed his press pass, and found a counselor.

A man who never failed to live his faith, Clinton said. The story of Graham's political ministry is a winding story of grace under pressure. To study its tensions, the temptations he faced, the balance he struck and the times when he stumbled, provides all kinds of signs and cautions for any traveler between the Two Kingdoms. It is hard to imagine that any preacher, or anyone in any field, will play the role that Graham did, or remain so close to such power for so long—close not only to politicians but to business leaders who courted him, global leaders who welcomed him as one of the few figures from any country at any time who was so universally known and admired. And yet "Graham never lost the sense of awe," said Charles Colson, a man with an acute understanding of what power can do to men's souls. "A friend of mine said one of the great miracles of the twentieth century is that Billy Graham remained a humble man."

In fact the greater miracle may be that Graham grew more humble as time went on, more willing to admit error, entertain doubt, welcome mystery where others wanted certainty. The fierce anticommunist so convinced of America's unique virtue became over the decades a global citizen, with a broader view: "When I go to preach the Gospel," he said in later years, "I go as an ambassador of the kingdom of God—not America." The same could be said of his White House ministry: he went as a courier for Christ, representing no constituency other than His own.

The persistent charge against him, leveled from both left and right over the years, was that he somehow lacked the moral courage to speak truth to power. He was too conciliatory, they said, he had the soul of a collaborator, so eager to please and comfort that he didn't know when to pause and confront. As the sleepy consensus of the 1950s gave way to sharp choices about war and peace and rights and culture, activists on the left wanted to know why Graham wasn't marching with Martin Luther King Jr., why he wasn't using his many golf games with Nixon to lobby for a bombing halt in Indochina. Later the armies of the right wanted to know why he did not throw his weight behind their crusades against abortion and gay marriage and liberal judges. Once the clergy took their seat at the political table, the most controversial thing about Graham was that he was noncontroversial. Passionate people were angry that he wasn't angrier, confronted him about being so nonconfrontational.

Graham himself would be the first to say that he was no prophet Nathan sternly rebuking various presidential Davids; but to the charge that he would not speak truth to power, he countered that this depended on what one meant by *truth*.

His reluctance to challenge presidents privately or chastise them publicly reflected his conviction that the truth that mattered most was the gospel truth; take up more earthly matters, he said, and he might lose his chance to witness. It was the basic nature of his faith that God had ordained these men to be president and his job was to pray with them and for them; the rest, he believed, would take care of itself.

To some who did not share the same view, Graham's ministry was more than frustrating: it could be dangerous. Encouraging presidents in the belief that they are divinely chosen might inspire them to make the worst decisions born of the best intentions; to ignore critics, exalt ends over means, might undermine the secular democratic premise that competition between conflicting ideas will yield the wisest judgment. After Watergate, when Graham confronted the evidence that an administration full of men he admired could behave in ways he abhorred, he pulled conspicuously back from his promotion of civil religion and rediscovered the genius of the First Amendment: by keeping church and state separate, we honor and safeguard both.

There were other, more personal reasons why Graham handled his presidents with such care. He was a man who hated conflict, hated to fire people, hated a fight. He could stand up in front of a hundred thousand people and throw down a gauntlet; but these men, these families, offered a rare opportunity to serve as pastor. Once elected, it was hard for them to go to church without creating a scene; and churches, Graham noted, can be pretty political places in their own right. He gave them a sanctuary; they gave him a congregation. But it's easier to brook no compromise from a stadium pulpit than in the intimacy of a friendship.

From the presidents' side, the alliance made sense at every level. They walked through a minefield when it came to people's appetite for public faith. Politicians of great confidence could be terrified by this terrain, fearful of saying the wrong thing, alienating someone, going too far or not far enough. Graham was guardian and guide, even to the most devout of them.

But that doesn't explain more than twenty visits to the Johnson White House; the bonds went beyond good company and comfort. Many of these presidents were men of high intelligence who disdained intellectuals, privately and sometimes publicly. The ones least inclined to do so—Kennedy especially—were the ones least close to Graham. Most saw themselves as men of action, willing to take risks, move history—an idealized image that fueled Eisenhower and Johnson, Nixon and Reagan, and George W. Bush. Pundits can sit on the sidelines—even Truman would cuss at the armchair statesmen who never made a hard decision in their lives—but history was made by the bold, and they recognized in Graham a fellow world historical figure, as transformational in his realm of the spirit as they were in the realm of the state. He was a man of action more than ideas. Or, more accurately, he acted fearlessly on the one great idea of his life: that God wanted him to spread the good news of the gospel. So when Graham's critics accused him of making things too simple, of not wrestling enough with the complexity of the human condition and soul, he still pushed on, fighting his way into countries not receptive to an American evangelist and drawing millions of people to hear him. The presidents all saw this and marveled: "How do you get them to come?" He was, almost uniquely, a peer, and so they sought him out in much the way that presidents bonded with each other once out of office, as members of the world's most exclusive club.

That still left the problem of election years. Again and again he vowed to stay out; again and again he was drawn back in. He always reminded people he was raised a Democrat and had friends in both parties, and while this was true, it became clear long ago he had the soul of a mainstream, moderate Republican. This meant that when his Democratic friends were running, the most he would do was resist pressure to help the Republican candidate. He did not assist Johnson or Clinton, much less Carter or Kennedy, in anything like the way he worked for Eisenhower or Nixon or, to a lesser extent, either of the Presidents Bush. On the other hand, when a president was in personal or political trouble, including Johnson and Carter and Clinton, Graham always answered their call and stood by their side.

As for his motives, the standard lures of politics did not really apply, beyond his basic love of the game. There is scant evidence that he had a social or legislative agenda he wanted to see enacted. He was not looking to get rich through his political connections, having passed up more chances for greater wealth than one can count. He could hardly become more famous than he already was; it was typically the presidents who came to him for some reflected glory, not the reverse. It's hard to imagine anyone he could not get on the phone if he wanted. When one measures what friendship with presidents could do for him, the agenda that emerges is the one he admitted to us the very first day we spoke to him: there were places he could not go without the power of the presidency behind him to open doors. That was the practical benefit of these friendships, and its impact was felt literally all around the world.

Even when he fell short and couldn't resist consulting behind the scenes, he professed neutrality as the ideal. But in the process he helped open the door for religious leaders to become political players, with no guarantee that they would abide by his rules. He witnessed the rise of a new generation of clergy that had no problem with aggressive partisanship. "I think we've lucked out with Billy Graham," said historian Martin Marty, "because he doesn't seem to have a mean streak in him." Marty divides American Christianity not between liberal and conservative, but between mean and "nonmean." "If Graham had chosen to be mean and to crusade against the humanist and secular world, then we would have had a culturally polarized America thirty years earlier." Graham would be the last person to boast of a political legacy; but if some of the acid were to drain from the debate, if there were less shouting, more listening, less anger, more humility, you sense he would be pleased to be seen as showing the way.

W e went back to see him for the last time in January 2007, just over a year after our first visit, with most of our questions answered, but one mystery to unravel.

Much about our return trip seemed identical to the first—or it felt that way for a while. Once again we met Graham's cheerful chief of staff, David Bruce, at the bottom of the big hill in Montreat and again we were driven up the steep mountain road, through the green rhododendrons and the stark and leafless hardwoods to the house in the sky.

The preacher's days were much the same: up in the morning for prayers, a light breakfast, and then devotionals. A nap followed, then lunch. He read the Bible in the early afternoon, met with visitors if they were on the schedule that day, breaking in the afternoon for exercise: a walk up and down the long driveway on the hilltop. If the sun was out, he might sit in an old wooden chair on the back porch, warming himself like a cat. After dinner, he glued himself to CNN, rarely missing Larry King. And then, more prayer before sleep.

When he met us again, right inside the door, he was smiling and looking as strong as eighty-eight years allow. He took us once more back to his private study, leading the way with a new walker sent to him by a manufacturer who had seen his old one on television and decided an upgrade was in order. The study had been redone: it was brighter and freshly painted, with more books and pictures. He told us his hearing was failing—and his vision wasn't far behind. The doctors at Mayo had recently begun to treat him for macular degeneration; he was having trouble reading even large-print Bibles now. "That's part of life, getting older," he mused, "which we expect."

While he seemed in some ways just as strong as a year before, Ruth was much more frail. This afternoon, she had been taken by ambulance for a procedure at a hospital in Asheville fifteen miles away. Her condition had consumed him since the fall; he gave her a huge saltwater fish tank for Christmas to keep right by her bed, a tropical escape for a woman who could no longer leave the mountain.

He kept a close watch on the news, and noted several times that it had been a hard year for his friend in the White House. George W. Bush had seen his presidency all but collapse in 2006, towed under by a war that much of the country had grown to doubt—and then deplore. His party had lost both houses of Congress in the midterm elections, and as the new year opened, Graham said he was embarrassed to report that he had not been able to arrange a meeting with Bush despite multiple attempts by both sides. "I just wrote him a letter because he's invited me to come and have lunch with him or afternoon tea or something private with him and Laura. We've postponed it three times now. I've not been able to do it because of my wife. I felt badly." But he was clearly disturbed by the course of the war and its impact on the president; he returned to the topic several times in the course of our last conversation, sometimes unbidden. Graham said he did not want to "take sides on this Iraq thing," but he acknowledged at another point that "I'm getting a little depressed about Iraq. . . . Think of what it is doing to Bush. There doesn't seem to be any way out." He did not mention that a grandson was serving as an army Ranger in Iraq.

He had also been following the start of the 2008 campaign closely and heard the echoes of races past. He did not know Mitt Romney of Massachusetts, he said, but he knew his father, George, and he offered that the former Massachusetts governor faced a challenge convincing Americans to vote for a Mormon. "He could [overcome it]. It will be somewhat of a problem for him like Jack Kennedy being a Catholic."

He was following the campaign of John McCain, though the two men had never met. "I ought to," he said, "because I have a story to tell him." During one of his Vietnam trips during the war, Graham explained, "I was stopping in Honolulu for three or four days on my way over. So the commander in chief of the Pacific theater was Admiral McCain and he invited me to come and see him. He told me the story of his son in prison, and we got on our knees, both of us did, and I prayed and he prayed. When I came back from Vietnam, I went to see him again. [John] was still in prison and we had prayer again. I never had the chance to tell that to Senator McCain."

Graham did not know Barack Obama but was watching the progress of Hillary Clinton, whom he knew the best after twenty years of friendship. "I keep up with her. I think a lot of Hillary."

Returning one last time to campaigns past, his memory was sharp in some places and fuzzy in others. He chose his words carefully and we were rewarded most when we waited for him to collect his thoughts and answer. What he wouldn't talk about much, no matter how long we waited, was himself. And any time we tried to give him credit for something, or get him to expound on how he accomplished this or that, he withdrew, saying that he doubted he had had any impact on anything at all.

And so late in our last session, we asked him the question that we had been living with for two years: How did he manage it? How did he handle the enormous cross-pressures of politics and faith, without sacrificing principle, cutting corners, being thrown off balance?

"I didn't sit down and try to manage it or think it through," he said flatly. "I just tried to be myself, I think. I have five children and each has their own temperament, their own ideas, they have grown up in different cultures . . . and they have different points of view and I accept all of them. And love 'em all. And I do the same with people."

We began to get a glimpse of where he was going. We had thought this was two stories, the private friendships of public men, the political ministry of the great evangelist. But to him the presidents were the same as family, the same as any friendships; the principles did not shift with the circumstances. He loved them, he forgave them, and he tried to be there for them, no matter what. In the end we are all the same, he said, and need the same things.

"I forget who it was, some famous man said he never met a man that he hated," Graham went on, and then for one rare moment, he turned the camera on himself: "And I felt that way. I haven't hated people. I haven't felt that I needed to take revenge on somebody. I never was jealous of people that I can remember.

"That was a gift from the Lord," he declared. "Jesus spent a great deal of his ministry talking about the need for love and working together and that's why he died on the cross—because of love. He loved sinners, people who didn't deserve it, that's what grace is. It means God gives us forgiveness that we don't deserve. And to me that's a wonderful thing."

At that moment Graham was leaning forward in his chair, his voice clear and strong as could be, no pauses now, no search for the right words. It was as though they had always been there. Because all along, there was really only one crusade.

Afterword

Under a blazing North Carolina sun a few months later, faith and power renewed their vows, as three former presidents—Carter, Bush the First, and Clinton—convened in Charlotte to pay tribute to their aging spiritual adviser. The occasion was the dedication of the Billy Graham library, modeled after the dairy farm where he had grown up, complete with a giant cross over the barn door, a museum chronicling his long and storied life, and even a comical, talking, mechanical cow.

Before the ceremony, ABC News anchor Charles Gibson pulled off a historic summit, gathering Presidents Carter, George H. W. Bush, and Clinton around a single table with Graham to discuss, among other topics, what a president prays for and what he needs most.

Bush paid tribute to the way that Graham's travels behind the Iron Curtain helped "tip the balance of history in freedom's favor." But he also thanked Graham for personally ministering to his family over more than fifty years. "Billy guided our kids, including our daughter, Doro, and the president, through their spiritual journeys." He choked up as he described his friend as "a spiritual gift to us all."

Clinton talked of his own journey. "I am here because of the public Billy Graham and because of the private Billy Graham. When he prays for you in the Oval Office or upstairs at the White House, you feel he is praying for you. Not for the president." Noting that he had attended crusades in 1959, 1971, 1989, and 2005, he added, "Billy has known me since 1985. But I have known him for nearly fifty years."

Carter recalled his own days as an organizer for a regional Graham crusade in the mid-1960s, and said, "I'm just one of tens of millions of people whose spiritual life had been shaped by Billy Graham."

When he finally rose to speak, the old preacher stole the show: "I feel like I've been attending my own funeral."

Three weeks later, he was attending one. On June 10, 2007, Ruth Bell

Graham turned eighty-seven. Battling pneumonia and bedridden for months with disease eating away at her spine, she nonetheless celebrated that day with her husband and children. That night, she began to slip. The next day, the tube that supplied her with food, fluids, and medicine came out while she was shifting in bed. Ruth asked that it not be put back in. The family talked it over and decided: She had battled long enough. The tube was replaced but only to deliver pain medication. Three days later, at dusk, she took her last breath. Graham asked the family to sing the Doxology, and they all struggled through it, praising God "from whom all blessings flow."

Graham was silent for weeks afterward, privately mourning his loss. But in early August, in his first public remarks after Ruth's death, Graham described for us the misery of life without his partner of nearly sixty years. "No matter how prepared you think you are for the death of a loved one, it still comes as a shock," he said. "And it still hurts very deeply." Graham told us that he regularly found himself "overwhelmed" with sadness without Ruth around the house. He was often inclined to pick up the telephone and call her, as he had done for so many years when he was traveling, only to realize he no longer could. "I realize now, in a way that I never could have before, that a very important part of me has been taken away."

And yet even in one of his most difficult passages, Graham was preaching, too, pointing out the way to others who would follow in his footsteps. "Over the years I've seen people lose a spouse and then withdraw and lose interest in life. And I believe we need to resist that." Soon, with the help of his five children, he was again making plans, talking of restoring parts of the house that Ruth had built. And there was talk of yet another book.

Besides, there were presidents—and their families—who still needed looking after. He had spoken to the Johnson daughters and Lady Bird herself just forty-eight hours or so before she died in July, one month after Ruth. And one morning late in October 2007, Graham once more slipped quietly into Washington, D.C. He had his long-postponed private lunch with George W. Bush upstairs in the White House residence, sharing conversation, prayer, and encouragement. As had so often been the case over so many years, neither the White House nor Graham's office announced the lunch to reporters.

Later that afternoon, while Graham was resting at a downtown hotel, former president George Herbert Walker Bush paid a surprise call on the man who taught the Bible to both the 41st president's mother and his son. The two men, one eighty-nine, the other eighty-three, spent thirty minutes talking.

That night, Graham made time for one more First Family. Driven over the Potomac River to McLean, Virginia, Graham spent a quiet evening with Lynda Bird Johnson Robb and her husband, Charles, the former senator. When he made it back to his hotel that night, it had been a long day, a three First Family day, a rare trifecta for the preacher to the presidents.

Acknowledgments

W e knew when we started this project that books don't write themselves. It turns out that authors don't really write books either;
they rely on the help of hundreds of other people to bring them forth.
Mr. Graham's chief of staff, David Bruce, and his longtime foreign policy
adviser, John Akers, were patient with our requests for times and dates
and documents. Larry Ross smoothed our way on our visits to Montreat—
and then helped shepherd our research and legal questions through the
BGEA. But, more than all that, Mr. Graham and his wife welcomed us
four times into their home as if we were old friends.

It will surprise few people that we owe a lot to three *TIME* managing
editors, and we could not have begun—or finished—this project without
their help. Our gratitude goes to Walter Isaacson for first suggesting a book
about Mr. Graham and then challenging us to meet the standards he set;
to Jim Kelly, for permitting us the time and space to dive into a book in the
middle of a war; and to Rick Stengel, for allowing us the time to finish it
as an election loomed. Each has been a father to the outcome; none bears
any responsibility for its faults.

From the start, we also benefited from the support of Time Inc. editors
in chief John Huey and Norman Pearlstine. We have been lucky to work
for two men who both love a good story.

We learned a long time ago that words mean more when accompanied
by strong images, and we had a team of six of the best in the magazine
business. *TIME* art director Arthur Hochstein worked nights and weekends to design the cover and came up with so many good ideas that we
almost regretted that we had but one book to write. Photo editors Michelle
Stephenson, Mary Ann Golon, and Katie Ellsworth helped us traverse
a bewildering photographic landscape, solving problems we didn't even
know we had. Jay Colton researched and found the wonderful pictures of
Mr. Graham and the presidents that are included inside. And ever game

for adventure, veteran White House photographer Diana Walker went with us to Montreat with her cameras and her keen eye.

Our other current and former colleagues at *TIME*, with whom we have worked daily for more than twenty years in both New York and Washington, pitched in to help whenever we needed advice or just some moral support. We are grateful to Priscilla Painton, Karen Tumulty, David Van Biema, Jay Carney, Mike Allen, Michael Weisskopf, Kathleen Dowling, Ratu Kamlani, Amanda Ripley, Lisa Beyer, Tim Burger, Ralph Spielman, Dan Goodgame, Lissa August, Camille Sanabria, and Judith Stoler. Andrea Sachs was our wise guide through the world of books.

Time Life archivist Bill Hooper helped us dig through more than fifty years of *TIME* and *LIFE* and *People* for information and interviews with Graham and the presidents. He also provided us with access to the notes and letters between Graham and Henry Luce, and Paul Siniawer and Edmund Behan were immensely patient working through the permissions to use them.

The book would not have been possible without the help of Penny Circle in President Ford's office, Deanna Congileo in President Carter's office, Joanne Drake and Wren Powell in Nancy Reagan's office, Jean Becker in President George H. W. Bush's office, Jay Carson at the Clinton Foundation, Lorraine Voles in Senator Hillary Clinton's office, and Karl Rove at the White House.

David Clark at the Truman Library, Valoise Armstrong at the Eisenhower Library, Barbara Cline at the Johnson Library, Paul Wormser at the National Archives/Pacific region, Sahr Conway-Lanz at the National Archives annex, Meghan Lee at the Richard Nixon Library and Birthplace, David Horrocks at the Ford Library, Albert Nayson at the Carter Center, and Shelly Jacobs at the Reagan Library helped us find letters and meetings we could not have located on our own. Roman Papadiuk at the Bush Library Foundation was helpful in every way.

We owe a particular debt to some eminent historians and journalists who pointed the way: Michael Beschloss encouraged us in this project from the beginning and then agreed to read the manuscript. Richard Ostling, who covered Mr. Graham's ministry for *TIME* and the Associated Press for decades, was a model of fairness and a very helpful reader; David Westin of ABC brought a lawyer's sharp eye, a journalist's curiosity, and an evangelist's enthusiasm to this enterprise from the very start. Tad Smith of

Reed Elsevier is one of the wisest readers and strategic thinkers we have yet encountered. Having launched us on this course, Walter Isaacson returned a marked-up manuscript, and we were reminded why every writer dreams of finding friends and editors with such a sharp mind and pencil.

Whenever we lost our way in trying to understand the role faith has played in politics, we relied on the generous advice and perspective offered by Randall Balmer, Will Billow, Joan Brown Campbell, Doug Coe, Michael Cromartie, Os Guinness, Richard Land, Martin Marty, Jon Meacham, Cal Thomas, Rick Warren, Jim Wallis, Joel Osteen, Jack Pannell, Richard Ostling, and Mark Noll.

Lending a hand when we needed it most were Martin Anderson at Stanford, Bo Baskin at Blue Sage Capital, Michael Deaver at Edelman, and Phyllis McGrady at ABC News.

We were saved from embarrassment numerous times by the dogged research skills of Jim Downie and Susan Kean Tonetti. Archivist Maria Wygand at the *Charlotte Observer* was willing and always thorough whenever we needed her help. Jack Valenti, Jim Cannon, Scott Haig, Craig Fuller, Robert Maddox, Bert Lance, Paul Kengor, Cal Thomas, E. J. Dionne, Doris Kearns Goodwin, and Jay Carney read all or some of the manuscript and made helpful corrections and suggestions to the text. What errors of fact or interpretation remain are ours, not theirs.

For sheer encouragement, perspective, patience, and sustenance in all its forms we owe a debt to Caroline Fitzgibbons, Carol McKeirnan, Sherrie Westin, Tim Smith, Jim Johnson, Maxine Isaacs, Mary Lukens, Jeff Wallbrink, Tom Casciato, Kathy Hughes, Mark Burstein, and Lori Beecher. Christopher and Helena Gibbs modeled patient scholarship and the spirit of academic adventure. Janet Gibbs and Robert and Nancy Duffy gave the gifts of unconditional love, unconventional insight, and the conviction that we are constrained only by the limits of our imaginations.

We had in Chris Park an editor from heaven who gently polished our prose and managed our worries without showing us any of hers. Managing editor Robert Castillo kept the manuscript on track through the production phase, copy editor Roland Ottewell saved us from many unforced errors, and Sarah Sper never lost her temper with the authors. Rolf Zettersten, Center Street's publisher, was excited about the project from the start.

As he has done for so many others, the incomparable Bob Barnett at Williams & Connolly steered us through the maze that is modern publishing not only with a cool head but with an infectious enthusiasm from the first day we pitched him on the idea. We slept better every night because we had Bob on our team.

But most of all we have our families to thank for letting us miss violin recitals and soccer games and countless other responsibilities to first report and research and then write and finish this project. Week in and week out for more than two years, Demetra, Waits, Niko, Charlotte, Luke, Galen, and Jake were the most helpful—and inspiring—of all.

With love and gratitude, we dedicate this book to them.

A Note on Sources

There have been dozens of biographies of Billy Graham, and he has written twenty-five books himself, many of which sold millions of copies. He is among the most interviewed people who has ever lived, a measure both of his popularity and his presence on the public stage for more than half a century. The Billy Graham Center at Wheaton College contains extensive records of his crusades. There is, in other words, a wealth of sources for anyone interested in tracing the course of his public life.

Of the biographies, William Martin's 1991 *A Prophet with Honor* remains the authoritative account. Exhaustively researched and reflecting hours of interviews with Graham, it is essential reading for anyone wanting a full account of the evangelist's life and ministry. Martin's *With God on Our Side*, the companion book to the PBS series, is equally useful as an account of Graham's place in the history of the religious right.

Among the first of the biographies was Stanley High's *Billy Graham: The Personal Story of the Man, His Message and His Mission*, published in 1956. High was the son of a minister and studied theology himself, before becoming a respected journalist and sometime speechwriter for Eisenhower; he was essentially charged by his publisher with determining whether Graham was for real, and his fascination with and admiration for his subject yield an account that is both skeptical and fair. William McLoughlin's 1960 *Billy Graham: Revivalist in a Secular Age* contains both sharper edges and insights, as did Noel Houston's long two-part profile of Graham in *Holiday* in 1958. John Pollock wrote an authorized biography, first in 1966 and then with various expanded and updated editions, including *Evangelist to the World* in 1979. That year also saw the publication of Marshall Frady's *Billy Graham: A Parable of American Righteousness*, which captured Graham as he was in recovery from his journey through the wilderness of the Nixon White House.

Graham's own memoir, *Just As I Am*, which became an instant best-seller when it was published in 1997, includes a chapter on every one of the presidents, and some candid reflections on the lessons he learned. Ruth Graham had the great good fortune of being rendered in print by her "adopted" daughter and later novelist Patricia Cornwell, who wrote *A Time for Remembering: The Ruth Bell Graham Story* in 1983.

David Frost conducted multiple interviews with Graham over several decades, and they provide real-time insight into his thinking about religion and politics as he wrestled with the proper contours of his role. Many are excerpted in *Billy Graham: Personal Thoughts of a Public Man*.

As for the other side of these relationships, we relied on presidential diaries and memoirs, and an all-star faculty of the great modern presidential historians: David McCullough, Robert Dallek, Robert Caro, Lou Cannon, Doris Kearns Goodwin, Stephen Ambrose, Richard Reeves, John Harris, and Michael Beschloss. Theodore H. White's *Making of the President* accounts of the campaigns of 1960 through 1972 were essential reminders of what those races felt like in real time. The presidential libraries each contain the correspondence between Graham and the presidents: many of these letters are formal, even perfunctory, especially during the early stages of the acquaintance. But there is typically a moment in each presidency when the tone changes, when Reverend Graham becomes Billy, when the correspondence feels less like a formality and more like a confidential memo—particularly some of the Nixon correspondence, which includes a letter of campaign political advice in the summer of 1960 and ends with the request that Nixon destroy it after he reads it. Then there are internal memos that talk about Graham's political activity, and their handwritten marginalia (as when Johnson was warned in 1968 that Graham might endorse Nixon, and scribbled back, "I can't control him").

It is even easy to listen online to Graham and Johnson chatting with each other on the phone, thanks to the Miller Center at the University of Virginia.

The following abbreviations are commonly used in the endnotes:

BG: Billy Graham
BGEA: Billy Graham Evangelistic Association
HST: Harry S. Truman
HSTL: Truman Library
DDE: Dwight D. Eisenhower

DDEL: Eisenhower Library
JFK: John F. Kennedy
JFKLA: Kennedy Library archives
LBJ: Lyndon B. Johnson
LBJLM: Johnson Library and Museum
WHCF: White House Central Files
RN: Richard Nixon
NPM: Nixon Presidential Materials
RNLB: Richard Nixon Library and Birthplace
HRH: H. R. Haldeman
HK: Henry Kissinger
JC: Jimmy Carter
JCL: Jimmy Carter Library
GF: Gerald Ford
GFL: Gerald Ford Library
RR: Ronald Reagan
RRL: Ronald Reagan Library
GHWB: George Herbert Walker Bush
GHWBL: George H. W. Bush Library
BC: Bill Clinton
HRC: Hillary R. Clinton
GWB: George W. Bush
PWH: *A Prophet with Honor*
JAIA: *Just As I Am*
MOP: *Making of the President*

Notes

INTRODUCTION: THE LIONS AND THE LAMB

vii. **"I have often gone on a three- or six-month crusade"** John Pollock, *Billy Graham: Evangelist to the World* (Minneapolis: World Wide Publications, 1979), p. 147.

x. **"I don't give advice"** Richard N. Ostling, "Graham Says NYC Revival Probably His Last," AP, June 16, 2005.

xii. **"I don't think presidents need anything"** BC, interview, April 23, 2007.

xii. **"I knew that they had burdens"** BG, interview, January 17, 2006.

xii. **"Every president needs some people"** *Christianity Today*, January 4, 1974.

xiii. **"build a wall of prayer around him"** David Frost, *Billy Graham: Personal Thoughts of a Public Man* (Colorado Springs, CO: Victor Books, 1997), p. 106.

xiii. **"I follow political trends carefully"** BG to HST, July 31, 1950, HSTL.

xiv. **"If I had not been a friend of the presidents"** BG, interview, January 18, 2006.

xiv. **"this was a way that God used me"** Frost, *Personal Thoughts*, p. 54.

xiv. **"into my own spiritual life"** BG, interview, January 19, 2006.

1: THE INVOCATION

1. **"I didn't have any other motives"** BG, interview, January 17, 2006.

1. **"The Boss says don't go away"** "A Little Something," *Time*, October 3, 1949.

1. **"the news hit the nation"** "The Thunderclap," *Time*, October 3, 1949.

2. **"this terrible job"** "The Terrible Job," *Time*, September 5, 1949.

2. **"more trouble than Pandora"** HST, letter to Nellie and Ethel Noland, September 8, 1949, quoted in David McCullough, *Truman* (New York: Simon and Schuster, 1992), p. 750.

2. **Charles Templeton** This account comes from Templeton's online memoir, *Inside Evangelism: Touring with Youth for Christ and Billy Graham*, www.templetons.com/charles/memoir/.

3. **rancous Youth for Christ rallies** "Youth for Christ," *Time*, February 4, 1946.

3. **"Christ's great commandment"** William Martin, *A Prophet with Honor: The Billy Graham Story* (New York: William Morrow, 1991), p. 111.

3. **"We are tired of religious revivals"** William G. McLoughlin Jr., *Billy Graham: Revivalist in a Secular Age* (New York: Ronald Press, 1960), p. 3.

4. **"Billy, you're fifty years out of date"** Billy Graham, *Just As I Am: The Autobiography of Billy Graham* (New York: HarperCollins, 1997), p. 138.

4. **"It was not too late to be a dairy farmer"** Ibid., p. 139.

4. **"Father, I am going to accept this"** Ibid., p. 139. There are many versions of this story, but the memoir seems most authoritative.

5. **"tall, slender, handsome"** Fact Sheet by Lloyd Doctor, Christ for Greater Los Angeles, November 21, 1949.

5. **no one wrote a word** *JAIA*, p. 143.

5. **"Russia has now exploded an atomic bomb"** McLoughlin, *Revivalist in a Secular Age*, p. 47.

5. **"Do you know that the Fifth Columnists"** Ibid., p. 48.

6. **had attended a crusade in disguise** *JAIA*, p. 150.

6. **"Thousands Hit Sawdust Trail"** *New York Sun*, November 2, 1949.

7. **"its foundation in the Bible"** Martin, *PWH*, p. 115.

7. **"Billy, you can't compete with us"** *JAIA*, p. 154.

7. **the dimensions of heaven** Martin, *PWH*, p. 126; see also "Heaven, Hell and Judgment Day," *Time*, March 20, 1950.

7. **"What I said was being quoted"** Marshall Frady, *Billy Graham: A Parable of American Righteousness* (Boston: Little, Brown, 1979), p. 204.

7. **"spend ourselves into a depression"** Martin, *PWH*, p. 128.

8. **"Keep prayin', fellas!"** Templeton online memoir.

9. **"There's a young fellow down here"** BG to Roy Rowan, unpublished transcript from "A Candid Talk with Crusader Billy Graham," *People*, November 26, 1975.

9. **"earnest, discouraged by lack of success"** William Howland memo, March 14, 1950.

9. **"I've been with statesmen, presidents, and kings"** McLoughlin, *Revivalist in a Secular Age*, p. 56.

9. **he feared that God would disapprove of him** Pollock, *Billy Graham: The Authorized Biography* (New York: McGraw-Hill, 1966), p. 71.

10. **"I think he was trying to pull me out"** Rowan, *People* transcript, November 26, 1975.

10. **"admirers of glib, arm-flailing Evangelist Dr. Billy Graham"** "The Whiskey Rebellion," *Time*, February 20, 1950.

10. **"hawk-nosed, handsome Evangelist"** "Heaven, Hell and Judgment Day," *Time*, March 20, 1950.

10. **"The Lord is working on our behalf"** BG to Henry Luce, March 31, 1950, Luce archives. Graham Letters 1950–1960, used by permission, all rights reserved.

2: HARRY AND BILLY

11. **"I know that I didn't have any fear"** BG, interview, January 18, 2006.

11. **a complete set of Mark Twain** McCullough, *Truman*, p. 83.

12. **"you'll never be a preacher"** Stanley High, *Billy Graham: The Personal Story of the Man, His Message and His Mission* (New York: McGraw-Hill, 1956), p. 103.

12. **"Sincerity is the biggest part of selling anything"** Ibid., p. 108.

12. **preached his first sermon** Noel Houston, "Billy Graham," *Holiday*, February 1958, p. 138.

12. **"I left his office disillusioned and dejected"** *JAIA*, p. 41.

13. **brought their campaigns to the farm belt** "Strategy Is Seen in Iowa Campaign," *New York Times*, September 12, 1948.

13. **"I'm going to give 'em hell"** "Truman Off on Western Trip Promising He'll 'Fight Hard,'" *New York Times*, September 18, 1948.

13. **"gluttons of privilege"** "Calls GOP Cunning," *New York Times*, September 19, 1948.

13. **"'with that message he's going to win!'"** BG, interview, January 18, 2006.

13. **"new unique powerful radio station KTIS"** BG, telegram to HST, February 8, 1949, HSTL.

14. **"God's choice for this great office"** BG to Charlie Ross, February 17, 1949, HSTL.

14. **his moment of ascension to the presidency** McCullough, *Truman*, p. 347; also "The Thirty-Second," *Time*, April 23, 1945.

14. **"I can't understand it"** McCullough, *Truman*, p. 390; also HST diary, May 27, 1945.

14. **He did harbor some suspicions** Merle Miller, *Plain Speaking* (New York: Berkley, 1973), p. 363.

15. **"call America to her knees"** BG, telegram to HST, December 31, 1949, HSTL.

15. **"to get President Truman's ear for thirty minutes"** Martin, *PWH*, p. 131.

16. **"he feared this was the opening of WWIII"** McCullough, *Truman*, p. 775.

16. **"God give you wisdom"** BG to HST, June 26, 1950, HSTL.

17. **the hardest decision of his presidency** McCullough, *Truman*, pp. 782–783.

17. **"It was quite an event for a country boy"** Ibid., p. 215.

17. **"the President was a haberdasher"** *JAIA*, p. xix.

18. **"he was receiving a traveling vaudeville team"** Ibid.

18. **"get a microphone and encourage the people"** "Evangelist Prays with Mr. Truman," *Washington Post*, July 15, 1950.

18. **"I know that I didn't have any fear"** BG, interview, January 18, 2006.

18. **"I am by religion like everything else"** McCullough, *Truman*, p. 83.

19. **"Look at little Truman now"** *Time*, April 14, 1946.

19. **"And as he got up"** "Evangelist Prays with Mr. Truman," *Washington Post*, July 15, 1950.

19. **"do it Lord"** Pollock, *Authorized Biography*, p. 77.

20. **"nobody had briefed me"** Rowan, *People* transcript, November 26, 1975.

20. **"very gracious, very humble"** "Evangelist Prays with Mr. Truman," *Washington Post*, July 15, 1950.

20. **"I just prayed to the Lord, and asked God to give him wisdom"** "President and Evangelist Pray in the White House," *New York Times*, July 15, 1950.

20. **"I prayed, a real prayer"** BG, interview, January 18, 2006.

20. **"National coverage . . . was definitely not to our advantage"** *JAIA*, p. xxi.

20. **"he's one of those counterfeits"** Miller, *Plain Speaking*, p. 363.

20. **"that I might proudly display in my office"** BG to Matthew Connelly, July 18, 1950, HSTL.

21. **"It is my privilege to speak"** BG to HST, July 31, 1950, HSTL.

3: TRUMAN'S REJECTION

22. **"I became strongly anticommunist"** BG, interview, January 18, 2006.

22. **"complete trust and confidence"** BG to HST, November 29, 1950, HSTL.

22–23. **"in your 'Emergency Address' you mention him with approval"** Edward Lindley to HST, December 14, 1950, HSTL.

23. **"Wouldn't it be good if they would hold a little prayer meeting"** Howland memo, December 7, 1950.

23. **"we are breaking apart from the inside"** McLoughlin, *Revivalist in a Secular Age*, p. 110.

23. **"We shall keep you abreast of fast-moving events"** Frady, *Parable of American Righteousness*, p. 225.

24. **"I even had a teletype machine in our house"** *JAIA*, p. 180.

24. **"The vultures are now encircling"** McLoughlin, *Revivalist in a Secular Age*, p. 108.

24. **"over 1100 social sounding organizations"** *Hour of Decision*, July 1953, quoted in McLoughlin, *Revivalist in a Secular Age*, p. 112.

24. **"While nobody likes a watchdog"** Ibid., p. 111.

24. **"I became strongly anticommunist"** BG, interview, January 18, 2006.

24. **"My job was preaching the gospel"** Ibid.

24. **"I fired him because he didn't respect"** Miller, *Plain Speaking*, p. 287.

25. **"He is one of the greatest Americans of all time"** Frady, *Parable of American Righteousness*, p. 253.

25. **"this twilight war"** McLoughlin, *Revivalist in a Secular Age*, p. 115.

25. **"some in Washington decided"** Ibid., pp. 115–116.

26. **"recent unpleasant headlines"** BG to HST, December 23, 1951. Graham also sent a telegram from Minneapolis, in which he had a proposal for saving U.S. pilots captured in Korea, and handling North Korean prisoners captured by the U.S. "Let's raise money to free our fliers held captive by public subscription," he wrote. "It would do more than anything I know to impress the seriousness of the present crisis on the American people. It would help unite us behind the defense program." [BG to HST, December 24, 1951, HSTL.]

27. **"The President does not want it repeated"** William Hassett to Connelly, December 28, 1951, HSTL.

27. **"In church there is no color line"** Richard Oulahan memo, January 11, 1952.

27. **"You're certainly rockin' the old capital"** "Rockin' the Capitol," *Time*, March 3, 1952.

27. **"the president will go down in history"** Memo for Connelly, January 31, 1952, HSTL.

27. **"Lead our people back to God"** Mary Schmit to HST, January 7, 1952, HSTL.

27. **"This country needs a revival"** Pollock, *Authorized Biography*, p. 93.

28. **"If I would run for president of the United States"** AP, in *New York Times*, February 4, 1952.

28. **"I believe we are missing a great opportunity"** Frank Boykin to Connelly, February 13, 1952, HSTL.

28. **"There's an absolute change in the cloakrooms"** Oulahan memo, February 22, 1952.

28. **"Once I spoke at a luncheon meeting in the Washington Hotel"** Ibid.

29. **"I want to give them the moral side of the thing"** "Rockin' the Capitol," *Time*, March 3, 1952.

29. **"I believe we can hold the balance of power"** Martin, *PWH*, p. 146.

29. **"I guess he was just too busy or something"** Oulahan memo, February 22, 1952.

29. **"I did not know how to conduct myself"** *JAIA*, p. 164.

29. **"history is beginning to show him now as a great president"** BG, interview, January 18, 2006.

30. **"I knew you hadn't been briefed"** Ibid.

4: CHRISTIAN SOLDIER

31. **"I didn't even know if he was a Democrat or a Republican"** BG, interview, January 18, 2006.

31–32. **he congratulated Graham on his efforts** DDE to BG, November 8, 1951, DDEL.

32. **"That was the damnedest letter"** *JAIA*, p. 189.

33. **"He was not a hypocrite"** William Ewald, interview, January 6, 2006.

33. **"I ask you this one question"** "Homecoming," *Time*, June 16, 1952.

34. **"he knew I had come all the way to see him"** BG, interview, January 18, 2006.

34. **"what you stand for is my mother's faith"** Rowan, *People* transcript, November 26, 1975.

34. **a mother whose faith rejected much of what her son stood for** In its April 7, 1952, issue, *Time*'s "Eisenhower: A Factual Sketch" identified Ida as a Jehovah's Witness. Among Ike's interests, he was described as "religious, but not a churchgoer."

34. **serious adult Bible study** Dwight D. Eisenhower, *At Ease* (New York: Doubleday, 1967), p. 305.

34. **"if each person were individually good"** Bela Kornitzer, *The Story of the Five Eisenhower Brothers* (New York: Farrar, Straus and Cudahy, 1955), p. 278.

35. **"the most honest and sincere pacifist I ever knew"** Eisenhower, *At Ease*, p. 106.

35. **"our dear old Mother likes to go to conventions"** DDE to Arthur Eisenhower, May 18, 1943, DDEL.

35. **Eisenhower as an "anti Christian Cultist"** Ralph Lord Roy, *Apostles of Discord* (Boston: Beacon, 1953), p. 20.

35. **"He used a lot of army language"** BG, interview, January 18, 2006.

35. **"solutions must be firmly based in spiritual and moral values"** DDE to Drew Pearson, March 27, 1952, DDEL.

35. **they had not talked politics at all** "Preacher Visits Eisenhower," *New York Herald Tribune*, March 26, 1952.

36. **"'Why do you go and talk to all these political leaders?'"** Sermon "The Holy Spirit and Revival in Our Time," preached to the National Association of Evangelicals convention in Chicago, 1952. From C. T. Cook, *The Billy Graham Story* (Wheaton, IL: Van Kampen Press, 1954), p. 100.

36. **"there's going to be the Jewish bloc"** Ibid.

36. **"The people are hungry for a moral crusade"** Ibid.

37. **"He appealed not to the mind but to the heart"** James Reston, "Eisenhower Opens 'Crusade' Amid His Boyhood Scenes," *New York Times*, June 5, 1952.

37. **"He [Carlson] thought I'd be a good speechwriter"** BG, interview, January 18, 2006.

37. **he wouldn't be getting tangled in partisan battles** *JAIA*, p. 191.

37. **"I hope to bring a message of militant faith"** "Plans 'Message of Faith,'" *New York Times*, July 15, 1952.

38. **"I will not hesitate to step to the forefront"** "Parties Are Warned by Billy Graham," *Washington Post*, July 10, 1952.

38. **"You have won so many people in this country"** Pollock, *The Billy Graham Story* (Grand Rapids, MI: Zondervan, 2003), p. 94.

38. **"Since all pastors must"** DDE to Arthur Langlie, August 11, 1952, DDEL.

39. **"I'm going to join a church"** BG, "Billy Graham's Own Story," *McCall's*, June 1964, p. 64.

39. **"I think a Bible should be read"** "The New Evangelist," *Time*, October 25, 1954, p. 54.

39. **Graham had marked up the margins** Frost, *Personal Thoughts*, p. 101.

39. **The Republican platform** From the American Presidency Project, University of California at Santa Barbara.

39. **"Faith in God and Country; that's Eisenhower"** William Lee Miller, *Piety Along the Potomac* (Boston: Houghton Mifflin, 1964), p. 19.

39. **"President who has the fortitude and moral courage"** McLoughlin, *Revivalist in a Secular Age*, p. 117.

40. **"voted to go into the Korean War?"** Ibid., p. 114.

40. **"I was not averse to publicly criticizing the U.S. State Department"** *JAIA*, p. 189.

40. **"survey of churchmen"** October 25, 1952.

40. **"Thanks again for backing Ike"** BG to Luce, November 20, 1952.

5: One Nation, Under God

41. **"I didn't feel that I could answer his question"** BG, interview, January 18, 2006.

41. **he painted a portrait** "Prayer for Peace by President," *New York Times*, December 25, 1953.

41. **"I have been recently studying"** BG to DDE, November 18, 1959, DDEL.

42. **"Either Communism must die, or Christianity must die"** Thomas Aiello, "Constructing 'Godless Communism': Religion, Politics, and Popular Culture, 1954–1960," in *Americana: The Journal of American Popular Culture, 1900 to the Present* 4:1 (Spring 2005), quoting *American Mercury*, August 1954, pp. 41–46.

42. **"Our forefathers proved"** "Eisenhower: 'The Miracle of America' Lies in Faith Fostered in Our Homes," *New York Times*, September 15, 1952.

42. **"inspire the American people"** Pollock, *Authorized Biography*, p. 96.

42. **"nowhere was there any representation"** "'God's Float' Will Lead the Inaugural Parade," *New York Times*, January 19, 1953.

42. **"Standing for all religions, it had symbols of none"** William Lee Miller, *Piety Along the Potomac*, p. 43.

43. **"I don't believe God cared what words Dwight used"** Kornitzer, *Story of the Five Eisenhower Brothers*, p. 308.

43. **"Please do not give that newspaper account another thought"** *JAIA*, p. 199.

43. **"we were scarcely home"** Robert H. Ferrell, ed., *The Eisenhower Diaries* (New York: W. W. Norton, 1981), February 1, 1953, p. 226.

43. **"we forgot the prayer!"** Ewald, interview, January 6, 2006.

44. **Foundation for Religious Action** "Three Faiths Will Join in Capital Parley," *New York Times*, November 11, 1954.

44. **"To see the President of the United States kneeling in prayer"** "Young Delinquents Billy's '56 Targets," *Charlotte Observer*, August 5, 1955.

44. **"a deeply felt religious faith, and I don't care what it is"** "President-Elect Says Soviet Demoted Zhukov Because of Their Friendship," *New York Times*, December 23, 1952. The rest of the quote reads, "With us of course it is the Judeo-Christian concept but it

must be a religion that all men are created equal. So what was the use of me talking to Zhukov about that? Religion, he had been taught, was the opiate of the people."

44. **"a very fervent believer in a very vague religion"** William Lee Miller, *Piety Along the Potomac*, p. 34.

44. **"the greatest demonstration of the religious character"** Ibid., p. 42.

44. **"the shortsightedness bordering on tragic stupidity"** Ferrell, ed., *The Eisenhower Diaries*, July 2, 1953, pp. 244–245.

45. **"Ours is a religious nation"** Kornitzer, *Story of the Five Eisenhower Brothers*, p. 137.

45. **"We are no longer going to be pushed around"** McLoughlin, *Revivalist in a Secular Age*, p. 117, from *Hour of Decision*, February 8, 1953.

45. **"Your interest in spiritual matters has helped tremendously"** BG to DDE, June 29, 1953, DDEL.

45. **"God is interested in the quality of converts"** Andrew S. Finstuen, "The Prophet and the Evangelist," *Christianity Today*, July/August 2006.

46. **"there has been a great increase in interest in religion"** Luce to Andre Laguerre, February 23, 1954, Henry Luce archives.

47. **Earl Warren led a prayer rally** Martin, *PWH*, p. 174.

47. **"Silly Billy"** Pollock, *Authorized Biography*, p. 118.

47. **"WHO WOULD WEAR THIS TIE???"** Dorothy Kilgallen, "Revival Altered Billy's Life, Dorothy Reveals," *New York Journal-American*, May 18, 1957, p. 4.

47. **"You'd think it was the Queen!"** "Billy's Britain," *Time*, March 8, 1954.

47–48. **"I have been praying a great deal for you"** BG to DDE, May 10, 1954, DDEL.

48. **"We live and learn"** High, *Billy Graham*, p. 184.

48. **"I am a man without hope"** *JAIA*, p. 236.

49. **"most talked-about Christian leader in the world"** "The New Evangelist," *Time*, October 25, 1954.

49. **"the only living American to whom Europeans seem willing to listen"** "Billy Emerging As No. 1 Enemy of Reds in Europe," *Chicago Daily News*, June 11, 1955.

49. **"if you will include the fire and the lightning"** High, *Billy Graham*, p. 53.

49. **"Mr. DeMille told me afterward"** Frady, *Parable of American Righteousness*, p. 271.

49–50. **"Billy Graham is different"** "The New Evangelist," *Time*, October 25, 1954.

50. **"Billy believes in going first class"** John Corry, "God, Country, and Billy Graham," *Harper's*, February 1969, p. 34.

50. **he was photographed more than Marilyn Monroe** "Sidelights, 10 Most Active Subjects," *New York Times*, March 24, 1956.

51. **"Isn't it a shame that he isn't in politics?"** High, *Billy Graham*, p. 19.

51. **"I'll keep him humble"** Pollock, *Authorized Biography*, p. 78.

51. **"restore intellectual respectability"** *JAIA*, p. 286.

51. **"Conservative Christians had failed"** Ibid., p. 291.

52. **his farm in Gettysburg** BG, interview, January 18, 2006.

53. **"not by anything we can do for ourselves"** *JAIA*, p. 204, and BG, interview, January 18, 2006.

53. **"I didn't feel that I could answer his question"** BG, interview, January 18, 2006.

53. **"you and Mrs. Eisenhower have paid a tremendous personal price"** BG to DDE, August 19, 1955, DDEL.

53. **"you are a better president from a sick bed"** BG to DDE, November 16, 1955, DDEL.

53. **"He just could not take it"** "The Return of Confidence," *Time*, July 4, 1955.

6: THE MAN WHO WAS GOING PLACES

54. **"Oh, I thought he was easy to know"** BG, interview, January 18, 2006.

54. **"There are few men whom I have loved as I love you"** BG to RN, 1962, pre-presidential papers of Richard Nixon, from RNLB, Yorba Linda, CA, November 11, 1962. All other Nixon correspondence prior to 1968 comes from this collection.

55. **"There's young Nixon"** BG, interview, January 18, 2006.

55. **"Keep your eyes on that young man"** From unpublished *Life* article, October 1960, RNLB.

55. **"And that was the beginning"** BG, interview, January 18, 2006.

55. **Graham himself called it "bittersweet"** *JAIA*, p. 462.

55. **"When Nixon's public and private personalities meet"** Stephen E. Ambrose, *Nixon: The Education of a Politician* (New York: Simon and Schuster, 1987), pp. 483–484.

56. **"the most calculating man I ever knew"** Christopher Matthews, *Kennedy and Nixon: The Rivalry That Shaped Postwar America* (New York: Simon and Schuster, 1996), p. 58.

56. **"the match was fixed"** Ambrose, *Nixon*, pp. 483–484.

56. **"His mind doesn't reach for political gimmicks"** Unpublished *Life* article, October 1960, RNLB.

56. **"Mr. Nixon is probably the best trained man"** "Billy Graham Says Nixon Well Trained," UPI, in *Charlotte Observer*, October 15, 1959.

56. **"He has been extremely reticent to speak out"** Charles P. Henderson, *The Nixon Theology* (New York: Harper and Row, 1972), p. 62.

56. **"You have gone far"** Richard Nixon, *The Memoirs of Richard Nixon* (New York: Grosset and Dunlap, 1978), p. 117.

57. **"the warfare of politics"** Nixon, *Six Crises* (New York: Simon and Schuster, 1962), p. 295.

57. **"other Quakers understand my son"** "A Worshiper in the White House," *Time*, December 6, 1968.

57. **went into a closet to say her prayers** Nixon, *Memoirs*, p. 8.

57. **Eisenhower urged him to work God into his speeches** Ibid., p. 14.

57. **"I tried to follow my mother's example"** Ibid., p. 6.

57. **he had made his commitment to Christ** Ambrose, *Nixon*, p. 41.

58. **"the modern world will find a real resurrection"** Nixon, *Memoirs*, p. 16.

58. **their passionate anticommunism** Nixon passed along to Graham some gossip from FBI director J. Edgar Hoover's monitoring of communist groups; they were noting Nixon's growing support in the churches and how he was benefiting from "his use of the propaganda machine built up by Billy Graham, the evangelist." RN to BG, August 7, 1958. Graham wrote back to thank him for sharing "the 'gossip' that is going the rounds in communist circles. I am honored to be identified with you in their ridicule." BG to RN, August 27, 1958, RNLB.

58. **"He has the rare gift"** Unpublished *Life* article, October 1960, RNLB.

58. **"who lets the people of the world see what Americans are"** Frady, *Parable of American Righteousness*, p. 439.

58. **"Oh, I thought he was easy to know"** BG, interview, January 18, 2006.

59. **"a far more complex and devious man"** Nixon, *Six Crises*, p. 161.

59. **"The President is a man of integrity"** Ambrose, *Nixon*, p. 564.

59. **"a week with Nixon fishing"** Ibid., p. 350.

59. **"a sponge"** Ibid., p. 618.

59. **"He just enjoyed the man"** Herb Klein, interview, January 31, 2006.

60. **"the most critical of your entire career"** BG to RN, October 8, 1955, RNLB.

60. **"seems to be a little fearful that you may be taken over"** Ibid. Graham shrewdly observed that he and Nixon were losing their trademark issue: the fear of Soviet aggression that lay beneath the political and revivalist currents of the decade. There is "so much goodwill bubbling out of Moscow that the issue of Communism is no longer as potent as it was politically in the US," Graham observed. "This, however, makes the political dilemma in America extremely critical, particularly for a man like you with strong convictions." He promised, however, to use his influence to show people that Nixon was a man of "moral integrity and Christian principle."

60. **"your political advice was right on the beam"** RN to BG, November 7, 1955, RNLB.

61. **"it is time that you move among these men"** BG to RN, June 4, 1956, RNLB.

61. **"From the opening crack of the gavel"** *Newsweek*, quoted in Nixon, *Memoirs*, p. 178.

62. "it would be best not only for our country" Ambrose, *Nixon*, pp. 406–407.

62. "some of the possibilities we talked about" BG to RN, November 10, 1956, RNLB.

7: AMBASSADOR AT LARGE

63. "I met all the [British] prime ministers" BG, interview, January 17, 2006.

63. a press conference in the spring of 1956 *New York Times*, March 22, 1956, p. 20.

64. "This was a long speech" John Steele memo, March 23, 1956.

64. "I'll be glad to see him any time" Oral History interview with Robert Gray by Ed Edwin, Columbia University Oral History project, DDEL.

65. "no American . . . has made so many friends for America" High, *Billy Graham*, p. 216.

65. a distinctive white train *JAIA*, p. 274.

65. "do more to demonstrate the friendliness of the Americans" McLoughlin, *Revivalist in a Secular Age*, p. 119, quoting *Christian Life*, April 1956.

65. "It is wretched politics and impossible Christianity" "Whose Ambassador," *Christian Century*, February 29, 1956.

65. to help arrange Graham's meeting with Nehru RN to Ambassador John Sherman Cooper, January 20, 1956, RNLB.

65. wrote to the Australian ambassador RN to Ambassador William J. Sebald, April 3, 1958, RNLB.

66. "Dr. Graham has made a very favorable impression" RN, memo to Ambassador Raymond Hare, April 23, 1959, RNLB.

66. "we could have another civil war" Ambrose, *Eisenhower: The President, Vol. II* (New York: Simon and Schuster, 1984), p. 308.

66. "He was not a racist" Ewald, interview, January 6, 2006.

66. "The Church should have been the pace setter" Cook, *The Billy Graham Story*, p. 88.

67. "Either these ropes stay down" Frady, *Parable of American Righteousness*, p. 408.

67. and you are following the shape of the cross High, *Billy Graham*, p. 61.

67. "I believe the Lord is helping us" BG to DDE, June 4, 1956, DDEL.

67. "maybe if you and Billy talked . . ." Boykin, letter to DDE, March 19, 1956, DDEL.

67–68. "What you say about Billy Graham interests me" DDE to Boykin, March 20, 1956, DDEL.

68. "matters we discussed" DDE to BG, March 22, 1956, DDEL.

69. "let the Democratic party bear the brunt of the debate" BG to DDE, March 27, 1956, DDEL.

69. The "foolish extremists" on both sides . . . "will never be won over" DDE, letter to BG, March 20, 1956, DDEL.

69. "I would like to caution you about getting involved" BG to DDE, June 4, 1956, DDEL.

70. "I shall do all in my power" BG to DDE, August 24, 1956, DDEL.

70. "I did write a brief note to each" "Billy Graham Says He Didn't Help on Keynotes," *New York Post*, August 22, 1956.

70. "I really can't compete" DDE to BG, August 29, 1956, DDEL.

70. "we might want to call on him for a little help" DDE to Leonard Hall, September 3, 1956.

71. "all thinking southerners" were appalled George Dugan, "Arkansas Events Disturb Graham," *New York Times*, September 25, 1957.

71. the White Citizens Council warned *JAIA*, p. 202.

71. "racial mixing has done much harm" Frady, *Parable of American Righteousness*, p. 409.

71. "God pity us [Christians]" McLoughlin, *Revivalist in a Secular Age*, p. 92, quoting *Charlotte Observer*, October 27, 1958.

71. "I have not come to make any inflammatory statements" Ibid., quoting *Arkansas Gazette*, September 13, 1959.

72. headhunters in Assam Murray Kempton, "Preparation of the Tabernacle," *New York Post*, May 14, 1957.

72. **the biggest "full-chorus"** "Billy in New York," *Time*, May 20, 1957.

72. **more than half . . . population of eight million was unaffiliated** "Billy v. New York," *Time*, February 11, 1957.

73. **"Our New York Campaign has been challenged by some extremists"** *Christian Beacon*, April 4, 1957.

73. **"God almighty wanted him"** Charles Wickenberg memo, August 14, 1954.

73. **Students at Bob Jones University were forbidden to pray for the crusade's success** Pollock, *Authorized Biography*, p. 174.

73. **"If by fundamentalist you mean 'narrow,' 'bigoted'"** *Look*, February 5, 1956, quoted in McLoughlin, *Revivalist in a Secular Age*, p. 70.

73. **"But I'm inclined to think the Almighty does"** High, *Billy Graham*, p. 100.

73. **The editors of the *Christian Century*** "Billy in New York," *Time*, May 20, 1957.

74. **"he could indirectly endorse what we were doing"** *JAIA*, p. 307.

74. **"setting an example of Christian love"** "As Billy Graham Sees His Role," *New York Times*, April 21, 1957.

74. **"one of the high points of my life"** Clayborne Carson et al., ed., *The Papers of Martin Luther King, Jr., Vol. IV, Symbol of the Movement: January 1957–December 1958* (Berkeley: University of California Press, 2000), p. 264.

75. **Said Jackie, "No comment"** "Great Medium for Messages," *Time*, June 17, 1957.

75. **1,941,200 people attended** "Crusade's Impact," *Time*, July 8, 1957.

75. **it would be politically dangerous to endorse "any religious promoter"** Henderson, *The Nixon Theology*, pp. 109–110.

75. **"most courageous spiritual ventures"** Ibid., pp. 106–107.

76. **"God will not share his glory with another"** Ibid., pp. 108–109.

76. **"He asked me to go see Nixon for him"** BG, interview, January 18, 2006.

76. **"'there's an old doughboy here'"** Ibid.

8: The Holy War

77. **"I did give political advice"** BG, interview, January 18, 2006.

78. **"only one way I can visualize religion being a legitimate issue"** Henderson, *The Nixon Theology*, p. 135.

78. **He was "casual about religious rituals"** Thurston Clarke, *Ask Not: The Inauguration of John F. Kennedy and the Speech That Changed America* (New York: Henry Holt, 2005), p. 63.

78. **"He made it a point to attend mass"** Theodore Sorensen, interview, July 20, 2006.

79. **Graham . . . remembers everyone celebrating** *JAIA*, p. 390.

79. **"Senator Kennedy is getting a fantastic buildup"** BG to RN, December 2, 1957, RNLB.

79. **"I have taken my stand"** BG to RN, November 19, 1959.

80. **"perfectly rational" for Protestants to oppose election of a Catholic** "Political Criticism of Catholic Backed," *New York Times*, February 6, 1960.

80. **"It would be a tragedy"** Houston, *Holiday*, March 1958.

80. **"I am desperately trying to stay out"** BG to Luce, September 16, 1960.

81. **Kennedy was hoping that Graham would consider making a statement** *JAIA*, p. 389.

81. **"The Pope will be running the country"** "Stop Signs," *Time*, April 25, 1960.

81. **Sorensen had quietly drafted a letter** Sorensen, interview, July 20, 2006.

81. **"an implied political endorsement"** *JAIA*, p. 389.

81. **urged Catholics to stay away** "Don't Be Half-Saved," *Time*, May 6, 1957.

82. **"We regarded Graham as a conservative"** Sorensen, interview, July 20, 2006.

82. **"unjust to discount any one of them"** Sorensen, *Kennedy* (New York: Harper and Row, 1965), p. 144.

82. **a $1,000 contribution from his father** Matthews, *Kennedy and Nixon*, p. 70.

82. **"We may be living at the end of history"** "Graham Deplores Crisis at Summit," *New York Times*, May 18, 1960.

83. **The convention unanimously adopted a resolution** "Baptists Question Vote for a Catholic," *New York Times*, May 21, 1960.

83. **"an implied, though unmistakable, endorsement"** Ibid.

83. **"But I'm not taking sides"** "Billy Graham Gives Implied Nod to Nixon for President," *Charlotte Observer*, May 21, 1960.

83. **"he had made up his mind to come out for you"** Hall to RN, May 23, 1960, RNLB.

83. **"I think this strategy carries greater strength"** BG to RN, May 27, 1960, RNLB.

84. **"you handled the subject with great skill"** RN to BG, June 4, 1960, RNLB.

84. **"a politically explosive town"** Anne Chamberlin memo, June 24, 1960.

84. **"Johnson invited me to his office"** BG to RN, June 21, 1960, RNLB.

85. **"This is not true"** LBJ Library Famous Names, BG to LBJ, August 8, 1960, LBJLM.

85. **"you could tip the scales"** BG to DDE, August 4, 1960, in Richard Pierard, "Billy Graham and the U.S. Presidency," *Journal of Church and State* 22 (Winter 1980), p. 120.

9: "I Am *for You*"

86. **"I wasn't necessarily involved"** BG, interview, January 18, 2006.

86. **"you will have my wholehearted support"** BG to JFK, from Pollock, *Authorized Biography*, pp. 218–219.

86. **"a highly financed and organized office is being opened"** BG to RN, August 22, 1960.

87. **Peale's church received more new members** "Crusade Adds 22 to Church's Rolls," *New York Times*, June 24, 1957.

87. **He was planning to come out squarely for Nixon** Carol V. R. George, *God's Salesman: Norman Vincent Peale and the Power of Positive Thinking* (New York: Oxford University Press, 1993), p. 198.

87. **"I informed them of your reticence"** BG to RN, August 22, 1960.

88. **"This completely avoids . . . religious prejudice"** RN to BG, August 29, 1960.

88. **"A man's religion cannot be separated"** Reuters, August 20, 1960.

89. **Graham had "plunged into politics"** "The Religion Issue," *Time*, August 29, 1960.

89. **"I am withdrawing myself from public involvement"** BG to RN, September 1, 1960.

89. **"a very knowledgeable straight shooter"** Sorensen, interview, July 20, 2006.

90. **"they were not anti-Catholic"** Deborah Hart Strober and Gerald S. Strober, *The Kennedy Presidency: An Oral History of the Era* (Washington: Brassey's, 2003), revised and updated edition of *Let Us Begin Anew: An Oral History of the Kennedy Presidency* (New York: HarperCollins, 1993), p. 41.

90. **"religion is the biggest issue in the South"** "Anti-Catholic View Found Widespread in Parts of South," *New York Times*, September 4, 1960.

90. **"he stands at the front door proclaiming charity"** "Truman Accuses GOP on Bigotry," *New York Times*, September 6, 1960.

90. **"don't believe in voicing prejudice"** "The Power of Negative Thinking," *Time*, September 19, 1960.

90. **"a disastrous political development"** Nixon, *Six Crises*, p. 327.

91. **"I don't know anything about Mr. Kennedy"** "Peale to Head Protestant Forum on Religious Issue in Campaign," *New York Times*, September 4, 1960.

91. **"The antagonism of the Roman church"** "The Power of Negative Thinking," *Time*, September 19, 1960.

91. **"Say one wrong word"** Ibid.

91. **called religion "a major factor"** "Protestant Groups' Statements," *New York Times*, September 8, 1960.

91. **"priests of the empty temple"** *New York Post*, September 9, 1960.

92. **Kennedy accused the group of challenging "my loyalty"** "Senator Says Religious Attacks Impugn His Loyalty As a Citizen," *New York Times*, September 10, 1960.

92. **"What kind of country do these Protestants want?"** "'Protestant Underworld' Cited As Source of Attacks on Kennedy," *New York Times*, September 11, 1960.

92. **Senator Henry Jackson** "Jackson Asks Nixon to Repudiate Peale," *New York Times*, September 13, 1960.

92. **"We can win or lose the election"**   White, *Making of the President 1960* (New York: Atheneum, 1961), p. 311.

93. **"as brilliant a performance as I've ever witnessed"**   Strober and Strober, *The Kennedy Presidency*, p. 45.

94. **"he ate 'em blood raw"**   Matthews, *Kennedy and Nixon*, p. 143.

94. **Peale . . . had been hit by a hurricane**   George, *God's Salesman*, pp. 207–208.

94. **"He had no disagreement with what was said"**   Sorensen, *Kennedy*, p. 189.

94. **"I wasn't necessarily involved"**   BG, interview, January 18, 2006.

94. **Graham . . . apologized to him**   *JAIA*, p. 392.

95. **"I cannot possibly get involved"**   BG to RN, September 24, 1960.

96. **"a hell of a lot of sense"**   RN to Hall, Bob Finch, October 5, 1960.

96. **Kennedy's talk of sacrifice**   BG to RN, June 12, 1961, RNLB.

97. **"you are going to sense supernatural strength"**   BG to RN, October 17, 1960.

98. **"your assiduous labor"**   Carson, ed., *Papers of Martin Luther King, Jr., Vol. IV.*

98. **"He would be a powerful influence"**   BG to RN, August 23, 1960.

99. **"We all have our fathers"**   Sorensen, *Kennedy*, p. 33.

99. **"I've got a suitcase of votes"**   White, *MOP 1960*, p. 387.

99. **"time for all of us to take off our Nixon buttons"**   Matthews, *Kennedy and Nixon*, p. 173.

99. **"a couple of phone calls"**   Frady, *Martin Luther King* (New York: Penguin Putnam, 2002), p. 77.

99. **"might have been avoided"**   Nixon, *Six Crises*, p. 362.

10: The Meaning of *LIFE*

100. **" 'The American people will call you again' "**   BG, interview, January 18, 2006.

100. **"possibly the greatest inward conflict"**   BG to Luce, October 24, 1960.

100. **"I was determined to stay out of politics"**   Unpublished *Life* article, October 1960.

101. **"I'm running it this coming week"**   *JAIA*, p. 392.

101. **Ruth was adamantly opposed**   BG to RN, June 12, 1961.

101. **"It's getting you into politics"**   Pollock, *Authorized Biography*, p. 219.

101. **Kennedy had called to protest**   Memo from William Furth to E. K. Thompson and Luce, October 22, 1960.

102. **"I never thought I'd be voting for a compulsive adulterer"**   William Sloane Coffin, quoting Reinhold Niebuhr in Strober and Strober, *The Kennedy Presidency*, p. 39.

102. **"would have a reverse reaction"**   BG to Luce, October 24, 1960.

102. **"the Lord had intervened"**   BG to RN, June 12, 1961.

103. **"That is bigotry at its worst"**   " 'We Are Electing a President of the World,' " *Life*, November 7, 1960.

103. **"citizens from all walks of life . . . are supporting candidates"**   *Charlotte News*, October 26, 1960.

103. **"some strong convictions"**   *Charlotte Observer*, October 27, 1960.

103. **the band played "Dixie Is No Longer in the Bag"**   "Kennedy, Billy Graham Lunch, Golf," *New York Herald Tribune*, January 17, 1961.

103. **"My appearance in Columbia should not be politically interpreted"**   "Dr. Graham to Aid Nixon Rally," *New York Times*, November 2, 1960.

103. **"my main responsibility is in the spiritual realm"**   *Charlotte News*, October 31, 1960.

103. **"there is great peace and this is all-important"**   BG to Luce, November 28, 1960.

103. **"any number of things could have made the difference"**   Luce to BG, December 9, 1960.

104. **"Probably the best and most effective statement"**   RN to BG, January 15, 1961, RNLB.

104. **"even gone so far as to exercise a veto"**   Nixon, *Six Crises*, p. 365.

105. **"he has said that in every state he's been in"**   Sorensen, interview, July 20, 2006.

105. **Grady Wilson claimed on a radio show**   "Billy Refused Kennedy Plea," *Charlotte Observer*, August 8, 1960.

105. **"television appearance Monday night"** BG to RN, November 2, 1960.
106. **"a campaign of unusual intensity"** Nixon, *Memoirs*, p. 214.
106. **"we would have been the heroes"** Nixon, *Six Crises*, p. 294.
106. **Tricia Nixon gave her Christmas money** Ambrose, *Nixon*, p. 644.
106. **"appreciated the spiritual inspiration"** RN to BG, January 15, 1961.

11: The Fourteen-Carat-Gold Photograph

107. **"I wanted to be used"** BG, interview, January 19, 2006.
107. **"Before we are inundated in weightier matters"** Hugh Sidey memo, January 18, 1961.
107. **"Billy accepted with some hesitation"** HRH, memo to RN, November 23, 1960, RNLB.
108. **"So don't think anything of it"** *JAIA*, p. 393.
108. **"a possible providential opening"** BG to Luce, November 28, 1960.
108. **"I told him he must make you one of his friends"** Rowan, *People* transcript, November 26, 1975.
109. **"it's in all their creeds"** BG, interview, January 18, 2006.
109. **"asked a hundred separate questions"** BG, "God Is My Witness," *McCall's*, June 1964, p. 145.
109. **"I tried to be a healer that night"** Transcript of BG interview with Gary Clifford, *People*, January 31, 1981.
110. **"a hurdle that has been permanently passed"** "Dr. Graham Says Election Aids Church Amity," *New York Times*, January 17, 1961.
110. **"Kennedy recognized him as a powerful influence"** Sorensen, interview, July 20, 1960.
110. **"pure 14-carat gold"** "Catholic View of J.F.K.," *Time*, January 19, 1962.
111. **"I really did not get to know John Kennedy"** James Michael Beam, "I Can't Play God Anymore," *McCall's*, January 1978, quoted in Frost, *Personal Thoughts*, p. 102.
111. **Sidey encountered him in the Oval Office** Sidey, "Beyond Politics, the Reality of Faith," *Life*, August 11, 1967.
111. **"I'll be your John the Baptist"** *JAIA*, p. 398.
111. **"Put the brakes on a little bit"** "Billy Graham Urges Restraint in Sit-ins," *New York Times*, April 18, 1963.
111. **"Negro's great stumbling block"** Martin Luther King Jr., "Letter from Birmingham Jail," April 16, 1963.
112. **"if King loses"** Adam Fairclough, *To Redeem the Soul of America: The Southern Christian Leadership Conference and Martin Luther King Jr.* (Athens: The University of Georgia Press, 1987), p. 136.
112. **"It is an insult to human dignity"** "Billy Graham's Work Sets a Pace in International Harmony," *Charlotte Observer*, August 16, 1963.
112. **"become our conscience"** Pollock, *Authorized Biography*, p. 223.

12: Tragedy and Transition

113. **"He was a very complex man"** BG, interview, January 17, 2006.
113. **"We'll wait for her"** "The Transfer of Power," *Time*, November 29, 1963; also "The Prudent Progressive," *Time*, January 1, 1965.
113. **"no plans showing how long the runways were"** "The Prudent Progressive," *Time*, January 1, 1965.
114. **"the most tragic day in American history"** "Graham Urges Prayer for America, Johnson," UPI, in *Charlotte News*, November 23, 1963.
114. **"Perhaps the American people will be awakened by this tragedy"** " 'I Had a Strong Feeling the President Should Not Go,' " *Charlotte News*, November 23, 1963.
114. **"Your message met the need"** LBJ to BG, December 9, 1963, LBJLM.
114. **"a goddamn raven hovering over his shoulder"** Doris Kearns Goodwin, *Lyndon Johnson and the American Dream* (New York: St. Martin's, 1976), p. 164.

114. ***Candid Camera* had trouble finding people** Robert Dallek, *Flawed Giant: Lyndon Johnson and His Times, 1961–1973* (New York: Oxford University Press, 1998), p. 44.

114. **"whatever happened to Lyndon Johnson?"** "A Different Man," *Time*, November 4, 1964.

114. **"at least his man wasn't murdered"** Dallek, *Flawed Giant*, p. 54.

115. **"Let's see what your cracker president is going to do for you now"** "City Goes Dark," *New York Times*, November 23, 1963.

115. **"The whole thing was almost unbearable"** Goodwin, *Lyndon Johnson*, p. 170.

115. **"I'd like for you to come over to the White House"** "God Is My Witness," *McCall's*, June 1964.

116. **"he will set a tremendous example"** "Graham Calls LBJ U.S. 'Moral Leader,'" *Charlotte News*, December 17, 1963. While Johnson would have heard Graham preside over prayer meetings in Washington during the 1950s, came to the 1952 and 1960 Washington crusades, and would indeed become the first sitting president to attend a crusade in Houston in 1965, it is unlikely that he had at this point attended "many" Graham crusades.

116. **"Pray for me, too"** LBJ to BG, January 3, 1964, LBJLM.

116. **"Graham was using Johnson"** Sorensen, interview, July 20, 2006.

117. **Graham's celebrity** Corry, "God, Country, and Billy Graham," *Harper's*, February 1969.

117. **"a man in transit between epochs"** Martin Marty, "Armageddon or Bust," *New York Times*, September 12, 1965.

118. **"Of all the things to which Kennedy was born"** White, *Making of the President 1964* (New York: Atheneum, 1965), p. 35.

118. **"a very insecure, sensitive man"** Dallek, *Flawed Giant*, p. 10.

118. **"Not many people in this country love me"** Patricia Cornwell, *A Time for Remembering: The Ruth Bell Graham Story* (San Francisco: Harper and Row, 1983), p. 192.

118. **"When I was being called a crook"** Marianne Means, "Pals: President and the Preacher," *New York Journal-American*, November 5, 1965.

118. **"People in power, who are larger than life"** Goodwin, interview, September 26, 2006.

118. **"He'd lie in bed and read the newspapers"** Rowan, *People* transcript, November 26, 1975.

118–119. **"we'd talk over the problems facing the country"** Edward Fiske, "The Closest Thing to a White House Chaplain," *New York Times*, June 8, 1969.

119. **"The decibels of anxiety"** Lucy Johnson, interview, September 12, 2006.

119. **"Billy was a comfort"** Cornwell, *A Time for Remembering*, p. 192.

119. **"do a little thinking of their own"** LBJ, call to BG, November 5, 1964.

119. **their father was rarely home** Robert Caro, *The Years of Lyndon Johnson: Master of the Senate* (New York: Alfred A. Knopf, 2002), pp. 229–231.

119. **"People in public life"** Lucy Johnson, interview, September 12, 2006.

120. **"my children have overcome this"** "He's Getting in Shape for Crusade," *Charlotte Observer*, April 2, 1972.

120. **"a lot of us felt his own sense of vulnerability"** Lucy Johnson, interview, September 12, 2006.

120. **"He could roar like a lion"** BG, interview, January 17, 2006.

120. **"I knew he was not a saint"** *JAIA*, p. 406.

120. **"unique in American political life"** Jack Valenti, interview, June 16, 2005.

121. **Graham received an album of photos** LBJ to BG, January 11, 1966.

121. **Goodwin herself had accumulated an even dozen toothbrushes** Goodwin, *Lyndon Johnson*, p. xi.

121. **"the 'Psychedelic President'"** BG to LBJ, June 21, 1968.

121. **"you have to be in that Pedernales River Valley"** Fiske, "The Closest Thing to a White House Chaplain," *New York Times*, June 8, 1969.

121. **a place of "nauseating loneliness"**   Quoting historian Walter Prescott Webb, "The Prudent Progressive," *Time*, January 1, 1965.

122. **"I was born in a manger"**   Dallek, *Flawed Giant*, p. 4.

122. **"things he would occasionally call 'the unforgettables'"**   Pollock, *Evangelist to the World*, p. 170.

122. **"a man of enormous personal faith"**   Lucy Johnson, interview, September 12, 2006.

122–123. **"It's just as solid as this"**   Sidey, "Beyond Politics, the Reality of Faith," *Life*, August 11, 1967.

123. **"an exquisite hole at his center"**   Dallek, *Lyndon B. Johnson: Portrait of a President* (New York: Oxford University Press, 2004), p. 190.

123. **he feared not just death**   Goodwin, interview, September 26, 2006.

123. **"the reason . . . was the bad weather"**   BG, interview, January 17, 2006.

123. **"He was always a little bit scared of death"**   Ibid., January 18, 2006.

123. **"he had a conflict within him about religion"**   Transcript, Billy Graham Oral History Special Interview, October 12, 1983, by Monroe Billington, LBJLM.

123. **"It's a once-for-all transaction"**   *JAIA*, p. 412.

124. **Johnson bowed his head over the steering wheel**   Martin, "Billy and Lyndon," *Texas Monthly*, November 1991.

124. **"only the Holy Spirit knows about that"**   BG, interview, January 18, 2006.

124. **"not ashamed to pray with each other"**   Marvin Watson, interview, August 15, 2006.

124. **"and I've just been out praying with him'"**   Harry McPherson, interview, June 19, 2006.

124. **"They have a babylike faith in me"**   "The American Dream," *Time*, May 1, 1964.

125. **"there is a great deal of the preacher in Lyndon Johnson"**   *New York Journal-American*, November 5, 1965.

125. **"Billy, I don't know how long I'll be in there"**   *JAIA*, p. 410.

125. **"Is that . . . our Billy?"**   McPherson, interview, June 19, 2006.

125. **"they just took turns baptizing each other"**   LBJ, remarks to members of the Southern Baptist Christian Leadership Seminar, March 25, 1964.

125. **"If you ever decide to run, I'll be your manager"**   Frady, *Parable of American Righteousness*, p. 266.

13: THE BATTLE FOR BILLY

126. **"'I don't think the country will elect a divorced president'"**   BG, interview, January 17, 2006.

126. **Gallup was conducting national polls**   Gallup poll, July 23, 1963.

126. **Draft Goldwater Committee called for a rally at the Armory**   White, *MOP 1964*, p. 97.

127. **Republican strategy session . . . discussed the merits of a Graham candidacy**   "Graham Weighs Idea of Running for President," *New York World-Telegram*, January 31, 1964.

127. **Republicans . . . would pledge their delegates**   Frost, *Personal Thoughts*, p. 48.

127. **By that winter it had been rumored for months**   "Issue of Marital Bliss Is Making GOP Unhappy," *Washington Post*, May 2, 1963.

127. **Hunt allegedly told Grady Wilson**   Martin, *PWH*, p. 300. Graham biographer William Martin went furthest in tracking the story down, and confirmed the offer with Wilson before he died in 1987.

127. **"As far as I can tell"**   Watson, interview, August 15, 2006.

127. **"Billy Graham Weighs Idea of Running for President"**   *New York World-Telegram*, January 31, 1964.

127. **"publicly disavow so improbable a possibility"**   Quoted in Frady, *Parable of American Righteousness*, p. 267.

128. **"I don't think the country will elect a divorced president"**   BG, interview, January 17, 2006.

128. **the two had met at the Biltmore for a breakfast** "Goldwater Hits Policies of Kennedy's," *Los Angeles Times*, September 17, 1963.
128. **"several key Goldwater operators"** Earle B. Mayfield Jr., memo to LBJ, July 21, 1966, LBJLM.
129. **"an animal in many ways"** Dallek, *Flawed Giant*, p. 138.
129. **"that's nothing compared to what I think of him"** Ibid., p. 136.
129. **"scared to death Bobby Kennedy would maybe come out with Jackie"** "The Preaching and the Power," *Newsweek*, July 20, 1970.
130. **"you're too stupid to be vice-president"** White, *MOP 1964*, p. 289.
130. **the Johnsons and Grahams took a well-photographed stroll** "Johnsons, Billy Graham Draw Crowds to Church," *Los Angeles Times*, August 24, 1964.
131. **"he was weary of being his brother's keeper"** James Wechsler, "The Message," *New York Post*, September 14, 1964.
131. **"Moral decay begins at the top"** *New York Times*, October 22, 1964.
131. **Graham went to Nixon's press conference and to his speech at the Augusta Armory** Frank Sleeper memo, October 22, 1964.
131. **"I doubt Goldwater can win"** *JAIA*, p. 443.
132. **"You've got this election . . . wrapped up"** LBJ, call to BG, October 20, 1964, University of Virginia, Miller Center.
132. **"Those visits spoke louder than words"** Means, "Pals: President and the Preacher," *New York Journal-American*, November 5, 1965.
132. **"'you kept me locked up here'"** Clifford, *People* transcript, January 31, 1981.
132. **"what goes on behind the scenes in politics"** *JAIA*, p. 407.
132. **"you know—Both sides of the road"** Bill Moyers to Ross Coggins, October 29, 1964, LBJLM.
132. **Western Union . . . had to open five extra wires** "Thousands Entreat Graham to Support Goldwater's Race," *New York Times*, November 3, 1964.
132–133. **Graham said he later met a man in Georgia** "Billy Says He'd Never Endorse a Candidate," AP, in *Charlotte News*, December 23, 1964.
133. **"I intended to stand by you 100 percent"** LBJ to BG, November 5, 1964 (WH 6411.08), LBJLM.
133. **he was maintaining strict neutrality** "Billy Graham Neutral on Choice of President," *Los Angeles Times*, November 2, 1964.
133. **"the church is getting too involved in politics"** "Billy's Advice to Churches: Shun Politics," *Charlotte Observer*, November 6, 1964.
133. **"you were not only the choice of the America people—but of God"** BG to LBJ, November 10, 1964, LBJLM.
133. **Ruth told people she never did know whom he voted for that year** "Billy's Political Pitch," *Newsweek*, June 10, 1968.

14: PREACHERS AND PROTESTERS

134. **"Johnson really loved black people"** BG, interview, January 18, 2006.
134. **"condemn you for your street demonstrations"** Frady, *Parable of American Righteousness*, p. 416.
135. **"If you go to the streets your people will desert you"** Frost, *Personal Thoughts*, p. 123.
135. **King shared Graham's idea** Taylor Branch, *Pillar of Fire: America in the King Years, 1963–65* (New York: Simon and Schuster, 1998), p. 24.
135. **writings of Gandhi disguised as Graham's books** Ibid., p. 122.
135. **"taking my cue from methods used by Billy Graham"** "Malcolm X Plans Muslim Crusade," *New York Times*, April 3, 1964.
135. **"No matter what the law may be"** Frady, *Parable of American Righteousness*, p. 412.
135. **"an unjust law is no law at all"** King, "Letter from Birmingham Jail," April 16, 1963.
135. **"With King there was a certain competition involved"** Goodwin, interview, September 26, 2006.
136. **"King was a most influential person"** Watson, interview, August 15, 2006.

136. **"I became mixed up in my thinking about him"** Frady, *Parable of American Righteousness*, p. 416.

136. **"it would have had a great impact on people"** Joseph Lowery, interview, July 11, 2006.

136. **"It was very difficult for the president to believe"** Watson, interview, August 15, 2006.

137. **"be on the receiving end of a fire hose"** "Never Again Where He Was," *Time*, January 3, 1964.

137. **"we wanted to change your behavior"** Lowery, interview, July 11, 2006.

137. **King, however, marveled at Graham's ability to win positive headlines** David L. Chapell, *A Stone of Hope: Prophetic Religion and the Death of Jim Crow* (Chapel Hill: University of North Carolina Press, 2004), pp. 142–143.

137. **He sent two lieutenants to Chicago** Branch, *Parting the Waters: America in the King Years, 1954–63* (New York: Simon and Schuster, 1988), pp. 594–595.

138. **"It is time now to write the next chapter"** Address before a joint session of Congress, November 27, 1963, LBJLM.

138. **"'to get it done, really done, we need your help and people like you'"** BG, interview, January 17, 2006.

139. **"Billy Graham turned us down"** LBJ, call to Luther Hodges, July 2, 1964 (WH 6407), LBJLM.

139. **"It's true I haven't been to jail yet"** Lowell Streiker and Gerald Strober, *Religion and the New Majority: Billy Graham, Middle America and the Politics of the 70s* (New York: Association Press, 1972), citing Religion News Service, March 3, 1965, p. 53.

140. **"The KKK went around and knocked our signs down"** *People* interview transcript, January 31, 1981.

140. **"the demonstrations have served to arouse the conscience of the world"** "Billy Graham Is Focusing on Rights," *New York Times*, April 17, 1965.

140. **"if the Ku Klux Klan will quiet down"** "Graham Discerns Gains in Alabama," *New York Times*, June 21, 1965.

141. **"this door is always open"** LBJ to BG, April 13, 1965, LBJLM.

141. **"How is it possible after all we've accomplished?"** Dallek, *Flawed Giant*, p. 223.

141. **Urban League the year before had ranked Los Angeles first in the country** White, *Making of the President 1968* (New York: Atheneum, 1969), p. 24.

142. **"We may have a blood bath"** "Graham Predicts Worse Violence," *New York Times*, August 16, 1965.

142. **"With words more hysteric than prophetic"** "Be Specific, Mr. Graham," *Christian Century*, September 1, 1965.

142. **invoked Dr. King** "Graham Asks Curb on Rioting," *Charlotte Observer*, August 15, 1965.

142. **"if Billy Graham can ride over them in a helicopter"** Branch, *At Canaan's Edge: America in the King Years, 1965–68* (New York: Simon and Schuster, 2006), p. 294.

143. **"a blind and misguided revolt"** "Curfew Lifted in Los Angeles," *New York Times*, August 18, 1965.

143. **By 1966 the number was 85 percent** Goodwin, *Lyndon Johnson*, p. 304.

143. **"national disorder for sinister political objectives"** "Graham Urges Johnson to Expose Extremists," *Los Angeles Times*, July 20, 1965.

144. **"the Social Gospel has directed its energies"** Martin, *PWH*, p. 343.

144. **"take some of the money we are giving away abroad"** "Graham and King As Ghettomates," *Christian Century*, August 10, 1966.

144. **"Graham has ever consented to so endorse a domestic program"** Sargent Shriver to George Christian, May 9, 1967, LBJLM.

144. **Johnson declined** Watson to LBJ, June 8, 1967, LBJLM.

144. **"It's not a giveaway program"** "House Hearing: Its Ritual and Reality," *New York Times*, August 21, 1967.

144. **America would "pay for it spiritually"** Martin, *PWH*, p. 343.

145. **"If you criticize the war on poverty"** "House Hearing: Its Ritual and Reality," *New York Times*, August 21, 1967.

145. **Graham immediately found himself under "tremendous pressure"** Shriver, memo to LBJ, June 15, 1967 (EX PR 12 WHCF Name File), LBJLM.

145. **Graham's lobbying helped save the OEO** Pierard, "Billy Graham and the U.S. Presidency," *Journal of Church and State* 22, p. 124.

145. **"nobody would have bet a nickel"** "How Poverty Bill Was Saved in the House," *New York Times*, December 25, 1967.

15: "THE STRONG ARM OF EMPATHY"

146. **"I knew that they had burdens"** BG, interview, January 18, 2006.

146. **"like some demonic, destructive suction tube"** "King Speaks for Peace," *Christian Century*, April 19, 1967.

146. **"Surely Negroes are divided"** "Graham Denounces Dissenters," *Christian Century*, May 17, 1967.

146. **"I was bound to be crucified"** Goodwin, *Lyndon Johnson*, pp. 251–252.

147. **"equally devout Christians were on both sides"** Rowan, *People* transcript, November 26, 1975.

147. **"I heard Billy Graham on a program"** George Smathers, call to LBJ, June 1, 1964 (WH 6406.01), LBJLM.

147. **The president "needs our prayers"** "Billy Asks Prayer Over Asian 'Mess,'" *Charlotte Observer*, February 15, 1965.

147. **"'I have come as a fire-setter'"** "President and Preachers," *New York Post*, November 17, 1967.

147. **"I began to feel the same way"** Rowan, *People* transcript, November 26, 1975.

148. **"I have been extremely careful"** *Christian Century*, Letters, March 29, 1967, and May 17, 1967.

148. **"half the [people] would not hear what I was saying about Christ"** Frost, *Personal Thoughts*, p. 131, quoting from Edward Watkin, "Revival Tents and Golden Domes," *US Catholic*, March 1976.

148. **landmark essay on civil religion** Robert N. Bellah, "Civil Religion in America," *Daedalus: Journal of the American Academy of Arts and Sciences* 96 (Winter 1967).

148. **"he had no stomach for it"** Dallek, *Flawed Giant*, p. 249.

148. **"they could make Hanoi confident"** "Graham Denounces Dissenters," *Christian Century*, May 17, 1967.

148. *America Hurrah* "America Hurrah Warmly Received by London Critics," *New York Times*, August 4, 1967.

149. **"I look forward to a full report"** LBJ to BG, November 28, 1966, LBJLM.

149. **"You have raised man's eyes"** LBJ to BG, January 1, 1967, LBJLM.

149. **"The stakes are much higher in Vietnam"** "Vietnam War Is Battle of World, Billy Says," *Charlotte Observer*, December 29, 1966.

149. **"we are on a collision course with China"** "Billy Says Big Disaster Is Pending," *Charlotte Observer*, December 31, 1966.

149. **"Now what do you think?"** Transcript, Billy Graham Oral History Special Interview, October 12, 1983, LBJLM.

149. **"the American people are getting restless"** Ibid.

149. **"Graham can give the Vietnam War the blessing"** "Danger on the Home Front," *Christian Century*, January 25, 1967.

150. **"they can sincerely be on either side"** "Graham Defends Mass Evangelism," *New York Times*, July 17, 1966.

150. **"bring awareness to Lyndon Johnson"** "Billy Refuses to Judge Moral Issue of Vietnam," *Charlotte Observer*, February 1, 1967.

150. **Watson told the president about a half-hour TV show** Watson to LBJ, February 28, 1967, LBJLM.

150. **he suggested . . . recruiting Graham** Fred Panzer to LBJ, March 10, 1967, LBJLM.

150. **give the South Vietnamese the benefit of the doubt** WHCF subject files, introduction to *Hour of Decision*, September 3, 1967, LBJLM.

150. **the CIA had funded Graham's Latin American crusade** "Pandora's Cashbox," *Time*, March 3, 1967. The group was the U.S. National Student Association, and it also funded the National Council of Churches and Harvard Law School and AFL-CIO affiliates.

150. **"funds from any government agency"** "Graham Denies Knowledge of C.I.A. Funds for Trip," *New York Times*, March 25, 1967.

151. **"Nobody could make Johnson feel"** Frady, *Parable of American Righteousness*, p. 422.

151. **"President Johnson had little choice"** "Billy Refuses to Judge Moral Issue of Vietnam," *Charlotte Observer*, February 1, 1967.

151. **"I need a little Billy Graham these days"** LBJ to DDE, February 15, 1965. From Michael Beschloss, *Reaching for Glory: Lyndon Johnson's Secret White House Tapes, 1964–65* (New York: Simon and Schuster, 2001), pp. 178–179.

152. **"the strongest personality that ever led this nation"** Watson, interview, August 15, 2006.

152. **"he would have been the greatest President"** Goodwin, *Lyndon Johnson*, p. 41.

152. **"I thought he was sounding like a fool"** McPherson, interview, June 19, 2006.

152. **"God had set out to torture him"** Goodwin, *Lyndon Johnson*, p. 342, and interview, September 26, 2006.

152. **"get through the sadness"** Valenti, interview, June 16, 2005.

153. **"There is division in the American house"** LBJ speech, March 31, 1968, www.lbjlib.utexas.edu/Johnson/archives.hom/speeches.hom/680331.asp.

153. **"'I come from a family of short livers'"** BG, interview, January 18, 2006.

153. **He'd even had a secret actuarial study done** Dallek, *Lyndon B. Johnson*, p. 328.

153. **"I don't think that's fair"** BG, interview, January 18, 2006.

153. **the air of "a prisoner let free"** Dallek, *Lyndon B. Johnson*, p. 332.

153. **"It was Lyndon Johnson's fate"** Tom Wicker, "In the Nation: The First and the Last," *New York Times*, April 2, 1968.

153. **"while the country desperately needs your leadership"** BG to LBJ, June 13, 1968, LBJLM.

154. **"There even come times of depression"** Pollock, *Evangelist to the World*, p. 147.

154. **"helped to lighten my load"** LBJ to BG, February 11, 1969, LBJLM.

154. **"My father had a sense of relief"** Lucy Johnson, interview, September 12, 2006.

155. **Graham told Julie Nixon Eisenhower that he had never seen Johnson so melancholy** Julie Nixon Eisenhower, *Pat Nixon: The Untold Story* (New York: Kensington, 1986), p. 378.

155. **He thought the Nixons would like it** *JAIA*, p. 416.

155. **overnight, everything would change** Goodwin, *Lyndon Johnson*, p. xiii.

155. **"so anyone who came, he triply valued"** Goodwin, interview, September 26, 2006.

155. **"will I ever see my mother and father again?"** Martin, "Billy and Lyndon," *Texas Monthly*, November 1991.

155. **"Don't use any notes"** Cornwell, *A Time for Remembering*, p. 195.

155. **"you tell 'em a few things I did for this country"** This version comes from Martin, "Billy and Lyndon"; also Pollock, *Evangelist to the World*, p. 170.

156. **"'Lord, remember me'"** BG to LBJ, March 18, 1971.

156. **"They're just too fickle"** Goodwin, *Lyndon Johnson*, p. i.

156. **"Forgive Us Mr. President"** Cornwell, *A Time for Remembering*, p. 196.

156. **"the Great Society was not a wild dream"** "Johnson Buried at Texas Ranch," *New York Times*, January 26, 1973.

16: The Return of Richard Nixon

157. **"The emphasis I tried to leave"** BG, interview, January 23, 2007.

158. **"It's the political thing to do"** "From Pulpit, Sen. Hatfield Calls on Nation to Repent," *Washington Post*, May 3, 1974.

158. **"I have no contemplation at all of being the candidate"** White, *Breach of Faith: The Fall of Richard Nixon* (New York: Atheneum, 1975), p. 72.

158. **"It would be very easy for you to become bitter"**   BG to RN, November 11, 1962, RNLB.
158. **"He was *so* dejected"**   BG, interview, January 18, 2006.
159. **he had doubts about sinking back into the political swamps**   Nixon, *Memoirs*, p. 291.
159. **"it is your destiny to be President"**   Ibid., pp. 292–293.
159. **"had a great deal to do with that decision"**   Streiker and Strober, *Religion and the New Majority*, p. 66.
159. **"I think his family and Billy Graham"**   "Julie: Graham Helped Persuade Father to Run," *Charlotte Observer*, October 18, 1968.
160. **"I don't really know . . . because he's never told me"**   Frost, *Personal Thoughts*, p. 49.
160. **Graham flatly denied**   *JAIA*, pp. 444–445.
160. **reserved rooms at the Miami Hilton Plaza**   "Now the Republic," *Time*, August 16, 1968.
161. **Carmichael . . . a fight to the death**   White, *MOP 1968*, p. 205.
161. **Nixon would talk about . . . those forgotten Americans**   Ibid., p. 325.
161. **"They are not out carrying placards"**   Frady, *Parable of American Righteousness*, p. 449.
161. **Graham went into the 1968 race**   Streiker and Strober, *Religion and the New Majority*, p. 67.
161. **"it muffled those inner monitors"**   *JAIA*, p. 445.
162. **"Graham will probably get the biggest write-in vote"**   Means, "Will Billy Graham Wield Influence to Help Nixon?" *New York Daily News*, May 21, 1968.
162. **"There is no American I admire more than Richard Nixon"**   *Charlotte Observer*, May 27, 1968.
162. **"This country is going through its greatest crisis since the Civil War"**   "Billy's Political Pitch," *Newsweek*, June 10, 1968.
162. **Graham declared that he would head to New York**   "Billy Graham Is Planning to Attend Kennedy Rites," AP, in *New York Times*, June 8, 1968.
162. **conducted a private service**   "Thousands Visit Kennedy Grave on Day of Mourning," *New York Times*, June 10, 1968.
163. **"he was about to do this in 1960"**   James Rowe, memo to LBJ, July 31, 1968, LBJLM.
163. **Gardner . . . led a key southern delegation**   John Sears, interview, September 21, 2006.
163. **"you just don't lie to Billy Graham"**   *Charlotte Observer*, August 18, 1968.
164. **"Rep. George Bush of Texas"**   Rowland Evans and Robert Novak, "Young Texas Congressman Bush Gets Nixon Look As Running Mate," *Washington Post*, June 5, 1968.
164. **"appeal to the strong Christian vote"**   *JAIA*, p. 446.
164. **"This will be a little bit of history"**   Ibid.
164. **"I believe that he's a moderate liberal"**   "Watergate," *Christianity Today*, January 4, 1974.
164. **the fact that Hatfield was so "square" . . . was politically fatal**   John Tower, *Consequences: A Personal and Political Memoir*, quoted in Eric Paddon, "Modern Mordecai: Billy Graham in the Political Arena, 1948–1980," dissertation for Ohio University, June 1999.
164. **asking that he pray about the choice**   *JAIA*, p. 447.

17: THE COURIER

165. **"I often talked to both of them"**   BG, interview, January 17, 2006.
165. **"No, that would hurt his ministry"**   William Safire, *Before the Fall: An Inside View of the Pre-Watergate White House* (New York: Ballantine, 1975), p. 68.
166. **he felt a pall over the convention**   *JAIA*, p. 449.
166. **"The unreality of Chicago"**   "Graham Describes Chicago as Unreal," *New York Times*, August 29, 1968.
166. **"The GOP may be of more help"**   Dallek, *Flawed Giant*, p. 571.
167. **"skullduggery and hidden actions"**   Ibid., p. 575.
167. **"one of the most cherished I have ever had"**   Streiker and Strober, *Religion and the New Majority*, p. 67.

167. **addition to Graham's television schedule** Martin, *PWH*, p. 353.
167. **"one of the most moving religious experiences"** Frady, *Parable of American Righteousness*, p. 447.
167. **"If any of you took the trouble to listen"** Safire, *Before the Fall*, p. 83.
167. **called the White House and asked to see Johnson** Bob Faiss, memo to Jim Jones, September 10, 1968, LBJLM.
168. **stopped to pay a visit to Graham's mother, Morrow** "'He's Homey . . . Easy to Talk To'—Mrs. Graham," *Charlotte Observer*, September 12, 1968.
168. **"will never embarrass him"** Famous Names Box 8, handwritten notes and an undated typewritten account, LBJLM.
168. **he doubted Humphrey had the ability** Dallek, *Flawed Giant*, p. 577.
169. **"Nixon's approach through Graham"** Ibid., p. 580.
169. **"in 1960 correspondents left Nixon"** White, *MOP 1968*, p. 327.
169. **the Democratic Party did not run a single national ad** Ibid., p. 353.
169. **"Politics is much more emotional than it is rational"** Ray Price, memo to RN, reprinted in Joe McGuinness, *The Selling of the President, 1968* (New York: Trident, 1969), p. 193.
170. **"my role is that of spiritual advisor"** "The Politicians' Preacher," *Time*, October 4, 1968.
170. **"Naturally my convictions . . . are strong"** Religion News Service, August 19, 1968, quoted in Streiker and Strober, *Religion and the New Majority*, p. 67.
170. **"There's nothing 'tricky' about him"** "Billy Graham Says Nixon Is Not Tricky," *Washington Post*, October 1, 1968.
171. **the wildest climax he'd ever seen** White, *MOP 1968*, p. 382.
171. **"the second most revered man in the South"** McGuinness, *Selling of the President*, p. 124.
171. **"that was all I needed"** "The Preaching and the Power," *Newsweek*, July 20, 1970.
171. **a *Christian Science Monitor* reporter** Dallek, *Flawed Giant*, p. 591.
171. **Intelligence from a bug** Anthony Summers, *The Arrogance of Power: The Secret World of Richard Nixon* (New York: Viking, 2000), p. 301.
172. **"If you lose I will be ready"** Pollock, *Evangelist to the World*, p. 172.
172. **"We did it"** McGuinness, *Selling of the President*, p. 163.
172. **gave thanks for "God's plan for the country"** *JAIA*, p. 450.
172. **"He is the only mass evangelist I would trust"** Templeton online memoir, www.templetons.com/charles/memoir/.

18: WHITE HOUSE OF WORSHIP

173. **"After Nixon was elected"** BG, interview, January 17, 2006.
173. **The Religious Observance Committee distributed ten thousand specially printed cards** "An Official Prayer Service to Open Nixon Inauguration," *New York Times*, January 15, 1969.
173. **"the most publicly prayed-over new President"** "Five Clergymen Plan Prayers at Service Before Inaugural," *Washington Post*, January 18, 1969.
173. **Bob Haldeman began to keep a diary** H. R. Haldeman, *The Haldeman Diaries: Inside the Nixon White House* (New York: G. P. Putnam's Sons, 1994), January 20, 1969, p. 18.
174. **"almost a political document"** Reston, "From Partisan to President of All," *New York Times*, January 19, 1969.
174. **"people would misinterpret his going to church"** "Billy Graham Cites Integrity: Nixon Seen As Shunning Political Use of Religion," *Washington Post*, November 16, 1968.
174. **Nixon had toyed with the idea** "Praying with the President in the White House," *New York Times*, August 8, 1971.
174. **"President Nixon . . . thought that church was so important"** Cornwell, *A Time for Remembering*, p. 197.
175. **Dwight Chapin and John Ehrlichman picked Graham's brain** Charles Wilkinson to BG, January 24, 1969, NPM.

175. **Graham sent them a list** "List Submitted: For President Nixon Only, CONFIDEN-TIAL and PRIVATE List of Suggested Protestant Clergymen to Be Invited for White House Services," NPM.

175. **"I've never heard of anything like it happening here before"** "Praying Together, Staying Together," *Time*, February 7, 1969.

175. **"I'll never forget the President sitting down on the spur of the moment"** BG, speech at RN funeral, April 27, 1994, BGEA archives.

175. **"trying mainly to pursue his religious commitment"** "Nixon Hopes Youth Turn to Religion," *New York Times*, April 28, 1969.

175. **"it was a social thing"** Herb Klein, interview, January 31, 2006.

175. **unnamed Protestant clerics** "Nixon Hopes Youth Turn to Religion," *New York Times*, April 28, 1969.

176. **"Sure, we used the prayer breakfasts"** Charles Colson to Martin, *With God on Our Side* (New York: Broadway Books, 1996), p. 98.

176. **"develop a list of rich people with strong religious interest"** Action memo, February 23, 1970 (Box 12), NPM.

176. **This would include top executives** Martin, *PWH*, p. 356.

176. **Haldeman complained . . . about the guest list** HRH to Alexander Butterfield, February 9, 1971 (HRH box 96), NPM.

176. **inspired Norman Mailer to describe Nixon** Quoted in McGuinness, *Selling of the President*, p. 31.

176. **both brothers were photographed with Nixon** "Praying with the President in the White House," *New York Times*, August 8, 1971.

176–177. **"would aid greatly in his campaign for this office"** Deborah Sloan to Butterfield, August 3, 1971 (Box 15), NPM.

177. **One Minneapolis Lutheran** "Praying with the President in the White House," *New York Times*, August 8, 1971.

177. **"an emasculated, non-denominational God"** Nicholas von Hoffman, "'Silent American,' with Sound," *Washington Post*, February 14, 1969.

178. **"I've been fairly close to two or three presidents"** "Billy Graham: The Man at Home," *Saturday Evening Post*, Spring 1972.

178. **"the principal spiritual influence"** Colson, interview, July 18, 2006.

178. **The president could run ideas past Graham** Klein, interview, January 31, 2006.

178. **Haldeman tried to enlist Graham** Haldeman, *Diaries*, December 21, 1970, p. 223.

178. **He received literally thousands of requests** "The Closest Thing to a White House Chaplain," *New York Times*, June 8, 1969.

178. **young men working full-time for Campus Crusade for Christ** Dwight Chapin, memo to HRH and John Ehrlichman, February 15, 1969, NPM.

178. **"to offset the bad influences now prevailing"** Harry Dent, memo to Ehrlichman, February 27, 1969 (Box 63), NPM.

179. **"I appreciate your willingness"** BG to Chapin, August 7, 1970, NPM.

179. **"Billy Graham raised with the president today"** HRH to Ehrlichman, February 1, 1972 (HRH box 199), NPM.

179. **Confidential Missionary Plan for Ending the Vietnam War** April 15, 1969, Correspondence File central files—confidential file (Box 1, NPM). Six months after Graham gave the plan to Nixon it was passed on to Kissinger, who responded that it "reflected a good deal of firsthand knowledge, and I found it quite useful. We are looking into the points which they raised."

180. **"this may be our best chance to make inroads into the Negro community"** HRH, memo to Len Garment, January 16, 1970, NPM.

180. **"He wants to see at least ONE of their projects approved"** HRH, memo to Ehrlichman, April 30, 1970, NPM.

180. **"I was aware of the risk"** BG, interview, January 23, 2007.

180. **Nixon had not consulted him on the sensitive appointment** "Billy Graham: The Appeal Is Still Very Strong," *New York Times*, June 28, 1970.

180. **He urged that Nixon invite . . . Carl Bates** BG to Chapin, June 18, 1970, NPM.

181. **"He had a very real affection for Billy"** Colson, interview, July 18, 2006.

181. **"The White House provides almost total isolation"** Haldeman, *Diaries*, January 29, 1969, p. 23.

181. **Nixon saw in Graham the skill set of a top politician** RN to Pollock, October 5, 1965, in Pollock, *Authorized Biography*, pp. 217–218.

181. **"the mood of the majority"** "Government in the Heartland," *Time*, February 16, 1970.

182. **When he saw a Gallup poll in the spring of 1970** BG to Garment, May 16, 1970, NPM.

182. **"The evangelical vote was the key to the southern strategy"** Martin, *With God on Our Side*, p. 99.

19: SUMMONS FOR THE SILENT MAJORITY

183. **"I was aware of the risk"** BG, interview, January 23, 2007.

183. **Nixon called Graham at home** "Billy Graham: The Appeal Is Still Very Strong," *New York Times*, June 28, 1970.

183. **Nixon went on television** His address was printed in the *New York Times*, May 1, 1970.

184. **National Guardsmen shot and killed four unarmed students at Kent State** "At War with War," *Time*, May 18, 1970.

184. **State Department . . . Peace Corps** Henry Kissinger, *White House Years* (Boston: Little, Brown, 1979), pp. 513–514.

184. **"The very fabric of government was falling apart"** Ibid., p. 513.

184. **"He's very disturbed"** Haldeman, *Diaries*, May 4, 1970, p. 159.

184. **on the edge of a breakdown** White, *Breach of Faith*, p. 131, and Walter Isaacson, *Kissinger: A Biography* (New York: Simon and Schuster, 1992), p. 259.

184. **"you want to get the war over"** "At War with War," *Time*, May 18, 1970.

185. **"They argue for more public presidential presentation"** Haldeman, *Diaries*, April 24, 1970, p. 154.

185. **Nixon told his staff that he wanted to try an idea** Ibid., May 12, 1970, p. 165.

185. **"he should probably go out into country"** Ibid., May 21, 1970, p. 168.

185. **Nixon sent Haldeman a memo** May 25, 1970, in Bruce Oudes, *From the President: Richard Nixon's Secret Files* (New York: Harper and Row, 1988), pp. 139–140.

185. **first appearance outside the White House since the invasion** "Nixon to Talk at Graham's Youth Rally," *Washington Post*, May 28, 1970.

185. **the largest public meeting in the history of the state** Pollock, *Evangelist to the World*, p. 107.

185. **"America needs to know something"** A transcript of Nixon's speech was printed in the *New York Times*, May 29, 1970.

185. **Several hundred demonstrators speckled the crowd** "Nixon Speech Cheered at Tenn. Rally," *Washington Post*, May 29, 1970.

186. **beaten by a policeman** "Nixon Emphasizes Youth Can Effect Peaceful Change," *New York Times*, May 29, 1970.

186. **it was televised later with the protests excised** Martin, *PWH*, p. 369.

186. **one even went on to become a minister** Pollock, *Evangelist to the World*, p. 109.

186. **"All Americans may not agree with the decision a president makes"** "The Preaching and the Power," *Newsweek*, July 20, 1970.

186. **"A number of presidents have looked to you for spiritual sustenance"** *JAIA*, p. 460.

186. **William Brock . . . Al Gore Sr.** "Nixon Emphasizes Youth Can Effect Peaceful Change," *New York Times*, May 29, 1970.

186. **"There were no political implications"** Streiker and Strober, *Religion and the New Majority*, p. 72.

186. **Gore had not been invited** "Nixon Emphasizes Youth Can Effect Peaceful Change," *New York Times*, May 29, 1970.

186. **Graham told Al Gore Jr. he was sorry** Al Gore Jr., interview, July 24, 2006.

187. **"to have [presidents] come and sit in the audience"**   Cornwell, *A Time for Remembering*, p. 201.
187. **"remarks were not as forthright a witness for Christ"**   *JAIA*, p. 459.
187. **called Graham from San Clemente**   Martin, *PWH*, p. 370.
187. **"It was a good forum for the President"**   "The Preaching and the Power," *Newsweek*, July 20, 1970.
187. **"If we destroy the system, a dictator is going to rise"**   Frost, *Personal Thoughts*, p. 130.
187. **"I don't guess anybody loves the flag more"**   "Graham Deplores Distortion of Patriotism," *New York Times*, June 24, 1970.
188. **"Let's keep it away from the war"**   Ibid.
188. **"Let's sing a little, let's wave the flag"**   "Gather in Praise of America," *Time*, July 13, 1970.
188. **Chapin sketched the plans for Haldeman**   Chapin, memo to HRH, June 9, 1970.
188. **he went to the Mall and visited**   "The Preaching and the Power," *Newsweek*, July 20, 1970.
188. **"They gathered in front of the Lincoln Memorial"**   "Gather in Praise of America," *Time*, July 13, 1970.
190. **"God, Guts and Gunpowder"**   Ibid.
190. **The "Huston plan"**   White, *Breach of Faith*, p. 138, and Church Committee Report 1976: Supplementary detailed staff reports on intelligence activities and the rights of Americans, April 23, 1976.
191. **"I never felt he was using me—*ever*"**   Cornwell, *A Time for Remembering*, p. 199.
191. **"He thought it would be appropriate to talk to you this morning"**   Memo to RN signed "A," January 1, 1971, NPM.
191. **"We have all had our My Lais"**   "Billy Graham: On Calley," *New York Times*, April 9, 1971.
192. **"They have told him that they are deeply troubled"**   HRH, memo to HK, November 11, 1971 (Box 197), NPM.
192. **Kissinger's confidential talking points**   HK to HRH, November 19, 1971, NPM.
192. **"The president wants to know which"**   Butterfield to Klein, July 15, 1969 (Box 1), NPM.
193. **"his comments are on my list of criticisms"**   Klein to RN, July 18, 1969, NPM.
193. **"Mitchell can stick his nose into this"**   Oval Office meeting, RN and HRH, September 13, 1971, transcript in Stanley I. Kutler, *Abuse of Power: The New Nixon Tapes* (New York: Touchstone, 1997), pp. 31–32.
193. **"What about the rich Jews?"**   Oval Office meeting, RN, HRH, and Colson, September 14, 1971, transcript in Kutler, *Abuse of Power.*
193. **"Conservatives for the President"**   Action paper, August 2, 1971, NPM.
193. **"'Billy, what job do you want?'"**   BG, interview, January 17, 2006.

20: 1972: The Race to the Bottom

195. **"I don't understand it"**   BG, interview, January 23, 2007.
195. **"the dinner may have had political overtones"**   "President, 7 Guests Take Cruise," *Washington Post*, August 11, 1971.
195. **As Haldeman remembered the night**   Haldeman, *Diaries*, August 10, 1971, p. 338.
196. **helped talk . . . Hatfield . . . out of challenging Nixon**   Martin, *PWH*, p. 392.
196. **"like a sheep led to the slaughter"**   Ibid., p. 399.
196. **He deplored the "awkward incident"**   HRH to Vern Coffey, August 11, 1971 (HRH box 197), NPM.
196. **"'Let others run your campaign'"**   Pollock, *Evangelist to the World*, p. 175.
196. **had taken to heart the advice Eisenhower and Johnson both gave him**   White, *Breach of Faith*, p. 108.
197. **"there have to be a few SOBs"**   White, *MOP 1968*, p. 132.
197. **"Perhaps that caused Haldeman"**   *JAIA*, p. 452.
197. **"Graham wants to be helpful next year"**   Martin, *PWH*, p. 391.

197. **"Don't ransom me"** "Round the Clock Guards Protecting Billy Graham," *Washington Post*, July 10, 1971.

198. **"All this for a preacher"** "'All This for a Preacher,' Billy Says," *Charlotte News*, October 13, 1971.

198. **"'I'm not going to let politics spoil it'"** "Billy Graham: The Man at Home," *Saturday Evening Post*, Spring 1972.

198. **"Jesus and Caesar weren't best friends"** Frady, *Parable of American Righteousness*, p. 458.

198. **"the genuineness of their admiration"** Editorial, "An Evangelist Is Honored by a Nation's President," *Charlotte Observer*, October 15, 1971.

198. **how vibrant it would look in the sunlight** Martin, *PWH*, p. 385.

198. **"'that would not be morally right'"** "Nixon Sees Graham in Peacemaker Role," *Los Angeles Times*, October 15, 1971.

199. **"We also wrestled with poverty"** "Hometown Honors for Billy Graham," *Washington Post*, October 16, 1971.

199. **"You have contributed to America"** Frady, *Parable of American Righteousness*, p. 460.

199. **"I have faith in [America]"** Remarks at Ceremonies Honoring Billy Graham in Charlotte, North Carolina, October 15, 1971, American Presidency Project, UCSB.

199. **"I'm sounding more like him"** *Washington Post*, October 16, 1971.

199. **daughter of a superior court judge** "Service Expected Trouble," *Charlotte Observer*, October 18, 1971.

199. **"a nice, greyhaired, everyday mother"** "Three Groups of Protestors Fail to Mar Graham Tribute," *Charlotte News*, October 16, 1971.

199. **Robert Scott** "Notes on People," *New York Times*, October 29, 1971.

200. **"Anyways you can't blame it on the president"** "Evangelist Backs Amendment for Prayer in School," *Charlotte Observer*, November 5, 1971.

200. **"they will have extremely *obscene* signs"** Ronald Walker, memo to HRH, reprinted in "Counterattack and Counterpoint," *Time*, August 13, 1973.

200. **"What mentality indicates 'good'"** "Haldeman Memos Heat Up Hearings," *Los Angeles Times*, August 1, 1973.

200. **"Graham's millions of religious followers also take his political advice"** "Honoring Billy Graham," Chicago Daily News Service, in *Charlotte News*, October 19, 1971.

200. **"Get Billy Graham in re politics today w/some of us"** HRH, handwritten notes, January 31, 1972 (HRH box 45), NPM.

201. **Graham went back to the White House** Conversation transcript, February 1, 1972, in John Prados, ed., *The White House Tapes* (New York: New Press, 2003), pp. 238–255.

201. **should "invite his elite group in for a Kissinger briefing"** HRH, "Memorandum for the President's File, Re: Meeting with Dr. Billy Graham," March 9, 1972.

201. **"terrible problem arising from the total Jewish domination of the media"** Haldeman, *Diaries*, February 1, 1972, p. 405.

203. **"I don't understand it"** BG, interview, January 23, 2007.

203. **"I will try to follow through faithfully on each point we discussed"** BG to RN, February 4, 1972, NPM.

203. **"Billy was . . . very careful in my dealings with him"** Colson interview, July 18, 2006.

204. **Haldeman wanted to know what Graham thought of it** HRH, "Talking Paper for Secretary Connally and Billy Graham (separately)," February 10, 1972.

204. **"Muskie's statements on the war disqualify him"** HRH, talking paper, February 15, 1972, NPM.

204. **"meeting with Billy Graham's religious leaders is going forward"** RN, memo to HRH, March 14, 1972, NPM.

204. **"Can McGovern really be nominated?"** HRH, talking paper, April 26, 1972, NPM.

205. **"recent attacks on certain members of the media"** Ibid., May 16, 1972, NPM.

205. **for Nixon to send a congratulatory telegram** Lawrence Higby, confidential memo to HRH, "re: Billy Graham phone call," June 14, 1972, NPM.

205. **"Graham has a line through to Wallace"** Haldeman, *Diaries*, June 19, 1972, p. 472.

206. **"I need to meet with Graham"** RN, action memo, June 25, 1972, NPM.

206. **"Should he be hit now or after the Democratic Convention?"** HRH, talking paper, June 26, 1972, NPM.

206. **Harry Williams** HRH, memo to Ken Rietz, July 26, 1972, NPM.

206. **also did some matchmaking between Nixon and Oral Roberts** Dent, memo to RN, August 11, 1972, NPM.

206. **Haldeman thought it was "a terrible idea"** HRH, memo to Chapin, August 17, 1972, NPM.

206. **"Wallace asked whether he would take more votes from the P"** Haldeman, *Diaries*, July 20, 1972, p. 484.

206–207. **"It's difficult to stay out of politics"** "Evangelist to Vote for Nixon," AP, August 13, 1972.

207. **"leader of the politically decisive majority"** Streiker and Strober, *Religion and the New Majority*, p. 189.

207. **Nixon's assiduous effort to be as closely associated as possible** "Billy Graham Values Seen Key to Election," *Los Angeles Times*, July 22, 1972.

207. **Nixon celebrated Johnson's sixty-first birthday** "Vacationer Nixon," *New York Times*, August 31, 1969.

207. **"the most inept politician, inept presidential candidate . . . in all of history"** Dallek, *Flawed Giant*, p. 617.

207. **The Democrats seemed to return the feeling** "Little Heard from Lyndon Johnson Among Delegates at Convention," *New York Times*, July 14, 1972.

208. **Nixon and Connally met to talk about how Graham could help** Haldeman, *Diaries*, August 14, 1972, p. 493.

208. **"I surely do want to thank you"** Cornwell, *A Time for Remembering*, p. 195.

208. **The president, Johnson said, should just ignore McGovern** Haldeman, *Diaries*, August 17, 1972, p. 494.

208. **"Hell, that's not going to hurt him a bit"** Nixon, *Memoirs*, p. 674.

208. **Nixon's acceptance speech** HRH, memo to RN, "Reverend Billy Graham's Suggestions Re: Acceptance Speech," August 19, 1972, NPM.

208. **"you will be making a serious mistake"** HRH to RN, August 19, 1972, NPM.

209. **"crazy as hell"** Dallek, *Flawed Giant*, p. 617.

209. **"But I'm not gonna do it"** BG, interview, January 19, 2006.

209. **Graham immediately called Haldeman** Haldeman, *Diaries*, August 22, 1972, p. 497.

209. **"It's too clouded"** Ibid., September 16, 1972, p. 505.

210. **"he'd be most happy to make a statement on my behalf"** Ibid., October 27, 1972, pp. 524–525.

210. **"Graham insists he's not campaigning for Nixon"** "*Christianity Today* Editor Sees Most Evangelicals Backing Nixon," Religion News Service, October 17, 1972.

210. **"How should the president handle McGovern"** HRH, talking paper, October 25, 1972, NPM.

210. **Graham had cast his absentee vote for Nixon** "'Born to Be President,'" AP, November 3, 1972.

21: THE RECKONING

211. **"I could sense that something was bothering him"** BG, interview, January 18, 2006.

211. **an open letter to Graham** Printed in the *Washington Post*, March 20, 1971.

212. **"Graham's White House Role Has Protestants in Quandary"** *Charlotte Observer*, April 22, 1972.

212. **"People have no idea what I say to the president"** "He's Getting in Shape for Crusade," *Charlotte Observer*, April 2, 1972.

213. **"Do we want a president in the White House who is not free to call on a clergyman"** Cornwell, *A Time for Remembering*, p. 198.

213. **Kissinger claimed in a television interview** HK, interview with Marvin Kalb, CBS, quoted in *Time*, February 12, 1973.
213. **"implore President Nixon to stop the bombing"** "U.S. Clerics Decry the Bombing and Urge End to Vietnam War," *New York Times*, December 23, 1972.
214. **"betraying the duty of peace"** Ibid.
214. **"An Open Letter to Billy Graham"** "100 War Protestors Hear Outdoor Mass Near St. Patrick's," *New York Times*, January 1, 1973.
214. **"lust for famous friends"** Pollock, *Evangelist to the World*, p. 155.
215. **"God has called me to be a New Testament evangelist"** "Statement to Define Dr. Billy Graham's Position Regarding the Recent Conduct of the Vietnam War," January 5, 1973, NPM.
215. **"The President doesn't call me up"** "Billy Graham's 'No Political Activist,'" *Charlotte News*, January 4, 1973.
215. **Graham was "very disturbed by some press reports"** Chapin to HRH, January 8, 1973.
216. **"getting a little depressed about it"** BG, interview, January 23, 2007.
216. **In mournful counterpoint across town** "Concerts Reflect Moods of Divided Washington," *New York Times*, January 20, 1973.
216. **"he knocked it out of my hand"** BG, interview, January 18, 2006.
216. **"judgment of God on America"** "Graham Tells of Reservations Over War," *New York Times*, January 21, 1973.
217. **"we can only patch and help"** "Nixon Is Praised at Capital Rites," *New York Times*, January 22, 1973.
218. **"I shall be eternally grateful"** RN to BG, January 22, 1973, NPM.
218. **"by your persistence, determination, courage and faith"** BG to RN, January 27, 1973, NPM.

22: The Man He Never Knew

219. **"I did misjudge him"** BG, interview, January 23, 2007.
220. **"They rest right here in this damn chair"** RN, phone call to Ron Ziegler, April 27, 1973 in Kutler, *Abuse of Power*, p. 350.
220. **"ethical principles wouldn't allow him"** "GOP Leaders Join Big Cry for Nixon Action," *Washington Post*, April 28, 1973.
220. **"We'll survive"** White, *Breach of Faith*, p. 327.
220. **"they wouldn't let me talk to him"** BG, interview, January 18, 2006.
221. **"I have marveled at your restraint"** BG to RN, April 6, 1973, NPM.
221. **"This is his great moment of glory"** RN, call to BG, April 4, 1973, in Kutler, *Abuse of Power*, pp. 302–303.
222. **"I personally do not think he knew about it"** Reported in the *Washington Post*, April 28, 1973.
222. **"This is a time for strong men, Ron"** RN to Ziegler, April 28, 1973, in Kutler, *Abuse of Power*, p. 353.
222. **"You're a strong man, goddamn it"** RN, call to HRH, April 30, 1973, in Kutler, *Abuse of Power*, pp. 381–382.
222. **"There can be no whitewash at the White House"** Transcript of the President's Broadcast to the Nation on the Watergate Affair, *New York Times*, May 1, 1973.
223. **"a commendable humility"** *New York Times*, May 1, 1973.
223. **"I had to tell Haldeman and Ehrlichman to resign"** RN, call to BG, April 30, 1973 (Tape #197 RC-3), National Archives.
223. **"He seemed to feel it was the right thing to do"** Haldeman, *Diaries*, April 30, 1973, p. 674.
223. **"Watergate situation is overblown"** Higby to RN, May 2, 1973, NPM.
224. **he wrote an op-ed** "Watergate and Its Lessons of Morality," *New York Times*, May 6, 1973.

224. **"This is the larger cover-up"** "Silence of the Leaders: The Other 'Cover-Up,'" *New York Times*, May 26, 1973.

224. **"I still have confidence in President Nixon"** "Graham Is Silent about Watergate," *Washington Post*, June 6, 1973.

225. **the headlines suggested the pressure he was feeling** "Graham to Abandon Crusades," *Washington Post*, July 13, 1973.

225. **"I tried to get in touch"** Pollock, *Evangelist to the World*, p. 178.

225. **"Nixon . . . would have leaned on Graham"** Colson, interview, July 18, 2006.

225. **"Democracy must have a moral basis"** "Impeach or Resign: Voices in a Historic Controversy," *Time*, November 19, 1973.

226. **"have the prayers of all Americans"** AP, November 22, 1973.

226. **Nixon's . . . charitable gifts** "President Concedes Material May Raise More Controversy," *New York Times*, December 9, 1973.

226. **used federal funds to upgrade his estates** "President Questioned by Graham," *Washington Post*, December 23, 1973.

226. **"I will go anywhere to preach the Gospel"** "Watergate," interview in *Christianity Today*, January 4, 1974.

227. **"I was feeling the strain"** Pollock, *Evangelist to the World*, pp. 178–179.

227. **"just a North Carolina country preacher"** "White House of Worship," *Washington Post*, December 17, 1973.

227. **"I was delighted to see you looking so well"** BG to RN, December 26, 1973, NPM.

228. **"I'm not so quick anymore to make political judgments"** "Watergate," interview in *Christianity Today*, January 4, 1974.

228–229. **"some of the news media carried only the negative aspects"** BG to RN, December 26, 1973, NPM.

229. **a rat deserting a sinking ship** George Stringfellow to BG, January 9, 1974, NPM.

229. **"I was saddened by your recent reported statements"** Norman Vincent Peale to BG, February 4, 1974, NPM.

229. **Graham sent two proposals of what Nixon could say** Suggested Remarks by the President at the Prayer Breakfast, January 31, 1974, NPM.

229. **"is totally unacceptable from my point of view"** Alexander Haig to RN, January 30, 1974, NPM.

230. **"To be President is a great and thrilling attainment"** BG to RN, February 2, 1974, in Oudes, *From the President*, pp. 609–610.

230. **"I remember how many times he quoted his mother"** BG, interview, January 23, 2007.

230. **"I wanted to believe the best about him for as long as I could"** *JAIA*, p. 458.

230. **"Those tapes revealed a man that I never knew"** John Dart, "Graham Finds It Difficult to Say Nixon Was 'Using' Religion," *Washington Post*, August 16, 1974.

231. **"Graham has been used for political image-building"** Ibid.

231. **"An evil spirit had somehow come upon him"** BG, interview, January 18, 2006.

231. **"whenever he spoke about the Lord, it was in pretty general terms"** *JAIA*, p. 442.

23: FORD AND FORGIVENESS

232. **"I never was sure that it really hurt [Ford]"** BG, interview, January 19, 2006.

232. **"honest faith of a Buddhist, a Hindu or a Jew"** BG, quoted in Ostling, "A Challenge for Evangelicals," *Time*, August 5, 1974, p. 48.

232. **"The gulf between it and the Evangelicals has deepened"** Ibid.

233. **"what he has convicted me of"** Pollock, *Authorized Biography*, p. 135.

233. **Billy Zeoli** Zeoli, interview, May 5, 2006.

233. **He dropped in on Ford** William Gildea, "And Now the White House Has Another Reverend Billy," *Washington Post*, January 29, 1975.

234. **Zeoli reported to Graham's office** Zeoli, interview, September 2, 2005.

234. **"I suggested we pray together when I returned to the States"** Zeoli, *God's Got a Better Idea* (Old Tappan, NJ: Fleming H. Revell Company, 1978), p. 16.

234. **"Sometimes I'd just go out and play baseball"** J. F. terHorst, *Gerald Ford and the Future of the Presidency* (New York: Third Press, 1974), pp. 31–33.

234. **Ford attended a weekly late-morning prayer session** James Cannon, *Time and Change: Gerald Ford's Appointment with History* (Ann Arbor: University of Michigan Press, 1994), p. 267.

235. **"much off the record group"** GF, quoted in Bob G. Slosser, "Weekly Session Held Amid Reports of Succession," *New York Times*, August 8, 1974.

235. **"It's hard to say when a man does that"** Zeoli, interview, December 28, 2006.

235. **"Billy Zeoli was the instrument"** Ford recalling weekly devotionals, in Zeoli, *God's Got a Better Idea*, p. 8.

235. **Ford's initial days as president** Betty Ford and Chris Chase, *The Times of My Life* (New York: Harper and Row, 1978), p. 162; and "Gerald Ford: Off to a Fast, Clean Start," *Time*, August 26, 1974.

235. **"services in the East Room for a select few"** Betty Ford, *Times of My Life*, p. 162.

236. **"He'll probably talk more about the Bible"** BG, quoted in Dart, "Graham Finds It Difficult to Say Nixon Was 'Using' Religion," *Washington Post*, August 16, 1974.

236. **Ford began each day in the White House** Cannon, *Time and Change*, pp. 36–37.

236. **a pardon for his friend Richard Nixon** Ambrose, *Nixon, Volume Three: Ruin and Recovery, 1973–1990* (New York: Simon and Schuster, 1991), p. 456.

237. **"commit hara-kiri"** Robert T. Hartmann, *Palace Politics* (New York: McGraw-Hill, 1980), p. 259.

237. **a pardon could be done** Cannon, *Time and Change*, pp. 373–375.

237. **"I told him how I felt"** BG, interview, January 23, 2007.

238. **At 11:05, he announced the pardon** "The Pardon That Brought No Peace," *Time*, September 16, 1974.

238. **"The Constitution is the supreme law"** GF, Nixon pardon statement, September 8, 1974, GFL.

238. **Graham watched Ford's announcement on television** *JAIA*, p. 555.

238. **"I never was sure that it really hurt [Ford]"** BG, interview, January 19, 2006.

239. **"important in my own reconciliation"** Lisa Singhania, "President Ford Toasted by the Reverend Graham," AP, August 20, 1999.

239. **"We would like to think it was an encouragement"** *JAIA*, p. 553.

239. **"disrespect has never been tolerated"** Ruth Graham, in Cornwell, *Ruth: A Portrait* (New York: Doubleday, 1997), pp. 234–236.

239. **"support me even physically!"** GF, letter to BG, June 6, 1975, GFL.

239–240. **"I think maybe she does, too"** BG, quoted in Jim Dumbell, "Graham, Mrs. Ford at Odds," *Charlotte Observer*, August 23, 1975.

240. **"What is story?"** GF, memo to Richard Cheney, September 1975, GFL.

240. **Ruth called to apologize** Ruth Graham, call to Ann Breen, December 3, 1975, GFL.

24: The Campaign That Changed Everything

241. **"Carter was very serious-minded"** BG, interview, January 18, 2006.

241. **someone asked the candidate if he was a born-again Christian** Martin Schram, *Running for President: A Journal of the Carter Campaign* (New York: Pocket, 1976), p. 111.

241. **"And I said, 'Yes'"** JC, interview, September 20, 2005.

242. **"transformed my life for the better"** Schram, *Running for President*, p. 111.

242. **"it's something he very deeply believed in"** Stuart Eizenstat, interview, Miller Center, University of Virginia, Jimmy Carter Presidential Oral History Project, January 29–30, 1982.

242. **"It wasn't a voice of God from heaven"** Schram, *Running for President*, p. 112; see also Wesley G. Pippert, *The Spiritual Journey of Jimmy Carter* (New York: Macmillan, 1978), p. 8.

242. **his 1966 defeat in a long-shot bid for governor** Rosalynn Carter, *First Lady from Plains* (Fayetteville: University of Arkansas Press, 1984), p. 54; also Jerry Rafshoon, interview, November 1, 2005.

243. **"I was really distressed"** JC, interview, September 20, 2005.

243. **"'devote yourself to God and see what happens?'"** Ibid.

243. **"A weak moment"** Ibid.

243. **racially integrated crusades** Ibid.

244. **asked organizers to simply screen the movie** Ibid.

244. **"to place their faith in Christ. Together"** *JAIA*, pp. 582–583.

245. **"sad duty of politics"** Niebuhr, *On Politics* (New York: Scribner's, 1960), p. 180; quoted in Pippert, *The Spiritual Journey of Jimmy Carter*, p. 91.

245. **Sister Ruth wrote letters** Myra MacPherson, "Evangelicals Seen Cooling on Carter," *Washington Post*, September 27, 1976.

246. **"When Jimmy Carter speaks"** Michael Novak, "The Hidden Religious Majority," *Washington Post*, April 4, 1976, p. 29.

247. **"almost like breathing"** Pippert, *The Spiritual Journey of Jimmy Carter*, p. 40.

247. **may stem from how they met** JC, interview, September 20, 2005.

247. **"personified success"** Ibid.

248. **"I looked on Carter . . . as the president"** BG, interview, January 18, 2006.

248. **"won't turn the White House into a Billy Graham Bible Class"** Rafshoon, quoted in Kenneth L. Woodward, "Carter's Cross to Bear," *Newsweek*, June 7, 1976, p. 56.

249. **"the other six days of the week"** BG, quoted in Ann Ray Martin, "Folding His Tent," *Newsweek*, June 21, 1976.

249. **"I learned my lesson the hard way"** BG, quoted in Woodward, "Politics from the Pulpit," *Newsweek*, September 6, 1976.

249. **"a hair's difference"** BG, quoted in Russel Chandler, "Graham Warns of Voting on Religion Basis," *Los Angeles Times*, August 11, 1976.

249. **Carter was poised to drain perhaps half the southern white vote** MacPherson, "Evangelicals Seen Cooling on Carter," *Washington Post*, September 27, 1976.

250. **"I didn't think it was appropriate to advertise my religious beliefs"** Gerald Ford, *A Time to Heal* (New York: Harper and Row, 1979), p. 417.

250. **"ask if he has any suggestions"** Richard Brannon, memo to GF, September 3, 1976, GFL.

250. **"Will help in many ways + has"** GF, memo to Cheney, September 5, 1976, GFL.

251. **"praying that God's will shall be done on November 2"** BG, note to GF, September 10, 1976, GFL.

251. **"looked on a lot of women with lust"** JC, quoted in *Playboy*, November 1976, p. 136.

251. **"It came off as goofy"** Anonymous Carter aide, interview, March 22, 2006.

251. **"I am quite disillusioned"** Jerry Falwell, quoted in MacPherson, "Evangelicals Seen Cooling on Carter," *Washington Post*, September 27, 1976.

251. **"people like Billy Graham"** Jeff Carter, quoted in "Jeff Carter Statement Causes Stir," AP, in *Asheville Times*, October 2, 1976.

252. **"Sure he has"** Jeff Carter, quoted in "Graham Is 'Unfair,' Carter Son Charges," UPI, in *Miami Herald*, September 30, 1976.

252. **"give Jeff a big hug"** BG, quoted in "Graham Shrugs Off Carter's Son's Remark," *New York Times*, October 8, 1976.

252. **"might be misunderstood"** BG, quoted in "Graham Likes Both Candidates— and Young Carter," Wire Services, in *Pine Bluff* (Arkansas) *Commercial*, October 10, 1976.

252. **Neither Ford nor Carter made it to the Pontiac crusade** Douglas E. Kneeland, "Dole Pictures Ford As Gaining on Carter," *New York Times*, October 31, 1976.

252. **"During the election period"** BG to GF, November 24, 1976.

253. **"I appreciate your wonderful understanding"** GF to BG, December 9, 1976 (PP10-3), GFL.

253. **"I'm very much for him"** "Carter Will Restore Confidence, Graham Says," *Miami Herald*, December 26, 1976.

253. **"Carter's summons to a moral revival"** *JAIA*, pp. 584–585.

253. **"it became the thing to do"** JC, interview, September 20, 2005.

25: The Next Great Awakening

254. **"I looked on Carter as the president"** BG, interview, January 18, 2006.

254. **Graham was not the first . . . to put his name and moral authority behind arms control** Jeremy Rifkin, *The Emerging Order* (New York: Ballantine, 1979), p. 252.

254. **"Why should any nation have atomic bombs?"** BG, interview, *CBS Evening News*, March 29, 1979.

255. **"the destruction and disruption that war brings"** Jim Wallis and Wes Michaelson, "A Change of Heart," *Sojourners*, August 1979, p. 12.

255. **"I've come to the conviction"** Ibid.

255. **"and Auschwitz just triggers this"** Wallis, interview, December 19, 2006.

256. **"That wasn't grape juice"** "Did Jesus Drink Wine?" *Time*, January 24, 1977.

256. **"I advised him that he should go"** JC, interview, September 20, 2005.

257. **"It signaled to the Hungarian government"** John Akers, letter to authors, April 2007.

257. **"Watergate changed me a little bit"** BG, unpublished portion of interview in *People*, January 31, 1981.

258. **"And that caught on"** James Robison, interview, April 5, 2006.

258. **"briefing and discussion"** JC to BG, May 9, 1979, JCL.

259. **"crusade and cannot possibly attend"** BG to JC, May 12, 1979, JCL.

259. **"even to suspect who I am for"** "Names in the News," AP, August 7, 1979.

260. **"Dinner . . . would please him"** Bob Maddox, memo to JC and Rosalynn Carter, September 5, 1979, JCL.

260. **"J"** JC, annotation to Maddox memo, September 5, 1979, JCL.

260. **Graham gathered twelve fellow preachers at a Dallas hotel** Robison, interview, April 5, 2006; see also Martin, *With God on Our Side*, pp. 205–206.

261. **"We did not see Carter as the necessary strong leader in the face of a grave threat"** Robison, e-mail to authors, June 6, 2006.

261. **"It was his ability to lead"** Robison, interview, April 5, 2006.

261. **"Graham could not afford the damage"** Ibid.

262. **"Conversation . . . should be most stimulating"** Maddox and Anne Wexler, memo to JC, October 26, 1979, JCL.

262. **"we shared our mutual faith in Jesus Christ"** *JAIA*, p. 586.

262. **White House sleepover** Terence Smith, "Inside White House, a New Tone Emerges," *New York Times*, November 6, 1979.

262. **"Thank you for an unforgettable evening"** Ruth Graham, note to Rosalynn Carter, November 6, 1979, JCL.

263. **"the beginning of the end"** Rosalynn Carter, *First Lady from Plains*, p. 324.

263. **"political and moral power of the evangelicals"** Maddox, letter to JC, January 2, 1980, JCL.

263. **Carter declined to actually join his guests for the meal** Maddox, interview, June 2006.

263. **"we are going to take over"** JC, quoted in Garrett Epps, "Born Again Politics Is Still Waiting to Be," *Washington Post*, March 30, 1980.

264. **"Hail to the Chief"** Cal Thomas and Ed Dobson, *Blinded by Might: Why the Religious Right Can't Save America* (Grand Rapids, MI: Zondervan, 1999), p. 25.

264. **Rosalynn met them** Maddox, interview, June 2006.

26: The Road to Moscow

265. **"The more I prayed about it"** BG, interview, January 23, 2006.

265. **Graham remembered Reagan** *JAIA*, pp. 626–627.

266. **"America needs you more"** Willard Rappleye, memos to *Time* editors, June 6–12, 1952.

267. **"needed to preach the Gospel"** Maureen Reagan, *First Father, First Daughter* (New York: Little, Brown, 1989), p. 61.

267. **"I admired his faith"** Nancy Reagan, *I Love You, Ronnie* (New York: Random House, 2000), pp. 85–86.

267. **"there will be those who will question"** RR, quoted in Dart, "Graham Launches 10-day Southland Crusade in Anaheim," *Los Angeles Times*, September 27, 1969.

267. **"I need a minute"** Jim Baker, interview, September 27, 2006.

267. **"'But it's all a part of God's plan'"** Mike Deaver, interview, July 2006.

268. **"they would spring forward and create great ministries"** Falwell, interview, June 2006.

268. **"He beat up Gorbachev on freedom of religion"** Frank Carlucci Interview, Miller Center, University of Virginia, Ronald Reagan Presidential Oral History Project, August 28, 2001.

268. **"perhaps there was a reason I had been spared"** Ronald Reagan, *An American Life* (New York: Simon and Schuster, 1990), p. 269.

269. **"irrational and suicidal"** Kenneth A. Briggs, "Growing Roles for Churches in Disarmament Drive," *New York Times*, April 10, 1982.

269. **Graham knew the conference** *JAIA*, pp. 593–594.

270. **"He may be correct"** James B. Nance to RR, February 4, 1982, RRL.

270. **"make the obvious propaganda objectives of this conference clear"** Warren Zimmerman, cable from American embassy in Moscow to secretary of state, February 9, 1982, RRL.

270. **"Since the conference will be rigged"** National Security Council, memorandum from William Stearman to William Clark, February 10, 1982.

270. **tried to make him think twice about going** "Billy Graham in Moscow?" *Newsweek*, March 22, 1982, p. 69. Graham said in one of his conversations with the authors that Bush had urged him not to go; in his autobiography, he reported that Bush did not tell him to cancel the trip.

271. **"If I go to Moscow, I will only preach the Gospel"** Ibid.

271. **Rather than offer a greeting** National Security Council, memorandum from Sven Kraemer to Clark, March 24, 1982.

271. **"So I finally decided to go"** BG, interview, January 23, 2007.

272. **"I'll be praying for you every step of the way"** *JAIA*, p. 596.

272. **"Please know that I have complete confidence in your decision"** RR to BG, April 26, 1982 (PHFII;3; Folder 35), RRL.

272. **"The President and I felt it would be counterproductive to insist Billy Graham not go to Moscow"** GHWB, cable to Ambassador Arthur Hartman, April 1982, RRL.

272. **On his first full day in Russia** Edwin Meese, interview, June 30, 2005.

272. **Carefully laid plans to preach twice the next day** Martin, *PWH*, p. 503.

273. **"We have more than 150 prisoners for the work of the Gospel"** BG, quoted in Serge Schmeman, "Graham Preaches at Church in Moscow," *New York Times*, May 10, 1982.

273. **"if we catch people doing things wrong"** Woodward, "Billy Renders Unto Caesar," *Newsweek*, May 24, 1982.

273. **"and here I have caviar with every meal"** Ibid.

273. **"respect the rights of religious believers"** *JAIA*, p. 598.

273. **"never get that in Charlotte"** Woodward, "Billy Renders Unto Caesar," *Newsweek*, May 24, 1982.

274. **"a special responsibility to bear the embarrassing burden of truth"** Safire, "All Things to All Men," *New York Times*, May 17, 1982.

274. **"he has used his prestige to announce his opposition to the arms race"** Editorial comment, "A Few Kind Words for Billy Graham," *Christian Century*, May 26, 1982.

274. **"I have not joined the Communist party"** Michael Shain, "Graham Red Faced on Soviet Freedom Quote," *New York Post*, May 20, 1982.

274. **"There is freedom of worship, but not of religion"**   James Duddy and Charles W. Bell, "Graham Insists Moscow Allows Worship Freedom," *New York Daily News*, May 20, 1982.

274. **"for giving absolution to the Soviet regime"**   "17 J.D.L. Protestors Seized," AP, in *New York Times*, May 20, 1982.

274. **"I don't think we need to get into that"**   Larry Speakes, White House Press Briefing, May 17, 1982, RRL.

275. **"worth taking a risk to preach the Gospel"**   Schmeman, "Graham Tour of Soviet Ends on an Upbeat Note," *New York Times*, September 22, 1984.

275. **"The fellow began pouring out the Soviet line"**   Erik Amfitheatrof, memo to *Time* editors, September 10, 1984.

27: THE SECRET AGENT

276. **"I turned him down several times"**   BG, interview, January 18, 2006.

276. **"evangelicals can't be closely identified"**   *New York Daily News*, January 30, 1981.

277. **"while the nations of the world spend $550 billion each year on weapons"**   Briggs, "Graham Warns on Arms and 'Dangers' in TV Evangelism," *New York Times*, January 29, 1981.

277. **"We dare not sit around"**   Ibid.

277. **"spiritual leaders have to speak out"**   "Billy Graham, First of the Big-Time TV Preachers," *People*, February 16, 1981.

277. **"Money is a means"**   Billy Graham, "TV Evangelism: Billy Graham Sees Dangers Ahead," *TV Guide*, March 5, 1983.

277. **Reagan was looking for a way**   Briggs, "Diplomatic Ties with the Vatican: For US, an Old and Divisive Question," *New York Times*, December 12, 1983.

279. **"We actually were surprised"**   BG to Clark, April 23, 1983 (System 2, 91492), RRL.

279. **"And I told him I just couldn't do it"**   BG, interview, January 18, 2006.

280. **"little jokes they don't mean"**   BG, quoted in "Graham Tells Estonia Reagan Didn't Mean It," *New York Times*, September 14, 1984.

280. **"May I impose on you further?"**   RR, letter to President François Mitterrand, July 7, 1986 (PHF Series I, Box 16, Folder 227), RRL.

281. **"Believe me, it helped and was, and is, most comforting"**   RR to BG, December 8, 1986 (PHF Series II, Box 17, Folder 268), RRL.

281. **"You don't face a problem but what God can help you solve it"**   BG to RR, March 6, 1987, RRL.

281. **"just a line, but a heartfelt line"**   RR to BG, March 11, 1987 (PHF Series II, Box 18, Folder 282), RRL.

281. **"Thank you for your prayers"**   Ibid., January 17, 1989 (PHF Series II, Box 21, Folder 346), RRL.

281. **"We're just more quiet about it now"**   Paul Hendrickson, "Billy Graham, Fundamentally," *Washington Post*, April 28, 1986.

281. **"Their relationship was beyond political"**   Nancy Reagan, interview, August 4, 2006.

282. **"Ronnie was just that kind of a person"**   Ibid.

282. **"Dad always had great respect for him"**   Michael Reagan, interview, June 2006.

282. **"You made us stand tall"**   BG, letter to RR, January 10, 1989.

283. **"Nancy comes home from Paris"**   RR, letter to BG, May 13, 1990.

283. **"not just to be there when they were president"**   Michael Reagan, interview, June 2006.

283. **"My thoughts and prayers are with you"**   BG, letter to Nancy Reagan, January 30, 1998.

28: THE FAMILY PASTOR

284. **"We went to Kennebunkport every summer"**   BG, interview, January 18, 2006.

285. **"water falling on dry ground"**   Doug Wead, interview, June 16, 2005.

287. **"an early signal"** Wead, *Vice President George Bush and the Evangelical Movement*, June 25, 1985.

289. **"She invited me to come and speak"** BG, interview, January 2006.

289. **"Billy was a good golfer and I know my father . . . enjoyed playing with Billy"** GHWB, e-mail to authors, October 24, 2006.

289. **Dorothy Walker Bush was a formidable Christian** Wead, memo to Craig Fuller, April 16, 1986, author's collection; and Mickey Herskowitz, *Duty, Honor, Country* (Nashville: Rutledge Hill, 2003), p. 9.

289. **"She loved the man"** GHWB, quoted in Vernon McLellan, *A Tribute from Friends* (New York: Warner, 2002), p. 23.

289. **Graham touted a forty-four-year-old Bush** Evans and Novak, "Young Texas Congressman Gets Nixon Look as Running Mate," *Washington Post*, June 5, 1968.

290. **both men were in Acapulco** Barbara Bush, *A Memoir* (New York: Scribner, 1994), p. 144; see also Cornwell, *Ruth: A Portrait*, p. 184.

290. **"we were around Billy in a rather informal setting"** GHWB, interview, October 14, 2006.

290. **"unfortunate things happen even to God's chosen people"** Barbara Bush, speech delivered in College Station, Texas, April 10, 2006.

290. **"We went to Kennebunkport every summer for a while"** BG, interview, January 18, 2006.

291. **"'Divorce? No. Murder? Yes'"** Barbara Bush, speech, College Station, Texas, April 10, 2006.

291. **"And heaven and sin. And wonder"** GHWB, quoted in McLellan, *Tribute from Friends*, p. 23.

291. **"Everyone left those meetings in awe of the Nation's Pastor"** GHWB, interview, October 24, 2006.

291. **"Good News was clear that night"** Doro Bush Koch, *My Father, My President* (New York: Warner Books, 2006), p. 211.

292. **"that fascinating study on the Evangelical Movement"** GHWB to Wead, September 14, 1985.

292. **"a chance to sit down with you at my house to go over this material"** Ibid., September 24, 1985.

292. **The vice president, Wead argued** Wead, second edition of memo to GHWB, November 1985.

293. **"I am no good at the breast beating bit, Doug"** GHWB to Wead, November 18, 1985.

293. **Bush's ground game for God** Bill Phillips, memo to Lee Atwater, Fuller, and Wead, March 10, 1986, GHWBL.

293. **"right to do it in a low-key way"** Fuller, interview, August 2006.

294. **"figure out how to do it"** Wead, memo to Atwater, Craig Phillips, and Ron Kaufman, April 2, 1986.

294. **urging Bush to make plans to attend** Wead, "Targets: The Vice President and Evangelical Leaders of Influence," December 28, 1985.

295. **"a situation where the leaders in a campaign want good things"** Bush campaign official, interview, January 21, 2007.

296. **"we are indeed one nation under God"** GHWB, quoted in "A Packed House for Graham," *Washington Post*, April 28, 1986.

296. **"this couldn't come at a more needed time"** Wead, memo to Kaufman, May 13, 1986.

296. **"I did not want to appear to be 'using' him"** GHWB, interview, October 24, 2006.

297. **"Graham was one of the few people who could get George Bush to confront his spiritual feelings or beliefs"** Fuller, interview, August 2006.

297. **"there have been many moments"** George H. W. Bush with Wead, *Man of Integrity* (Eugene, OR: Harvest House Publishers, 1988), p. 34.

297. **"become politicized"** Ibid., p. 45.

298. **"that idea should be dissipated"** "Christians Don't Have to Belong to GOP, Democrat Graham Says," *Los Angeles Times*, July 23, 1988.

298. **"Naturally, I was overwhelmed, but terribly unprepared"** BG, letter to GHWB, December 12, 1988 (3255), GHWBL.

298. **"'He'll need it'"** *JAIA*, p. 703.

29: "It Was Billy I Reached Out To"

299. **"And I decided to talk on peace"** BG, interview, January 23, 2007.

299. **"That is something not only needed, but very special indeed"** GHWB, letter to BG, January 25, 1989 (FG001-03), GHWBL.

300. **"All's well, though!!!!"** GHWB, memo to John Sununu, January 29, 1989 (TR001 190991), GHWBL. Wead's miscalculation was a harbinger of things to come; he would be forced to resign a year later when he criticized White House officials for allowing homosexual rights activists to attend a hate crimes bill signing ceremony.

300. **"perhaps we can say hello to each other on the telephone"** BG to GHWB, May 25, 1989, GHWBL.

300. **"I will be seeing you somewhere along the way"** GHWB to BG, May 25, 1989 (TR021-04), GHWBL.

300. **"the person without an agenda had greater standing"** Fuller, interview, August 2006.

300. **"I never felt Billy Graham had 'an agenda'"** GHWB, interview, October 24, 2006.

301. **"his teaching and his faith gave me strength"** Ibid.

301. **"Bush is easy to talk to about spiritual things"** BG, interview by David Aikman, *Time*, March 30, 1990.

301. **"This will not stand"** George H. W. Bush and Brent Scowcroft, *A World Transformed* (New York: Vintage, 1998), p. 333.

301. **the looming war remained unpopular** Dart, "Clerical Opposition to War in Gulf Builds Quickly," *Los Angeles Times*, December 22, 1990.

302. **"It does hit me pretty hard—That moment's upon us"** George H. W. Bush, *All the Best* (New York: Scribner, 1999), p. 501.

302. **a full-page advertisement in the *New York Times*** "War Is Not the Answer," *New York Times*, January 7, 1991.

302. **"No sane person wants war"** BG, quoted in "U.S. Religious Leaders: Let There Be Peace on Earth," AP, January 10, 1991.

302. **Only one was invited to the White House** BG, "Hands On," *Washington Post*, January 18, 1991.

303. **"rolling me up to the Blue Room to watch some TV?"** Barbara Bush, quoted in Joe Treen, "America's Crusader," *People*, October 7, 1991.

303. **"watching as lights were blacked out all over Baghdad"** Ibid.

303. **"And I decided to talk on peace"** BG, interview, January 23, 2007.

303. **"We wanted Billy Graham by our side"** GHWB, interview, October 24, 2006.

304. **"[Billy] helped me realize that life would go on"** Ibid.

305. **"I choke up very easily at this stage in my life"** Ibid.

30: Bill and Hillary

306. **"I loved those two people"** BG, interview, January 18, 2006.

306. **"elected to our highest office"** Terry Mattingly, "Inaugural Prayer Put Graham in a Tight Spot," *Chicago Tribune*, January 22, 1993.

306. **"in all godliness and holiness"** *JAIA*, p. 771.

307. **"He's the easiest guy to get to know"** Jim Morrill, "Graham Dines with Old President, Welcomes New," *Charlotte Observer*, January 21, 1993.

307. **"in public life, I think"** BC, speech delivered at Ministers Leadership Conference, Urbana, Illinois, August 10, 2000.

308. **"I loved Billy Graham for doing that"** Bill Clinton, *My Life* (New York: Knopf, 2004), p. 39.

308. **"relationship between your faith and your work"** BC, from Q&A session following Illinois conference, August 2000.

308. **"good chunk of what I had"** Clinton, *My Life*, p. 46.

308. **spending the summer of 1971 in Berkeley, California** Ibid., p. 185.

309. **"I wanted her to see Billy"** BC, interview, April 23, 2007.

309. **"His quick mind and warm personality"** *JAIA*, p. 769.

309. **"extremely important for your future"** BG, letter to BC, August 1, 1988.

310. **Worley Oscar Vaught** Clinton, *My Life*, p. 294.

311. **a thirty-minute Bible lesson** *JAIA*, pp. 770–771.

311. **"outside the Eastern Gate"** BG, recounted by Clinton in *My Life*, p. 39.

311. **"could have given to his pastor"** *JAIA*, p. 771.

311. **The experience sealed the bond** BC, interview, April 23, 2007.

311. **"If his wife cannot rely upon him"** James Kennedy, in Priscilla Painton, "Clinton's Spiritual Journey," *Time*, April 5, 1993.

312. **"When Clinton talked about Graham"** Dee Dee Myers, interview, November 2006.

312. **"He was the only recent national Democrat"** Mike McCurry, interview, January 31, 2007.

313. **"No hurry. No agenda"** Dan Poneman, interview, July 2005.

313. **When Graham finally sat down privately with Kim in Pyongyang** Joel S. Wit, Poneman, and Robert L. Gallucci, *Going Critical* (Washington: Brookings Institution, 2004), p. 132.

314. **"he understood the limits"** Poneman, interview, July 2005.

314. **"This could be your finest hour"** BG, quoted in Wit, Poneman, and Gallucci, *Going Critical*, p. 148.

314. **When Nixon died** *JAIA*, pp. 547–548.

315. **"one of the most charismatic people I've ever met"** BG, interview with Larry King, *Larry King Live*, CNN, May 25, 1996.

316. **"who to vote for"** BG, quoted in "Graham Neutral on Clinton, Dole," AP, in *Los Angeles Times*, September 28, 1996.

316. **"Clinton really jumped on him"** McCurry, interview, January 31, 2007.

31: MENDING THE BREACH

317. **"I said one word"** BG, interview, January 23, 2007.

317. **Reverend Don Jones** Hillary Rodham Clinton, *Living History* (New York: Scribner, 2004), p. 23.

318. **"a positive feeling about him"** HRC, interview, January 10, 2007.

318. **"draw those parallels"** HRC, interview.

318. **"pitiless"** Hillary R. Clinton, *Living History*, p. 167.

319. **she joined a bipartisan prayer group** Ibid.

319. **"individual responsibility and caring"** HRC, speech delivered at the University of Texas, Liz Carpenter Lecture Series, April 7, 1993.

319. **"He had such a charismatic presence"** HRC, interview, January 10, 2007.

320. **"'How about sitting here and talking with me?'"** BG, interview, January 21, 2007.

321. **"I know how hard it is"** BG, quoted on the *Today* show, March 5, 1998.

321. **"I said one word"** BG, interview, January 23, 2007.

321. **a quiet signal of support for the president** Isaacson, interview, February 5, 2007.

322. **her approval ratings** For an excellent discussion of the impact of 1998 on the Clintons' relationship, see John F. Harris, *The Survivor* (New York: Random House, 2005).

322. **"she relies on her strong religious faith"** Statement by Marsha Berry, HRC's spokeswoman, August 18, 1998.

322. **On vacation the next week** Clinton, *My Life*, p. 803; see also Hillary R. Clinton, *Living History* (New York: Scribner, 2003), pp. 468–469.

322. **He told a church gathering** BC, speech at Union Chapel, Oak Bluffs, Massachusetts, August 28, 1998.

323. **"the secular saint and the religious saint"** HRC, interview, January 10, 2007.

323. **"indefensible, but not unforgivable"** "President in Peril," *Charlotte Observer*, September 18, 1998.

324. **Graham was "incredibly supportive"** HRC, interview, January 10, 2007.

324. **"everybody has to make his or her decision"** Ibid.

32: THE MUSTARD SEED

326. **"I can see him back there now"** BG, interview, January 18, 2006.

328. **a "Bush Bash"** Bill Minutaglio, *First Son* (New York: Random House, 1999), pp. 190–192.

329. **"on the road to nowhere at 40"** John Ellis Bush, quoted in Sam Howe Verhovek, "Is There Room on a Republican Ticket for Another Bush?" *New York Times*, September 13, 1998.

329. **Graham and Ruth spent a few days at Kennebunkport in August 1985** BG, interview, January 20, 2006.

329. **"That was our beginning"** Ibid.

329. **"one of the questions came from [George W. Bush]"** Ibid.

329. **"They had a conversation"** Karl Rove, interview, February 2007.

330. **"Sin is sin"** Aikman, *A Man of Faith* (Nashville: W Publishing Group, 2004), p. 75.

330. **"It was the wonderment of Graham's watching him"** Ibid., p. 74.

330. **"I don't remember what we talked about"** BG, interview, January 20, 2006.

331. **"He made it a point to call me aside and ask how things were going"** GWB, quoted in George H. W. Bush, *Man of Integrity*, pp. 45–46.

331. **"'Get me Billy Graham'"** Barbara Bush, reported in Verhovek, "Is There Room on a Republican Ticket for Another Bush?" *New York Times*, September 13, 1998.

332. **"'I want to remind both of you never play God'"** Ken Herman, "Bush and Baptists Concur," *Austin American-Statesman*, June 18, 1997.

332. **Bush unwrapped this story . . . in part to signal to voters** Ibid.

332. **the campaign of Ann Richards** Fred Barnes, "The Gospel According to George W. Bush," *Weekly Standard*, March 22, 1999, p. 22.

332. **"It gets the story of the governor's faith out there early"** Wead, memo to GWB, April 18, 1999.

333. **during a fund-raising trip to California in 1997** Rove, interview, February 5, 2007.

333. **"He led me to the path"** George W. Bush and Herskowitz, *A Charge to Keep* (New York: HarperCollins, 1999), p. 136.

334. **"When you are dealing with a skeptic, it takes a while for the message to sink in"** Barnes, "The Gospel According to George W. Bush," *Weekly Standard*, March 22, 1999, p. 20.

334. **"it was a wonderful answer"** "Graham Rejects Farrakhan As 'Unifying Force,'" *Ottawa Citizen*, January 3, 2000.

334. **"They think he's a man of little substance"** BG, quoted in David Von Drehle and Dan Balz, "Bush, McCain Clash in Debate; Campaign Finance, Taxes Draw Fire in Spirited Forum," *Washington Post*, January 7, 2000.

335. **"That was my whole purpose"** Brian Jacobs, interview, May 5, 2006.

335. **he got down on his knees and prayed** Jacobs, interview, December 13, 2006.

336. **"If you call Graham"** Wead, memo to GWB, October 25, 2000.

336. **"I've made mistakes in my life"** GWB, quoted in Tim Burger, "In the Driver's Seat: The Bush DUI," chapter 4 of Larry Sabato, *Overtime! The Election 2000 Thriller* (New York: Longman, 2002), p. 79.

337. **"It's comforting to be with a close friend"** Ibid.

337. **"I'm going to do everything in my power to help them make it a successful presidency"** BG, quoted in Jake Tapper, "Bush makes a final push in Florida," Salon .com, November 5, 2000.

338. **"The governor had things to do and Mr. Graham had things to do"** Rove, interview, February 5, 2007.

338. **"Dr. Graham will be able to purge all that evilness from my brother's soul"** Jeb Bush, interview with Bob Schieffer, *Face the Nation*, CBS, November 5, 2000.

338. **"every little bit counts"** Ari Fleischer, interview with Larry King, *Larry King Live*, CNN, November 7, 2000.

Conclusion: Lessons of a Lifetime

341. **"Graham never lost the sense of awe"** Colson, interview, July 18, 2006.

342. **"an ambassador of the kingdom of God"** "A Challenge from Evangelicals," *Time*, August 5, 1974.

344. **"I think we've lucked out with Billy Graham"** "American Revival: A Life Spent Bringing That Old-time Religion to Everybody," *Minneapolis Star-Tribune*, June 16, 1996.

Index